The Joy
of Oysters

The Joy of Oysters

Lori McKean
Bill Whitbeck

SPEED GRAPHICS
Seattle, Washington

PHOTO CREDITS

Except as noted below, all photographs in The Joy of Oysters were taken or provided by author Bill Whitbeck. Illustrations of oyster character cartoons by Don Smith. Other illustrations as noted below. We gratefully acknowledge contributors from the shellfish industry for providing photographs and illustrations that help document and clarify the history of North American oystering and the techniques, old and new that brought these tasty morsels to our tables.

Cover: Front cover illustration by Don Smith.

Back Cover: 1. Sign at Samish Bay oyster grower; 2. Oyster stew label from Northern Oyster Company; 3. Sign from O'Sheridan's Oyster Bar, South Bend, WA; 4. Hand-drawn chalk sign from The Brooklyn Oyster House, Seattle; 5. Oyster Bill and Half Shell Lori by Chuck Hill

Page 14, Burleigh Bros. Seafood; page 18 (top) Burleigh Bros. Seafood; page 18 (bottom) Tallmadge Bros. Oyster Co.; page 19, Tallmadge Oyster Co.; page 27, Pacific Coast Shellfish Growers Assn.; pages 28-29, Olympia Oyster Co.; page 40, PCSGA; pages 43-45, Taylor Shellfish Co.; page 47, 49, Washington D.N.R.; page 49 (mid) Pearl Seaproducts; page 50, Olympia Clam Co.; page 52 (bottom) PCSGA; page 54, Glidden Point Oyster Co.; page 57, Tallmadge Bros. Oyster Co.; page 60, Gulf of Mexico Program; page 65, Pearl Seaproducts; page 69,75 PCSGA; page 87, 93, Chuck Hill; page 97, McIlhenny Co.; page 155, Dan & Louis Oyster Bar; page 159, Rodney's Oyster House; page 160, Ray's Boathouse; page 181, Wildwood Restaurant; page 243, Shaffer City Oyster Bar; pages 279,281, Anthony's Restaurants; page 286, Galway International Oyster Festival; page 287, Annual Milford Oyster Festival; page 288, North Carolina Oyster Festival; pages 292-293, Annual Oyster Festival, Oyster Bay, NY; page 297, Shaw's Crabhouse; page 302, Testical Festival, Rock Creek Lodge;

Speed Graphics, 17919 2nd Ave. NW, Shoreline, WA 98177 • 206-546-8523 • speedgraph@aol.com

Printed in the United States of America   Published by Speed Graphics

Cover illustration and design by Don Smith

Publishers Cataloguing in Publication Data
McKean, Lori, 1955 -
Whitbeck, William, 1950 -

Joy of Oysters, The   Text by Lori McKean and Bill Whitbeck, recipes by Lori McKean
ISBN 1-929258-00-3
Includes index

1. Cookery, Seafood   2. Cookery, American   3. Oysters, History

*Wooden-hulled oyster dredge boats heading out of Norwalk,
Connecticut through a channel cut in ice by steel-hulled boat.*

Table of Contents

ACKNOWLEDGMENTS

So many thanks are due to friends and family. First, a big thank you to Peter Auguzstiny of Westcott Bay Sea Farms, and Paul Blau and his late brother, John, of Blau Oyster for providing inspirational oysters for tasting and recipe testing. Also, thanks to the many gracious oyster-loving chefs who contributed recipes, especially to Doug Charles, formerly of the Oyster Creek Inn, for hosting our oyster wine tastings. And to Mother Nature, for providing us with the miracle of oysters and the ability to enjoy them.

Thanks to my Aunt Dorres and Uncle John (Captain Hook) for initiating me into the world of oysters. To Jon (Glycogen) Rowley for his ongoing inspiration. To our magnificent publisher Chuck Hill for his diligence, patience and encouragement. Way to go Chuck! To my delightful slurping cohort and co-author Oyster Bill. To my next favorite slurping buddy, my mastiff Kuma, who learned to love oysters during recipe testing for this book. Most of all, thanks to my loving, supportive family, Linda, Little Mother (Jan), and Bill. Here's to elbow benders around the world!

Half Shell Lori

My sincere thanks go out to many who were instrumental in the publishing of this book. I'd like to thank oystermen Hill Bloom, his late brother Norm, and their families, who remain long time friends and neighbors down the street in East Norwalk. Thanks to their company, Tallmadge Brothers, and their employees, especially Dave Hopp and Jim Riley, for allowing me to photograph and study every aspect of the business for nearly thirty years, and for the many wonderful hours spent out on the oyster boats. Thanks too, for providing us with perfect oysters for the recipe testing and wine tastings for the book. I'd also like to send a big thank you to Norman Bloom, Jr., for his generosity in providing boats used for the more recent photo shoots in Connecticut, and for the lobsters and clams on the Fourth of July.

In his memory, I'd like to thank my uncle Stan Dawson, a Pacific Northwest native who introduced me to oysters on the west coast, for taking me in 1977 to Blau Oyster Co. on Samish Island for the first time, and for showing me his favorite places to find oysters on Hood Canal. My thanks also go to Paul Blau and his late brother John, and plant manager Peter Nordlund for all the help (and oysters) they provided. I want to thank Sue for the opportunity to pursue oysters in Chile, and also for the encouragement and support she gave me beginning with these words, "Don't wait for your ship to come in..... swim out to it."

Artist Don Smith deserves a tip of the hat for his wonderful cover art and many illustrations throughout the book. This project could not have been done without fellow oyster lovers Lori McKean (co-author) and Chuck Hill (publisher). Thanks to both of them for their inspiration, professionalism, and hard work, and for the friendship that developed among us during the past two years.

Thanks to you Mom, in loving memory, for your help and support with everything I've achieved, and for making me eat fish and vegetables when I was a little kid. I especially want to give thanks and love to my Dad, who taught me so much about life on the water, and who shared his love of boats, the sea, and oysters with me as only a father could.

Oyster Bill

Introduction
The Pearl Between the Shells

Not everyone loves oysters the way the authors of *The Joy of Oysters* do. Categorically there are those who hate oysters (won't eat them in any form), those who eat oysters cooked, and those who enjoy oysters on the half shell. Half Shell Lori McKean and Oyster Bill Whitbeck are in a completely different category. It doesn't matter whether oysters are served on the half-shell, baked, grilled, or fried, they LOVE oysters in every shape and form.

As a result of this passion their book discusses every facet of oysterdom. You will find over 150 recipes for oysters and accompaniments covering a dozen categories and cooking styles. The best wines and beers to consume with oysters have been investigated and reported, as have the tastiest hot sauces.

In *The Joy of Oysters* you will learn about the history of oystering and the changes that have occured over 300+ years of recorded North American oyster harvesting. Shucking, serving and slurping of the tasty morsels is covered and there is even an "Oyster Sensory Appreciation Wheel" for those who would like to describe their oyster experience in precise terminology.

The cultural side of oysters is sprinkled liberally throughout the book. You'll find quotes about oysters, songs about oysters, oyster poems and oyster rhymes. An entire section of *The Joy of Oysters* details oyster events held throughout the United States and abroad. Appendices list oyster growers, oyster organizations and oyster regulatory boards.

The Joy of Oysters puts you knee-deep in oysters. Not over your head, but just a comfortable wading depth through a world of briny bivalves. This is a book that brings together oyster lovers with facts, fun and good taste.

Come on in and shuck a few of your favorite oysters to enjoy with your new friends, Half Shell Lori and Oyster Bill.

For Love of Oysters

Lori McKean

As I sit writing about my love affair with oysters, summer has just given way to autumn, my favorite season. The change is marked by cold dewy mornings filled with silvery spider webs, the sweet, musty smell of tumbling leaves, the muted golden rays of the sun, a brisk salty breeze off Puget Sound, my garden giving one last brilliant thrust at bearing fruit or vegetables before going to seed – the autumnal equinox.

These same triggers that alert me to the changing seasons, also signal to oysters that spawning season is over. It is time to settle back in their snug shells, safe in their cold, watery homes, feasting on nutritious plankton – growing plump and healthy in preparation for next summer's mating season. For oyster lovers, autumn marks the beginning of oyster season – when the briny bivalves are at their prime in taste and texture.

My senses and taste buds are aroused just thinking of eating oysters. I'm excited. Salivating. Hair bristles on my skin. The exhilaration of eating freshly shucked oysters is so vivid. I feel the crisp, icy cold oyster meeting my lips, sliding gently into my mouth, then slithering down my throat. The cucumber-fresh, briny meat smacks of the sea and tangy minerals. I am alive . . . after a sip of steely, icy cold wine, I'm back for more oysters. This is heaven.

Like the beginning of the universe, the awakening of my oyster consciousness started with a big bang. I use the term "awakening" because at the age of ten, although I'd never tasted an oyster, somewhere deep in my subconscious, dull and slumbering like Rip van Winkle, dwelt a primordial awareness of oysters. When I tasted my first briny Willapa Bay oyster there was a sudden taste recognition that seemed to transcend time. It's the same sort of feeling I've had when first meeting people I fall in love with – a very sensual, yet unexplainable combination of touch, scent, taste, rhythm, sound . . . magic.

The cosmic chain of events leading up to my "big Bang" went like this. In honor of my grandparents' 50th wedding anniversary, our extended family had gathered on Long Beach Peninsula – home of the incredible Willapa Bay Oyster – for a weekend camping trip. Dinner the first night involved oysters.

My Uncle John, "Big Bad John," as my dad called him, a husky, good-natured, maritime fellow, who happens to love oysters, stood watch over the barbecue like a helmsman. "More oysters mates," he shouted to his enthusiastic crew, who helped him toss handfuls of chalky oyster shells over the hot coals. The hiss and sputter of the salty steam rising from those cool oysters as they met the hot fire is still delectably fresh in my mind.

Eagerly we watched as, one by one, the oysters reluctantly opened, revealing their soft, creamy meat. Convinced that all was under control, Uncle John joined the adults inside the main cabin. Wasting no time, my cousin Coyne, who was always up to mischief, carefully withdrew three small firecrackers from his pocket. He inserted the firecrackers into several of the oysters atop a platter bound for Uncle John. With a flick of a match, the oysters became a ticking time bomb.

Utter chaos followed – screaming, flailing arms and oysters flying everywhere, followed by the Big Bang – the seeding of my oyster awareness. We returned to the barbecue to feast on the remaining oysters. Outside, breathing in the cool ocean mist, with the pulse of Pacific surf surging through us, we slurped those hot, juicy oysters straight from the fire – the beginning of my love affair with oysters.

Lori McKean

Oysters East, Oysters West

To achieve success and well being during your lifetime, you need to maintain good relationships with a benevolent banker, an aggressive attorney, a crafty CPA, and...a superlative supplier of the freshest and highest quality oysters available. Maybe you could do without the first three, but heaven forbid going through life without access to fresh oysters. Life, in my opinion, would not be worth living without oysters. Gotta have 'em.

Bill Whitbeck on ship rounding Cape Horn in December, 1999 on his way to taste Chilean oysters at the source.

Looking back on my childhood, oysters were always a part of my surroundings. I grew up in Norwalk, Connecticut on Long Island Sound during the 1950s and 60s, and my family always had a boat of some sort. We spent the warm months of summer on the water, cruising around islands and protected inlets that were home to some of the finest oyster grounds in the world. The right supply of nutrients, proper water temperature and salinity, an excellent gravelly sea bottom, and the proximity of freshwater rivers made this corner of Long Island Sound prime oyster territory. It was while camping or picnicking on the boat with my family that we would watch the old wooden oyster boats lower and raise their dredges, releasing their catch on deck, while busy deckhands sorted and bagged the oysters according to size. The boats worked most every day, all year, and even when the harbor froze during some extremely cold winters, arrangements were made for a steel hull boat to clear a path through the ice so that the more fragile wooden boats could make their way to the open water around the oyster beds.

My father knew all the old oystermen and sea captains on the waterfront in Norwalk. He was involved with the repair and installation of marine electronic equipment, and kept the radios, depth sounders, radar, and other electronic gear on most of the oyster fleet in working order. As a boy I would go with him on weekends down to the oyster house docks and "help" him work. Mostly I just got in the way, but it was exciting for me to hang around with my dad and these colorful old salts. Growing up on the water only forty miles or so from New York City also enabled my dad and me to make an annual event of attending the big boat show, usually held in mid January at the New York Coliseum at Columbus Circle. We would take the train from Norwalk into Grand Central Station, and in less than an hour, exit into the dark subterranean bowels of New York City, and onto the long walkway that led to the main terminal. It was there that we always stopped at the Grand Central Oyster Bar for a hot lunch before the twenty block trek to the boat show. Closing my eyes today, the aroma of the pan roasts being prepared by the chefs at the "bar" fill my head. Heavenly.

During the summertime, the Hungarian Reformed church we attended would have several outdoor bazaars and dances. My father would usually bring a couple bushel bags of oysters and clams, and would shuck them for anyone who asked. Topped with a bit of my mom's horseradish laced cocktail sauce, they were always a special treat at these outings to those who really loved to eat them raw, while the more faint of heart enjoyed stuffed cabbage and chicken paprikash. It was at one of these summer church functions that I ate my first raw oyster, shucked by my dad, and it was truly a religious experience!

During my college years I developed an interest in cooking while working summer jobs at various restaurants and resorts around Boston, Cape Cod, and on the island of Martha's Vineyard. I had always enjoyed eating good food, but after working at several of these establishments, I learned the finer points of preparing good food as well. I experimented on my own, and over time began to turn out some pretty tasty dishes. Fresh

The Joy of Oysters

seafood, being readily available in that part of the country, became my main focus of attention in food preparation.

Returning to Norwalk after graduating college, I negotiated the use of some unused space in the old Radel Oyster Company building, and operated a small photography studio, print shop, and graphics studio there for eight years. There was a working oyster company right next door, and a fresh seafood market downstairs, and I was able to moor my boat at the marina on the opposite side. Needless to say, working there was a very enjoyable experience. The closeness to this salt air environment on a daily basis encouraged me to expand not only my cooking abilities, but also to learn as much as I could about the food I was preparing. By now I had also discovered that I really liked oysters!

Oysters fascinated me, and I spent many hours out on the oyster boats taking photographs, observing the shuckers as their skilled hands quickly removed the oyster meats from their shells, and talking with the old timers that had been oystering for 60 years. Until that time, so much about the oyster business was unknown to me, but the more I was exposed to its inside workings, the more I wanted to learn. The eight years that I worked in that idyllic location was my inspiration toward a lifelong goal, and culminates with the publishing of this book. This goal is--- to introduce the world of oysters to as many folks as possible from East Coast to West, to tell the story of the oyster's history in a way that is easily understood, to educate readers in the selection and purchasing of oysters, to make tummies happy by presenting recipes from basic to classic, and to instill my love of this wonderful bivalve to oyster lovers everywhere.

My home is no longer in New England. Twenty-three years ago my travels brought me to the Pacific Northwest, to another region that has an equally impressive history of oystering. The species of oysters are different here, as well as the growing methods, planting of the seed, and harvesting. Since oystering is basically a farming operation, problems that are familiar to agricultural farmers are also of concern to oyster growers on both coasts. These include pests and predators, availability of nutrients, crop diseases, and pollution, which can greatly effect the quality of the growing conditions. Specific problems sometimes differ from one oyster growing area to another, but exist as common elements of the business and must be dealt with wherever oysters are commercially grown. Certain areas that were once thriving oyster grounds 100 years ago became choked with pollution, sediment, and non-native predators, (introduced either naturally or inadvertantly by humans), unable to support the growth of oysters. Through the efforts of the growers, environmental groups, private watchdog organizations, commercial industry and the public, many of these areas are once again growing oysters. Some of these areas though, continue to be plagued with problems, and may never return to the highly productive nutrient rich grounds they were in the past.

In this book we also discuss clean water and how clean water is so vital to the healthy growth of not only oysters, but to so many other species of sea life that are eaten by people all over the world. We, as consumers, must do our part to insure that the bays, rivers, salt marshes, estuaries, lakes and oceans that provide life to these species remain clean. The final part of my earlier-mentioned goal is that all of us find out through local, state or federal programs and agencies how we can contribute to the cause of clean water for the new millennium.

Certain ways of life are sometimes difficult to modify, but through education, communication, contribution and participation, we can make these changes in our lives to ensure that the world's precious sea dwellers will prosper in an environment of clean, life-supporting water.

Bill Whitbeck

The Oyster's Tale - East and West

Retelling, in detail, the entire history of oystering throughout all of North America would require an entire book the size of this one, and to read such a lenghty tome might cause our dear audience to miss many delicious oyster meals. Instead, we present two essays that tell much of the oystering story as it has unfolded since the arrival of white settlers in North America. Following these detailed chronologies – one East Coast and one West Coast – you can enjoy brief descriptions of each oystering area with histories limited to the most important events.

Oystering in New England

Throughout the oyster producing regions of North America, archeological excavations reveal that there were oyster lovers on these shores thousands of years before Daniel Webster slurped them at Ye Olde Union Oyster House in Boston. It was during that time period that bands and tribes of native North Americans on both coasts harvested "wild" oysters. These oysters grew naturally, without being planted and cultivated, and because of their abundance in some areas, sustained the natives for centuries.

The excavations of "middens," which were tribal dumping grounds for shells, char-coal, bones, and other artifacts, have turned up large piles of oyster shells along the ancient banks of many rivers and tributaries.

In northern New England, one such midden was located at the current site of an oyster company in Maine. Glidden Point Oysters, in Edgecomb, Maine, reports that the Damariscotta River estuary provided the natives of the Pemaquid area with these wild oysters, and that the shell piles found along the river banks are estimated to be 2,100 years old. The remains of these Native American artifacts have been studied by historians and archeologists, and are considered local treasures to the present day communities surround-ing these areas.

We all remember from our high school American History classes that the Indians of coastal New England traded with "wampompeag," or wampum. The material used for making these small beads were made from the purple and white shells of clams and oysters, polished smooth, and then used for the trade and exchange of property and other goods as we use money today. The Shinnecock tribe, once a part of the Metoac Indians of Long Island, New York, were probably the most well known of these "money makers" because of the great abundance of oysters and other shellfish that grew wild on their shores.

For many years the natural growth of these wild oysters kept up with the natives' consumption, but as more European settlers arrived along the Atlantic coast of North America, more oysters were consumed. The colonists found the oysters easy to gather, especially during the colder winter months, since they grew in the shallow waters of pro-tected bays, and were more easily obtained than other food during those frigid times of the year. It was thought that there would always be a supply of oysters to meet any demand, but as early as the mid-1700s, colonists realized that there was a serious depletion of these natural oyster beds occurring along the entire Atlantic coast. This happened not only as

coastal consumption increased, but as methods of packing and shipping improved, large quantities of these oysters found themselves on the dinner plates of inland settlers. What was once a seemingly inexhaustible supply of oysters from Maine to Texas, was beginning to fail at a surprising rate. Each state or territory along the coast made attempts to curtail the elimination of these natural oyster beds (or bars and rocks as they were referred to in the south) by passing legislation to that effect. Prohibiting the use of dredges to harvest oysters, which was believed to damage oysters, was one such law passed in Rhode Island in 1766. This allowed only hand-operated tonging devices to scoop the oysters from the bottom.

Shipping oysters in the barrel by sailing ship from Prince Edward Island, Canada. c. 1900

Two other factors which led to the depletion of the natural oysters' population were that the oysters were gathered all year from all areas, and those who harvested the oysters did not return the shells to the original tidal areas that the oysters were taken from. This threatened the survival of both the newly fertilized oysters by not providing a suitable surface to attach too (ideally an empty shell), as well as the older adults that spawn or reproduce during the summer months.

Before we continue with our history lesson, let's jump to biology class for awhile so that we understand what was happening here.

When native Americans were this continent's only residents, there were only two edible wild oyster species in North America that warrant any attention. The oysters that we consume belong to two distinct genera, *ostrea* and *crassostrea*. They differ not only in appearance, but also in the method by which they reproduce. Ostrea shells are more round, and somewhat symmetrical, while crassostrea are more elongated and generally larger than ostrea. Oysters that grew on the Atlantic coast were of the species *crassostrea virginica*. This is the same dominating species that continues to be commercially grown and harvested today on the East Coast. This oyster is commonly called the American or Eastern oyster. In protected inlets of the Pacific coast, the native oyster that grew for centuries was the tiny *ostrea lurida*, or Olympia oyster. This oyster's shell rarely exceeds one inch (2.54 cm) across and is considered a true delicacy to many oyster lovers. Currently there are several other commercially marketed species grown in North America, but they will be discussed in a later section of this book.

"Oysters, down in Oyster Bay, do it. Let's do it, let's fall in love."

Let's Fall in Love
Cole Porter

For either of these genera of oysters to become amorous, the water in which they live must reach a temperature of somewhere between 68° - 70° F. (20° - 21° C.). It is during this period of a warmer environment that the reproductive cycle is triggered, and the oysters begin spawning. With the genus crassostrea, both female and male oysters spawn by releasing their respective egg and sperm cells into the surrounding waters. During a single spawning season, depending on how long the water remains at that temperature, females will release up to 80 million eggs, and the males a seemingly countless number of sperm. These egg and sperm cells float about freely, and if by chance they meet during their seagoing travels, they biologically join and become a fertilized egg, or larva. The vastness of the sea and the constantly moving currents which carry unfertilized cells prevent all but one or two in several million eggs from becoming impregnated with a sperm cell. We need to thank Mother Nature for that, for if every oyster egg were to become fertilized, in a relatively short period of time the sea bottom that provides growth for these critters would rise up out of the sea, covered with tiny oysters! An interesting point regarding the sexuality of *crassostrea* is that they all begin life as males, then change to females during the next season, and may even go back and forth several more times during their life-span.

The genus ostrea reproduces in a different manner. Where the genus crassostrea are trans-sexual, ostrea are bi-sexual, and during a single spawning season can change between male and female. When spawning begins, the ova are created and remain within the shell during the oyster's female stage. The males release their sperm into the water, and once again by chance, they enter the female's shell and fertilize the eggs. The fertilized egg remains in the parent shell for an incubation period of about 12 days until it is released as a free-swimming larva.

Now we have these tiny free floating larva, or "spawn," being carried along by tide and current. At this stage they have already developed a shell, although soft and translucent, and also a way of feeding themselves as they drift through the sea around them. Tiny hairs, or cilia, protrude from the shell and through the constant movement of these cilia, the baby oyster filters algae and plankton from its surroundings, and feeds on these nutrients.

As the oyster eats it gets larger and heavier until it can no longer be suspended in the water. This free swimming stage lasts about two weeks, and as it approaches the length of about 1/75 of an inch (.38 mm), its weight finally causes it to sink to the bottom, and it attaches itself to whatever it lands on. This is probably the most crucial point in the life of an oyster, because if what they attach to is not a suitable hard surface, or if the bottom is very soft and muddy, they will eventually die. Another reason that makes this such an

The Joy of Oysters 15

important event to an oyster is that wherever the oyster attaches itself is where it will spend the rest of its adult life. No vacations to the Bahamas for these guys. They become totally sedentary, unless moved by some outside force. As mentioned in our earlier history lesson, the ideal setting material, or cultch, is another clean oyster shell. It is what oyster larvae prefer in the wild, and seems to provide the best material for commercial growing. The size and shape of an adult oyster is greatly influenced by the cultch onto which it originally attaches.

So, what does all of this have to do with the depletion of oysters on the Atlantic coast during colonial times? Back to our history class.

Now we have a better understanding of what was happening when the wild oysters were harvested all year, and the shells were not returned to the spawning grounds. By consuming oysters during the summer months, the young ones were not given a good chance to survive, and by not returning the shells, the larvae had no suitable place to hang their hats for the remainder of their lives, so supplies of oysters dwindled.

"Hear Ye! Hear Ye!" During Feb. 1762 in New Haven, Connecticut, a law was passed to curb the rapidly reducing oyster population. The law simply stated that "....no person shall be allowed to Rake up and Catch any oysters in the Harbour of New Haven or the Cove from the first day of May to the first day of September upon a penalty of 20/ Bushels...." and that "....nothing in this vote Shall hinder the Selectmen of the Town or any one of them to Give Liberty to any person to Catch a Small Quantity of oysters in the Case of Sickness or Necessity." Also that "....no person Shall carry off any oyster shells or Culch from the oyster Banks below the New Wharf and East Haven Wharf and below a parrelel line from the oyster point to the Lower Building yard at the west....." This law from 1762 is probably the earliest reference to the old wive's tale that you should only eat oysters during months that have the letter "R" in them. (All months, except the warm weather months of May, June, July, and August.) Although oysters are not as firm and visually appealing while spawning, they are perfectly safe to eat during those months, and this tale may have been created originally to protect the species of the shellfish, rather than the health of the oyster eater. The harvesting of wild oysters continued along the Atlantic coast with these certain laws in effect to keep the oyster population in check, but it wasn't until the 1820s that oystermen attempted to "plant" oysters by harvesting small seed oysters from natural growth beds and transplanting them to their own beds. The oysters then grew on those beds until reaching market size, or for a period of between 3 and 5 years, depending on the water conditions and temperature (oysters grow faster in warmer water, so southern grown oysters reach market size more quickly than northern oysters grown in colder water).

During the 1860s, a more advanced method of oystering was developed which in many ways paralleled the planting and rotation of agricultural crops on farms. This type of cultivation maintained the supply of oysters, and became a profitable business to many oystermen along the coast. In many areas along the eastern seaboard, this became the most successful method of oyster farming, and for the most part continues to this day with little

change. This process of aquaculture utilizes privately owned or leased oyster grounds that are maintained by individual oystermen or their companies.

The selected oyster grounds are chosen for a good hard bottom that is neither muddy or prone to silt accumulation. Good food supply must also be available, as well as the water having the proper salinity. The beds are then cleaned of any debris and their boundaries accurately marked off by long poles anchored in place in the water. They are then carefully mapped and recorded in the local town records. Once the beds are prepared, a layer of clean shells is spread out to cover the bottom.

Oyster shells are hosed off the deck onto the beds in this 1970s shelling operation on Long Island Sound.

The "shelling" operation has to coincide with the free swimming stage of the larvae in the water. In early years of oystering this time was more of an educated guess, but with more recent advancements in biological testing and sampling equipment, larvae can be physically detected in the water, and the proper time to begin shelling can be calculated to within a day or two. Hopefully, the larvae will attach to the clean shell cultch and begin their growth. These setting beds are usually in fairly shallow water close to shore, so the oysters need to be moved to slightly deeper water before their first winter. When the baby oysters reach the age of two or three months, they are transplanted to beds farther offshore where the water salinity increases, and food is more plentiful. They remain in these beds for two to three years, then are moved again to even deeper water where their growth rate rises even more due to the greater concentration of nutrients in water that is found farther offshore. These are the "fattening" beds where the oyster meat becomes firm and plump, ready for market, then onto our plates!

Oystermen quickly learned how to produce the most oysters per acre of ground by experimenting with variations on this basic method of cultivation. Each major oyster growing area was unique, and each had its own slightly different geographic, ecologic, and environmental factors. In many areas of New England, the oysters were collected off the bottom by steel or rope nets or "dredges." Three types of dredges were used - the hand dredge, which was usually favored on sailing vessels, the hand dredge with a winding mechanism, and the power dredge. In many of the shallower areas farther south, hand operated tongs were used to collect the oysters from small shallow draft boats. A long handled rake with a forked bucket on one end was also used to collect oysters.

Along with the many ways of harvesting oysters came the even larger number of types of boats used. There was no typical "oyster boat," but many varieties evolved along the Atlantic coast depending on the water depth, sea conditions, and local regulations. During the mid to late 1800s every imaginable design of boat was modified and used for oystering. Pine dugout canoes that held less than 50 bushels could be seen oystering along with single and two masted "sharpies." The sharpie was a sailing vessel whose sole purpose of design was for oystering. These boats had a very shallow draft and were ideal tonging vessels. The style of the sharpie even varied from one location to another. Catboats, canoes, rowing skiffs, sloops, skipjacks and larger freighters were all part of the oyster fleet. The freighters were usually schooners, from 50 to 100 feet (15.2 to 30.2 m) in length, and were used not to harvest oysters, but to ship them along the more open unprotected routes between Boston, New York, and Chesapeake Bay.

Tonging oysters on Malpeque Bay, Prince Edward Island, Canada, c. 1900

As the demand for oysters increased, so did the need for faster, more productive boats. The age of the power driven oyster vessel began in 1874, when Peter Decker of Norwalk, Connecticut installed a steam engine on his sloop "Early Bird." This became the first totally steam powered oyster boat, and initiated a flood of sail-to-power conversions. The power steamers were used not only to maintain the cultivated beds on private grounds, but also to gather oyster seed from the natural growth beds, and within a few years the depletion of natural beds began again, because the steam powered vessels were so much more productive than sailing vessels.

The oyster steamer "Mildred."

Once more legislation was passed first by restricting the number of weeks in a year that power vessels could gather seed from natural-growth beds, and finally by banning it all together. Today most oyster growing areas still prohibit the use of power driven vessels to harvest oyster seed from natural beds. As we move farther south, the greater abundance of natural-growth reefs in warmer waters kept many of the sail powered oyster boats from converting to power. Since cultivation of oysters taken from natural beds was not practiced in southern waters as much as it was in the north, many of the areas in Chesapeake and Delaware Bays chose to stay with sail as the power of choice. The sailing oyster vessel still plys the waters of Chesapeake Bay.

By the turn of the century, oysters were becoming one of the mainstays of food consumption along the east coast. Oyster saloons and bars sprung up all throughout coastal areas, and once again the increased demand required a greater supply, so shipbuilders produced faster, larger and more powerful boats. In the early 1900s oyster boats were being built with steam engines. These were eventually replaced by gas engines because of the gas engines' much smaller size, higher efficiency, and the fact that no coal or water for the boiler was needed to be stored aboard. Diesel engines later replaced gas because of their long lasting reliability, fuel efficiency, safety, and better adaptability to cool, damp marine environments.

In Norwalk, Connecticut this massive shell pile accumulated with the bountiful oyster harvest. c. 1914

The oystering industry reached a peak along the Atlantic coast during the years between 1905 and 1920. Life was good, and grandiose stories abound about the heyday of the oyster eater. "Diamond" Jim Brady and his mistress Lillian Russell consumed oysters by the hundreds on a daily basis. New York City's Grand Central Oyster Bar, which opened in 1913, served oyster stews and pan roasts to the social elite and working

In this view from the water side, the shells are loaded by conveyor onto boats to shell the beds. c. 1940

commuter sitting shoulder to shoulder at the restaurant's landmark bar. Northeastern oyster companies maintained the largest fleet of steam powered oyster vessels in the world.

The oyster was the king of seafood, but along with its rise to the throne came a rise in industrialization. Mills and factories were choking the eastern seaboard with pollutants, and little was done at that time to curb their release. Oyster beds that once thrived around New York's Staten Island and in New York Bay, were polluted and declared unsafe by 1927. The economy was changing as well. Wooden shipbuilding was on the decline, turning more toward iron and steel vessels. The many yards that built those wooden oyster boats that were so pleasing to the eye were closing their doors, so maintenance and repairs of existing vessels suffered. Workers once lured to the high profits of the oyster business were turning to more lucrative industrial jobs.

Other factors leading to the oyster's decline were related to its own industry. There were several years of bad oyster sets on certain grounds, overharvesting, not replacing the spawning oysters, and lastly, one of the most destructive natural forces witnessed during modern times - the great hurricane of 1938. On September 21 of that year, a hurricane slammed into Long Island, New York and southern New England with little warning. With winds gusting to over 150 miles per hour (240 kph), it destroyed nearly everything in its path, killing an estimated 700 people and creating a tidal surge that left Providence, Rhode Island, which lies 40 miles (64 km) from the ocean, under 13 feet (3.96 m) of water.

The 40 mile (64 km) wide "eye" brought with it an almost unheard of barometric pressure of 27.94 inches of mercury. Salt-damaged crops and vegetation were detected 50 miles (80 km) inland, and property loss exceeded 400 million dollars (based on 1938 dollars). Because of the shallow water in which most of the oysters grew, this massive turbulence literally carried acres of oysters out to sea, and deposited a layer of life threatening silt and debris over hundreds of square miles of delicate oyster and other shellfish habitats. Years of hard work carefully preparing and maintaining these grounds for successful oyster cultivation was destroyed in several hours.

The advent of World War II, just several years after the hurricane, directed much of America's work force toward military oriented positions, and those struggling few oystermen that continued to operate had to redesign harvesting equipment on the boats as well as on shore toward a more automated system, so that the same amount of work could be done with fewer hands involved. This led to the development of newer designed mechanical dredges and also hydraulic suction as a means to harvest oysters off the bottom.

Deckhand emptying oyster dredge on an oyster boat on Long Island Sound during the 1970s.

Utilizing more modern automated techniques, the boats could now operate with only two men on board, a pilot in the wheelhouse and a deckhand operating the dredge. Since oystering in warmer southern waters depended mostly on harvesting from natural growth beds, where the oysters spawn more frequently, the rise and fall of the oyster empire was more drastic and had more of an impact in the northern states, where cultivation of the beds played a more important role in the success of the business.

The increase in pollution had dramatic effects on the oyster business in all northeast states, reducing the areas where oysters could be profitably cultivated to areas of Long Island Sound, Oyster Bay and Wellfleet in Massachusetts. As if pollution weren't burden enough, two diseases: MSX, *Hasplosporidium nelsoni* and Dermo, *Perkinsus marinus*, arose in almost all areas along the eastern seaboard to further devastate oyster populations.

Today, cleanup of polluted areas and environmental consciousness by both industry and individuals is making possible a comeback in oystering in the northeast. Better understanding of MSX and Dermo is helping control those threats and hatchery operations are providing seed oysters rather than relying on natural sets. Our discussion of regional oyster fisheries elaborates on the industry status as the new millennium unfolds, beginning on page 53.

West Coast History - A Tale of Two Oysters

In discussing the history of oystering on the west coast of North America, we need to examine two very distinct accounts. Unlike the Atlantic coast, which saw the native American oyster (*crassostrea virginica*) dominate the market for over three hundred years, the Pacific coast has two oyster species that have been of great importance to the oyster industry, and each one has a very interesting story behind it. One species (*ostrea lurida*) is native to the area, while the other (*crassostrea gigas*) has its origins in Japan. The native oyster, commonly called the Olympia oyster, and the immigrant, known as the Pacific oyster, need to be looked at separately, since the history of each one is so unique.

The west coast of North America has been home to a small native oyster for thousands of years. Petrified shells of ostrea lurida have been found from coastal Alaska to the deserts of Southern California and Mexico, in areas that were once covered by the sea during prehistoric times. During the time that European and early American explorers arrived to the Pacific coast, the Native Western oysters, as they were called before obtaining the name "Olympias," grew naturally in many locations along the coast. They were found in greatest abundance in the Crescent Bay and Ladysmith areas of British Columbia, numerous protected bays of Washington's Puget Sound, Samish Bay and Willapa Bay, and in Oregon's Yaquina Bay. The tidal estuaries of California's Humboldt Bay, Tomales Bay, and San Francisco Bay also offered protected tidelands that supported the growth of these oysters.

The physical size of this oyster and its method of reproduction were factors that limited the areas in which they grew naturally. The shell size of an adult ostrea lurida is from 1 to 2 inches (2.54 cm to 5.08 cm) in length, and they grow wild in shallow tidelands and flats between the tidal range of mean high and mean low water. Unlike the Pacific oyster that can survive out of water for many hours during extreme low tides, the tiny Olympia oyster can only be exposed to air for relatively short periods of time. Because of the near constant submersion underwater, this oyster feeds continuously, so the flow of current passing over them must be just enough to provide a steady supply of nutrients, but not too strong as to wash these little creatures away.

The Pacific Coast Native Americans, as did their Atlantic Coast counterparts, consumed great quantities of native oysters, along with clams and fish. Large shell deposits have been excavated near productive natural oyster beds, indicating that the Indians settled near these beds, and after feasting on the oysters and clams they harvested, left their shells in piles nearby. In the Pacific Northwest, stories were told to early settlers of how the peaceful fish-eating Siwash Indians of the coastal areas would be raided by the more warlike Indians of the Yakima tribes. The inland Yakimas, being unfamiliar with the rise and fall of the tides, would steal the canoes of the Siwashes, thinking they were keeping them from their food supply, but the Siwashes would go out at night on the low tide and gather a supply of oysters and clams while in hiding. After the Yakimas caught their fill of shellfish by using the stolen canoes, they would return home, believing they had defeated the Siwashes.

"A beatific smile over his face! Man had tasted the oyster!
In half an hour, mankind was plunging into the waves searching for
oysters. The oyster's doom was sealed. His monstrous pretension
that he belonged in the van of evolutionary progress was killed forever.
He had been tasted and found food. He would never again battle for
supremacy. Meekly he yielded to his fate. He is food to this day."
Don Marquis

Another tale describes a fierce British Columbia tribe that plundered the Indians of Mud Bay (known today as Eld Inlet in southern Puget Sound), not only by foraging their oyster supply, but by capturing some of the tribe's women and children and holding them as slaves. Shortly after one of these raids, according to legend, a well-liked leader of the Mud Bay Indians passed away, remained dead for three days, then returned to life. When he "awoke," he spoke of how the Great Father told him to preach to all the tribes in the region, and tell them they must stop fighting among themselves, for they were all brothers. This "born again" man organized what later became the Indian Shaker Church, a new religion based on a mixture of Catholicism and Protestantism, which were both being introduced to Native Americans by early Christian missionaries at that time. The church promoted righteous living, and seemed to appeal to the Indians' peaceful ways. The Indian Shaker Church became popular among the many Northwest tribes, and the first church building was erected at Mud Bay within sight of the oyster beds. Invitations to meetings with other tribes were a regular occurrence, attracting many from surrounding areas. These gatherings were usually followed by feasts of oysters, promoting unity and friendship among the tribes.

By the mid 1800s, native western oysters were already being harvested on thousands of acres of tidelands in San Francisco Bay. California, especially San Francisco, was in the midst of rapid growth because of the Gold Rush. The appetites of the hungry gold seeking "forty-niners" placed such a demand on these oysters that the supply was being consumed faster than the beds were being replenished, and within a short period of time, the natural oyster beds around San Francisco had been depleted.

The search was on for more oysters! Farther to the north in Oregon and Washington Territories, major native oyster producing areas were just beginning to see the influx of newly arrived settlers. The smaller bays of coastal Oregon had some natural beds, but could not provide anywhere near the amount of oysters that San Francisco demanded. Southern

22 *The Joy of Oysters*

Puget Sound, being a more inland waterway separated from the Pacific Ocean by the Juan de Fuca Strait, was not practical as a source for oysters being shipped to San Francisco. There was one body of water in Washington Territory that contained great numbers of natural oyster beds and was easily accessible to the ocean and to the direct shipping route to San Francisco. This beautiful, unspoiled arm of the sea was known then as Shoalwater Bay (currently called Willapa Bay), a large estuary located north of the mouth of the Columbia River, easily approachable by ships sailing in from the open ocean. A narrow peninsula, rarely more than 2 miles (3.2 km) wide and stretching 30 miles (48 km) to the north, protected the tranquil bay from the often raging Pacific. Entering Shoalwater Bay from the ocean was accomplished by crossing the bar at Ledbetter Point, on the northern tip of this long peninsula, and sailing south into the bay.

In 1850, there were only a handful of white settlers on Shoalwater Bay, mostly loggers, hunters, and trappers, who were not particularly interested in the abundance of oysters that the Native Americans had been eating and harvesting for centuries. The "oyster rush" to the markets of San Francisco began in 1851, when several Chesapeake Bay oystermen arrived at Shoalwater Bay after their futile attempt to find gold in "them thar hills of Californee." These men, known as the "Bruce Boys" (named after the first two-masted schooner they purchased in San Francisco, the "Robert Bruce") began shipping native western oysters from Shoalwater Bay to San Francisco. An interesting bit of history tells how shortly after the Bruce Boys arrived in Shoalwater Bay, their ship, the Robert Bruce, burned to the waterline before any oysters were ever shipped out of the bay. No one is exactly sure what happened that rainy night in December 1851, but the fire was believed to have been started by a fellow named Jefferson, who was the cook aboard the ship. It seems that Jefferson had been mistreated during the journey from San Francisco, and wanted to get even with his fellow crew members who had given him just one too many orders. Jefferson disappeared after this little incident, and the Bruce Boys, now "Shipless in Shoalwater," managed to acquire two more schooners within the next few years.

This was the beginning of what became the very profitable business of delivering oysters from Washington Territory to the booming city of San Francisco. Bruceport, the first settlement on Shoalwater Bay, was started by the group near the wreckage of their ship, and the rush was on. Other oyster schooners were soon making the run, filling their holds with oysters, and returning to California. In 1853, a dollar in gold was paid for each bushel basket of Shoalwater oysters delivered to an oyster schooner, which could hold up to five thousand baskets. Each basket contained roughly 1,500 native oysters. The same basket would sell for ten dollars when off-loaded in California, and gourmet diners would then pay a silver dollar for each oyster they ate at the many fine restaurants and eateries in San Francisco.

While the Bruce Boys were successful in their oyster shipping ventures, they were not very well liked by their neighbors. The natives and the settlers constantly seemed to be at odds with these fishermen from the Chesapeake. Anyone else that tried to harvest oysters would mysteriously find themselves minus their boats or their collected oysters, and this discouraged any serious competition. Robert Espy, a logger working at Shoalwater Bay for an Oregon timber firm, sought employment by the Bruce Boys, but had no success. Espy in the meantime had developed a close friendship with one of the Siwash tribal chiefs, Nahcati, who confided in him that there were many more natural oyster reefs on the peninsula side of the bay, the oysters there being much tastier than the ones being harvested by the Bruce Boys on the opposite shore. Nahcati then made an offer to Espy. If Robert Espy would hire men from the tribe to work for him in the oyster trade, Chief Nahcati would reveal the location of these great oyster reefs. In April 1854, Espy, his good friend Isaac Clark, and Chief Nahcati, visited the oyster beds on the peninsula side of the bay during a morning low tide. Espy and Clark could not believe what they saw — oysters stretching as far as they could see, to the north and south. They made good on the chief's offer, and established a settlement at the north end of the peninsula. Soon after, as newcomers began

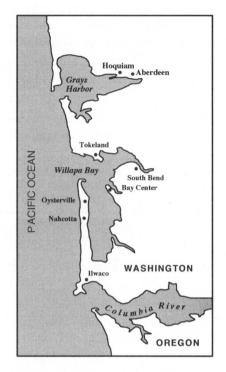

arriving to this oyster growing community, Espy named the little town "Oysterville." Hiring the hard working men of Nahcati's Siwash tribe, Espy and Clark gave the Bruce Boys some stiff competition. During the next few years, several minor altercations erupted between the two factions, but as the word about the magnificent oyster reefs spread, it became more difficult to maintain any semblance of order in Shoalwater Bay. Everyone wanted a piece of the oyster pie, and Oysterville thrived. The Bruce Boys continued their operation, but the severe high tides of winter eventually eroded away the shore on which Bruceport had been settled. All that remains today as you drive along the road to Long Beach is a historical marker and sign that tells the quirky tale of Bruceport.

Meanwhile, Oysterville became a very prosperous town, replacing the fishing village of Chinook as the county seat of Pacific County in May 1855. In 1858, over 75,000 bushels of oysters were shipped to San Francisco from Oysterville. So plentiful were these oysters that a rail line was constructed from Oysterville to the town of Ilwaco, along the mouth of the Columbia. The railroad tracks extended onto a trestle at the water's edge in Oysterville, allowing oysters to be loaded directly onto awaiting rail cars for shipment to other points in the west. Chief Nahcati and Robert Espy remained beloved friends until the chief's death in 1864, and the settlement just south of Oysterville was named Nahcotta in his honor. This oyster trade down the Pacific Coast to San Francisco reached it's peak in 1891, with 130,000 bushels shipped, but soon after that the beds became depleted by overharvesting and several extremely cold winters. By the mid 1890s, there were not enough native oysters left to support the commercial oyster harvesters that prospered just 40 years earlier.

In 1894, an attempt was made to introduce Eastern oysters from the Atlantic coast to Shoalwater, and although they grew successfully once planted, they did not reproduce well, since they were not suited for the very soft and silty bottom that was found in most of the bay. Three hundred and sixty railroad cars filled with barrels of young eastern oysters were shipped to Shoalwater Bay between 1902 and 1912, but because of the high transportation costs and the amount of labor required, profits were minimal. In 1919, almost all of the eastern oysters and what remained of the western native oysters were killed as a result of a mysterious toxic marine plankton that invaded the bay, although the exact cause was never confirmed. This ended a brief but very important chapter in the history of the native oyster on the Pacific coast.

While the native oysters of Shoalwater Bay were on the decline, quite a different scenario was unfolding in southern Puget Sound, about 120 miles (192 km) to the northeast. Prior to Washington becoming a state in 1889, all titles to tidelands were held by the United States government. As previously mentioned, these tidelands of southern Puget Sound were occupied by Native Americans for thousands of years, and they gathered oysters, clams, and fish from these shores in great numbers. As the white settlers arrived, the Indians would sell their shellfish to these eastern pioneers as they developed communities throughout coastal Washington. In the larger towns of Seattle, Olympia, and Tacoma, Indians could sell these wonderful small native oysters at the markets for as much as twenty five cents a basket. We need to remember that the Easterners were accustomed only to the larger Atlantic oyster, so these delicious tiny oysters quickly became sought after by these newcomers to the Northwest.

The Indians had never cultivated or tried to "farm" these native oysters. They grew wild and had always been in such abundance, that nothing was ever done to replenish the supply. There were natural oyster reefs in areas that had been protected by small gravel "dikes." These dikes formed from the natural wave action in uneven tidal areas, forming small ridges of gravel that surrounded and protected the beds of oysters within. On an incoming tide, the water would rise above these natural dikes, and fill in the ponds that contained the oysters, providing a new supply of fresh plankton and algae for the oysters to feed on. As the tide receded, the dikes would keep the water from draining out so the oysters were almost always covered, even during the extreme low tides that the Pacific coast is famous for. This was the way of nature, and it remained virtually unchanged for thousands of years. The Native American Indians always had a plentiful supply of oysters for themselves and, with the advent of new settlers to the region, also developed a market for selling these very popular oysters to the pioneers.

In 1889, Washington became the 43rd state admitted to the Union, and as early as 1890, the state government recognized the need to carefully develop Washington's natural resources, which included oyster harvesting. Two laws that were fundamental in the development of oystering in Washington were introduced within the first few years of statehood. The Callow Act, passed by the state's first legislature in 1890, stated that land containing natural oyster beds which had been occupied and cultivated after March 26, 1890, could be sold by the state. This meant that anyone having occupied and cultivated oyster tidelands

The Joy of Oysters 25

after that date could apply for the purchase of that land through the Land Office of Washington State. The land was surveyed, and these maps were provided along with the purchase application. The sale price of this land was extremely low so that oyster entrepreneurship was highly encouraged. The caveat to this purchase of cheap oyster land was that if the land was ever used for anything other than oyster cultivation, the state had the right to take back the land from the owner.

The second law that dealt with the purchase of oyster tidelands was the Bush Act, passed on March 2, 1895. This allowed any citizen the opportunity to apply for the purchase of oyster land, whether he had previously cultivated oysters on it or not. To maintain the land for oyster production, this act provided that if the land was used for anything other than oystering, pending a hearing, the deed could be revoked, and the land resold. The Bush Act also contained a clause providing that if the land was later found unsuitable for oyster production, the purchaser could cancel his claim and receive another plot of land.

These two legislative acts set the stage for what became a rush to purchase these choice oyster tidelands. Both white settlers and native Indians filed applications to purchase oyster land, and almost immediately oyster houses, oyster bars, and oyster packing and shipping plants dotted the shores of these narrow inlets and bays of southern Puget Sound. When Washington became a state in 1889, there was debate as to where the state capital would be. Olympia had been the capital of Washington Territory, but many other cities in Washington wanted the opportunity to become the capital city. The decision was to be voted on by the residents of the state, and so each prospective capital city launched a campaign promoting itself. The folks of Olympia, wishing to keep the capital where it was, organized meetings throughout the state, including some distant locales in Eastern Washington. To these assemblies they brought native oysters, and served great oyster dinners at the meetings' end. The popularity of the merits of Olympia as the State Capitol, along with the oyster dinners, were enough for Olympia to win the peoples choice in the voting. Washington State's capital was to remain in Olympia, and the oysters received such rave reviews that from then on, the native oysters were referred to as "Olympia Oysters."

The methods used during the early years of oystering in Puget Sound were very primitive, and as in other oyster growing regions of that time, little was done to replenish the supply of oysters as they were harvested. This was a new venture for many of those involved, and it required a learning process that never seemed to end. Many techniques of cultivation, opening and packing that evolved over the next thirty years were developed as the business grew. More practical and less labor intensive means were needed as demand increased, and it was discovered early on that catching oyster seed and planting it to propagate the future generations of oysters would be necessary. One of the first major breakthroughs of the west coast oyster industry came late in 1898, with the construction of the first Olympia oyster opening house. Originally, all oysters were sold in the shell. When they were purchased at the markets and taken home for family dinners, many housewives struggled with these tiny shellfish just to get them open. Any restaurant that served oysters in cocktails, stews, or pan roasts had an oyster shucker in the kitchen. As the demand for oysters being used in home cooking increased, the need for market available shucked

oysters was established. The Olympia
Oyster Company, established by pioneer
oysterman J.J. Brenner, shipped fresh
oysters both in the shell, and opened. As
many as thirty shuckers at one time
worked in the large well lit opening
room of Brenner's plant.

At nearly the same time that oyster
opening plants appeared, oystermen
noticed that some of the greatest oyster
sets took place in areas containing old
shells, barnacles, and other shellfish

Oyster harvest by tonging. c. 1900

remains. Now that Olympia oysters were being shucked for sale at the market, a supply of
good clean shells was becoming available. It was quickly discovered that these shells, when
spread over the beds during the summer spawning months, were the perfect material, or
"cultch," for the oyster larvae to attach to. The shells from the opening plants were then
stockpiled during the year, being returned and distributed over the clean beds during the
spawning season, greatly increasing the supply of oyster seed. This procedure, known as
"shelling," continues to this day in nearly all of the oyster producing areas around the world.
As the demand for more seed exceeded the supply of shells, variations of artificial cultch
were devised and used quite successfully. They usually consisted of a lightweight material
or some type of netting dipped in cement, providing just the roughness needed for the
juvenile oysters to attach to.

Another significant advancement which greatly
increased Olympia oyster production was the building of
man-made diking systems that improved on what was
already being done naturally with wind, tide, current,
and the gravel bottom. The gravel ridges that held in
water at low tide were simulated by building dikes out of
creosote treated timbers. The uneven oyster beds behind
these dikes were leveled to maintain a uniform depth of
water of about six inches (15.24 cm) covering the oysters
when tides were low. As more oyster grounds were
created, the dikes became very intricate in their construction, with some beds revealing up to five dike levels at
low tide. Higher levels were usually reserved for the seed
oysters, while the deeper lower levels held the four to
five year old market oysters. Wooden dikes yielded to
ones made of cement, and diking was soon standard
practice for all Olympia oyster growers.

*Dike building in southern Puget
Sound.*

The complexity of the dike systems, and the fact that they all had to be constructed at
very low tides, made for a tedious and difficult task. Depending on the time of year and the

The Joy of Oysters

The Great Dike holding water for Olympia oysters. c. 1920.

height of favorable low tides, there were only between four and six hours of usable construction time, and during the winter months, these low tides occurred at night. Forms had to be set and concrete poured during this time frame, allowing for only fifty to one hundred feet (15.25 to 30.5 m) of dike to be built in one day by a four man crew. The construction and maintenance of dikes was very costly, but these complex systems allowed oyster production to keep up with the increasing demand, and also maintained the beds for future Olympia oyster cultivation.

The companies that cultivated, grew, harvested, maintained, and provided Olympia oysters were managed by a select group of hard-working individuals who truly loved their work. In 1905, a group of these oyster pioneers met in Olympia, Washington, and called to order the first meeting of what was to become the Olympia Oyster Growers Association. This group of eight men were aware of the many problems facing the oyster industry, and recognized the need for cooperation between the growers to face the challenges and to solve these problems by civil, organized means. As stated in its initial Constitution, the Association's purpose was ..."to protect and foster the interests of all engaged in the production and sale of the Olympia oyster, and to promote friendly and fraternal relations among them." This Association grew into a strong and well-organized group of oyster growers that became the official representative of the Olympia oyster industry for over fifty years.

During those years, the Olympia Oyster Growers Association worked closely with other organizations both statewide and nationally to produce an oyster that was one of the most flavorful and nutritional foods available. The business became so productive that during the latter part of 1921 it became evident that the supply of oysters was exceeding the demand. The industry was on the brink of a competitive price war which, if it occurred, would destroy much of the "friendly and fraternal relations" that the association had worked so hard to maintain. At a meeting in Shelton, Washington on December 14, 1921, Association President Dr. G. W. Ingham presented his thoughts on how to resolve this immediate problem of supply and demand.

The minutes of that meeting reveal President Ingham's pleading "for united rather than divided effort, for cooperative effort throughout the Association; for faith in the future of the Olympia oyster, the most wonderful food created by the Almighty and cultured by man! All that is needed is that the public be told of its virtues, and demand will increase beyond our ability to supply!" In other words... ADVERTISE. The Association's advertising committee then introduced two executives from J. William Sheets, a well-known Seattle advertising agency. They proceeded to expound on the virtues of successful advertising, and outlined their proposed strategy. The Association approved, and on January 1, 1922, one

of the most effective advertising cam-
paigns in the food industry was
launched.

Although limited to just the Pacific
coast states, the public interest in the
subject matter of oysters was so great
that well-written stories about Olympia
oysters appeared in newspapers from
Seattle to Los Angeles. This caused even
greater reader interest, and soon articles
with photos and artwork were found in
magazines and other publications
throughout the West. Display banners

Olympia oyster trade exhibit. c. 1925

were created for seafood restaurants. Roadside billboards touting Olympia oysters sprung
up throughout the countryside, and cooking schools began to incorporate oyster recipes in
their classes. Many oyster companies developed beautiful color labels for their packaging,
and each year the first week of September was declared Olympia Oyster Week throughout
the Northwest for "feasting, celebration, thanksgiving, and good cheer in memory of the
occasion." This festivity set the stage for the future of oyster festivals and events that occur
around the world to this day.

The Association had initially established an assessment of one dollar per sack of
oysters be set aside to cover the cost of this extremely expensive yet highly effective ad
campaign, and the records show that this amount allowed for advertising expenses was
paid religiously for almost fifteen years. By the mid-1930s the demand for oysters had once
again exceeded the supply, and so advertising efforts were reduced accordingly.

The members of the Olympia
Oyster Growers Association faced
other challenges during the rise of
the Olympia oyster industry. Sanitation and cleanliness standards for
oyster growers nationwide were
being established by the U.S. Public
Health Service following an outbreak
of typhoid fever in several East Coast
cities during 1924 and 1925. These
cases were reportedly traced to
contaminated shellfish beds in highly
populated Northeast areas. Waters
in which Olympia oysters grew were

Oyster company dock in Olympia, WA, c. 1910

very clean compared to those of the problem areas on the East Coast, yet the Association
realized that uniformity established on a national level was necessary. Washington, along

with each oyster growing state, needed to adopt minimum requirements for health and sanitation that met or exceeded the requirements established by the Federal Government. Along with these requirements, water samples taken from oyster grounds would be tested by the State for purity, and if the water is found clean enough to allow taking of oysters for market use, the oyster grower would be issued a State Certificate that declares the growers beds are safe for oyster consumption. Also issued are individual numbers that must appear on any container or bag of oysters from these certified beds. This allows the source of each oyster to be readily traced should a problem arise, or as a check to guarantee that the oysters were harvested, processed, and packed according to Federal and State Departments of Health. This State Certification of water purity and uniform sanitary requirements is a practice that continues today in every aspect of the industry, including growing, harvesting, shucking, packing, and shipping.

During most of the forty-plus-years that the Olympia oysters rose to becoming the most sought after mollusk in America, the threats on its existence were usually controlled by the growers. In the case of Mother Nature dealing a blow with several consecutive winters of extreme cold, it rebounded in the following years of warm weather with good sets. One event that drastically reduced the production of Olympia oysters was the construction of a sulphite pulp mill in 1927. This mill, located on Oakland Bay in Shelton, Washington, discharged waste water from the pulp manufacturing process, including bleaching agents and other toxic chemicals directly into the water. Almost immediately, natural oyster sets ceased, and adult oysters began to die. Several years prior to the opening of the mill, production of Olympia oysters was roughly 50,000 bushels per year. Between 1927 and 1933, it had declined to about 19,000 bushels. A slight improvement to 23,000 bushels per year was achieved during the mid-1930s because the mill rerouted its discharge into a small lake west of Shelton, but contaminants leached through groundwater systems and found their way back into the bay.

The mill temporarily closed during part of World War II, and resumed partial operations in 1945. Many Olympia oyster growers filed law suits against the owners of the mill, seeking damages for tideland and crop loss. It became a very emotionally charged issue within the community. Settlements were made out-of-court to the oyster growers, and the threatened closure of a mill that provided jobs for local workers caused the townspeople to raise $150,000 to help pay for these damages. In 1948, the mill once again resumed full production, and the oysters that had started to return to Oakland Bay, once again disappeared.

Several investigations and experiments connecting the possibility of the oysters' decline to the pulp mill's discharge were carried out by State and Federal agencies. In the 1949 Washington State Fisheries Bulletin 49-A, it was summarized that after all possible causes of the reduction of oysters were examined, all were found ... "to be inadequate to explain any but a small fraction of this alarming decrease. Sulphite pulp mill waste alone appeared to offer a sufficient cause."

The Joy of Oysters

The Shelton mill closed its doors in 1957, and within three years, water quality improved enough to see a gradual return of the Olympia Oysters. In 1961, an outstanding natural set of oysters occurred once more in southern Puget Sound, but by this time, most of the Olympia oyster growers that suffered losses during this long ordeal had replanted their beds with heartier Pacifics. There are currently less than a half dozen growers cultivating Olympia oysters in Washington State, and they must supplement their operations with other more predictable products such as Manila clams, mussels, or Pacific Oysters. The yearly production of Olympia oysters rises and falls like the tide. During the winters of 1983 and 1986, bitter cold temperatures swept in from the north, and these bad freezes depleted nearly 75% of the total harvest. Even worse was the winter of 1989, when minus 3.5 foot tides coincided with 40 knot winds and temperatures falling below zero degrees F. Nearly all of the Olympias perished that winter during their exposure to such harsh conditions.

As of this writing in January 2000, only Totten Inlet and Skookum Inlet in southern Puget Sound supports the commercial cultivation of native Olympia oysters. The growers who choose to harvest Olympia oysters today are demonstrating their love and devotion toward these tiny native oysters that once grew in great abundance. They are both protecting and providing an oyster that has nearly become exterminated more than once. Recent reports from California tell of several natural sets of Olympia oysters in San Francisco Bay, but it remains to be seen if they'll ever return to a point where they will be commercially grown in that location. Since the entire procedure of cultivating and harvesting Olympias is done by hand, profits are small, and over the years the market has been greatly reduced. In spite of all the hardships they've endured, Olympia oysters are still available, and well worth a visit to the Olympia area of south Puget Sound.

While the popularity of the Olympia oyster on the west coast was never in question, there still remained a market for a larger oyster that could be used in ways for which the tiny Olympia oyster was unsuitable. The raw oyster cocktail was the Olympia oyster's claim to fame. Oyster recipes that were popular in restaurants on the east coast called for them to be cooked in one way or another. Many oyster dishes were either baked, fried, broiled, or grilled, and although the Olympia oyster was used in pan fries, stews and pan roasts, try making Oysters Rockefeller with Olys! They're just too darned small. During the 1920s, eastern oysters were shipped to the west coast by rail, but many wholesalers encountered problems with marketing this larger oyster. Since a great number of folks who settled on the west coast were originally Easterners, they were accustomed to a larger oyster, and were willing to buy oysters shipped from the Atlantic states. To make any profit, the oysters needed to be sold at a high price to offset the cost of shipping. Refrigeration, which consisted of re-icing the cargo along the way, was poor by today's standards, and the quality of the oysters deteriorated before reaching the west coast. This was an even greater problem during warm weather months, when entire shipments spoiled during the heat of summer.

We already know that earlier attempts to plant oysters from the east coast had been unsuccessful in Washington's Willapa Bay, and shipments were also planted in San Francisco Bay and certain areas in Puget Sound. Wherever the young eastern oysters were planted, the results were the same — high mortality rate before reaching market size. They also did not reproduce well, even though the growers tried to maintain similar conditions on the west coast to what was found back east. The fact that eastern oysters didn't do well on the west coast had been a head scratcher for years. Oysters are very environmentally sensitive animals, and each species has its own quirks and characteristics. The means of propagation, temperature of the water, tides, current, salinity, food supply, type of sea bottom, and water depth are all factors that determine which species of oyster can live where. There is one major difference between the Atlantic and Pacific coasts that contributes more to this quandary than any other, and that difference is TIDE.

For those of you who do not live in salt water coastal areas, let's first explain a little about tides, what they are and what causes them. According to Bowditch's *American Practical Navigator*, "The tidal phenomenon is the periodic motion of the waters of the sea due to differences in the attractive forces of various celestial bodies, principally the moon and the sun, upon different parts of the rotating earth. In its rise and fall, the tide is accompanied by a periodic horizontal movement of the water called tidal current." And...."to avoid misunderstanding, it is desirable that the mariner adopt the technical usage: tide for the vertical rise and fall of the water, and tidal current for the horizontal flow. The tide rises and falls, the tidal current floods and ebbs." Got that? Tide rises, tide falls. Current floods, current ebbs.

"An oyster is what happens
  when the ocean finishes with the moon."
Tom Robbins, 1993

The difference between a pair of successive high and low tides, or range, varies greatly throughout the world. It may be as little as several inches, or in excess of 60 feet (18.3 m). In most coastal areas, there are two high and two low tides each day. This type of tide is called semi diurnal. The duration of the average tidal day is 24 hours and 50 minutes. This causes corresponding tidal events to take place approximately 50 minutes later each day. So, if the tide is high at 2:00 PM on Tuesday at a certain location, on Wednesday it will be high at about 2:50 PM at that same location. If you were to plot a tidal curve for various ports along the Atlantic Coast , you would see that the range for most locations is pretty uniform, meaning the heights of the highs and lows are roughly the same from one day to the next. There are exceptions during certain phases of the moon where you may find higher or lower tides, but not extreme differences. The species of oyster that grow on the east coast live underwater all the time, feeding constantly. During periods of low tide, they are never exposed to the heat or cold of the air. The Pacific Coast tidal curves tell a different story. The distinguishing characteristic of Pacific tides is the varying differences in heights of successive high tides or successive low tides. This type of tide is said to have diurnal inequality, resulting in greater and more rapid changes in the tidal heights. Diurnal inequality is a result of many factors including the funneling effect caused by complex positioning of land masses, slope of the sea bottom, wind, barometric pressure, rotation of the earth, distances the tidal bulge must travel, and the time lag between different points along the tidal current's route.

To demonstrate this, let's look at a tide table for Olympia, Washington on two different days of 1999. The heights are given in feet, and are referenced to an average low tide of 0.0 feet. Plus or minus numbers are heights above or below this low tide reference. Tides with minus numbered heights are referred to as minus tides. On Wednesday March 10th, there was a high tide of +11.9′ at 12:16 AM, followed by a low tide of +7.3′ at 5:25 AM. The next high occurred at 10:13 AM, with a height of +12.1′, then a low of +1.9′ at 6:07 PM. The differences in height between the two highs and two lows were 4.6′, 4.8′, and 10.2′. The first two tide changes show a rather modest range of slightly more than 4.5′ each, while during the third change, the tide dropped a little more than 10′. Examining the table for Olympia on June 15th, we notice something quite different. At 1:32 AM, there was a low tide of +6.9′, followed by a +14.6′ high at 6:18 AM. The next low tide was at 1:42 PM, but the height was a whopping -3.7′! That's almost 4′ below average low tide. The following high at 8:55 PM was also very extreme, with a height of +16.4′. The first range was 7.7′, the second, 18.3′, and the third was 20.1′! That's a lot of water movement in just over seven hours.

What this means to oyster beds on the Pacific coast is that at certain low tides during the year, many tidal flats that are usually submerged become exposed for varying amounts of time, this being dependant on the height of the low tide. During an extreme minus tide like the one mentioned above, entire inlets and estuaries empty their waters, uncovering gradually sloping sea floors, including oyster beds, that can extend for miles. This is a wonderful time for beachcombing, as many forms of sea life are visible during a

Minus tide at Blau Oyster Co. on Samish Bay, WA with Mount Baker in the distance.

big minus tide that are usually hidden by the sea the rest of the year. Another aspect of this tidal phenomenon that affects oysters in the Northern Hemisphere is caused by the 23-1/2 degree tilt of the Earth as it rotates on its axis while traveling around the sun. Because of this tilt, the greatest range of tides occurs not year round, but during the hottest part of the summer (mid-June through mid-July), and the coldest part of the winter (mid-December through mid-January). On top of that, the summer minus tides take place during the midday sun, while the winter ones are in the middle of the bitter cold night. Those Atlantic oysters that are used to being snug in their watery beds day and night just can't take exposure to heat and cold that are a normal occurrence in Pacific waters. This diurnal inequality of west coast tides is common not only to the North American coast, but to the entire Pacific

Rim. The fact that Japan is included in this unusual tidal situation and also lies closely between the same north latitudes of the United States makes for a fascinating question. Could oyster seed from Japan (where species of larger oysters were already being grown commercially) be successfully transplanted to similar conditions on the Pacific Coast in the United States?

As early as 1899 inquiries from officials in the U.S. were made to Japan asking what type of larger oysters would best be suited and available for export to the shores of North America. Between 1902 and 1920 attempts were made at transporting small shipments of oysters from a number of locations in Japan to the west coast of the United States, as well as to Hawaii. Very little is known about these early experiments, and they had no major impact on the west coast oyster industry. Generally these transplants did not do well, due to either a high mortality rate during the 15 to 20 day ocean crossing, or not surviving for long periods of time once they were planted in their new homes.

In spite of low survival, two lessons were definitely learned from these experimental operations. First, the younger the oysters were when they were shipped, the greater was the chance of survival. Older oysters did not take to the ocean crossing as well as the younger ones. Second, an oyster's chance of survival was greatly increased if it spent its first winter months in the same water and environment in which it was fertilized. You loving parents were always correct in saying that baby's first Christmas should be spent at home! Since oysters begin their lives during the summer, those first few months leading into winter are very crucial to the development of a healthy juvenile. By the early spring, the shell has hardened and they've had good growth during the winter, allowing them to withstand being out of the water for longer periods of time. The most successful transplants were done during the spring, and the species that had the lowest mortality rate was *crassostrea gigas*.

While these experiments with transporting small shipments of oysters were going on, two young Japanese men residing in Olympia had their own plans. Joe Miyagi and J. Emy Tsukimoto had been researching areas in Washington that had once supported the growth of Olympia oysters, comparing them to familiar oyster growing regions in their native Japan. While still in school, Joe and Emy worked for several Olympia oyster companies during their summer vacations, learning as much as they could about the business. They visited many shorelines within Washington taking temperature and salinity readings, and obtained corresponding information from areas in Japan.

In the spring of 1919, these men shipped to the U.S. cases of oysters from the Miyagi Prefecture near Sendai, Japan. Their first endeavor was a failure, or so they thought. Almost all of the oysters were dead upon arrival to Washington, so the men discarded them at their intended destination in Samish Bay, thinking all was lost. This dumping site was on the tide flats of the former Olympia oyster farm, the Pearl Oyster Company. Soon, something remarkable happened that was the root of the successful future of oystering on the west coast. Several months after the dead shells were dumped, workers at Pearl Oyster noticed increased growth of the originally unseen spat that had been attached to the shells of the larger dead oysters. Young Japanese oysters were growing in U.S. waters, and their size increased at a surprising rate! It was decided by Joe and Emy that Samish Bay, a northwest-erly exposed tidal area southeast of Lummi Island and the San Juan archipelago, would be most suitable for establishing a commercial oyster company utilizing imported seed from Japan.

It must be said at this time that whenever you slurp a wonderfully plump Pacific oyster (*crassostrea gigas*), you should tip your hat and offer a quick "thank you" to these two men, Joe Miyagi and J. Emy Tsukimoto. It cannot be determined what exactly made their efforts successful while others failed. Many times when a discovery or invention is devel-oped, we can't put our finger on the one aspect that made it work, and this is also true with oystering. As we mentioned, their initial shipment was thought to be a loss, but later proved to be a great success. The bottom line is that whatever these two did, it worked. Emy and Joe were very well educated and hard working young men, and knew much about oystering in both Japan and the United States. If they had not been successful in 1919, someone else probably would have been down the road. But they were the first. Pioneer Olympia Oysterman E.N. Steele wrote in his book *The Immigrant Oyster*, "Whether they were smart, or lucky, or both, they succeeded, and are entitled to that acknowledgment." Thanks, guys.

Between 1919 and 1920, Miyagi and Tsukimoto organized a small company with several Seattle area businessmen, raised enough money to purchase the 600-acre Pearl Oyster Company, and shipped 400 cases of oyster seed from Japan to Seattle in the spring of 1921. The wooden cases, each holding approximately two bushels of seed, were carefully packed and thoroughly soaked with sea water before being loaded onto the open deck of an American ship, "President McKinley." Covered with a matting that could be hosed down with ocean water to keep the cargo cool, the cases made the ocean crossing in 16 days, passed customs inspection in Seattle, and made their way north to Samish Bay on a scow. At their final destination, they were spread across their new homeland, and immediately began to grow very quickly. Not only was their growth rate greater than in their native Japan, but they developed a delicious flavor that was considered superior to their previous taste. For the first time on the west coast of North America, a large oyster comparable in size to its highly demanded east coast cousin, was being commercially grown.

An unfortunate event in American history occurred very soon after the formation of this new business and the purchase of the oyster grounds. Due to political issues taking place around the world, the popularity of Japanese people living in America, especially on the west coast, was on the decline. In 1921, legislature passed the anti-alien law, which prevented the leasing or ownership of any land in the United States by an alien. The oyster land on Samish Bay had been purchased under contract by several Japanese men, and now they could no longer maintain legal ownership. The owners negotiated the sale of Pearl Oyster Company, and in May 1923, sold both the business and the 600 acres to J.C. Barnes and E.N. Steele.

Tsukimoto returned to Japan to set up an oyster seed procurement operation for Barnes and Steele, who immediately began to develop a marketing plan for their new business. Until this time, these transplanted oysters were referred to as "Japanese Oysters." Because of the growing sentiment against anything from Japan in the United States, Barnes and Steele marketed the oysters as "Pacific Oysters," and named the newly purchased operation "Rock Point Oyster Company," after a prominent rocky projection that extended out from the hillside above the oyster beds.

Steele had grown and sold Olympia oysters since 1907, and had many prospective buyers in the Northwest for his new Pacifics. They were much larger than the Olympias, and Steele knew that if marketed properly, could replace the need for expensive eastern oysters that were still being shipped to the west coast. They would be much fresher, and the cost would be quite a bit less. As sales manager for Rock Point, Steele traveled north to Bellingham and south to Everett, Seattle, and Tacoma. It was more difficult than first expected, but over time the Pacific oysters were accepted by more buyers and markets. Steele would bring samples to restaurants and cafes and demonstrate to skeptical chefs how to prepare these oysters that were the new kids on the block. We remember the great ad campaign that the Olympia oyster industry initiated in 1922. Steele used some of the same tactics for his Pacifics, and created beautiful packaging for his containers, which ranged in sizes from one gallon to half pint. One visible difference between eastern oysters and Pacifics is that the Pacific oyster has a dark, purplish rim around the oyster meat that is not present on the eastern oyster. Many restaurant patrons thought that there was something wrong with the oyster, so the oysters were advertised by the statement, "Look for the oyster with the velvet rim. It assures you that it is grown in the pure waters of Puget Sound, and that it is fresh! It has a velvet rim the same as the Olympia oyster."

Dick Steele,
son of E.N. Steele

As the Pacific oyster grew in popularity, Steele and Barnes expanded their market farther south into Oregon, and California, and east into Idaho, where some folks had never seen or even knew what oysters were. In 1926, Rock Point Oyster Company had a small truck built as their traveling demo vehicle. Loaded with lots of oysters, coolers, advertising material, cooking demonstration equipment, and sleeping accommodations for two, E.N.'s brother and sister-in-law hit the road and peddled Rock Point oysters hither and yon. Once, while demonstrating in a San Francisco market, a traffic jam developed from the large crowd of onlookers that had spilled out into the street.

While the Steeles were busy marketing and selling, our friend Emy was back in Japan, obtaining not only prime seed oysters, but also determining what cultch material would be best suited for Pacific oyster larvae growing in the Northwest. Along with cases of oysters, Emy shipped mussel shells, cherry tree branches, cement covered matting, bamboo, and oyster shells to Rock Point, all of which were tried as cultch. A good percentage of time during Rock Point's early years was spent experimenting with various growing methods, cultch materials, and harvesting techniques.

This was new territory to explore, and every effort was made to obtain the most productive oyster beds possible. The Pacific Oyster adapted very well to its new home, and soon had all but replaced the eastern oyster market in the western states.

During the first eight years that seed oysters were transported from Japan, Rock Point Oyster was the sole company involved in the operation, and Samish Bay was the only destination of the young oysters. Willapa Bay on the Washington coast had supported the growth of Olympia oysters for many years, even though the 1920s saw virtually no more Olympia oysters remaining. A few oyster companies on Willapa Bay that still had their oyster grounds, equipment, and shucking houses available, quickly learned of the success of the Pacific oyster in northern Puget Sound. Test plantings were done at Willapa, and the growth of the baby oysters was even more remarkable than in Samish Bay, reaching market size in less than two years. In 1931, four oyster companies on Willapa Bay imported seed oysters from Japan, and the successful results encouraged other growers in prospective locations to plant Japanese seed. It seemed that wherever the seed was planted, the oysters grew, and by 1935, almost 72,000 cases of oyster seed were shipped from Japan and planted in various waters on the Pacific Coast. The number of buyers for this seed totaled 156, and seed planting was carried out in California, Oregon, Washington, Alaska, and British Columbia. The plantings outside Washington State were carried out just a few years after the expansion into Willapa Bay.

In Oregon, the first Japanese seed was planted in 1934 on tidelands that once supported native western oysters. Locations around Coos Bay, Bay City, Ocean City, Yaquina Bay and Tillamook proved most productive for the newly arrived Pacific oyster. For over sixty years, family members at Qualman Oyster Farms, founded in 1937 in Coos Bay, have harvested and processed Pacific oysters from the same waters as their grandfather. The Wachsmuths were another pioneer family in the early days of Oregon oystering. Louis Wachsmuth had cultivated Olympia oysters in Yaquina Bay until Pacifics were planted during the 1930s, and also operated "Dan & Louis Oyster Bar" a fine oyster bar and restaurant in Portland that continues to sell oysters today.

California followed with successful plantings in 1935. The Pacific oyster quickly replaced the depleted supply of the native oyster in California, with Tomales Bay, Humboldt Bay, Morro Bay, and Elkhorn Slough near Monterey receiving the majority of seed. Within twenty five years, California became one of the largest oyster producing states in the country, with nearly 2,500,000 pounds (1,132,500 kg) of oyster meat processed between 1952 and 1959.

We spoke earlier of the construction of a sulphite pulp mill in 1927 at Shelton, Washington, and its effect on the Olympia oyster industry. The beginning of the Olympia oyster decline coincided with the rise of the Pacific oyster on the west coast. The Pacific oyster was never meant to replace the Olympia oyster market, but the Pacific withstood more environmental changes and required less hands-on maintenance than the more delicate Olympia. The growing methods for the two oysters are quite different, and for many years they did not "grow up in the same neighborhood." This had kept them somewhat at a distance from each other. While the yearly production curve of the Olympia oyster has resembled a roller coaster since the early 1930s, the introduction of the Pacific oyster to the West Coast demonstrated no adverse effect on the pre-existing Olympia oysters.

As the number of Pacific oyster growers increased, common problems and challenges arose, along with the need for standard practices to be developed within the industry. The North Pacific Oyster Growers Association was formed in 1931 to meet these needs. The Association, as did its predecessor the Olympia Oyster Growers Association, established uniform packaging and naming standards, wages being paid to shuckers, amounts to be set aside for advertising purposes, and most importantly, how to handle the recent rapid expansion of the oyster business, with supply exceeding demand, and the great depression looming just ahead.

During the depression, Congress passed the National Industrial Recovery Act in 1933, requiring all businesses to operate in accordance with a Code of Fair Competition. This established codes of ethical marketing and fair prices for goods produced. The oyster industry, not excluded, felt the need to cooperate in this patriotic effort. At the 1933 National Oyster Convention in New York City, E.N. Steele represented both the Pacific and Olympia Oyster Growers Associations, and offered their support in the creation of a National Oyster Code. This became a very serious matter, and the West Coast growers were proud to participate in a national program that was the first step towards the recovery of the oyster industry and the end of the price wars that reduced the price of oysters to below the cost of producing them. The National Code was established, all parties approved the final draft, and President Franklin Roosevelt put his pen to the paper on February 26, 1934.

Although a National Code of Oysters had been established, the years that followed were years of stabilization, not growth. Oyster growers suffered extreme hardships as the price of oysters remained between $1.10 and $1.50 per gallon. This was due in part to the over supply of oysters resulting from heavy plantings in 1934 and 1935. Production costs were much greater than that, and many smaller operations were forced to go out of business. Rock Point Oyster Company sold approximately 50,000 gallons of oysters during the 1935-1936 season, and showed a loss of over $1,000 for the year. In May 1935, the U.S. Supreme Court declared the National Recovery Act unconstitutional, which nullified the National Code, and the Pacific oyster industry slipped into another period of disturbing confusion. The contributing factors that saw the industry through these hard times were the patience and perseverance of the Association membership, their strong commitment and hard work, and incorporating clauses of the Fair Competition Code into their by-laws and constitution. By the end of 1938, the west coast oyster companies that remained in business were either operating at a loss or barely breaking even. Decisions had to be made and made quickly. One of the options that several of the larger companies chose was to turn the ownership of the business over to the employees, form a cooperative organization, and offer profit sharing. This was the route that Rock Point Oyster Company took, and over the next three years, the market slowly took a turn for the better.

From 1936 until the surprise attack by Japan at Pearl Harbor on Dec. 7, 1941, Japanese seed oysters continued to be shipped to the West Coast, but the number of cases had declined yearly until 1941, when only 10,400 cases were imported. The thrusting of the United

States into war with Japan presented a new series of problems for the west coast oyster industry. Obviously, seed shipments from Japan would not be made during the time of war, and millions of men were taken out of the civilian work force to join the military operations. Oyster companies produced food for our nation, and that food supply could not just come to a halt. The fact that the war came on the heels of a huge surplus of oysters was a saving grace, and with one-and-a-half million gallons of oysters growing on the West Coast, it was estimated that the available supply would last, at most, three years. It was feared that if the war lasted longer than three years, without Japanese seed, the industry would die.

From the time that the first seed oysters from Japan were successfully planted in 1919 until the war broke out in 1941, spawning and natural oyster sets took place only in rare instances. There were some small areas where the water temperature reached the necessary 68-70 degrees F. (20-21 degrees C.) to trigger spawning, but the waters on the Pacific coast are generally cooler than on the Atlantic, so these natural sets were undependable as a source of future oysters. At times mother nature offers us just rewards instead of crushing blows, and the years during the war was a time to appreciate her generosity. Warmer than normal summers resulted in natural oyster sets in areas where previously there were none. This continued throughout the war years, and by combining these natural sets with the existing surplus, the oyster industry was able to maintain a stable supply during the war. The military also contracted with members of the Pacific Coast Oyster Growers Association, insisting that at least 60% of their production be reserved for the armed forces, and agreed to purchase frozen oysters for $3.75 per gallon. This arrangement continued until the war ended.

After the war, the Pacific oyster industry needed to resume relations with Japan to re-establish the shipment of seed to the United States. The demands of war had diminished our west coast oyster supply, and soon after the war ended, communications between oyster growers and Japanese seed producers were entered upon once more. It took over a year to iron out postwar problems that were a result of the conflict, but seed shipments began again in the spring of 1947, when nearly 57,000 cases of seed were shipped to the West Coast. The years after World War II saw the west coast Pacific oyster industry enter another period of increased Japanese seed planting. We already know that the Pacific oyster beds had become depleted during the war, but also the Olympia oyster supply in southern Puget Sound had nearly been destroyed due to pollution. As a result, more companies that grew Olympias replanted their beds with Pacifics, with hopes that these oysters could survive in areas which once supported the tiny native Olys. As more Pacifics were planted on the West Coast, natural sets occurred with greater frequency, gradually reducing the need for foreign seed oysters. Empty oyster shells obtained from opening houses were spread out over the beds, or strung on lines suspended above the bottom to catch as many young larvae as possible during spawning season. The introduction of oyster hatcheries that regulated spawning, larvae growth, and attachment to cultch in a controlled environment, also contributed to an industry less dependent on shipments of seed from Japan. The Pacific oyster was here to stay. A once foreign immigrant had become a naturalized citizen. With the advent of canneries that opened along the West Coast, cooked oysters and oyster stew could be processed, canned, and shipped to any destination without fear of spoilage. Individually quick frozen oysters appeared in market freezers during the early 1960s, and although not as flavorful as fresh, they were pretty darned good, especially if you lived in Alpena, South Dakota and that's all you could get.

There was another species of oyster whose seed was introduced to the United States from Kumamoto, Japan to augment the dwindling Olympia oyster supply. The *crassostrea sikamea* is a small, deep-cupped variety that makes for an excellent half shell oyster. Experimental seed shipments began in 1949, and increased to approximately 1,200 cases of seed by 1961. The last import of Kumamoto seed was in the mid-1960s, after which all seed was obtained from hatcheries. Currently, the Kumamoto oyster remains very popular as a half shell or cocktail oyster, and has become the perfect oyster for those adventuresome first time oyster eaters, or "virgin slurpers."

Hand picking Pacific oysters in southern Puget Sound.

As we enter the 1970s, oyster hatcheries provided most of the seed for Pacific oyster growers, and natural sets, although unreliable, produced healthy juveniles as well. During this same period of time in Europe, the supply of European oysters (ostrea edulis) had diminished to a degree that Japanese seed was needed to supply growers across the Atlantic. A bidding war between Japanese seed providers and the U.S. and European oyster growers raised the cost of seed to an unaffordable level in this country, forcing Pacific oyster growers to halt seed imports from Japan. The importation of Japanese seed oysters to these shores ended in 1979, when 4,900 cases were shipped.

The past twenty years of Pacific oystering on the West Coast have been very productive, but not without challenges and confrontations. Coastal development, both residential and commercial, has impacted the water quality in both rural and urban areas. Logging and other timber related operations have altered the landscape, effecting erosion and watershed runoff into saltwater estuaries. Poor management of fisheries and overfishing certain species have caused imbalances within the ecosystem as well as the food chain for marine plants and animals. Pollution from human and industrial waste must be constantly checked and monitored. All of these factors play a part in the success of oystering. Oyster growers are farmers of the sea, and must maintain a fertile and nutritious habitat for their crop. If this environment is not maintained to safe and healthy standards, the beds are deemed unfit to grow oysters for consumption.

We also need to realize that Pacific oyster farming on the west coast is still relatively young for a commercial enterprise. The first successful plantings of Japanese oysters took place in 1919, less than one-hundred years ago. Much has been learned regarding planting seed, cultivation, and growing techniques, but it's a continuing educational process. Shellfish labs and hatcheries on both coasts utilize scientific technology, research and environmental information, and genetic engineering that was not available fifty years ago. During the early 1980s, for example, research began on the development of a Pacific oyster with an extra set of chromosomes that prevent the oyster from spawning. These *triploid* oysters maintain their marketability all year, instead of becoming soft and milky during the spawning season. Choice, firm, plump oysters are now available year round, including months containing an "R"!

It is this writer's feeling that the Pacific oyster industry on the West Coast is a healthy one. During the 1970s and 1980s, Eastern oysters produced in Chesapeake Bay nearly disappeared due to pollution and overharvesting. Long Island Sound's supply, which had been depleted during the mid-1900s, was showing steady, but slow signs of recovery. Problems with shellfish disease and bacteria in the Gulf Coast caused concern with oyster lovers in the south. The previously hidden virtues of sweet West Coast Pacific oysters soon became evident to oyster eaters across America. While citizens, environmental agencies, and oyster growers on the Atlantic Coast worked tirelessly to clean up their local waters and reopen previously closed oyster beds, Pacific oysters from clean waters of the Northwestern United States and British Columbia made their way across the continent to oyster aficionados everywhere. There was even a point in time during the early 1980s that the Northwest shipped seed oysters to Japan, to help meet their demand. At the beginning of the new century and the year 2000, we are experiencing an Oyster Renaissance in North America and around the world. Pacific oyster growers have pledged themselves to the highest standards of quality and freshness, and continue to educate themselves in their ability to produce and maintain a world class oyster.

Many of these current developments and procedures are detailed in other segments of this book, but in the meantime, take a reading break, pour yourself a stout beer, and eat some oysters.

Oyster Nomenclature, Species and Varieties

Forty years ago, if we ordered oysters in a seafood restaurant, there would probably be few, if any, choices available. Oysters were usually advertised as "fresh" or "local," and historically were identified by the town, bay, or body of water they were harvested from. On the East Coast, we've eaten Apalachicolas from Florida's Gulf coast, Malpeques from Canada's Prince Edward Island, Chincoteagues from Virginia, and Oyster Bill's beloved Blue Points from Long Island Sound (although Blue Points originally came from Long Island's Great South Bay). The oldest "brand name" oyster in the U.S. is the Cotuit, from the Cotuit Oyster Company, founded in 1837 on Massachusett's Cape Cod. All of these Eastern oysters belong to the species *crassostrea virginica*, but each variety takes on a unique taste, size, texture, color, and shell appearance. These characteristics are dependant not only on the surrounding waters, but also the method by which the oysters are grown and cultivated.

The *ostrea lurida*, or native Olympia oyster, dominated the commercial West Coast market for nearly a century, until Japanese seed oysters, *crassostrea gigas*, were transplanted to locations from California to Alaska. Quilcenes from Washington's Hood Canal, British Columbian Lasquitis from Lasquiti Island, and Tomales Bays from California were popular Pacific oysters on western menus for many years.

The Europeans, especially the French, classify their oysters more by shell shape or environment, than by a geographic location. *Huitre plate*, French for plate or flat oyster, refer to *ostrea edulis*, commonly referred to as European Flats. The European deep-cupped oyster is *huitres creuses*, Latin name *crassostrea angulata*. This oyster is similar in shape and shell texture to the Japanese oyster *crassostrea gigas*, and history tells of how it was introduced to Europe in 1868 when a Portuguese ship returning from Asia was forced to dump it's cargo, which included oysters, while weathering out a storm off the Bay of Biscay. The oysters that survived began to spawn, and a new variety of oyster was soon appearing in European markets.

The French also have a classification that rates the quality level of the oyster. Oysters from Marennes, France have a subtle green hue caused from the high concentration of chlorophyll in the algae on which the oysters feed. To many oyster bon vivants, they are considered the finest oysters in the world, and receive the highest classification of quality, or *fines de claires*. Oysters with this designation are lovingly cared for and grown in dredged out and thoroughly cleaned salt basins, also called parks. They remain there for three to four years, and then are taken to market.

When visiting an oyster bar today, especially in the Pacific Northwest, you will find more varieties and market names than ever before. Some oyster eateries may offer as many as fifteen local varieties of Pacific oysters, all belonging to the same species, but each one unique to the area in which it was grown, and cultivation method employed during that growth.

If by now you are somewhat confused by all of these Latin names and oyster varieties, hold on to your hats folks, for we've only just begun! Let's begin by briefly describing each of the five species of oysters that are planted, cultivated, and harvested in North America, plus one that comes to us from South America. This Chilean oyster is just beginning to make its appearance at some of the finer oyster bars and seafood restaurants on this continent.

Crassostrea virginica

This species of oyster is native to the East Coast of North America from Prince Edward Island to the Gulf of Mexico, and may well be called The All-American Oyster. Hatcheries provide much of the seed, but many naturally occurring beds are still used as a source for young oysters. The shells are relatively smooth, thick and somewhat asymmetrical in shape. Market size is from three to five inches (7.6 to 12.7 cm) in length. Commonly called Atlantic, Eastern, or American oysters, they are eaten raw on the half shell, or cooked. Most varieties of Eastern oysters have a solid, definitely salty flavor, and taste like you're "biting into the sea." Because of the large geographic area in which they are found, variation among Eastern oysters from different locations is great. Generally, northern oysters are firmer and considered better for eating raw than southern oysters because of the colder water temperatures. The Eastern oyster is the most widely cultivated species grown in North America. In markets, they are available alive in the shell, or shucked and packed fresh in various sized containers. Eastern oysters are now successfully cultivated on the West Coast by Taylor Shellfish Co. in Puget Sound, Washington and Hog Island Oyster Co. in Tomales Bay, California.

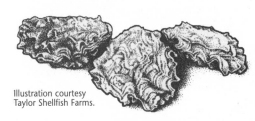

Illustration courtesy
Taylor Shellfish Farms.

Crassostrea gigas

Originally from Japan, this species was commercially introduced to the West Coast of the United States in 1921. The majority of these cupped oysters are grown along the Pacific coast on privately owned or leased oyster beds, with the seed coming from hatcheries. There are some natural sets that take place in areas where the water reaches the proper temperature, but these are not reliable enough to provide a dependable source of seed. It is a very hearty oyster, adapting well to many environments, and is the most widely cultivated oyster in the world. Shells are more brittle and usually thinner than the Eastern oyster shell, and the great number of cultivation methods produce oysters that vary in shape, flavor, size, and shell color. They may have a somewhat smooth and almost symmetrical shell, but the majority have fluted ridges with a more elongated shell. The common name for these oysters is Pacific, and market size is anywhere from three to twelve inches (7.6 to 30.48 cm). Smaller Pacifics are normally eaten on the half shell or in oyster cocktails, while the larger ones are used for cooking, or cut up for stews and chowders. Pacifics traditionally have a milder flavor when compared to Eastern oysters, and are sold either in the shell, or shucked and graded by size.

Crassostrea sikamea

Another species native to Japan, these oysters reached the shores of the West Coast as a shipment of seed in 1949. Kumamotos, or Kumos, are named for the bay on the island of Kyushu, in which they were originally cultivated. They are highly prized for their fruity, sometimes buttery flavor. Kumos are a small oyster, measuring two to three inches (5 to 7.6 cm) in length and are usually eaten raw on the halfshell. Shells are highly sculptured and easily identified. There is little variance among Kumamotos grown in different locales. All Kumamoto oyster seed is produced in hatcheries, with the majority of growers being on the West Coast. They are sold live in the shell. If you've never eaten a raw oyster, and had but one oyster to choose from for that honor - choose a Kumamoto.

Illustration courtesy
Taylor Shellfish Farms.

Ostrea lurida

This diminutive oyster is the true native oyster of the West Coast of North America. Its history can be traced back thousands of years, when they grew wild from Alaska to Mexico. Originally referred to as Native Western Oysters, the common name today is the Olympia oyster, or Olys. With a shell size rarely exceeding two inches (5 cm), the Olympia is grown commercially in protected gravel beds, surrounded by man-made dikes that retain water at low tide. Although there are a few locations where these native oysters continue to reproduce on the Pacific Coast, only a handful of oyster growers in Washington State cultivate and harvest Olympia oysters. The entire operation of raising and harvesting Olympias is done by hand. Spawning occurs naturally, usually during the second or third week of May. The small size of their shells makes shucking Olympias a time consuming task, and usually a standard oyster knife is whittled down to a smaller size for shucking purposes. Olys are ideally served on the half shell, but if cooked, use only in stews, pan roasts, or pan fry very quickly. Never bake or deep fry. The market for Olympia oysters is rather limited, since the cost to grow and pack them is so high. They can be purchased in the shell, or shucked, but be prepared to pay a dear price. In January 2000, retail prices were running approximately $32.00 per pint of shucked Olympias, with roughly 275 oysters per pint. Olympia oysters are difficult to obtain outside of the vicinity in which they grow. They are a true Pacific Northwest delicacy, and considered by many to be the finest tasting oyster grown today. With today's common use of overnight air freight, even Olympias can be procured for your pleasure from Taylor Shellfish Company and a few other suppliers in Washington State.

Illustration courtesy
Taylor Shellfish Farms.

The scientific community is constantly updating and sometimes changing the Latin names for species of both animals and plants. One such change that may appear in current reports or scientific journals is the more modern name for the Olympia oyster. *Ostreola conchaphilia* is the same species as ostrea lurida, and should not be confused. For the sake of consistency in writing this book, the more familiar name, *ostrea lurida*, will be used in reference to the Olympia oyster.

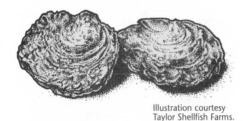

Ostrea edulis

When ancient Greeks and Romans began to cultivate oysters as early as 300 years BC, it was most likely the species *ostrea edulis* that they harvested from the Adriatic Sea. These particular oysters are native to the continent of Europe, the choicest ones coming from the estuaries along the Bay of Biscay. Today they are grown on both coasts of North America, with seed coming from hatcheries. The great State of Maine and the Pacific Northwest are especially known for the successful cultivation of these European oysters. The common name is the European Flat, although sometimes they are referred to as Belons. This is actually a misnomer, since true Belon oysters must have matured at the mouth of the Belon River in Finistere, France. They are closely related to the Olympia oyster, in that the parent holds the fertilized eggs within the shell for about two weeks before releasing them as free swimming larvae. European Flats are easily identified by their symmetrical, almost round shell, and are very flat in thickness compared to a Pacific or Eastern oyster. Market size for Flats range from three to five inches (7.6 to 12.7 cm) in diameter, and they are sold live in the shell. Many oyster lovers feel they should never be cooked, only eaten raw on the half shell. Their flavor is very light and mild, and very often have a pleasant metallic aftertaste. Because the tiny larvae are developing shells during their two week incubation period, Flats may have a gritty texture if eaten during spawning season.

Ostrea chilensis

During a recent visit to South America, this writer, Oyster Bill, had the opportunity to sample a plateful of freshly harvested Chilean oysters while wandering through the fish market stalls of Puerto Montt, Chile. Grown off the Island of Chiloe (pronounced chee´-lo-way) on Chile's rugged inside passage, these oysters resemble Eastern oysters (*c.virginica*) in appearance, but are much smaller in size. The average sized shell was about two inches (5 cm) in length. After the fish monger shucked a few for me to sample (with a very large chef's knife), I ordered a plate. Several minutes later no less than three dozen perfect oysters arrived at my table, accompanied only by fresh lemon halves. Wonderfully plump, they had a very firm texture with a true briny finish. The lemon was all that was needed, and most were eaten au naturale. To my knowledge, no Chiloes are cultivated in North America, but probably in the near future our hatcheries will be producing seed for growers to plant.

Oyster Culture Methods

Our friend and object of desire, the oyster, is somewhat picky about where he/she wants to live. Native Americans discovered the places that oysters occurred naturally and availed themselves of many fine oyster dinners. It wasn't until Europeans arrived and populations grew that natural oyster beds were endangered on both east and west coasts. Depletion of natural oysters in Long Island Sound, coastal New England and Chesapeake Bay was almost complete in just 200 years.

To bring oysters back to levels where we oyster lovers can enjoy them with regularity, it became necessary to invent methods of culturing or "farming" the sea. You will see how many different methods have been used to raise a crop of oysters in different areas.

The Picky Mr./Ms. Oyster

Oyster habitat is particular in many ways. The mollusk only survives in water that is partly salty (brackish) by dilution with fresh water from rivers or streams. The salinity

requirements for each oyster varies but the survival range is generally considered to be between 5 and 40 parts per thousand (salt in water). Water temperature is rarely the cause of oyster mortality, but extreme low temperatures will inhibit growth rate and reproduction. Oysters require unpolluted water and are, in fact, used as an indicator if marginal pollution conditions exist.

Water-borne nutrients on which oysters feed arrive via tidal current or from streams and rivers emptying into the bays. Nutrient-rich areas provide for fast growth of oysters to marketable size.

Stable sea bottom conditions are critical for oyster survival and have been a major contributing factor to destruction of natural oyster beds. Specifically, oysters must remain uncovered. Rocky beds, shell beds and sandy bottom conditions are the most favorable. Mud, clay and other soft substrates present the potential for oysters to sink into the bottom and suffocate. Silt deposits originating from rivers and streams (often due to destruction of stable, non-eroding river banks) frequently have been the cause of severe oyster mortality in bottom-grown oyster habitat.

Natural Oyster Culture – Oyster "Reefs"

Over thousands of years, indigenous oyster populations formed large colonies on the bottoms of bays and estuaries referred to as oyster "reefs." These oyster colonies had naturally found suitable water conditions and thus were able to reproduce and thrive. Layers of shells and living oysters accumulated on the bottom, providing an excellent surface for oyster spat to grow on. Life was good for Mr./Ms. oyster.

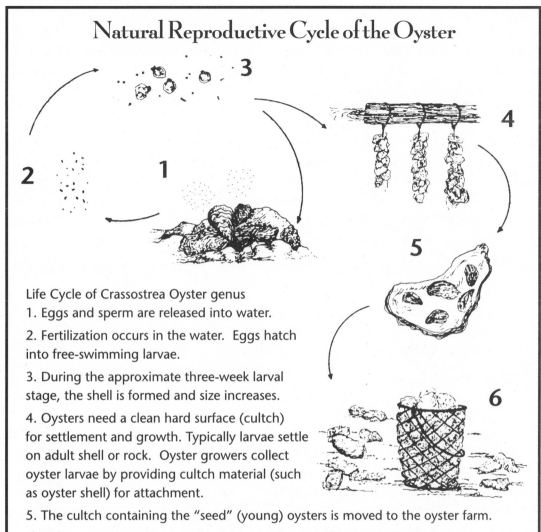

Natural Reproductive Cycle of the Oyster

Life Cycle of Crassostrea Oyster genus

1. Eggs and sperm are released into water.

2. Fertilization occurs in the water. Eggs hatch into free-swimming larvae.

3. During the approximate three-week larval stage, the shell is formed and size increases.

4. Oysters need a clean hard surface (cultch) for settlement and growth. Typically larvae settle on adult shell or rock. Oyster growers collect oyster larvae by providing cultch material (such as oyster shell) for attachment.

5. The cultch containing the "seed" (young) oysters is moved to the oyster farm.

6. Oysters are planted on rearing beds and harvested in two to four years.

Increased population by man affected these colonies primarily by over harvesting. Worse, original oyster harvesters unknowingly destroyed the bottom conditions by removing oysters, shells and all. Free swimming oyster spat no longer had a suitable surface to which they could attach and grow. Add a good dose of silt and sawdust from nearby mills (along with a little chemical pollution thrown in) and natural oyster production came to an end.

Successful regeneration of oyster reefs has been accomplished by regulating harvests and harvesting methods, along with cleaning up the water around bays and estuaries. In some areas of the south (Gulf of Mexico) oyster harvesting has returned to a semi-natural condition. In most other places, oyster reefs are now "farmed" by man.

Bottom Culture

Shallow bays and estuaries in the Northeast were prime habitats for oysters. Vast tracts of Long Island Sound, Chesapeake Bay and other areas were literally covered with native oysters when the first white men arrived in the 17th century. As described earlier, depletion took less than 200 years.

Many of these same bodies of water are still suitable habitat for growing oysters. Today they are "farmed" by "seeding" or "planting" small oysters attached to shell fragments (cultch) and allowing them to grow over several years to marketable size. During this time the growing oysters are often relocated to different beds where environmental conditions suit their stage of development. Finally, the "fattening" beds are then "dredged" with a rake-and-bucket like tool to collect the oysters for market. Then the process begins again.

In some areas, hatchery grown spat must be placed in the beds to grow larger. In other areas, cultch (bare oyster shells) are spread on the bottom just prior to the oyster's spawning season to "catch" free swimming spat looking for a place to settle down.

This "oyster farming" method has proved successful in most oyster growing regions with minor variations between producers and/or growing areas.

Intertidal Beach Culture

In areas where tidal ranges are often a dozen feet or more, as in the Pacific Northwest, oysters can be grown on rocky or hard gravel beaches. At low tide, 100 feet or more of beach may be exposed and oysters can be tended to or harvested by the oystermen. One method of harvesting this type of beach culture is that the oyster company will set out large metal containers by boat at high tide, each one having a floating buoy attached to mark their location. At low tide, workers go out to the exposed beds and fill up the containers by hand, leaving them on the oyster grounds. When the tide comes in, the floating buoys are visible, and the full containers are hoised on to the deck of the oyster boat as it passes by. The containers are emptied on shore, and are once again taken back out to the oyster beds to be filled at the next low tide.

The conditions for beach culture are not right for every oyster species and not just any beach will do. (See oyster growing requirements above.) Beach culture sometimes utilizes natural oyster set (after an adult population is established), and in other instances cultch with attached spat is spread on the beach seasonally. Marine predators can be a problem with this type of culture, as well as poaching by organized or unknowing oyster lovers.

Suspended Culture

In certain growing regions where the water is very deep or where oyster predators abound, bottom culture of any kind is not possible. Innovative oyster growers have, over the past 40 years, developed methods of growing oysters that do not rely on laying the oyster down on the bottom. Several methods are popular including the use of lines and cables strung just off the bottom, and plastic trays and nylon nets of various shapes and sizes.

Long Line Culture

Developed by the Japanese oyster industry during the late 1940s, long lines are economical to construct, and can be used in rougher, more exposed waters, since no rigid structures are used. In this method of oyster farming, growers attach the cultch. In this method of oyster farming, growers attach the cultch (with growing oysters aboard) to cables or lines strung near the bottom. When the oysters have grown to marketable size, the lines are

Long line intertidal culture near East Sound on Orcas Island, Washington.

retrieved and the oysters are separated and made ready for sale. This method is very labor intensive and results in oysters that are most often destined for the more-profitable half shell trade.

Many East coast oyster companies growing European flat oysters for the half-shell trade have been successful using one or more of the long line culture methods. On the Pacific coast where long lines are relatively new, experimentation is still being carried out to determine the most suitable method for a variety of water conditions.

Suspended Tray, Lantern Net Culture

Two methods of oyster culture that are gaining in popularity for the single oyster half-shell trade is the use of stacked trays and nets suspended in deep, cool waters of tidal inlets. Trays may be either commercially made, usually of plastic, or constructed with wood frames covered with some type of mesh or wire that keeps the baby oysters from being washed away. Nets are available in several shapes, the most common being the lantern net. In appearence they resemble decorative hanging Japanese lanterns. While the large stacks of trays require specialized, heavy-duty equipment to handle them, they produce a very high quality product and offer the grower flexibility in production and harvesting.

Lifting stacked trays at Pearl Seaproducts in British Columbia.

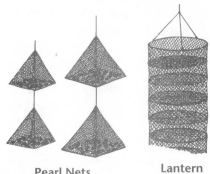

Pearl Nets

Lantern Net

Rack & Bag Culture

Growing oysters in bags hanging from racks is another method of suspended culture. These oysters are often "singles" grown to a certain size in hatchery-like conditions and then placed one by one into bags or nets to spend an additional two years in the water. Such unattached oysters are pristinely beautiful and command a premium price for half shell service. The maintenance of the growing equipment and vulnerability to damage by storms or careless boaters increase the produc-

Pacific oysters in rack and bag growout on Eld Inlet in Washington State.

tion cost and limit this method to certain protected areas of the west coast.

While the oysters grown in suspended culture develop beautiful shells with a minimum of mud and seaweed attached, the animals must be handled carefully before going to market. Suspended culture oysters don't develop thick protective shells like their bottom-grown counterparts since they are not exposed to current and tidal flows that toss them about. Also, since the oysters don't have to deal with being exposed to air at low tide, they have weak adductor muscles and must be "hardened" by several weeks of intertidal life prior to shipment or they would lose their precious liquor in transit.

Oyster Predators and Pests

Like a slug on your favorite lettuce leaf or aphids eating your prized roses, oysters must contend with a variety of organisms that either enjoy eating the oyster as much as Diamond Jim Brady did or threaten the habitat on which the oyster grows.

Oyster eaters include starfish, crabs and drills (snails). Starfish grab the oyster with their powerful tube-feet and force the shell open, allowing them to digest the oyster. Crabs similarly are able to open the shells of small oysters and extract the oyster meat. Several species of snails (referred to as a group called drills) attach to the oyster shell and use their powerful rasp-like tongue to bore a hole into the oyster shell. The contents are then removed for the snail's nourishment.

Salinity of the water where oysters grow has a lot to do with presence of various predators. If the salinity is less than 15 parts-per-thousand (ppt), oysters are happy but starfish and oyster drills stay away. Also, starfish are less of a problem for intertidal (shallow water, exposed at low tide) oysters than for sub-tidal (always under water) oysters.

Ghost shrimp are a bane for oyster growers attempting bottom culture on a stable mud seabed. The shrimp burrow into the bottom in such great numbers that the oysters fall through the lattice-like labyrinth and are suffocated by the mud. Periodic treatment of these oyster beds to kill the shrimp is a controversial issue as we enter the new millennium.

Non-native organisms are a continual problem in some oyster growing areas. One of these is spartina grass, a harmless looking cordgrass native to the east coast that is destroying certain oyster habitats out west. It is believed that spartina was introduced to western oyster beds when it was used as packing material for east coast oysters shipped to the Pacific coast. The grass was tossed aside when the oysters were unpacked and it began to grow. Spartina develops massive root systems that virtually fill in open water along shorelines with solid earthlike material. Since west coast oysters grow in these inter-tidal areas, they compete with spartina grass for living space. The thick grass also acts as a dike, trapping silt deposits, and steals nutrients that are vital to the growth of oysters. One of the regions hardest hit with spartina infestation is Washington State's Willapa Bay. Attempts are continuously underway to mow the grass, pull up the seedlings by hand, and rake it from the shoreline. Herbicides are being tested experimentally, but overall success has not yet been achieved, and the use of chemical sprays is always controversial.

Another non-native predator with an appetite for oysters and other shellfish is the European green crab. Invading the Atlantic coast during the 1930s, this crab most likely arrived on North America's shore in the ballast holds of large ocean crossing ships. After wreaking havoc along the east coast, European green crabs have recently been discovered on the west coast, working their way up from San Francisco Bay, and most recently being seen in Coos Bay, Oregon, and Willapa Bay, Washington. Although no large scale damage has been observed, shellfish growers are keeping a close watch on their shell stock for any sign of these unwanted pests. If left uncontrolled, the crabs may have a devastating impact on the future of the west coast oyster industry. In addition, the green crab is expected to compete with native Dungeness crabs and possibly affect that fishery as well.

Oyster Diseases

Two diseases have been responsible for the severe decline of oyster populations in the eastern U.S. during the 20th century. MSX, (*Hasplosporidium nelsoni*) a protozoan parasite, affects oysters of all ages and is nearly always fatal. It has shown to be less viable in waters with salinity below 15 ppt, providing some relief from complete destruction of oystering. The fungal disease transmitted by the southern oyster parasite *Perkinsus marinus*, Dermo is also a fatal disease to many oysters and is especially active in years of warmer weather. Like MSX, Dermo is less viable in waters with low salinities.

Extensive research has been undertaken to find ways of combatting these diseases with promising results from several sources. A universal cure is on the horizon, however, and oystering in the Northeast U.S. will no doubt be affected for years to come.

Oyster Hatcheries - The Whys and Hows

When the first settlers arrived in New England and the Mid-Atlantic, the bays and estuaries were teeming with marine life. Increasing immigrant populations at first didn't stress the resource, but further exploitation by commercialization of the fishery spelled trouble ahead for the great reefs of oysters in Long Island Sound and Chesapeake Bay.

Efforts were made in the 19th century to manage the resource by "farming" the bays and taking advantage of "natural sets." Natural breeding of oysters during the warm summer months resulted in a renewal of the population and provided a source of oyster "seed" for commercial oystermen to transplant onto their leases. It was the declining frequency of the best of these natural sets, coupled with the catastrophic effects of MSX and dermo in the 1950s that necessitated intervention by scientists and eventual creation of shellfish hatcheries.

Bottles of different algae cultures are prepared to feed the baby oysters.

The goal of both commercial firms and university programs in creating hatcheries is to help renew the shellfish resource. By controlled breeding of oyster stock, the millions of larvae can be saved from natural predation and allowed to "set" on cultch that has been specially prepared. The resulting oyster spat are then grown out in controlled conditions (tray or net culture) or are reared for a time then planted out on the beach or bottom to reach harvestable size.

The hatchery is part laboratory and part shellfish aquarium. A major portion of hatchery resources are involved in producing food for the tiny oyster larvae and spat. This food consists of special types of algae grown in large tanks and "fed" to the microscopic baby oysters as they grow. Devices known as "upwellers" are used to circulate the food and keep nutrients available to the spat. Keeping these offspring happy and healthy leads to thousands of spat ready to be reared at the oyster farm or planted out in the bay.

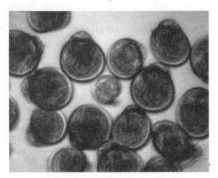

Oyster larvae under the microscope.

The advantages of hatchery production include: choosing what oyster species to produce, avoiding changes in climate that might prevent natural spawning in the wild, and developing selective breeding programs to create an animal that can resist diseases or retain a robust meat during the warmer months of summer.

A maze of pipes, pumps and tanks awaits the visitor to an oyster hatchery since fresh seawater is distributed to nearly every area for production of food (algae) and the creation of favorable conditions for the brood oysters to spawn. A female oyster releases about 120 million eggs and a male oyster releases over a billion sperm. If an egg receives multiple fertilizations, it will not survive, so controlled spawning conditions are monitored closely.

Some oyster hatcheries break up cultch into tiny pieces so that only one oyster spat can "set" on each piece. As these oysters grow, they will be perfect individuals instead of clumps of a dozen or more stuck to a single shell. The resulting oysters are idealfor the half-shell trade where the beauty of the oyster shell helps to establish the value of the product.

Advanced hatchery operations, combined with further efforts to clean up waters where oysters are grown, promise more enjoyment for oyster lovers of future generations.

  The Joy of Oysters

Oyster Producing Regions of North America

Enjoying oysters on the shores of North America predates white recorded history of the area by thousands of years. Many of the same bays and estuaries visited by Native Americans for oyster gathering are today producing shellfish of superior quality and variety. Oyster farmers operate from cold northern waters of the Canadian Maritimes to the warmer shoals of the Gulf of Mexico on the Atlantic Coast, and from the Gulf of Alaska to the bays and inlets of Northern California on the Pacific Coast. For details on specific oyster growers in each region, see the index of growers beginning on page 308.

Canada's Maritime Provinces

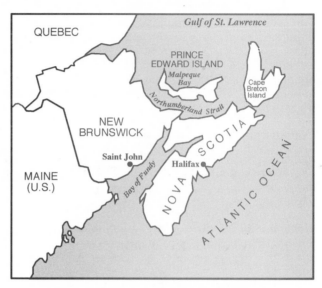

Though the industry is relatively small in harvest size, superior quality oysters are shipped far and wide from this area. Prime oyster habitat is along the Northumberland Strait, separating New Brunswick and Nova Scotia from Prince Edward Island. This area is part of the Gulf of St. Lawrence and is called the "Acadian Pocket" for it's warmer temperatures as related to its latitude of roughly 46° north. Oysters are harvested from both public ground and private leases.

Oystering on Prince Edward Island has a long history as the reputation of Malpeque Bay oysters and those from other areas is renowned. A destructive disease – termed "Malpeque disease" caused almost complete oyster mortality in the early 20th century, but the natural resurgence of resistant stock is returning the areas along the Northumberland Strait to commercial productivity. Oystermen collect the oysters from bays and estuaries during the fall by tonging from small dories. The harvest is sold mainly to markets in Eastern Canada, though the best quality oysters serve the restaurant half-shell trade across the continent in both Canada and the United States.

The oyster industry in New Brunswick and Nova Scotia was affected by Malpeque disease during the 1950s and resistant stock was brought in from Prince Edward Island to revive the industry. The first aquaculture efforts were employed in New Brunswick using cement-coated plastic cones to attract free-swimming spat from each year's ample natural spawning.

Oysters are tonged at many locations in New Brunswick and in Nova Scotia at Pugwash, Wallace Harbor, Caribou-Pictou and Antigonish. Pollution has adversely affected oyster survival in selected areas.

The Joy of Oysters 53

New England Coast

Among Native Americans, those living along the coast of Maine may have been the most appreciative of the fine taste of fresh oysters. Middens of oyster shells discovered at Salt Bay in the Damariscotta River are considered the largest in the world dating from about 100 A.D. Many of these fine oyster grounds produced their last harvest in the mid-19th century. By-products of local sawmills (sawdust and wood debris) being dumped into the bay was the probable cause of the demise.

From the Piscataqua River on the south coast to Bar Harbor and further north, oystering is making a comeback. The University of Maine has supported hatchery and aquaculture programs to increase the chances of survival of oysters planted out by commercial growers. American oysters and European flat oysters are both raised in the Damariscotta River estuary. Juvenile oyster disease is less of a problem than it once was and MSX and Dermo are being held in check. Glidden Point Oyster Company is achieving great success and their oysters are available on the half shell in many East Coast cities. Near Kittery, Maine, Spinney Creek Shellfish is raising American oysters for regional shipment.

Sorting Eastern Oysters at Glidden Point Oyster Co., Maine

Since colonial days, the region between Massachusetts Bay and Raritan Bay has been one of the largest commercial oyster growing areas in North America.

On Cape Cod, Massachusetts, small oyster fisheries exist in Barnstable Harbor, Wellfleet Harbor, and Cotuit Harbor. Seed oysters are obtained from natural beds in other states and planted on leased grounds, where they grow to market size. The Cotuit Oyster Company, founded in 1837, is the oldest oyster company in the United States.

The State of Rhode Island began leasing oyster grounds to fishermen in 1822, and a substantial local market was developed in Narragansett Bay, with oyster seed coming primarily from Connecticut. Rhode Island took a direct hit from the 1938 hurricane, and most

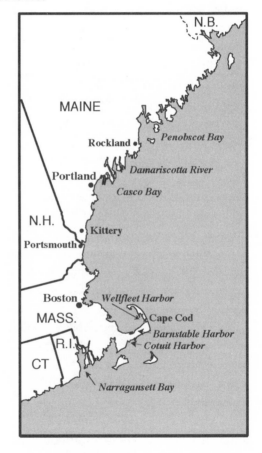

The Joy of Oysters

of the oysters were either buried under tons of silt and suffocated, or were carried out to sea by the turbulent waters. Since Connecticut's natural beds were also affected by the same storm, oyster seed for Rhode Island's oystermen became unavailable in the years following the hurricane. Since then, oystering in Rhode Island has been slow to recover, but during 1993 and 1994 an increase in seed oysters from natural beds in Narragansett Bay occurred, and in 1996, nearly 30,000 bushels of oysters were harvested. This is a far cry from the roughly 2,000,000 bushels harvested by that tiny state in 1910.

Long Island Sound is bordered by Connecticut to the north, and Long Island, New York, to the south. Its eastern entrance is marked by a narrow body of water called The Race, where swift currents, during their twice daily ebb and flood, transport nutrient rich water to a region that is home to some of the highest quality oysters grown anywhere. The Sound is relatively shallow, with depths rarely exceeding 140 feet (43 m).

On the Connecticut side of the Sound, commercial oyster beds are primarily found on leased beds from New Haven, following the coast southwest toward Greenwich. Numerous islands, reefs, and river outlets provide an ideal environment for oyster cultivation. Water depth around the growing beds ranges from 8 to 25 feet (2.5 to 7.6 m). Hydraulic dredging is the primary method of harvesting. Natural beds still provide most of the seed oysters, but several hatcheries have become a source for seed when natural sets are poor. This has been one of the hardest hit regions during the late 1990s for oyster mortality due to the Dermo (*perkinsus marinus*) and MSX (*minchinia nelsoni*) parasites, and currently, the larger commercial operations have had to rely on hard-shell clams as their primary fishery, while the oysters recover. These diseases have no effect on human life, but can kill oysters to such degree that in some beds as much as 95% of the oysters have been destroyed.

The Long Island Soundkeeper, an organization that keeps a close watch on the water quality of the Sound, has developed the Yankee Oyster Project, which was designed to protect and sustain healthy oyster aquaculture on Long Island Sound. This project is basically a co-op oyster hatchery run by small commercial growers, non government organizations, and State and Federal agencies. Their primary goal is to create a disease tolerant strain of oysters that can be re-bred over a long period of time, hopefully producing a strong, healthy and disease resistant oyster population. This particular hatchery is still in the early stages of development, but Soundkeeper Terry Backer reports that their first season was successful, having produced nearly 100,000 baby oysters, of which 30-40% appear to be disease tolerant. This was reportedly confirmed by the State of Connecticut's Department of Aquaculture. If this hatchery accomplishes its goal, one more step will be taken to preserve the fragile oyster industry that has seen so much turbulence during the past 100 years.

For many years the primary oyster producing bay on Long Island was the Great South Bay, located on the south side of the island. Extending for nearly 40 miles (64 km) and protected from the Atlantic Ocean by a narrow barrier beach island, this shallow bay averages only 5 to 10 feet (1.5 to 3m) in depth. It was in this bay that the well-known Blue Point oyster was first harvested, coming from the waters off the town of Blue Point, near Patchogue. The name of Blue Point as an oyster became so famous, that soon any oyster grown in New York was called a Blue Point. To prevent other New York regions from using

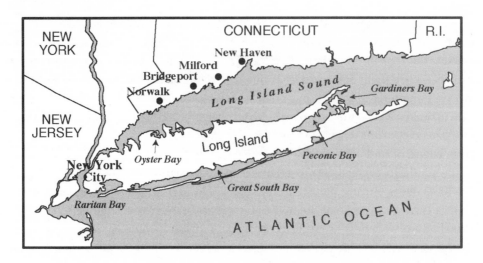

the Blue Point name, the state legislature passed a law in 1908 that prohibited anyone from selling oysters marketed as "Blue Points" unless they were planted and cultivated for at least three months in the waters of the Great South Bay in Suffolk County. Since this law applied to sales only in New York State, it wasn't long before oysters from Connecticut's coast were being sold as Blue Point oysters. Blue Point is still the common name used for oysters harvested on either side of the Sound.

The hurricane of 1938 opened up large inlets in the barrier island, causing ocean water to rush in, and increasing the salinity of the bay to levels that supported the small snail-like oyster drill. This predator quickly spread throughout the bay, and killed the remaining oysters. Replanting efforts during the 1940s were met with minimal success, and during the 1960s the disease MSX wiped out nearly all of the cultivated oysters that remained.

Today on the Sound's New York side, only a handful of oyster companies operate in Northport, Peconic, Gardiner's, and Oyster Bays. The largest, Frank M. Flower and Sons, is the only seed production operation left in New York, producing seed for small companies as well as for planting on their own beds in Oyster Bay. Some seed is also available from naturally occurring sets near Northport and Oyster Bays.

Until recently, another body of water that was too polluted to sustain healthy shellfish is Raritan Bay, lying between the southern shore of Staten Island, New York, and New Jersey. Up until the late 1800s over 800 oystermen worked the waters between Raritan and Newark Bays, supplying the many oyster bars and saloons in Manhattan, just a stone's throw away. Industrial activity increased in surrounding areas, and by 1925 several people died from typhoid fever, as a result of eating polluted oysters from Raritan Bay. As more people became ill, the oyster companies in the Bay and neighboring waters went out of business. Today, Raritan Bay is cleaner than it has been in nearly 100 years, but it will take many more years before it returns to the condition it was in before the mid 1800s. Since the beginning of the year 2000, reports from that area tell of healthy oysters living once more in Raritan Bay. If the efforts continue in keeping Raritan Bay pollution free, as in Long Island Sound to the east, chances are good that clean, healthy oysters may once again be harvested from those waters.

  The Joy of Oysters

The Saviours of Long Island Sound Oystering

The waters off Rhode Island, Massachusetts, Connecticut, and Long Island, New York continue to play an important role in the North American oyster fishery, but as with other once highly producing regions, this area has not been without its problems. From the mid 1800s to the early 1900s, this region was the leader in oyster production on the Atlantic Coast. The great hurricane of 1938 buried much of the prime oyster grounds in silt. By the end of World War II, profitable oystering in southern New England had nearly vanished. There were a few small operations that struggled to survive, but the future health of the oyster business was in serious jeopardy. A slow increase in production is the late 1940s was curtailed once more by several more hurricanes during the 1950s, destroying a good percentage of the oyster set, and again in 1957, when starfish, which had not been a threat for many years, suddenly became more abundant, and eliminated most of the seed oysters. During the 1960s, the starfish population was reduced by extensive mopping (dragging large mops over the beds thus entangling the rough surfaced starfish) and the use of quicklime to destroy the animals on contact. From the 1970s to the present, the oyster fishery has made a slow but steady return to this part of New England.

The Bloom brothers aboard "Eaglet."

The success of this return is largely due to the efforts of two hard working men from East Norwalk, Connecticut. Twin brothers Hillard and Norman Bloom were born into an oystering family in 1928, and as young boys worked with their uncle Wally Bell on his oyster sloop "Seabird." Working off the natural beds between Bridgeport and Stratford, Connecticut, they learned the oyster business from their uncle, as well as from the old timers that still lived in East Norwalk.

They loved the hard work, and the life on the boats as "natural growthers," dredging seed oysters from natural beds, and selling them by the bushel to larger oyster companies who then transplanted them to their own leased beds. After graduating from high school in 1946, they bought their first boat, an old oyster sloop, the "Eaglet" and started out on their own, dredging oyster seed while under sail. Several years later, they acquired another sloop, the "Suzie C." Their own experiences and what they learned from their predecessors were invaluable in creating an oyster operation that has become the largest and most successful oyster company in the world today. The major difference between these two brothers and so many other oystermen that had tried to make a go of the business during difficult times was that these boys were really smart. Smart in a way that is hard to put into words. Instinctively smart. Not only did they work very long hours, they also modified their business tactics when nature dealt them a bad hand. For example, after the hurricanes of the 1950s that wiped out acres of oyster beds, they converted their boats to clam dredgers, and continued harvesting hardshell clams (quahaugs, cherrystones, and littlenecks). Since the clams lived under the sea bottom, they were not affected by the storms as much as the oysters were. While clamming, the Blooms worked to re-establish the oyster grounds that were destroyed by the storms.

To assure some sort of steady income, the Blooms had other part time jobs in their "spare time." Norman ran a small plumbing business, working evenings and weekends, and for awhile they even had a band, performing dance jobs on Saturday nights. Their days on the boats were exhausting. Even after Hillard contracted polio in 1950 and lost the use of both legs, they worked on the water seven days a week, from 10 to 12 hours a day, 52 weeks a year. They bought out one small oyster company after another, refusing to let the business die in spite of many setbacks. In 1967, they bought the company that was owned by their grandmother's family, Tallmadge Brothers, which became the name of their business.

Tallmadge Brothers in South Norwalk, CT.

In March of 1973, a fire totally consumed their offices, shucking house, and processing plant in South Norwalk, and once again they were determined to keep the business going. Within a week of the fire, they had a temporary office set up and used refrigerated trailers for storage of their oysters and clams. Soon after that, a modern facility was built at the same location. By the mid-1970s, the oysters had returned to their beds, clamming continued, and the Bloom brothers had proven to the shellfish industry that hard work and foresight could bring back a dying way of life that had been all but lost just 25 years prior.

They were also instrumental in controlling and fighting pollution and in helping to establish watchdog organizations to keep tabs on the environment. It was during the 1970s that public awareness regarding clean water was brought to the forefront. The Federal Clean Water Act of 1972 set the recovery of New England's oyster industry in motion. As a result of the efforts of all involved, the state of Connecticut's oyster production tripled between 1989 and 1995, accounting for 94% of the total harvest in the Northeast. Norman Bloom died in 1989, but his brother Hill (as he prefers to be called) continued the family business. In 1991, much of Long Island Sound's oyster beds were destroyed when a group of gas transmission companies constructed a natural gas pipeline across the Sound. A lawsuit brought against the large corporate consortium by Tallmadge Brothers and other oyster companies lead to a $5.5 million settlement paid to the oystermen. Hill Bloom donated his company's share of the settlement to the State of Connecticut for the construction of a modern water quality testing laboratory in Milford.

Today, Tallmadge Brothers leases over 40,000 acres of oyster grounds in the northeast, and has modern plants in Norwalk, as well as in Bivalve, New Jersey. Their fleet of over twenty wooden boats is maintained by their own shipwrights to yacht-like standards. A few of their boats are over 100 years old, and remain working symbols of the golden age of oystering on Long Island Sound.

Hill Bloom at work in his waterfront office.

Until cancer struck in 1999, Hill worked 80 to 90 hours a week, occasionally taking a holiday off. This author, Oyster Bill, visited him in July of 2000, and although his battle with cancer continues, he still runs the business while bedridden. In 1994, when Hill was honored at the dedication of the State's new water quality lab, then Connecticut's Governor Lowell Weicker, Jr. referred to him as "a modern day man of the sea, one of Connecticut's treasures." The governor told the crowd at the dedication, "Whatever you do in the future, be sure to hang on to the Hill Blooms of this world. When they're gone, we're gone."

New Jersey and Delaware

The oyster fishery of New Jersey was once a very important part of the state's economy. Barnegat, Great and Little Egg Harbor Bays along the Atlantic coast were protected by barrier islands that created a low salinity that favored oysters over their predators. As in Great South Bay, NY, severe storms just after the turn of the century breached the barrier islands raising the salinity of the bays and effectively ending a thriving oyster industry. Great Bay still supports a small commercial oyster harvest.

Delaware Bay on the border between New Jersey and Delaware was another great oyster ground of huge size. Millions of bushels of oysters were once harvested from Delaware Bay on both the New Jersey and Delaware shores. The importation of seed oysters from Virginia and other areas brought in the 20th century scourge of east coast oystering: MSX (*Hasplosporidium nelsoni*) and Dermo (*Perkinsus marinus*). These two oyster diseases sequentially affected Delaware Bay (coming and going with changes in temperature and other factors) to nearly end oystering on the bay. Through changes in cultivation practice and better scientific understanding of oyster diseases, the bay is once again producing oysters although at a fraction of the levels of the turn of the century.

Chesapeake Bay – Maryland and Virginia

The history of commercial oystering in Chesapeake Bay dates from the early 1800s. Shipment of oysters to other markets was most easily facilitated from Baltimore due to its status as a center of transportation, most notably the Baltimore and Ohio Railroad. Oysters were shipped in the shell and also as shucked meats. Providing oysters to the shippers and shucking houses was the domain of Chesapeake Bay oystermen. These hardy individuals initially used hand-operated tongs to collect oysters from the rich oyster reefs

A Chesapeake Bay skipjack.

along the mouths of many bay tributaries. The advent of dredging as a harvest method coincided with the growth of the commercial oystering industry. Initially dredging was allowed only on oyster grounds in the bay proper. Harvesting activity in the river mouths and upriver was reserved for those harvesting with tongs. As the bay oyster grounds depleted, dredgers began harvesting in the rivers and consequently had conflicts with both tongers and the state officials who were trying to enforce the regulations.

Patent tongs are used for harvesting oysters on Chesapeake Bay.

The traditional dredging boats used on Chesapeake Bay remained unchanged for over a century. Single-masted skipjacks and schooner-rigged "pungies" and "bugeyes" plied the bay dredging under sail (by regulation) even though the boats had engines.

The romance of life working on the water in Chesapeake Bay is now a subject more for museums. The glory days of hundreds of boats oystering and huge shipments being sent out of Baltimore for points north and west have ended.

While there are still Chesapeake Bay watermen making their living oystering, the oyster diseases MSX and Dermo have diminished the harvest and make the continued success of the industry uncertain.

The Virginia portion of Chesapeake Bay has had a similar oystering history to that of Maryland. The turn of the twentieth century saw grand harvests and hundreds of Virginia residents employed in the oyster industry. As the quality of water in the bay declined, the abundance of oysters decreased, with MSX and Dermo wielding a stunning blow to the industry in the early 1960s. Adjusting oyster seed gathering to lower salinity river areas has been one remedy, and recent efforts to clean up the water in the bay will also help restore the oyster industry along the Chesapeake.

The fame of Chesapeake Bay as a source of oysters has continued to this day despite a relatively small modern industry compared to that of a century ago. Maryland's annual harvest of four to six million bushels of oysters in the 1890s has declined to just 200,000 bushels in the 1990s. Some oyster reefs in the bay were several thousand years old and up to 10 feet thick when modern harvesting began. Insufficient shell planting to catch set and deforestation of the bay's tributaries (resulting in silting-over of oyster beds) initially reduced the harvest. Invasion of MSX and Dermo in the second half of the 20th century has frustrated efforts to revive the industry to its former size and glory.

Today, commercial oystering in Maryland takes place at the mouths of the Choptank, Chester and Patuxent Rivers and in Eastern Bay. Tangier Sound and areas off Annapolis and Baltimore still support small commercial harvests each year. Tonging and dredging are limited to certain areas.

The history of commercial oystering in Virginia parallels that of Maryland with record harvests in the 1880s and 1890s (approaching 10 million bushels per year) and the slow decline from overharvesting during the first half of the 20th century. Rapid decline occurred in the second half of the 20th century due to MSX and Dermo. Today, Virginia produces annual commercial harvests of only 45,000 bushels.

Production areas currently harvested are all on the James River. Former oyster grounds on Hampton Roads, Mobjack Bay, Chincoteague Bay and the Rappahannock, Piankatank and York Rivers have declined to non-commerically viable levels.

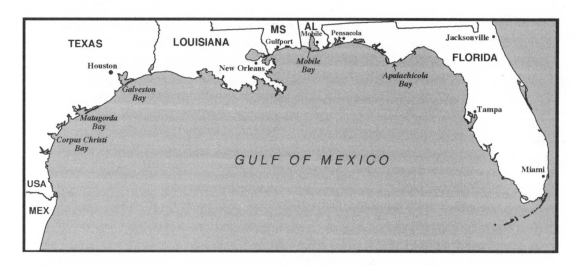

South Atlantic Region – North and South Carolina, Georgia and Florida

The South Atlantic states enjoy warmer waters and a more prodigious natural oyster set than their neighbors to the north. Oyster banks on the coasts of the Carolinas have been harvested for generations by simply gathering the bivalves at low tide. Depletion of the natural beds has not been a particular problem though pollution of coastal waters by increased development for recreational purposes is a concern. For the most part, oysters harvested in the South Atlantic states are opened by steaming whereby the cooked meats are canned. Comparatively few oysters make it to the half-shell trade.

Oysters grow on natural, intertidal beds on the South Atlantic coast. Before pollution and increased activity of Dermo, natural set on the beds seemed to keep the oyster supplies at a sustainable level. Today, coastal development is directed toward recreational industries with priorities that do not coincide with preservation of natural oyster stocks. Small quantities of oysters are still harvested locally for oyster roasts and a few half-shell operations.

Gulf of Mexico – Florida, Alabama, Mississippi, Louisiana and Texas

The Gulf Coast with its warm waters and solid substrate has seen the accumulation of dramatic oyster reefs that have been continuously harvested since the arrival of white settlers. Many small areas along Florida's west coast have modest oyster harvests while Apalachicola Bay has long been famous for its oystering industry. Damage to oyster beds by hurricanes and mortalities due to drought conditions (changing the bay's salinity) have been occasional drawbacks. Oysters are harvested mostly by tonging with a few dredging operations in Apalachicola Bay.

The earliest French settlers in Louisiana enjoyed the oysters they found in the bayous and inlets as had the native Americans in the area for over 2,000 years. Coastal fishermen eventually added oysters to their catch-for-sale, and harvesting of the tasty bivalves for profit was underway. Many Yugoslavian immigrants arrived in Louisiana beginning in 1840 and took up the fishing industry they had known in the old country. This third wave of

settlers developed methods of transplanting natural oyster seed from one area to another to promote faster growth and better flavor. This familiar pattern of relocating oysters is one repeated throughout the North American industry.Now the largest producing area of American oysters (*crassostrea virginica*), the U.S. Gulf Coast lands several million bushels per year. The primary producer among the five states is Louisiana with about 50% of the harvest followed by Florida at 20%, Texas at 18%, Mississippi at 8% and Alabama at 4%. Oysters are grown on natural reefs and banks that have been the source of food for local residents for over 4,000 years.

Florida's primary production area for oysters is at Apalachicola Bay on Florida's panhandle. Most of the oysters are harvested off public reefs which are supported by shelling with cultch to maintain the fishery. Oyster harvesting on public grounds is by hand tonging or by hand while diving or wading. Some dredging takes place on private leases. The annual Florida Seafood Festival is held in Apalachicola and celebrates the oyster and shrimp industries there.

The Alabama oyster fishery is primarily on the western shore of Mobile Bay and Mississippi Sound inside Dauphin Island. The sites are Cedar Point Reef, King's Bayou, Portersville Bay and Whitehouse Reef.

The primary oyster grounds of Mississippi adjoin those of Alabama inside the barrier islands on Mississippi Sound. Graveline Bayou and Bayou Cembest Tonging Reefs are adjacent to Pascagoula and the Square Handkerchief, St. Joseph Point and St. Stanislaus Reefs are southwest of St. Louis Bay. Oysters are harvested primarily by tonging.

The vast oystering industry of Louisiana dates back to the arrival of the original French settlers of the area who recognized the American oyster growing in the bayous as a cousin of their familiar European oyster, *ostrea edulis*. The abundance of rich oyster reefs is harvested mostly by dredging with public seed grounds supplying oysters for grow-out on private leases. Various areas all along the coast of Louisiana provide abundant harvests of oysters.

Commercial oystering in Texas is limited to several bays although oysters can be found all the Texas Gulf Coast. About 90% of the public reef acreage is in Galveston, Matagorda and San Antonio Bay systems. Oysters are relocated from public reefs to private leases for grow out.

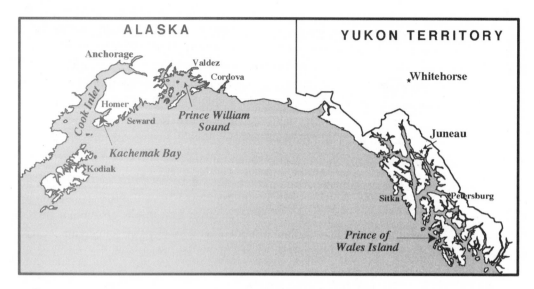

Pacific Coast - Alaska

While most seafood aficionados seek out wild Alaska king salmon from select runs in the springtime, oyster lovers know that small growers in the region are producing some delicious bivalves in the icy waters. Traditional native shellfish include scallops, abalone, geoducks, razor clams and butter clams. Oysters in Alaska must be grown from seed obtained from hatcheries since the water is too cold for oysters to spawn at any time of year.

Seed oysters procured from Japan were first planted on Alaska beaches around 1910 with limited success. This method proved not to be commercially viable. Today, seed oysters purchased from hatcheries in Washington, British Columbia and California are grown out in several locations using almost exclusively lantern nets. These devices are suspended from bouys and rafts in waters along the southeast Alaska coast (Prince of Wales Island) and also in Prince William Sound and Kachemak Bay off Cook Inlet.

The nutrient-rich, unpolluted waters of Alaska produce a delicious oyster that arrives in a beautiful shell since they are singly grown off the bottom. These delectable bivalves are a natural for the half-shell trade. Pacific oysters (*crassostrea gigas*) are the only species grown since an import ban on shellfish has been in place since 1978. Afraid to infect naturally occuring species of fish and shellfish with diseases or pests, the State of Alaska has been adamant about these restrictions. Pacific oysters were "grandfathered in" to the regulations due to the history of the fishery dating back so many years.

Growers in Southeast Alaska include Tenass Pass Shellfish and Canoe Lagoon Oysters on Prince of Wales Island and and Elfin Cove Oysters and other small growers along the panhandle. Pristine Products, Aquabionics and the Native Alaskan enterprise Tatitlek Oysters produce oysters on Prince William Sound and numerous small growers make up the Kachemak Bay Shellfish Mariculture association.

The Native Alaskan Qutekcak Shellfish Hatchery near Seward is now producing seed stock for Alaska oyster growers.

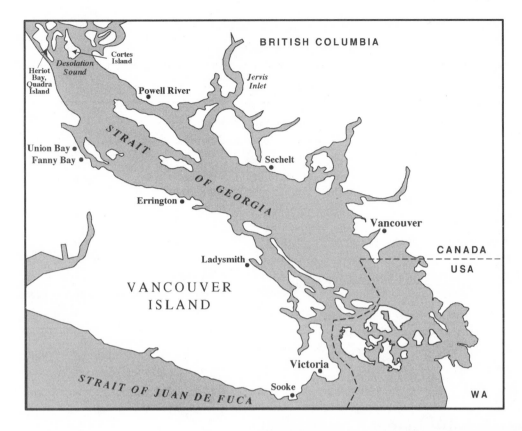

British Columbia

Oysters have been grown for about 100 years in the Strait of Georgia between the mainland and Vancouver Island. Various early plantings of Pacific oysters yielded moderate success of beach culture in protected areas near Ladysmith Harbour and Pendrell Sound. Seed was collected from natural sets in Pendrell Sound and Pipestem Inlet for transplanting to other areas. Unpredictable spawning and costs involved in seeding from purchased or locally collected spat caused these initial ventures to decline.

Pearl Seaproducts suspended culture operation at Jervis Inlet, British Columbia.

Currently oysters are grown using suspended culture from rafts or floats in areas from the southern Georgia Strait up to Desolation Sound. Species include Pacifics, Kumamotos and European Flats. Deep water suspended culture produces superb half shell oysters with unique flavors and distinctive appearance. Fanny Bay Oyster Company practices traditional intertidal beach culture at their locations on the east coast of Vancouver Island. Seed oysters are currently purchased from hatcheries in Washington or British Columbia. Pearl

Seaproducts farms the pristine waters of Jervis Inlet producing oysters grown at three different depths by tray culture. Oysters grown at shallow depths (slightly warmer water, different nutrient and salinity levels) are offered as a milder flavored alternative to "Sinku" oysters grown at medium depth (15 to 20 feet) which exhibit a more salty and full flavor. Oysters grown at depths of 60 feet (19 meters) are in very cold water and are harvested in summer only since they don't exhibit watery characteristics from spawning.

Smaller growers like Brent Petkau of Cortes Island in Desolation Sound produce unique oysters using suspended culture techniques. His Royal Myiagis, Golden Mantels and Whaletown Gems are highly prized for quality and flavor.

Washington State

Washington is America's oyster success story for the last quarter of the 20th century. Clean water, new growing techniques, dependable hatchery seed and a strong market for oysters have helped create an oyster heaven for consumers. Oyster growers on Willapa Bay, Grays Harbor and dozens of Puget Sound locations offer many choices for the oyster lover.

Willapa Bay & Grays Harbor

These large, shallow tidal estuaries were once literally covered with native Olympia oysters. Native Americans had availed this abundant source of shellfish for centuries and white settlers in the 19th century grew to appreciate the tiny bivalve as well. Oyster-hungry San Franciscans provided motivation for many oyster entrepreneurs to harvest the oyster reefs of Willapa Bay and ship the precious cargo south on sailing vessels. From the 1850s to the 1870s the area was an oyster boomtown. Overfished and under-protected, Willapa Bay gave up its final commercial harvest of native oysters before the turn of the century.

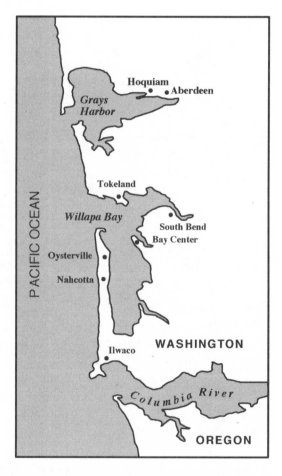

Attempts were made to introduce Eastern oysters to the natural reef areas, but today the business has changed to farming Pacific oysters using intertidal bottom culture as well as several methods of suspended culture. Thousands of acres of Willapa Bay are oyster farmed producing a significant percentage of America's annual oyster harvest. Two pests of these oyster farmers are ghost shrimp and Spartina grass. Ghost shrimp burrow in the oyster bed making it soft

The Joy of Oysters

so the oysters sink into the mud and die. Spartina grass grows over the bed making it difficult to farm. Controls for these pests have been controversial and questionably effective. Alternatives to bottom culture have been suggested as the ultimate solution with seed oysters grown out in mesh bags, protected from predators and suspended above the mud bottom by various devices.

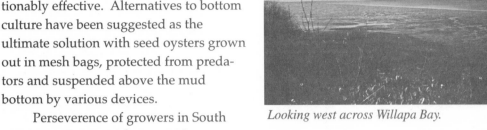

Looking west across Willapa Bay.

Perseverence of growers in South Bend, Bay Center, Nahcotta and Oysterville indicates that this area will continue to thrive as an oyster-producing region. To the north, several producers are doing well in the waters of Grays Harbor.

Nisbet Oyster Company of Willapa Bay is trying a unique marketing technique with their Goose Point brand, shipping oyster "shooters" prepackaged with cocktail sauce in shot glasses. The product is available fresh or frozen offering the retailer or restaurant a reasonable shelf life for the normally highly-perishable product.

South Puget Sound

The bays and inlets around Olympia and Shelton, Washington were the first home to oystering in the Puget Sound region of the state. Extensive harvesting of native Olympia oyster reefs preceded cultivation of the same animal as natural stocks declined. Preparation of diked growing areas and organized promotion of the resulting product were hallmarks of Washington's early 20th century shellfishing

Olympia Oyster Co., near Olympia, WA.

industry. Rapid population growth along Puget Sound combined with industrial growth and resulting pollution dealt a serious blow to the industry from the 1950s to the 1970s. Today, oyster growing has finally recovered thanks to several insightful and determined growers and the efforts of anti-pollution agencies. Seasonal blooms of naturally-occurring toxic algae and pollution levels from industrial and metropolitan sources are strictly monitored.

The health of the waters in this area is, for the most part, good, and the expansion of the oyster industry is encouraging to oyster lovers throughout North America. Hatchery and growout operations by the Taylor Shellfish Company at their

Shucking Olympia oysters.

The Joy of Oysters 67

Shelton headquarters produces a variety of oysters to harvest and seed for growout at other Puget Sound locations. Different species are grown using different methods of bottom and off-bottom culture, as well as the latest technologies for oyster health. Many smaller operations produce Pacific oysters for sale to local restaurants in the areas around Shelton and Olympia.

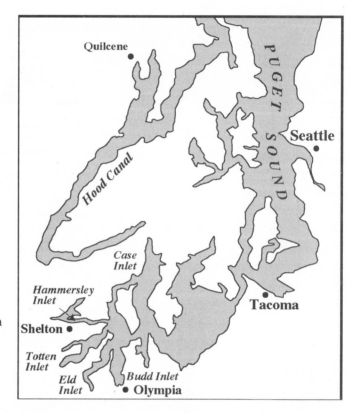

Hood Canal has long been a source of delicious Pacific oysters after it was discovered in the first half of the century that the species would successfully spawn and set on the rocky bottoms from the "Great Bend" of the canal in the south to Dabob and Quilcene Bays in the north. The growing conditions are so good in the northern reaches of Hood Canal that two oyster hatchery operations make their home near the town of Quilcene. Many Washington residents remember their first oyster experiences harvesting oysters from the beaches near Seal Rock and Brinnon. Fresh oysters are for sale all along the canal today either in the shell (large sized Pacifics) or shucked by the pint.

North Puget Sound

As the latitudes grow more northerly different oysters and culture methods are favored. The extensive tidal flow from the ocean via the Strait of Juan de Fuca provides ample nutrients to northern bays and inlets. Shallow waters such as those found in Samish Bay provide hundreds of acres for bottom culture of Pacific oysters and other species as well. Taylor Shellfish and Blau Oyster Company both have extensive operations in this area.

Beach culture on Hood Canal near Quilcene.

The Joy of Oysters

Small growers on several islands in the San Juan archipelago, and in bays and inlets along the strait, grow out tasty oysters of several species, each reflecting the waters of the particular area of culture. The largest of these growers is Westcott Bay Sea Farms on San Juan Island. They grow several oyster species in lantern net and tray culture for the half shell trade.

Floats suspending lantern nets dot scenic Westcott Bay off the northwest corner of San Juan Island, Washington.

Oregon and California

The great reefs of native oysters that once covered the coastal bays of Oregon and Northern California were depleted during the California gold rush years. This resource was no doubt enjoyed by 19th century settlers and by the wealthy "forty niners" who paid dearly for oysters in San Francisco that had been shipped south in barrels. Today, oystering has been restored to several locations on the Oregon coast and to Humboldt, Tomales and Morro Bays and Drake's Estero in California.

The 1990s has seen much activity on the Oregon coast with oyster operations growing in several locations. Rivers flowing from Oregon's mostly-undeveloped Coast Mountain

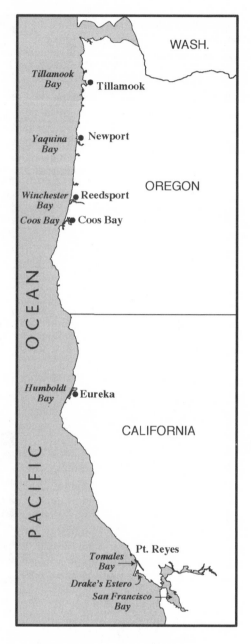

Range feed the coastal bays, so industrial pollution is minimal, though dairy farms and logging operations sometimes foul the streams.

Tillamook Bay on the northern coast is home to oystering firms at Garibaldi, Bay City and Pearl Point on the south side of the bay. Pacific oysters are grown out here along with Kumamotos and European Flats. Yaquina Bay at the city of Newport offers a large estuary that is currently home to three oystering operations. Off-bottom culture is used for production of half shell oysters and oysters are shucked for by-the-jar sales as well. Pollution from a recent shipwreck on the coast suspended harvests for a time but everything now shows signs of recovery.

Winchester Bay is the estuary of the Umpqua River at the town of Reedsport. Oystering has been restored to this famous location and shows promise of success. Coos Bay is home to Clausen Oyster Company at North Bend and Qualman Oyster Farms.

The center of California's oyster industry is in the area around Point Reyes just north of San Francisco. The long, narrow Tomales Bay on the coastal side of Marin County offers protection from the Pacific Ocean, ample nutrients brought in by tidal exchange and a salinity that seems to please several species of oysters. The Hog Island Oyster Company practices intertidal and off-bottom culture of Pacific, European Flat and Kumamoto oysters. This company has been very successful at producing oysters for the half shell trade of the West Coast and beyond. Tomales Bay Oyster Company also produces oysters here.

Around the corner of Point Reyes, one finds the south-facing entrance to Drake's Estero, a bay named for explorer Sir Francis Drake after his visit hundreds of years ago. The northeast part of this body of water is named Home Bay and is home to Johnson Oyster Company. Johnson Oyster has been farming the bay for several generations.

Oysters have been grown commercially in other areas of California, most notably the north part of Humboldt Bay near the Oregon border and in Morro Bay near San Luis Obispo.

Oysters at the Dinner Table

Now that we know the history of oysters, what their names are and how they're grown, we can get down to the business of inviting them to dinner! Preceding our collection of over 150 oyster recipes are sections devoted to the fine art of handling and shucking oysters, matching up libations with bivalves and some choices of spicy hot sauces to try with half shell oysters.

Buying Oysters
Shucking Oysters
Half Shell Oyster Service
Oyster Accompaniments
The Oyster Appreciation Wheel
Favorite Oysters
Matching Wines with Oysters
Matching Beers with Oysters
Hot Sauces to Accompany Oysters
Oyster Recipes

Buying Oysters

Nothing beats buying oysters at the source. Taste is a very complex sensation that involves emotion, knowledge, memory, smell, sound, sight, and much more. The more we know about how a food is grown and harvested, the better it tastes. When we fully experience the "sense of place" or spirit of a food or wine, it becomes a part of us, greatly enhancing our enjoyment.

When you buy oysters at the source, you inhale the briny kelp and brisk foggy air off the bay. You hear the lonely cry of the gulls and the chalky clink of oyster shells as they are pulled from the sea. You feel the silty mud of the estuary oozing between your fingers, and breath the rich nutrients and minerals from the sea that give an oyster its trademark taste. You hold the oysters, heavy and compact in your hand, and feel the ruggedness of their beautiful fluted shells. Eat one of these freshly shucked oysters, and all your senses come alive again. Each half shell holds much more than flavor.

If you don't have an opportunity to purchase oysters directly from a grower, there are plenty of other options. Check with your local seafood merchant or grocer to find out what they offer. Often they can special order oysters, so you're assured of freshness. Some oyster companies around the country even ship fresh oysters overnight, via UPS or Fed X. (For a listing see page 322.)

"I do not have a favorite oyster. Any good oyster, fresh and crisp from cold waters, is pure bliss for me."

Consider the Oyster
M.F.K. Fisher

Dos & Don'ts

Whenever you buy live oysters, inspect the oysters to make sure they are alive and their shells are intact. Shells should be tightly closed, or should close readily when tapped. Oysters should feel heavy and full in your hand. Since an oyster loses moisture once it is removed from the sea, this suggests they are freshly harvested. Oyster meats should be tan to cream-colored, heavy and plump. They should smell sweet and briny like the sea. Discard any oysters that do not close, or that emit a bad odor.

Fact or Fiction? The "R" Months

There is an old saying that you should never eat oysters during months without an "R" in them. This was true in the days before refrigeration, when oysters shipped during the heat of summer spoiled quickly, but there is really no basis for this now. Yet some people still prefer not to eat oysters during the warmer months. The reason is that in the summer oysters are leaner and milder tasting. During the spawning season, which is triggered by summer heat, oysters consume their own sweet stores of glycogen, a starch that gives them energy to reproduce. The by-product of this glycogen consumption is lactic acid, the same acid found in milk. This gives oysters a milky appearance and less assertive flavor. It's not bad; just different.

We recommend serving oysters on the half shell during the cooler months, when oysters are at their peak in flavor and texture. During the warmer months oysters are great for grilling and cooking.

First Communion

Hardly any food makes a greater impression than our first raw oyster. Good or bad, we never forget the experience — vividly recalling the time of day, the season, the weather, our age, who we were with. We tremble with fear of the unknown. What will it feel like? Will it make me sick? Can I really swallow something that's alive? Foremost in our minds is the incredible sensation of that first slurp — the surprisingly slippery, yet crisp, texture and brisk ocean flavor that instantly takes us back to the stuff-of-life, the primordial ooze. It is our first communion with the sea: a powerful initiation into the fellowship of elbow benders.

Storing Oysters

Store live oysters in the refrigerator between 34 and 40-degrees F. Place them deep side down (to retain their juices) in an open container. Cover the oysters with a damp towel or layers of damp newspaper. Remember, oysters are alive and need to breathe, so never seal them tightly in a plastic bag. Fresh oysters stored this way will keep up to seven days.

Never immerse live oysters in fresh water or melted ice; it will kill them.

Freshly shucked oyster meats in jars or plastic tubs should be packed in their own liquor, which should be clear. Stored at 34° - 40° F., these will keep up to two weeks (look for an expiration date stamped on the container).

An Important Warning About Raw Oysters

Very old or very young persons, or persons with compromised immune systems should not eat raw oysters. Several organisms occur in shellfish that are harmless to the creature but can be very dangerous to humans. Vibrio vulnificous can cause severe illness in anyone and can be fatal to those whose ability to fight disease is reduced. Thoroughly cooking shellfish (including oysters) is recommended to lessen the chance of bacterial infection. Occurence of these organisms in oysters from clean, cold waters (and those that have been properly stored and handled) is rare, but the warning should be heeded by those at risk.

The Art of Shucking Oysters

They say shucking oysters does not require an understanding of rocket science, but if you've ever tried opening an oyster without a good oyster knife in hand, you know what a heroic combination of strength and ingenuity it takes to pry open these stubborn mollusks. Just handling an oyster alerts it to tighten or "clam up"— forming a seemingly impenetrable fortress.

"The man has sure a plate covered o'er
With brass or steel, that on the rocky shore
First broke the oozy oyster's pearly coat,
And risked the living morsel down his throat."

18th century British poet, *John Gray*

Unfortunately for oysters, we have been enamored of their succulent taste of the sea since time began, and are relentless in our search to get at their sweet, briny meat. Since early man cracked oysters open with rocks, we have tried every way we can think of to open oyster shells. We stab them, stick them, pry them, crack them . . . even resort to can openers and other makeshift tools . . . anything we can do to savor their sea-fresh flavor.

To make oyster shucking quicker and more profitable, commercial oyster growers have tried in vain to invent some sort of mechanical oyster shucking device. Many attempts have failed simply due to the varying shape and thickness of oyster shells. Some years back, the Pacific Northwest Oyster Growers Association presented their shucking dilemma to the Battelle Memorial Institute — a worldwide organization of top scientists and engineers. They figured if anyone could invent a superior shucking method it would be them.

For two years, those great minds, who have engineered everything from atom bombs to artificial heart implants, experimented with possible high-tech shucking methods. They tried blow torches, carbon dioxide and cryogenic freezing, explosive decompression, ultrasonic vibration, even electric shock. But nothing, not even microwaving oysters worked. When a microwaved oyster finally blew up, splattering itself about their pristine laboratory, Batelle admitted, when it comes to shucking, they'd found nothing to surpass the human hand and a good oyster knife.

Still, others continue the search for a new-and-better shucking method. Most recently we heard about a new method of "super steaming" oysters open. We haven't yet sampled the evidence, but are suspicious that, like microwaving, the process might render a partially cooked oyster.

To date, human hands fitted with a good oyster knife, remain the best shucking tools. Like any master of the arts — for example, cellist YoYo Ma, ice skating star Michelle Kwan, or basketball's Michael Jordan, a skilled oyster shucker has a knack for making oyster shucking appear effortless and flawless. In contrast to a beginning shucker's awkward movements, a skilled oyster shucker acquires grace and purity of movement. Their magic combination of balance, skill, timing, speed and perfection -- leaves each oyster quivering on the half shell, primed for some grateful palate.

"An oyster should look as though it never even knew it was shucked," says Food Consultant Jon Rowley. A perfectly shucked oyster glistens with life, cradled like a jewel in its pearly cupped shell. The brisk scent of the sea wafts from its briny nectar. Eat one of these oysters and the vital elements of the air, earth and sea are unleashed on your palate. Sweet and succulent, they taste at once of melon, cucumber, tangy minerals, the salty sea, and more.

In the trade, shucking oysters is known as "doing it." And people who have mastered the art of shucking are said to have "the hands." One shucker who had "the hands," was Billy Lowney of Providence, Rhode Island who, in 1913, opened 100 oysters in just over three minutes. Like any art, oyster shucking requires lots of practice. Besides manual dexterity, timing, speed and balance, it requires a good understanding of an oyster's architecture.

Oyster Architecture

Tucked snugly in its seemingly impenetrable fluted shell, an oyster is a marvel of design. By the time it has reached the size of a poppy seed, each young, naked oyster, or "spat," begins building its own home or environment by secreting a shell composed of ninety-five percent calcium carbonate. Inside, the shell is pearly and smooth, while the outer shell is sharp and fluted. The deep, cupped portion of each shell cradles the tender mollusk,

A sampling of oyster varieties: large Pacific, medium Pacific, Kumamoto, European Flat, Olympia.

while the flat shell serves as a beautiful tiled roof. Each year an oyster adds a layer or "shoot" to its shell, much like a tree grows rings. Like a tree, you can count the number of shoots to learn an oyster's age.

Each oyster shell is fitted with hinges for opening and closing. A large, scallop-like muscle, called the adductor muscle, is attached to both shells and fastens the fragile oyster firmly to the safety of its compact home. The adductor is fastened on both top and bottom shells about half way down on the right side (hinge or "beak" pointed toward you). Once opened, each oyster shell reveals a small indentation where the muscle attaches. With the hinge, the muscle serves as a sort of bellows for opening and closing the solitary bivalve. This allows the oyster to filter hundreds of gallons of sea water each day that, brimming with plankton and other tasty microscopic morsels, provides an endless buffet.

The art of shucking an oyster is to open the shells with a skillful, yet delicate touch, then quickly release the oyster meat from the shell by slicing through the adductor muscle (also known as the eye). The oyster is left perfectly intact in the half shell, plump and vigorous, swimming in its own flavorful liquor.

Oyster Knives

Oyster knives have evolved with the oystering industry so that today there are several blade shapes and handle styles available. Long, thin "stabbers" and the heavier "Galveston" and "New Haven" blades each have their proponents. Regional styles exist reputedly to handle the shell qualities of oysters harvested in particular areas.

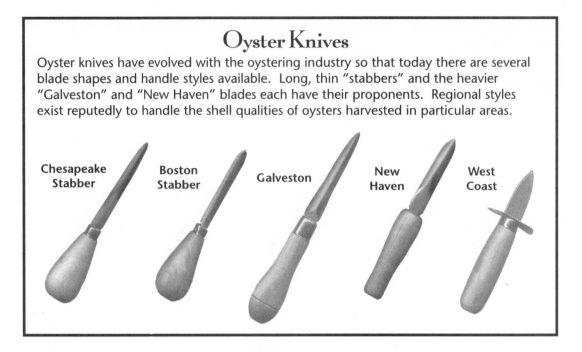

Chesapeake Stabber   Boston Stabber   Galveston   New Haven   West Coast

Tools of the Trade

There are a variety of tools available to facilitate oyster shucking. Most important is a good oyster knife, of which there are several varieties. During "The Great Oyster Craze" of the 1800s, when America's mania for oysters reached its zenith, each oyster region, including Chesapeake, New England, and New York, developed its own shucking techniques and tools. Find any old salt who has shucked oysters all his life, and he'll no doubt swear by his traditional shucking knife.

The Chesapeake or Boston Stabbers are long, narrow-bladed knives tempered for strength and resiliency. They come with rounded handles of wood or plastic (which is now required in the industry for sanitation). The New Haven oyster knife, with a wide, stubby blade and longer handle is popular with New Englanders, while in the southern and Gulf Coast regions, shuckers preferred the Galveston shucker. The stubby West Coast style featres a protective guard and a short, wide blade. A solid steel Crack Knife (see page 79), is preferred for the cracker method of shucking and for breaking apart clumps of oysters.

Besides these traditional oyster knives, modern day oyster knives of varying shapes and sizes are also available. With so many styles to choose from – short blades, long blades and, in between, the most important thing is to find a sturdy, well-built knife that feels comfortable in your hand. For example, if you are a woman with smaller hands, you might prefer a shorter, stocky blade that offers better control, to a longer blade. If the blade is made of carbon steel, you'll need to dry it and oil it before storing it to prevent rust. Stainless steel blades, on the other hand, are nearly maintenance free.

Other factors to consider when choosing an oyster knife are the variety, shape and size of the oysters you will be shucking. Shucking a tiny, quarter-sized Olympia oyster, for example, requires a lot more finesse than does shucking a large, crusty Pacific oyster or sturdy European Flat oyster. If you enjoy eating a variety of oysters, it's worth investing in several different styles of oyster knives, so you always have one on hand that best suits the shucking job.

Shucking Oysters:
"The Art of Revealing the Tender Mysteries of the Oyster"

Always shuck oysters just before serving time: You want them as cold, crisp and fresh as possible.

Start by preparing a plate to hold the opened oysters. You can fill a chilled plate with a bed of crushed ice or fresh seaweed. An old-fashioned method was to make indentations in a large block of ice to hold each oyster, using a large heated spoon or ladle. The ice block was used to serve both half shell oysters and oysters out of the shell.

Oyster plates fitted with receptacles for holding oysters were extremely popular in the late 1800s to early 1900s. Oyster plates are still available new at specialty cooking stores and can be found at some antique stores. Line each receptacle with chipped ice, or place the whole plate in the freezer to chill before use.

Let the Shucking Begin

Always begin by scrubbing oysters thoroughly under cold running water, using a stiff brush to remove any mud or grit. Then, choose your shucking method. No matter what method you choose, it is always a good idea to protect the hand that's holding the oyster with a folded kitchen towel or a heavy glove. This helps prevents cuts, in case the knife slips, and keeps sharp, jagged shells from slicing into your hands. Some people prefer to cup the oyster in their hand while shucking, but placing an oyster firmly on a non-stick surface offers better leverage. And always, ALWAYS remember to keep the oyster's deep shell on the bottom to catch every drop of that delicious oyster liquor.

Most importantly, relax and have fun. Each oyster is a special gift from the sea and deserves to be enjoyed in a spirit of thanks and celebration.

Hinge Method

This is the most popular and easiest method of shucking for amateurs. It is also the best for half shell presentation and enjoyment. It takes a bit of practice, but once you've mastered the technique, it is very effective. Hinge entry helps prevent damage to the oyster meat.

Place the oyster on a firm, non-slip surface with the hinge or "beak" pointing toward you. Wedge the tip of the oyster knife into the depression on the hinge of the oyster, pushing and wiggling side-to-side until you feel the knife slip into the soft spot in the hinge. Twist the knife 90 degrees until the hinge pops, releasing the two shells.

Once the hinge has popped, slide the knife blade, flat, across the underside of the top shell, keeping the blade in the center of the shell and as close as possible to the top shell. Move the knife to the right and slice the adductor muscle from the top shell in one quick motion. (The muscle is usually attached near the center of the shell, a bit closer to the wide

The Joy of Oysters 77

How to Shuck an Oyster (Hinge Method)

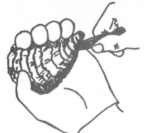

1. Scrub the oyster well under cold, running water to remove mud, dirt and algae. Using a sturdy oyster glove (on the hand holding the oyster), hold the oyster flat side up with the narrow end toward you. (Some shuckers hold the oyster down on a tabletop for more stability.) Insert the tip of the oyster knife into the small opening at the hinge of the oyster. Twist the knife to pop open the shell.

2. To sever the muscle that connects the oyster to its shell, slide the knife blade along the underside of the top shell.

3. Remove the top shell and sever the muscle that attaches the oyster to its lower (cupped) shell. Be careful not to spill out the oyster "liquor" in the bottom shell.

Alternative methods: Some shuckers like to insert the knife at the side or front (opposite end from the hinge) of the oyster to slide it in and sever the top adductor muscle. In commercial shucking houses this is often facilitated by breaking off the edge of the shell to provide an opening for the knife. Finding the separation of the two shell halves without breaking off the edge is quite difficult for most oyster species.

end, on the oyster's right side.) The top shell is now free and can be flipped off easily.

You will be able to see the adductor mussel in the upper right hand quadrant of the oyster. Loosen the oyster from the bottom shell by sliding the knife under the oyster in front of the muscle and drawing the knife towards you along the underside of the oyster, as close as possible to the shell. (Be careful at this point not to tip the shell and loose any of the succulent nectar). With the oyster knife, carefully nudge the oyster down into its delicious juices, retaining as much liquor as possible. Use the tip of the oyster knife to remove any bits of shell or grit that may have fallen into the oyster. Carefully flip the oyster over in its shell to reveal its plumpest, most inviting side. (This also assures eaters that the adductor muscle is completely severed and the oyster is ready for slurping.) Set the freshly shucked oysters in their shells on a prepared bed of crushed ice or fresh seaweed.

NOTE FOR LEFT HANDED PEOPLE: Open the shell as above, however, before severing the adductor muscle, turn the oyster so that the hinge is pointing away from you. This will place the muscle on your left side, making it easier to cut the muscle.

  The Joy of Oysters

Stabbing Method

In this method, the tip of the oyster knife is pushed between the top and bottom shells at the wide end or "mouth" of the oyster.

Place the oyster on a non-slip surface with the flat side up and wide end facing toward you. Bracing the hinged end against a wooden stop will help prevent the oyster from sliding.

Pushing and wiggling, force the point of the knife between the two shells, repeating until you have entered the oyster. Push the blade in firmly and slice sideways, keeping the blade close to the top shell to cut the muscle. Follow the Hinge Method for severing the muscle on the bottom shell.

Prying or Side Method

Here, the tip of the knife is pushed between the top and bottom shells near the muscle. It is perhaps the most difficult method to learn and, if shells are fragile, allows more fragments to get into the meat. This method is best for oysters that you are going to rinse and cook.

Place the oyster on a slip free surface with the wide end facing toward you. Insert the point of the knife between the two shells on the left side of the oyster -- the side opposite the adductor muscle. Push the knife in and over the meat to sever the muscle. Pry the shell off, removing any loose shell particles. Follow the Hinge Method for severing the muscle on the bottom shell.

The Cracker or Breaking Method

This is a method often employed by commercial shuckers because it offers quick entry into an oyster. It requires the use of a thick block of wood with a metal insert on top, called a cracking iron, and a sturdy hammer designed for cracking shells. Place the edge of the shell on the block, extending the mouth or wide end of the shell about 1/2-inch over the edge of the block. Give the shell several sharp taps with the hammer to chip off the tip of the shell, leaving a slot for entry. Once that's accomplished, follow instructions for the Stabbing Method.

Cracking Hammer

Cracking Block

Weighted Cracking Knfe

Alternative Methods

The following two methods of opening oysters should not be used for half-shell service, when it is crucial that oysters are absolutely fresh and crisp. They can, however, be used for cooked oyster dishes, especially if you have lots of oysters to open and are short on time. Neither of these methods fully cooks the oysters.

The Microwave Method

Place the oysters, deep side down, in a glass casserole dish lined with rock salt. Microwave for 5 minutes at a warm temperature setting. Remove oysters from the oven and pry open the hinges immediately.

The Joy of Oysters 79

The Fire and Ice Method

Preheat oven to 400° F. Place the oysters, deep side down, on a baking sheet lined with rock salt. Bake for 5 minutes. Remove oysters from the oven and immediately plunge them into a bowl of ice water. Pry open the hinges.

Many oyster lovers find oyster shells lovely to behold, but not Maria Parloa, author of Miss Parloa's New Cook Book, published in 1880. In this amusing recipe she offers her remedy for doing away with what she refers to as "those unsightly shells in which raw oysters are usually served."

Oysters on a Block of Ice

"Having a perfectly clear and solid block of ice, weighing ten or fifteen pounds, a cavity is to be made in the top of it in either of two ways. The first is to carefully chip with an ice pick; the other, to melt with heated bricks. If the latter be chosen, the ice must be put into a tub or a large pan, and one of the bricks held upon the centre of it until there is a slight depression, yet sufficient for the brick to rest in. When the first brick is cold remove it, tip the block on one side, to let off the water, and then use another brick. Continue the operation till the cavity will hold as many oysters as are to be served. These should be kept an hour previous in a cool place; should be drained in a colander, and seasoned with salt, pepper, and vinegar. After laying two folded napkins on a large platter, to prevent the block from slipping, cover the dish with parsley, so that only the ice is visible. Stick a number of pinks, or of any small, bright flowers that do not wilt rapidly, into the parsley. Pour oysters into the space in the top of the ice, and garnish with thin slices of lemon. This gives an elegant dish, and does away with the unsightly shells . . . "

"Secret, and self-contained, and solitary as an oyster."

A Christmas Carol
Charles Dickens

Half Shell Service

"How do we like our oysters? Raw! Raw! Raw!"

1930s Campus Cheer

For many oyster enthusiasts nothing is more delicious and exhilarating than downing a freshly shucked oyster on the half shell. Purists insist that an oyster needs no accompaniment other than its own briny liquor. Others prefer a refreshing drop of fresh lemon juice or peppery Tabasco Sauce, which has been served with oysters since it was first bottled in 1878. Still others, craving a bit more oomph, relish a pungent Mignonette Sauce or spicy cocktail sauce. No matter what your preference is, the secrets to enjoying oysters on the half shell are few and simple. Oysters should be absolutely fresh, perfectly shucked and icy cold.

Throughout the history of slurping, from the ancient Greeks, to the "Great Oyster Craze" of the 1800s, when America's oyster mania reached its zenith, to our current "Oyster Renaissance," we have celebrated these luscious bivalves with gusto. "Let us roister with the oyster — in the shorter days and moister," began a poem first published in The Detroit Free Press in 1889 and roister we did. In a boisterous air of festive merrymaking, crowds frequented early oyster cellars and houses, heartily downing raw oysters and ale while engaged in rousing conversation. Happily, oysters are experiencing a renewed enthusiasm.

"Oysters are the only meat that men eat alive,
  and yet account it no cruelty."

Thomas Fuller

"I will not eat oysters. I want my food dead — not sick,
  not wounded — dead."

Woody Allen

Oyster Accompaniments

Traditionally, oysters on the half shell are served with crisp, dry white wines, such as Meursault and Chablis, or with thick, creamy stouts and lighter ales. These spirits work as natural palate cleansers, slicing right through the briny flavor of the oysters, readying the palate for more. Brown or rye bread and butter, or oyster crackers are also traditionally served with oysters. Bread works with the wine or beer, keeping the palate refreshed. This combination of oysters, bread and spirits is so delicious, it is considered by many as the "holy trilogy" of oyster service. Fresh lemon, Hot Pepper Sauce and Mignonette Sauces are also traditional accompaniments. You can serve lemon in slices or turn a whole lemon into a lemon squeezer by rolling it on a hard surface to loosen the juices and poking a large hole in the top to squeeze the juice through.

For more information regarding sauces to serve with oysters, please refer to the oyster recipes section beginning on page 203.

Putting Together an Oyster Tasting

When serving oysters on the half shell, you can offer a variety of oysters for comparison, or simply serve one variety of oyster with a sampling of sauces. In preparation, a good way to find your favorite oysters for half shell service is to visit your local oyster bar where they offer a selection of oysters and often provide information regarding the different varieties.

Serve six to one-dozen oysters per person as an appetizer.

Small Is Beautiful

For half shell service, select single oysters that are one to three-inches in length. Many oyster growers raise oysters solely for half shell consumption, and label them as such. Others label them as "mediums," "smalls," "petites," "cocktails," " or "extra smalls." This provides the perfect slurp: Not too big, not too small. Just so.

Temperature Is Crucial, As Is Freshness

Oysters should be no more than seven days out of the sea, and should be shucked as close to serving time as possible. Serve them icy cold on a bed of shaved or crushed ice. Cold temperatures preserve an oyster's complex volatile flavors and keep the oyster firm and crisp.

If oysters have not been chilled in the refrigerator before serving, you can bury them in ice for about 15 minutes before shucking.

"The dunkers-in-catsup are probably not aware that oysters from different beds have different tastes.

The Oyster Book
Louis P. DeGony

Consider the Source

Similar to wines, oysters develop unique flavors and qualities depending on their variety and where they are grown. Factors that influence an oyster's color, shape and flavor include salinity levels of the water, the presence of algae or eel grass in the growing beds,

the cleanliness of the water, soil type and rainfall. Different growing methods, such as bottom culture, raft or tray culture, and lantern net culture, also affect flavor. An oyster raised on the bottom of a bay, for example, often has an earthier flavor than one that never touches land, such as those raised in a lantern net suspended from a raft.

Oyster flavors range from salty brine, to the cold slap of the sea, kelp, iodine and flinty minerals. Some hint of cucumbers, mushrooms, tapioca, watermelon, roses and toasted nuts, even chrysanthemums. Oysters are vegetarians, feeding mostly on one-celled plants called diatoms, which in turn are nourished by various minerals including copper, iron and iodine. All these elements contribute to the distinct flavor and color of each oyster.

To learn when and where oysters where harvested, ask to see the purveyor's shellfish harvest certificate. This lists the date of harvest, origin, and verifies that the oysters came from safe, clean waters.

Optional Enhancements

When serving oysters on the half shell, you may want to provide oyster or cocktail forks for your guests. Long and slender, they are perfectly designed for skewering oysters, for slurpers who would rather not use their fingers. Napkins for wiping fingers and mouths are a good idea, as are bowls or buckets for discarding empty shells. Beyond these basic items, you'll want to consider things such as lighting, music, table settings, and such, always keeping in mind that oysters are romantic, sexy and fun.

The Joy of Slurping

Eating an oyster on the half shell is a simple act. You lift the oyster shell to your mouth, "tasting" with your fingertips, inhaling the cool sea breeze that wafts from the oyster. You tilt your head back and slurp, taking in the icy cold oyster and its briny liquor, nudging it gently in with your fingertip.

Wet and quivering, each succulent sea-plum unfolds in a burst of flavor, blossoming like a bouquet on your tongue. As you chew the oyster slowly, the power of the sea is suddenly unleashed, surging through your senses in frothy waves of taste and emotion. Your palate is tingling and alive, cucumber crisp and bristling with the salty tang of the surf. Layers of flavor lap at your senses — earthy mushrooms, sassy minerals, cool, damp ocean mist . . . You chase the oyster with a cold, refreshing swig of steely wine. It rushes through you like the wind, carrying with it all the scents and flavors of the sea, leaving you exhilarated and clamoring for more.

"According to the French," writes food author M.F.K. Fisher, "all oysters should be eaten this way . . . plucked from its rough, irregular shell at once, so that its black gills still vibrate and cringe with the shock of air upon them. It should be swallowed, not too fast, and then its fine salt juices should be drunk at one gulp from the shell. Then, of course a bit or two of buttered brown bread must follow and then of course, of course a fine mouthful of white wine."

The Joy of Oysters 83

The Oyster Sensory Appreciation Wheel

When tasting wines, many people enjoy picking out the different flavors and aromas in each glass. An awareness of the different components of wine leads to greater enjoyment. You can do the same thing with oysters, concentrating on the different textures and flavors of each variety. Is it briny? Does it taste fruity? Like minerals? You'll be surprised how quickly you develop an oyster vocabulary — what we call "oysterspeak."

Illustrated below is our soon-to-be-famous "Oyster Sensory Appreciation Wheel." Oyster lovers can hone their own skills in recognizing the sight, touch, smell and flavor of their favorite bivalves. There are certainly many more terms to describe oysters than the nearly-90 presented here, so feel free to add your favorites in the margin!

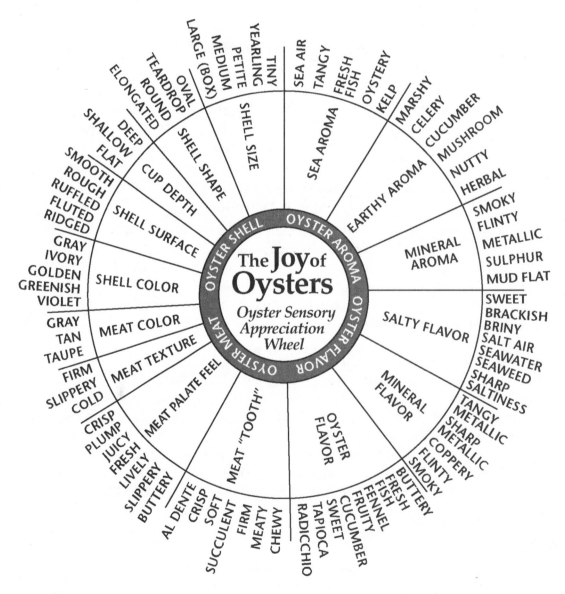

The Joy of Oysters

Some of Our Favorite Oysters

East Coast

(*crassostrea virginica* unless noted)

Blue Point- Long Island Sound, CT

Cape Breton - Nova Scotia, Canada

Chincoteague - Chincoteague Island, VA

Glidden Point Damariscotta Belons - ME

    (*ostrea edulis*)

Malpeque - Prince Edward Island, Canada

Mountain Island Flat - Nova Scotia, Canada

Pine Island, New York

Raspberry Point - Prince Edward Island

Spinney Creek Oysters - Eliot, ME

Wellfleet - Cape Cod, MA

West Coast

(*crassostrea gigas* unless noted)

Hog Island Kumamotos - Tomales Bay, CA

    (*crassostrea sikamea*)

Hog Island Sweetwater - Tomales Bay, CA

Coos Bay Pacifics - Coos Bay, OR

Pearl Point - Netarts Bay, OR

Umpqua Flats - Winchester Bay, OR

    (*ostrea edulis*)

Yaquina Bay Pacifics - Yaquina Bay, OR

Eagle Rock - Eagle Rock,. AK

Elfin Cove - Port Althrop, AK

Tenass Pass - Tenass Pass, AK

Baywater Sweet - Hood Canal, WA

Blau Selects, Samish Bay, WA

Dabob Bay - Hood Canal, WA

Discovery Bay Flats - Discovery Bay, WA

    (*ostrea edulis*)

Goose Point - Willapa Bay, WA

Hama Hama - Hood Canal, WA

Judd Cove - Orcas Island, Puget Sound, WA

Kumamoto (Taylor) - Shelton, WA

    (*crassostrea sikamea*)

Maple Point - Shelton, WA

Miami Beach - Hood Canal, WA

Olympias (Taylor, Olympia Oyster Co.)

    (*ostrea lurida*)

Penn Cove Select - Whidbey Island, WA

Quilcene - Hood Canal, WA

Samish Bay - Samish Bay, Puget Sound, WA

Shoalwater Bay - Willapa Bay, WA

Snow Creek - Discovery Bay, WA

Sund Creek - Hood Canal, WA

Westcott Bay Flats - Westcott Bay, WA

    (*ostrea edulis*)

Westcott Bay Petites - Westcott Bay, WA

Fanny Bay - Vancouver Island, BC

Golden Mantel - Desolation Sound, BC

Lesqueti Goldens - Lesqueti Island, BC

Pearl Bay Oysters - Strait of Georgia, BC

Royal Miyagi - Cortez Island, BC

Sinku Deep - Strait of Georgia, BC

Matchmaking Oysters

Ever since oysters were first cultivated by the ancient Greeks in the fourth century B.C., and presumably long before, people have chased the succulent bivalves with their favorite local beverage. A common tradition in the British Isles is the marriage of oysters with a rich, creamy stout — Irish-made Guinness is a favorite. Oysters are also downed with refreshing ales and with "Black Velvet" — a mixture of stout and Champagne. In Scandinavia, oysters on the half shell are customarily served with icy-cold Aquavit, a caraway flavored liquor, while in Japan, fresh oysters are downed with chilled sake (rice wine). Dry sherry and steely dry white wine are also enjoyed with oysters.

There is no question that drinking a refreshing beverage with oysters greatly enhances the oyster experience. Whether it's a swig of wine, beer, or some other suitable spirit, a great oyster beverage refreshes the palate and prepares the oyster lover's palate for another tasty morsel.

Oyster Wines

"A loaf of bread the walrus said is what we chiefly need.
Pepper and vinegar besides are very good indeed.
Now, if you're ready oysters dear, we can begin to feed."

The Walrus and the Carpenter
By Lewis Carroll

The conniving, oyster-slurping walrus in Lewis Carroll's The Walrus and The Carpenter certainly had his priorities straight when it came to eating oysters. Unfortunately, he and his wily colleague, the carpenter, were negligent is assembling their picnic: They forgot the wine and, in doing so, missed one of the greatest gastronomic pleasures of all times — oysters slurped with wine. Washing down a freshly shucked oyster with a crisp, cold, steely white wine is nothing less than exhilarating.

Technically, raw oysters are alive when we eat them and their brisk, lively flavor calls for an equally zesty wine that cleans the sea from your palate like a frothy wave. Since wine is also a living, breathing entity that continually changes in the bottle, it is not surprising that oysters and wine make excellent partners. Both reflect the elements of place in which they are raised — the soil, the water, the climate, what winegrowers call terroir. Wine and oysters are even similar in chemical makeup. Both are rich in vitamins A and B, and contain fair amounts of calcium, zinc, iron, magnesium and phosphorus. Best of all, wine offers a lilting edge of crisp acidity that counterbalances the soft, egg-yolk pH of oyster meat.

Awash in its own ecosystem of saltwater, minerals and oyster juices, each oyster exhibits its own lively flavor, while sharing similar qualities of "oysterness." This enables great oyster wines to match nicely with more than one type of oyster. An oyster wine should work as a condiment for the oyster, never over powering the oyster, or vying for attention on your palate, but rather enhancing the oyster's flavor, much like a dash of salt or a squirt of lemon enhances food.

A Dating Service for Northwest Wines & Northwest Oysters

Jon Rowley

Seafood marketer Jon Rowley is a strong advocate for enjoying locally grown fish and shellfish with wines produced by local vintners. His Pacific Coast Oyster Wine Competition was helpful to both shellfish growers and to the Northwest wine industry by promoting a natural affinity between the two products.

Jon also was among the first to recommend wines to accompany wild Northwest salmon. His promotion "Tale of Two Pinots" played across the country helping to establish both Pinot Noir and Pinot Gris as superb accompaniments for salmon.

Today Jon casts a wider net by promoting the most perfectly ripe Northwest peaches and pears.

Historically, the beverage of choice for oyster lovers has been dry white wine. Tasters prefer crisp, clean wines with refreshing acids and flinty minerals that clean the palate, leaving them wanting more oysters. French favorites include crisp Burgundian whites — including Chablis, Meursault and Pouilly Fuissé — all produced from chardonnay grapes. Interestingly, eons ago, the Chablis region of France was under water. When the sea receded, it left behind a shell-rich chalky soil that imparts crisp, mineral flavors to the wines produced there — providing the perfect compliment to the metallic tang of oysters.

Other French favorites include Champagne, Graves, of which sauvignon blanc is the principal grape variety, Muscadet or Melon, and Sauternes, which is produced from semillon and sauvignon blanc. Reportedly, Sauternes was the favored oyster wine during the 19th century in France. Although we primarily associate Sauternes with ultra-rich, nectar sweet wines, it is more likely that the wine drunk with oysters in the 1800s was produced in a dry style, much like a modern day semillon-sauvignon blanc.

During the 1990s, famed oyster promoter and devotee, Jon Rowley, of Jon Rowley and Associates in Seattle, conducted a series of American oyster/American wine competitions in seven major cities around the country, including Seattle, Chicago, Boston, New York, Washington, Los Angeles and San Francisco. His goal was to find regional American oyster wines that had the same magic with oysters as the great oyster wines of France — notably Muscadet and Chablis. During each competition, both oysters and wines were served icy cold. "Cold temperatures create a one-dimensional effect on the palate, bringing the wine and food together in a focal point, " explained Rowley. "Once a wine warms up, it releases many more volatile flavors that compete with the oyster."

While favorites among oyster wines differed from taster to taster and from region to region, similar patterns began to develop. When asked "What is an Oyster Wine?" Judges responded with like comments such as: "Dry as a whistle, clean as a bone." "Crisp, clean, refreshing." "Lean, austere." "Lets the oyster be an oyster." "Clean, slicing finish." "Seeringly dry." "Makes you want to eat more oysters."

Judges continually selected lean, white wines with crisp acids that sliced right through the briny, metallic flavor of the oysters, favoring crisp, steely sauvignon blancs and

The Joy of Oysters

semillons, lean chardonnays without oak, light fragrant gewurztraminers and mineral-scented pinot blancs and pinot gris. For the record, a red wine was never selected, though a few dozen were entered.

Some contend that oysters from different shores pair better with wines from the same region. Historically, the quintessential match is a light, crisp Muscadet, made near Nantes on the northwest coast of France, paired with oysters from the region's world-class oyster beds. Locals hardly consider drinking anything else with oysters. The question is, does a crisp pinot blanc from the Pacific Northwest taste better with plump Pacific oysters from Puget Sound? Or is a Long Island sauvignon blanc better for washing down briny Pine Island oysters than, say, an Australian semillon? The ballot is still out regarding this theory, but we hope oyster and wine lovers everywhere will dedicate themselves to a lifelong pursuit of matching regional oysters with local wines.

This brief discussion of wine varietals and growing regions is designed to help you find your favorite oyster wines for half shell service: Keep in mind that oysters on the half shell call for uncomplicated, dry, refreshing wines that have been influenced by little or no oak aging. Cooked oyster dishes, however, often call for richer, oakier and spicier wines. When serving cooked oysters, consider the sauce and other ingredients when selecting a wine. For more specific wine recommendations, please refer to each recipe.

Sauvignon (Fume) Blanc

Grown in many regions throughout the world, this sassy varietal is made in a number of styles. Typically, they are seductive, sophisticated wines with zesty acidity and fresh, crisp flavors. Some Sauvignon Blanc is oak-aged, adding richness to the wine's flavor. These richer wines are best saved for oyster dishes with rich, creamy sauces, but lighter, crisper sauvignon blancs, with bracing acidity, and perhaps a tiny kiss of oak, call out for freshly shucked oysters.

Semillon

Blended with sauvignon blanc, semillon makes the great white wines of Sancerre and Bordeaux in France. On its own, semillon can offer rich flavors of melon and fig, or it can be lean and citrusy. The latter style is the most successful with oysters, serving as a condiment to enhance the oyster and highlight its delicate flavors. Barrel-fermented semillons (especially those that have undergone malolactic fermentation) are rich, buttery and powerful — usually too much of a good thing when it comes to pairing with raw oysters.

Chardonnay

Though it is the queen of white wines in popularity, chardonnay is often made in a rich, oaky style that overpowers the delicate flavor of oysters on the half shell. Those with lighter, crisper flavors and citrus notes tend to be more successful with raw oysters. For cooked dishes with cream sauces of other stronger flavored ingredients, chardonnays offer a wide range of possibilities in both style and price range.

Pinot Gris

This cousin of Pinot Noir produces a crisp, white to slightly pinkish wine with exotic fruit flavors, flinty minerals and crisp, lemony acids. Currently Oregon's rising star, Pinot Gris is planted throughout Western Europe, where it is best known as the grape of Alsace, and as Italy's Pinot Grigio. This grape lends itself to oak aging and is also delicious aged in stainless steel tanks. It is these stainless steel fermented, citrusy, mineral-scented versions that make great oyster wines.

Pinot Blanc

Another transplanted Alsatian, pinot blanc is grown in the cooler regions of California and in Oregon. Confused with Melon de Bourgogne by American growers during the 1980s, pinot blanc has now been decisively identified and winemakers are making some terrific wines from the varietal. Made in a dry, crisp fashion, pinot blanc is a great oyster wine.

Chenin Blanc

It takes a clever winemaker to craft a chenin blanc in a dry style that offers complexity and flavor. Unfortunately, chenin blanc is often produced in a semi-sweet style with sweet pear and marshmallow flavors — one that is definitely not friendly to half-shell oysters. To accompany oysters, look for dry chenin blanc from California or the Pacific Northwest. Because this grape is greatly influenced by weather conditions and cellar practices, it is best to evaluate chenin blancs on a vintage-by-vintage basis.

Gewurztraminer

Another classic grape varietal from Alsace and Germany, gewurztraminer made in a dry style can be a superb oyster wine. It offers an kick of Asian spice, with lychee and tea-like flavors that, when present in light amounts, pair beautifully with an oyster's delicate, briny flavor.

Riesling

Riesling is another northern European varietal that works great with oysters when it is made in a dry style with the barest hint of sweetness. These elegant, sophisticated wines have crisp acids and layers of complex fruit and spice, with refreshing mineral notes that pair splendidly with oysters.

Viognier

This French Rhone varietal is crisp and dry with a lilt of refreshing minerals. Sometimes, however, it has a bitter flavor that does not pair well with oysters on the half shell. We recommend this with cooked oyster dishes, especially those with lively seasonings. Fortunately, winemakers are constantly producing new and more oyster friendly viognier wines. We look forward to seeing it poured more in the future.

Muscadet (Melon de Bourgogne)

Grown near Nantes at the mouth of the Loire River in France, home to some of the world's finest oyster beds, French Muscadet is the quintessential oyster wine. It is delicious, uncomplicated and racy — always great with half-shell oysters. In the U.S., this varietal, sometimes called "melon," is made by just a handful of producers. When made in a dry style it offers fresh aromas and flavors that lead to a crisp, acidic finish. If you can find it, it is definitely worth trying with oysters.

Champagne and Sparkling Wine

This can be a delightful match if you keep a few things in mind. When matching Champagne or sparkling wine with half-shell oysters, the rule is the drier and less complicated the wine, the better. Forget the qualities you typically look for in great Champagne — rich yeasty character and complex, lingering flavor. Remember that oysters work best with light, lean, uncomplicated wines. Our best luck pairing oysters with sparkling wines has been with less expensive bottlings from California and the Pacific Northwest.

Sake

Made from pure spring water and polished rice, sake (or rice wine) varies in flavor, dryness and acidity, much like different wines. Styles range from very acidic sake with complex notes of licorice and fruit, to full bodied sake with hints of pears, to slightly sweet with mango and guava undertones. Some are lighter and more refreshing, with subtle flavors of nuts. For the most part, these lighter, nuttier sakes pair best with oysters on the half shell. However, with sweeter, more flavorful oysters, such as European Flat oysters, try a more complex sake with notes of fresh fruit.

Stronger Spirits

As mentioned earlier, many oyster aficionados, both past and present, enjoy stronger spirits with oysters. American statesman and diplomat, Daniel Webster, a daily visitor to the Union Oyster House in Boston during the early 1800s, downed a tall tumbler of brandy and water with each half-dozen oysters. Many Americans prefer a shot of icy-cold vodka, or single malt scotch with their oysters.

People who drink hard alcohol with oysters may, in fact, be on to something. A report written by a team of medical researchers in the late 1980s regarding an outbreak of hepatitis A in Florida discovered that alcohol acted as a preventative against the virus. From their studies, they concluded that by chasing oysters with a glass of wine containing over 10 percent alcohol, or with a cocktail, oyster eaters could reduced the risk of hepatitis by a whopping 90 percent.

"Reminds me of my safari to Africa. Someone forgot the corkscrew and for several days we had to live on nothing but food and water."

W. C. Fields

1999-2000 Oyster Wine Judging for The Joy of Oysters

To select wines for inclusion in The Joy of Oysters, the authors and publisher sampled many bottlings from around the U.S. and some from foreign shores. We were fortunate to have a tasting session at The Oyster Creek Inn before the restaurant closed for remodeling. Their former chef/manager Doug Charles sat in to add his wine-and-oyster expertise to our selection process. Wine expert Kurt Krause also contributed his expertise in assessing the wines sampled. The recommended wines (and beers a few pages hence) are not the final word on beverages to accompany oysters, but, instead, should serve as a starting point to select some appropriate oyster-friendly libations to enjoy.

Recommended Oyster Wines (by varietal)

Sauvignon Blanc
Benziger 1998 Fume Blanc, CA
Caterina Winery 1998 Sauvignon Blanc, WA
Chateau Ste. Michelle 1997 Sauvignon Blanc, Horse Heaven Hills Vineyard, WA
Chateau Benoit 1998 Sauvignon Blanc, OR
Columbia Crest 1997 Sauvignon Blanc, WA
Compte LeFond 1997 Sancerre, France
Covey Run 1997 Fume Blanc, WA
Hogue Cellars 1998 Fume Blanc, WA
Hoodsport 1998 Sauvignon Blanc, WA
Kenwood 1998 Sauvignon Blanc, Sonoma Valley, CA
Ladoucette 1997 Pouilly Fume, France
La Poussie Blanc 1997 Sancerre, France
R. H. Phillips Night Harvest Sauvignon Blanc, CA
Raymond 1998 Sauvignon Blanc, Napa Reserve, CA
Robert Mondavi 1997 Fume Blanc, Napa, CA
Robert Mondavi 1997 Sauvignon Blanc, Stag's Leap District, CA
Powers 1997 Fume Blanc, WA
Wente 1998 Sauvignon Blanc, Central Coast, CA
Yorkville 1998 Sauvignon Blanc, Mendocino, CA

Semillon
Columbia Crest 1997 Semillon, WA
Hogue Cellars 1998 Semillon, WA
Washington Hills Cellars 1998 Semillon, WA
Yorkville 1998 Semillon, CA

Blended Wines

Hedges Cellars 1998 Fume Chardonnay, WA
Washington Hills 1998 Semillon Chardonnay, WA

Pinot Blanc

Adelsheim 1998 Pinot Blanc, OR
Amity Vineyards 1998 Pinot Blanc, Willamette Valley, OR
Foris Vineyards 1998 Pinot Blanc, Rogue Valley, OR
Tualatin Vineyards 1998 Pinot Blanc, OR
Valley of the Moon, Pinot Blanc, CA
Wild Horse 1998 Pinot Blanc, CA
WillaKenzie Estate 1998 Pinot Blanc, OR
Yamhill Valley Vineyards 1998 Pinot Blanc, OR

Chardonnay

Ivan Tamas 1997 Chardonnay, Central Coast, CA
R. H. Phillips NV Barrel Cuvee, CA
Trefethen 1997 Chardonnay, CA
Willamette Valley Vineyards 1997 Chardonnay, OR

Rhone Varietals

R. H. Phillips 1998 EXP Viognier, CA
Zaca Mesa 1998 Rousanne, Santa Barbara, CA
Zaca Mesa 1998 Viognier, Santa Barbara, CA

Pinot Gris

Autumn Wind Vineyard 1998 Pinot Gris, Yamhill County, OR
Eola Hills Wine Cellars 1998 Pinot Gris, OR
King Estate 1997 Pinot Gris, OR
King Estate 1997 Pinot Gris Reserve, OR
Rex Hill Vineyards 1998 Pinot Gris, OR
Silvan Ridge 1998 Pinot Gris, OR
Yamhill Valley Vineyards 1998 Pinot Gris, Willamette Valley, OR

Sparkling Wine & Champagne

Champagne Deutz 1993, France
Korbel Natural, CA
Louis Roederer 1993 Blanc de Blancs, France
Mumm Cuvee Napa Blanc de Blancs, CA
Mumm Cuvee Napa Brut Prestige, CA
Mumm Cuvee Napa DVX, CA
Schramsberg Blanc de Blancs, CA

A Tribute to a Friend of Wine and Oysters

Wine writer and oyster lover Tom Stockley died tragically with his wife Peggy in the crash of Alaska Airlines Flight 261 in February of 2000. Tom was an excited participant in Jon Rowley's first oyster wine competition, serving on both the preliminary judging committee and the final judging group in Seattle. The poem below was written by Tom and Peggy's daughter Dina describing family oyster outings to Hood Canal and the surrounding area. She read the poem at the couple's memorial service at St. Mark's Cathedral in Seattle.

Known Only To God

By Dina Stockley Moreno

On my plate I have
oysters
Shucked on a sharp and rocky beach
salty and mixed with blood
from an oyster shell cut.

Oysters that my father opens
my sister and I bringing them
saying
Open this one first
and this is a good one.

Oysters that I eat raw
holding the stone it clings to
and swallowing
soft and cold
slipping from its smooth home.

We wash our cuts in the canal
stepping carefully on
barnacled rocks.
Count grey lumps
into my cupped hands
getting our limit each.

In our minds we see
Mrs. Swift's old house
Grandpa Stockley sitting on a log
and smoking
and Joe.
We know the cemetery as if we were
buried there
between the BABY GIRL
and the BODY OF A MAN FOUND ON BEACH
WITH KNIFE WOUND IN NECK
KNOWN ONLY TO GOD.

I have always stood here
rattling oysters shells
and composing poetry.
My sister has always claimed
the abandoned houses
the wood swings
the deep water.

We eat memories
with our oysters.

Beer with Oysters

We have seen happy tavern-goers tossing down oyster shooters by the dozen (with cocktail sauce) and chasing each mouthful with a big swig of Budweiser. Given the right moment and the right company, we regard this as an enviable pursuit that requires little of the participant other than to have a jolly good time. The authors know of many Northwest taverns that fit into this style and we are sure that numerous establishments exist in each seaside community where oysters are grown.

Those with more time - and inclination - to explore oyster and beer combinations, can expand their taste horizons by trying selected imported beers and craft brews with freshly shucked oysters. Centuries of oyster consumption in Europe and a slightly shorter span in the Eastern United States have created some traditions in beer styles that flatter oysters.

Stout

Stout is a dark ale, made heavy with flavor and color by the addition of roasted and burned malt to the mash and the boil. The most famous stout throughout the world is Guinness. Touted throughout the British Isles as being great with oysters (and nearly every other food), Guinness has undoubtedly washed down more bivalves than any other single beer. Many other imported stouts are admirable in their ability to accompany oysters such as Tooths Sheafstout from Australia and Murphy's Stout from Cork, Ireland.

The microbrew or "craft brewing" revolution that took place in America in the 1980s launched many exciting stouts brewed from recipes both traditional and innovative. Dark, toasty beers with bodies thick and thin feature flavors of chocolate, coffee and spice. Not all are great with oysters and we leave it to the reader to identify their favorite local dark ale for oyster slurping.

Porter

If stout is a dark, dry and bitter ale, then porter is a dark, off-dry and smooth ale. The brewer's craft that produces the difference is not the issue, but the style is as old as stout and just as popular when it comes to accompanying oysters. Sweetness of this genre is mitigated by the bitterness imparted by the brewing with dark malts, as in stout, and doesn't affect the ability to wrap itself around an oyster like a dark little coat. Samuel Smith's brewery in Tadcaster, Yorkshire produces a

quintessential version in their Taddy Porter. This well balanced, dark and toasty ale offers a smooth and flavorful accompaniment to oysters.

Lighter Styles of Oyster Beer

Some oyster lovers prefer lighter styles of beer than the traditional heavy stouts and porters. Full bodied pale ales take various forms, with the hoppier versions finding the most success as oyster beers. India Pale Ale most often denotes this style with examples from breweries both American and continental. Light lagers brewed in the true pilsner tradition often have the right bitterness to refresh the palate of oyster eaters and prepare them for the next bivalve.

Regional Brews

With the revival of craft brewing in America, breweries in each area of the country have developed specialty ales and lagers to please the local clientele. While it is beyond the scope of this book to research and recommend "oyster beers" from hundreds of regional breweries across the U.S., we can recommend some from the Pacific Northwest that are favorites of local oyster  aficionados. Born in Seattle but now well distributed throughout the country is Redhook Brewery's Blackhook Porter. A deliciously dark and flavorful ale with notes of coffee and chocolate, it is delicious with oysters on the half shell or many cooked oyster preparations. Pike Brewing Company offers their XXXXX Stout, a dark and dry version in the style of Imperial Stout, for oyster lovers to enjoy along with their hoppy Pale Ale. Bert Grant's Perfect Porter and Imperial Stout are also on the top of the list for accompanying oysters on the half shell, as is their superb India Pale Ale.

We strongly recommend that oyster lovers explore the offerings from their local breweries, in addition to sampling the internationally recognized beers that have paired with oysters for generations.

Favorite Beers to Accompany Oysters

Stout
Grant's Imperial Stout
Guinness Stout
Murphy's Stout
Pike Brewing XXXXX Stout
Pyramid Espresso Stout
Redhook Double Black Stout
Samuel Smith Imperial Stout
Samuel Smith Oatmeal Stout
Skookum Stout, LaConner Brewing

Porter
Grant's Perfect Porter
Redhook Brewing Blackhook Porter
Samuel Smith Taddy Porter

Lighter Oyster Brews
Grant's Scottish Ale
Grant's India Pale Ale
Pike Brewing Pale Ale
Pilsner Urquell

"What contemptible scoundrel stole the cork from my lunch?"

W. C. Fields

The Joy of Oysters

An Oyster Lover's Companion

If ever two products were linked together in the minds of consumers, TABASCO® brand pepper sauce and oysters on the half shell join as one. Ask almost anyone "What sauce should you use to spice up raw oysters?" and the answer is inevitably, "Tabasco sauce." Almost no other condiment – a specific brand, at that – has ever dominated a niche like "That Famous Sauce that Mr. McIlhenny Makes."

Edmund McIlhenny came to New Orleans from his birthplace in Maryland in 1841 and through hard work and marriage became a successful member of a prominent landowning Louisiana family. While the Civil War disrupted the family business of sugar cane farming and salt mining at their ancestral home of Avery Island, the conflict led to a chance meeting of Mr. McIlhenny and a traveler returning from a visit to Mexico. This traveler offered him some favorite pepper pods to season his cooking. Saving the seeds from the pods, Edmund McIlhenny grew the plants in the plantation garden and began experimenting with producing a hot sauce from the resulting peppers.

Combining salt from the Avery Island salt mines with the mashed peppers (red peppers now identified as *Capsicum frutescens*) and white wine vinegar, the foundation for Tabasco sauce began. Beginning with a family-run production line McIlhenny bottled some of his sauce and impressed wholesale grocers in New Orleans and south Louisiana. He patented the sauce in 1870 and increased both its production and distribution.

From the post-Civil War beginnings of Tabasco, several heirs to the McIlhenny family have helped the company grow and prosper. The family estate at Avery Island now includes a sanctuary for snowy egrets and the Jungle Gardens designed for the enjoyment of visitors in 1900. These features were the work of Edward (Ned) Avery McIlhenny – "Mr. Ned" – second son of founder Edmund. Visits to Avery Island now include organized tours of the Tabasco operation and a visit to the Tabasco Country Store, home to dozens of delicious, decorative and fun Tabasco-branded items.

Today the Tabasco brand is a trademark recognized the world over. Tabasco pepper sauce is labeled in 20 languages and is sold in more than 100 countries and territories around the world. Members of the U.S. military are offered Tabasco to spice up their MREs. The most famous politicians, movie stars and musicians swear by Tabasco to add spice and good taste to their meals wherever they travel.

For millions of oyster lovers, Tabasco is a tradition that is part of the flavor of oysters on the half shell. The condiment helps "first timers" slurp their first bivalve, and it is an ingredient in countless oyster preparations that are baked, boiled or fried.

The Joy of Oysters   97

Taste Test: Hot Pepper Sauces for Oysters

Modern cooking styles embrace the addition of heat and spice to many dishes. While Tabasco® brand pepper sauce is established as the original and leader in the area of "hot sauce on the half shell," there is a new wave of flavors and heat intensities to sample. Many new hot sauces offer the heat and flavor of particular pepper varieties (Cayenne, Habanero, Jalapeno), and others combine popular flavors of garlic, lemon, mustard and exotic foreign spices. Our tasting revealed that many different flavors are complementary to oysters, both on the half shell and cooked. Whether oysters are freshly shucked, grilled, baked or sauteed, adding a little heat and flavor just before slurping can add considerable enjoyment.

Almost every major city has a shop or two specializing in hot sauces with varieties topping 1,500 or more selections. A sampling of about 20 pepper sauces that were recommended for oysters by their manufacturers yielded some beginning recommendations for your fire-eating slurp fest. The many different flavors and styles in just this small sampling suggested that descriptions were more appropriate than ratings.

Peppers in Rehoboth Beach, Delaware
http://www.peppers.com

Another Bloody Day in Paradise - Designed originally for making the perfect Bloody Mary Cocktail and for topping cooked seafood, this sauce made from red peppers, green chile peppers, lemon juice and black pepper is quite assertive on oysters. A nice flavor alternative and a fun label on the bottle.

Hot Buns at the Beach - Besides the great label art, this sauce has a complex flavor from two Habanero varieties, Cayenne pepper mash, ginger, garlic, molasses and other ingredients. A powerful Habanero sauce for those who can stand the heat and a great match for the smoky nuances of barbecued oysters.

Kiss Your Ass Goodbye - In numerous tastings this award winning sauce emerged as Half Shell Lori's all-time favorite sauce for half-shell oysters. It offers a perfect combination of heat from habanero peppers with complex flavors of garlic, just

The Joy of Oysters

the right amount of acidity from vinegar, and salt -- flavors that never overwhelm the oyster - just "kiss" or enhance it. Half Shell never slurps without it.

A Taste of Thai - With a touch of garlic, sugar, vinegar and salt, this tangy chili pepper sauce from Thailand is very nice on half shell oysters. Fired by sirachi peppers and garlic, this flavorful sauce is not super hot, but it definitely livens up the palate.

Crabanero - Created especially for crab and shellfish, this lively sauce is seasoned with Old Bay Seasoning. With a peppery finish and complex flavors offered by habanero peppers and vinegar, it matches great with half shell oysters.

Half Moon Bay Trading Company
in Jacksonville, Florida
http://www.halfmoonbaytrading.com

Iguana Red Cayenne Pepper Sauce - The classic style of red pepper sauce balancing flavor and heat. Popular in Florida and rapidly gaining a wide following. Great Iguana artwork graces the label.

Iguana Mean Green Jalapeno Pepper Sauce - A balanced Jalapeno sauce with that pepper's famous "delayed heat," it's blended with onion, garlic and other ingredients for complexity. Straight Jalapeno blends don't seem to work as well with oysters as red pepper varieties or Habaneros.

Iguana Gold Island Pepper Sauce - Golden Habaneros, mustard and a variety of vegetables and spices are blended together to create this hot sauce with curry-like flavors in a West Indies style. A bit too much for topping half shell oysters, but a winner with grilled or sauted bivalves.

Iguana Lightning Hot & Spicy Catsup - From the label art of their Iguana flipping burgers to the mild-yet-spicy flavor profile of this sauce, it's hard to believe someone didn't invent this long ago. It's a good choice for beginning oyster lovers who like to add a little more sauce to their half shell treats.

Panola Pepper Sauces in Lake Providence, Louisiana
www.southernnet.com/panola_peppers

Panola Extra Hot Sauce - Made from Habanero and aged red pepper mash in Northeast Louisiana, this sauce offers clean flavors and ample heat to spice up oyster slurping. It's quite hot, so just use a dash or two.

Panola Cajun Hot Sauce Piquant - A Louisiana medium hot sauce made from aged red pepper mash. This sauce is noticeably salty, which may help complement oysters from certain regions.

Panola Cajun Hot Sauce Green - Lots of heat – both up front and delayed – from Louisiana red peppers and Jalapenos with balanced flavors and not too salty. Jalapeno flavors once again seemed odd with oysters.

Panola Vampfire Sauce - This sauce is made just up the road from Graveyard Bayou near Transylvania, Louisiana – check the map! A blend of Habanero, Cayenne and Louisiana red pepper mash makes this a potent sauce for oyster lovers who really like heat.

Panola Bat's Brew - This is a very hot sauce made from Habanero and Jalapeno peppers with some lemon to temper the heat.

The Pepper Plant in Gilroy, California
www.pepperplant.com

Pepper Plant Original California Style Hot Pepper Sauce - This rich, hearty sauce offers the delayed heat of Jalapeno peppers with a variety of other ingredients to create body and complex flavor. This sauce is best used with cooked oyster dishes since the bold flavors overwhelm the subtleties of oysters on the half shell.

Pepper Plant Habanero Extra Hot Pepper Sauce - Basically the original sauce with Habanero spice added for extra, up-front burn. Good on cooked oyster dishes; too much for half shell.

Pepper Plant Hot Pepper Sauce with Fresh Chunky Garlic - Basically the original sauce with lots of fresh garlic added (remember this company is in the garlic capitol of the world!). Good for garlic lovers on cooked oyster dishes.

Oyster Musing - The Bivalve Blues

Music and Lyrics by Patti Payne, Seattle Radio Personality and
Columnist for the Eastside Journal - © 1993

If chocolate slips between your lips
and lodges squarely on your hips,
Then where, oh where do oysters go?

I've got the oyster, cloister, shuck 'em, jive 'em, slurp 'em,
suck 'em, baby, bivalve blues.

When in the mood, I like them stewed,
But oysters raw are slightly lewd.
You gotta try 'em in the nude

I've got the oyster, cloister, shuck 'em, jive 'em, slurp 'em,
suck 'em, baby, bivalve blues.

The oyster's of the bivalve strain.
Inside, divine.
Outside, pure pain.
Inside delicious,
Outside, vicious.
It's one of nature's finest dishes
Without the smell of certain fishes

I've got the oyster, cloister, shuck 'em, jive 'em, slurp 'em,
suck 'em, baby, bivalve blues.

What's in a name?

On a map you can find these communities, bodies of water and landmarks named for our favorite shellfish!

Oyster, Virginia
Oyster Bay, New York (on Long Island)
Oyster Bay Cove, New York
Oyster Creek, New Jersey
Oyster Creek, Texas
Oyster Creek, Washington
Oyster Creek Landing, North Carolina
Oyster Harbor, Maryland
Oyster Harbor, Massachusetts
Oyster Inlet, Bremerton, Washington
Oyster Point, California
Oyster Point, New Haven, Connecticut
Oyster Point, South Carolina
Oyster Point, Virginia
Oyster Ridge, Wyoming
Oyster River, British Columbia
Oyster River, New Hampshire
Oyster River, Maine
Oyster Rock, Delaware
Oysterville, Oregon (Lincoln County)
Oysterville, Washington (Willapa Bay)
Bivalve, California
Bivalve, Maryland
Bivalve, New Jersey
Royster, Florida

Introduction To Recipes

The recipes included in this book are a combination of our own recipes and those of prominent chefs and oyster growers across the country. We hope you will be as inspired as we were by the creativity expressed in these recipes, and by the enthusiastic love and support these people share toward oysters and the environment in which they are grown and served.

The basic premise of good cooking is always to start with the freshest, highest-quality ingredients you can find. The goal in cooking is to showcase the food in the best way possible to highlight its unique qualities, texture, and flavor. Please keep in mind when following these recipes that all cooking is based on improvisation. Recipes are intended to guide and inspire you; ingredient lists are not written in stone. If you feel that a certain herb, vegetable, or other ingredient is better suited to a dish, or is fresher than the one suggested, feel free to substitute.

While compiling these recipes, I jotted down a few notes that I felt should be mentioned. Listed below are general cooking tips for oysters. More specific cooking tips are listed at the beginning of each chapter.

I hope you experience as much joy cooking and eating these oyster dishes as we did. Enjoy!

Half Shell Lori

Butter

Some recipes in this cookbook call for salted butter, others for unsalted. Generally, I've specified unsalted butter if the chef recommended it, and for delicately flavored dishes. You can substitute one for the other: Simply adjust seasonings accordingly.

Oil for Frying and Sautéing

Peanut oil works best for deep fat frying because it can be heated to higher temperatures without smoking. For other uses, I prefer safflower oil, canola oil, corn oil, or mild flavored olive oil.

Freezing Oysters

Oysters can be frozen either shucked or in the shell, but we do not recommend it, as it compromises texture and flavor.

Amount of Oysters Per Serving

Of course this depends on the eater, and the size of the oysters, but the general rule is six oysters per person for appetizers, and eight to 12 per person for entrees.

To Keep Oysters Upright During Cooking

Most recipes recommend spreading a bed of rock salt on baking pans, but Kosher salt or crinkled aluminum foil can also be used.

Salt

I recommend Kosher salt or sea salt for cooking. They have a pure, clean flavor and contain no additives like iodized salt.

Cream and Butter versus Low-Fat Substitutes

If you are on a restricted diet, you can substitute low-fat or nonfat dairy products for cream, butter and other dairy products. Please understand, however, that the texture and flavor of certain recipes may be compromised.

Non-Reactive Pans or Bowls

Many recipes call for using a non-reactive pan — meaning that the material will not react with acidic ingredients such as lemon juice or vinegar. Choose bowls or cooking pans made of glass, ceramic, or stainless steel, or those lined with enamel.

"So if you go for oysters, and I go for ersters,
I'll order oysters, and cancel the ersters,
Oysters, ersters. Ersters, oysters.
Let's call the whole thing off!"

George & Ira Gershwin
Let's Call the Whole Thing Off, 1937

The Joy of Oysters

Oyster Appetizers

Oysters, eaten on the half shell with or without seasoning or sauce, are still the favorite appetizer among true oyster lovers. Others prefer their oysters sauteed, baked, broiled or barbecued, and there are many variations on these themes.

Our selection begins with a few classic recipes then loosely organizes the remaining 40 or so by method of preparation. A complete listing of all recipes can be found in the index on page 324.

Oysters Kirkpatrick
Oysters Rockfeller
Oysters Casino
Oysters Soaked in Sake
 with Slivered Scallions
Oysters Laphroaig
Shaffer City Oyster Martini
Pacific Oyster Cocktail
Oysters on the Half Shell with:
 Citrus-Coriander Sauce
 Frozen Raspberry Mignonette
 Iced Apple Cider Mignonette
 Spicy Italian Sausage
 Three Sauces
Singapore Slurp
Shirred Oysters with Saffron
Whistling Oyster Dip
Potted Oyster and Shrimp Spread
Baked Oysters with Beurre Blanc
 & Parsley Gremolata
Smoked Oysters
Baked Oysters with
 Chanterelle Mushroom Sauce
Oyster Stuffed Mushroom Caps
Baked Oysters with Toasted Pecan Pesto

Baked Oysters Klondike Style
Oyster Bill's Baked Stuffed Oysters
Oysters Provencal
Roasted Oysters with
 Garlic Parsley Butter
Brooklyn Baked Oysters
Hot Oysters with Beurre Blanc,
 Cucumber & Swiss Chard
Oysters Rockefeller (Shuckers,
 Four Seasons Olympic Hotel)
Poached Oysters with
 Champagne Cream Sauce
Steamed Oysters with Leeks
Oysters in Sweet Riesling Sauce
Oyster Fritters in Beer Batter
Curry Fried Oysters

Oysters Kirkpatrick

*This dish was named in honor of John C. Kirkpatrick,
who once managed the Palace Restaurant in San Francisco. There are many
renditions of this classic recipe, but the basic ingredients are baked oysters, catsup,
green pepper and bacon — cheese and onion are optional. In our version, the oysters
are roasted in a bed of hot rock salt, then topped with all the goodies.*

Serves 4

24	medium oysters in the shell
2	cups rock salt for lining serving dishes
6	slices bacon
2	teaspoons butter
1/2	cup minced green pepper
1/2	cup minced green onion
1/2	cup catsup
1/4	cup freshly grated Assiago or Parmesan Cheese

Preheat oven to 400° F. For four servings, fill four pie plates or deep ovenproof plates with 1 to 2 inches of rock salt. Place the plates in the oven for about 15 minutes, until they are very hot.

Meanwhile, slice the bacon into 1-inch slices. Heat a skillet over medium-high heat. Cook the bacon, stirring often, until it is almost cooked, but still limp and not yet golden brown. Drain the bacon on paper towels, reserving 2 teaspoons of bacon grease. Return skillet to medium-high heat; add the butter and, when sizzling, stir in the green pepper and onion. Cook, stirring often until soft and golden on edges. Remove from heat and stir in catsup; set aside.

Rinse and shuck the oysters, leaving the meat in the deep, cupped shells. Carefully set 6 oysters in each hot roasting pan. Top each oyster with 1 table-spoon of the catsup mixture. Top with bacon pieces and sprinkle with grated cheese. Bake in the oven until the cheese is nicely browned and oysters are heated through, about 12 minutes. Serve hot.

Recommended wines: Viognier (dry style), Dry Riesling, Dry Gewurztraminer, Sauvignon Blanc, Pinot Gris.

The Joy of Oysters

Oysters Rockefeller

This is no doubt the most sought-after oyster recipe in the world.
Chefs and oyster lovers have tried unsuccessfully for over three generations to coerce
the original recipe from Antoine's in New Orleans. Others have tried to duplicate the recipe,
but so far, none are quite identical to the original. Rumors prevail that the closest recipe
to the original was developed by former Antoine's owner, Roy Alciatore, and published
in Life Magazine's "The Picture Cookbook" more than 30 years ago. Although Alciatore's
recipe included spinach, it is believed that the secret ingredient is actually green onions,
not spinach. We'll probably never learn the truth, but it's delicious trying.
Note: Originally, topping ingredients were ground by hand in a mortar and pestle,
but a blender or food processor make much quicker work of the process.
Oysters Rockefeller is believed to be an adaptation of Oyster Florentine, a very old recipe,
of which no one quite knows the origins. It is made by placing poached oysters back
in their shells on a bed of cooked shredded spinach. The oysters are topped with Mornay
sauce and grated cheese and broiled until the cheese is golden brown.

Preheat oven to 425° F. Heat the butter in a saucepan over medium heat; when sizzling add the leeks, fennel and parsley. Cook about 5 minutes, until tender. Remove from heat and stir in bread crumbs and Pernod. Transfer mixture to a blender or food processor and process until finely chopped, about 1 minute. Season to taste with salt, pepper and hot pepper sauce.

Rinse and shuck oysters, leaving meat in the deep cupped shells. Line 4 pie tins or baking dishes with 1-inch rock salt. Set 6 oysters in each dish. Top each oyster with an equal amount of topping mixture, about 1 tablespoon. Bake for about 10 minutes, or until the oysters are heated through and topping is golden brown.

Recommended wines: Light bodied Chardonnay, Pinot Blanc, Pinot Gris, Sauvignon Blanc.

Serves 4

- 24 medium oysters in the shell
  Rock salt for lining baking pans
- 6 tablespoons butter
- 1/2 cup finely sliced leeks or green onion
- 1/2 cup finely sliced fennel bulb or celery
- 1/4 cup finely chopped parsley
- 1/3 cup bread crumbs
- 1/3 cup Pernod or anisette
  Salt, freshly ground pepper and hot red pepper sauce to taste

Oysters Casino

Like other classic oyster recipes, this has many versions, but two standard ingredients are bacon and green pepper. Optional ingredients include finely chopped celery, lemon juice, Worcestershire sauce and Tabasco® brand Pepper Sauce.

Serves 4

24 small to medium oysters in the shell
  Rock salt to line baking dishes
4 slices bacon
2 tablespoons butter or butter mixed with vegetable oil
1/3 cup finely diced shallots or onion
1/4 cup finely diced green pepper
1/4 cup chopped fresh parsley
1 teaspoon fresh lemon juice
1 teaspoon Worcestershire sauce
  Few drops of TABASCO® brand Pepper Sauce

Preheat oven to 425° F. Slice bacon into 1-inch pieces. Cook in a skillet over medium heat until almost cooked through, then drain on paper towels, reserving 1 tablespoon bacon grease. Return the skillet to medium heat; add butter and, when sizzling, stir in the shallots and green pepper. Cook, about 5 minutes, until tender. Stir in the chopped parsley, lemon juice, Worcestershire sauce and Tabasco sauce.

Rinse and shuck oysters, leaving meat in the deep cupped shells. Line 4 pie tins or baking dishes with 1-inch rock salt. Set 6 oysters in each dish. Top each oyster with an equal amount of topping mixture, about 1 tablespoon. Top with pieces of bacon. Bake for about 10 minutes, or until the oysters are heated through and bacon is golden brown.

Recommended wines: Sauvignon Blanc, Semillon.

Oysters Soaked in Sake with Slivered Scallions

Located on the lower level of New York's Grand Central Station, this restaurant is renowned for its varied and delicious oyster dishes. While this recipe calls for few ingredients and is simple to prepare, it offers an incredible complexity of flavor and texture. Punctuated by the hot bite of slivered scallions, the sweet, nutty flavor of sake delicately wraps around each oyster's essence of the sea. Grand Central recommends serving Humboldt Bay Kumamotos from California.

Rinse and shuck the oysters, leaving them in their deep cupped shells. Set the oysters on a serving dish lined with a bed of crushed ice. Top each oyster with 1/4 to 1/2 teaspoon of slivered scallions and finish by sprinkling 1/4 to 1/2 teaspoon chilled sake over each oyster. Serve at once.

Serves 2

12 small oysters in the shell
1/2 cup finely slivered scallions
  (green onions)
1/4 cup dry sake, chilled
  (Use a good quality dry sake)
  Shaved ice to line serving
  platter

Preparing oyster stews and pan roasts to order at the Grand Central Oyster Bar & Restaurant in New York City. See Grand Central Oyster Bar Pan Roast recipe on page 253.

The Joy of Oysters 109

Oysters Laphroaig

Shoalwater Restaurant, Seaview, WA

"Don't let the simplicity of this recipe fool you — the flavors of the fresh oysters and the peaty, iodine-y quality of this particular single-malt Scotch whiskey complement each other perfectly," say owners Tony and Ann Kischner. Located on Washington's Long Beach Peninsula, the restaurant is situated deliciously close to Willapa Bay, where some of the region's finest oyster beds are found. The instructions call for roasting oysters in the oven, but the Kischners also recommend grilling the oysters over a hot fire until they pop open. "Simply pull off the top; drizzle the Scotch over the top — and it's Heaven!" they say.

Serves 6

24 to 36 fresh small oysters (at the Shoalwater they serve Willapa Bay raised Pacifics or Kumomotos)

6 cups rock salt (to line baking sheet and serving plates)

1/2 to 3/4 cup Laphroaig single malt Scotch whisky

Preheat oven to 500° F. Scrub the oysters well to eliminate mud and sand. Place the oysters on a baking sheet lined with rock salt.

Bake for about 10 minutes, or until the shells pop open slightly. Remove from the oven. Using an oven mitt and a sharp knife, cut the muscle at the back of the oyster and remove the top shell. Arrange the oysters on serving plates lined with rock salt. Using an eye dropper or spoon, drizzle several drops of Scotch over each oyster. Serve hot.

Recommended beverage: Laphroaig Scotch

Shaffer City Oyster Martini

Shaffer City Oyster Bar and Grill, New York

For an extra smooth martini, chill the vodka in the freezer well ahead of time. It won't freeze, but the icy-cold vodka will acquire a thick, silky texture. "Start sipping, and you will wade deeper and deeper into the sea. For the ultimate trip, make sure to eat that drunken little devil. Wow!" says A. Jay Shaffer, Shaffer City's Executive Chef and Host.

Swirl the vermouth in a chilled martini glass, then discard the vermouth. Shuck the oyster and place the oyster and its liquor in the glass. Fill the glass with chilled vodka. Enjoy.

For each martini:

4 ounces Kettle One vodka, or other high quality vodka or gin, chilled

2 drops dry vermouth

1 West Coast oyster with liquor

"Oyster dear to the gourmet, beneficient Oyster, exciting rather than sating, all stomachs digest you, all stomachs bless you."
Seneca
Roman Orator

Pacific Oyster Cocktail

Layered with briny, extra-small oysters and spicy cocktail sauce, this oyster cocktail is a specialty of bars and taverns up and down the Pacific Coast. Traditionally, the oyster cocktail is served with oyster crackers or saltines and ice-cold draught beer. This may not be the most elegant dish, but when made with really good fresh oysters, it certainly is tasty.

Serves 2

12 ounces extra-small oysters, shucked

Pacific Cocktail Sauce:
3/4 cup catsup
1-1/2 tablespoons fresh lime juice
2 teaspoons hot red pepper sauce, or to taste
1 tablespoon prepared horseradish sauce
1 teaspoon Worchestershire sauce
1 teaspoon celery seed
1 tablespoon grated onion
Salt and freshly ground black pepper to taste
Lime wedges for garnish

In a non-reactive bowl, whisk together the catsup, lemon juice, hot red pepper sauce, horseradish, Worchestershire sauce, celery seed and grated onion. Season to taste with salt and pepper. Chill the sauce for at least 1/2 hour to marry flavors.

Meanwhile, chill 2 cocktail or parfait glasses. Beginning and ending with a layer of sauce, layer the oysters and sauce in each glass. Serve chilled with lime wedges.

Recommended beverage: Chilled beer.

Oysters On The Half Shell with Citrus-Coriander Sauce

Canlis Restaurant, Seattle, WA

Chef Greg Atkinson delighted former oyster grower Doe Webb, of Westcott Bay Sea Farms in Friday Harbor, Washington, with this bright citrus sauce laced with garlic and ground coriander seed. Doe used to tell Greg that she loved it because it didn't mask the flavor of the oysters. When Greg lived and worked in Friday Harbor, near Westcott Bay, he served this sauce with Westcott Bay's "petite" oysters which, as the name implies, are quite small, about 2-inches in length.

With a citrus zester (available at kitchen shops) or grater, carefully remove the colorful outer rind from each citrus fruit. Place the zest in a small, non-reactive bowl and set aside. Slice each fruit in half, horizontally, and, using a juicer, squeeze the juice from the fruit. Add the citrus juice to the zest. Stir in the garlic, sugar, coriander, salt and white pepper. Chill and serve with freshly shucked oysters arranged on a bed of crushed ice.

Serves 6

1 lemon
1 lime
1 orange
1 teaspoon minced garlic
1/2 teaspoon sugar
1/2 teaspoon ground coriander seed
1/4 teaspoon each, salt and
   white pepper
36 small oysters, freshly shucked

"God help me, I love them oysters!"

David Letterman
The David Letterman Show, 1997

Oysters On The Half Shell
with Frozen Raspberry Mignonette

Canlis Restaurant, Seattle, WA

Greg Atkinson, Executive Chef for Canlis, one of Seattle's most elegant restaurants, adds a Northwest twist to a traditional mignonette, by using a tangy raspberry vinegar in place of the usual red wine or champagne vinegar. He freezes the sauce to a slushy consistency to provide an icy topping for freshly shucked oysters, which he arranges in a circle, hinge-sides facing in, on a chilled plate lined with crushed ice. After spooning a teaspoonful of frozen mignonette on top of each oyster, he garnishes the center of the plate with a few fresh raspberries. Note: If you can't find raspberry-flavored vinegar, you can make you own by steeping one cup of raspberries in two cups of red wine vinegar for 24 hours.
Allow six freshly shucked oysters per person.

Frozen Raspberry Mignonette

Makes about 2 cups

- 1 cup raspberry-flavored red wine vinegar
- 1 cup sparkling water
- 2 tablespoons finely chopped shallots
- 1 tablespoon coarsely ground black peppercorns

Combine all ingredients in a non-reactive bowl. Place the bowl in the freezer and freeze until the mixture is slushy and, almost frozen solid. Stir to break up the ice crystals, then spoon 1 to 2 teaspoons of mignonette over each freshly shucked oyster.

Oysters on the Half Shell
with Iced Apple Cider Mignonette

Legal Seafoods, 19 Eastern Seaboard locations (see restaurant directory)

A family owned business based on the Eastern Seaboard, Legal Seafoods has filled a welcome niche in the restaurant and mail-order business for people who love great seafood. This is one of Chef Rich Vellante's specialties for half-shell oysters. He recommends Cotuit, Wellfleet or Waquoit oysters, but this tart mignonette sauce is also delicious on oysters from many other regions. For an elegant presentation, Chef Vellante suggests topping the oysters with a dollop of caviar. The apple cider needs to be frozen for this recipe, so plan to start at least four hours in advance.

"If it isn't fresh, it isn't Legal!"

Pour 1-1/2 cups of the apple cider into two ice cube trays, fitted with cube dividers, and freeze until solid (about 4 hours.) To make the mignonette: Place the remaining 1/2 cup of apple cider in a non-reactive bowl. Whisk in the diced apple, pepper, and chives. Cover and chill until needed.

Once the apple cider is frozen, empty the cubes into a blender, ice shaver, or food processor. Process until cubes have become shaved ice. Transfer to a chilled bowl and reserve in the freezer.

Scrub and shuck the oysters, leaving the meat in the deep cupped shell. Set the oysters on a serving plate lined with shaved ice. Whisk the mignonette to distribute the cracked pepper, and pour 1 teaspoon over each oyster. Place a dollop of the Apple Cider Ice over each oyster and top with a sprinkle of chives. If desired, top with a small spoonful of caviar. Serve at once.

Recommended wines: Viognier (dry style), Dry Riesling, Pinot Gris.

Serves 4 to 6

24 small to medium oysters in the shell
2 cups apple cider
1 tablespoon finely diced shallot
2 tablespoons apple cider vinegar
2 tablespoons finely diced apples (use tart apples, such as Granny Smith)
1 teaspoon cracked black pepper
1/4 cup finely sliced chives
2 ounces caviar, optional
Shaved ice to line serving dish

Iced Oysters on the Half Shell with Spicy Italian Sausage

This is a delicious, classic combination that my friend Fred Carlo — sausage maker extraordinaire, and I served to restaurateur Mark Miller on one of his visits to Portland, Oregon. Fred made the sausage, and I prepared my favorite Dijon Spice Bread (see recipe page 265) to accompany the ice-cold Willapa Bay oysters and hot, spicy sausages. The combination was a big hit with everyone. If you aren't as lucky as I was to have a sausage maker for a friend, you can make your own without too much trouble. If you'd rather not grind your own pork, ask your butcher to do it for you.

Half Shell Lori

Serves 4

Sausage:

5 pounds coarse ground pork butt
2 teaspoons crushed red peppers
1 tablespoon anise seed, crushed
1-1/2 tablespoons salt
1-1/2 tablespoons coarsely ground black pepper
2 tablespoons paprika
5 garlic cloves, minced
1 cup cold water

20 small oysters in the shell
Parsley sprigs for garnish
Lemon wedges
Crushed ice to line serving plate

Make the sausage: In a large mixing bowl, combine all the ingredients, mixing well. Cover the sausage mixture and refrigerate at least one hour to marry flavors and diffuse saltiness. To make patties, shape scant 1/2-cup mixture (about 3 ounces) into 3-inch rounds, approximately 1/4-inch thick Set aside 2 per serving and keep chilled until ready to cook. Form the extra sausage mixture into patties; wrap individually in plastic wrap and freeze.

Preheat oven to 200° F. Heat a lightly oiled heavy skillet over medium heat. When hot, add the sausage patties, working in batches, if necessary. Cook, turning once, until golden, about 5 minutes on each side. Drain the sausages on paper towels and discard any fat in the pan before proceeding with the next batch. Keep warm in a 200° F. oven.

Meanwhile, prepare the oysters. Scrub the oysters and shuck them, leaving the meat in the oyster's deep cupped shell. Arrange the oysters on a chilled plate lined with shaved or crushed ice. Garnish with parsley sprigs and lemon wedges. Pass the sausages on a separate serving plate.

Recommended beverages: Champagne or sparkling wine, Pinot Gris, Sauvignon Blanc, chilled beer.

Oysters on the Half Shell with Three Sauces

Ray's Boathouse, Seattle, WA

Ray's Boathouse began as a boat rental and bait house on Shilshole Bay in 1939. In 1945, the original owner, Ray Lichtenberger expanded the business, adding a cafe featuring fresh seafood that offered an incredible view of Puget Sound and the Olympic Mountains. Now a Seattle landmark, Ray's serves some of the finest seafood in the country. For this recipe, Chef Charles Ramseyer suggests serving a variety of seasonal oysters and having your guests help shuck them. He lines a 2-inch deep serving dish with crushed ice, garnished with seaweed or fresh rosemary sprigs and lemon slices, then arranges the freshly shucked oysters on the ice. He serves the sauces on the side. Each of these sauces can be prepared one day in advance.

Place the cilantro leaves and garlic in the bowl of a food processor. With the motor running, slowly drizzle the lemon juice and olive oil through the feed tube, processing until the cilantro and garlic are pureed. Transfer the pesto to a bowl and stir in the salt and pepper. Refrigerate, covered, until ready too use.

Cilantro Pesto

Makes 1/2 cup

- 2 cups cilantro (fresh coriander) leaves
- 3 garlic cloves, minced
- 1 tablespoon fresh lemon juice
- 1/4 cup extra virgin olive oil
- 1/2 teaspoon salt
- 1/2 teaspoon freshly ground black pepper

Combine the tomato puree, vodka, lime juice, celery seed and salt in a small bowl. Stir in the black pepper and mix well. Refrigerate, covered, until ready to use. Whisk before serving.

Bloody Mary Sauce

Makes 1/2 cup

- 1/2 cup tomato puree
- 1/4 cup vodka, chilled
- 2 teaspoons fresh lime juice
- 1/2 teaspoon celery seed
- Pinch of salt
- 1/2 teaspoon freshly ground black pepper

Whisk all ingredients together. Cover and refrigerate until ready to use.

Recommended wines: Sauvignon Blanc/ Sancerre.

Balsamic Mignonette Sauce

Makes 1/2 cup

- 1/2 cup balsamic vinegar
- 1 large shallot clove, finely diced
- 1/2 teaspoon freshly cracked black pepper

Singapore Slurp
Printer's Row, Chicago, IL

Award winning Chef Michael Foley of Printer's Row in Chicago was in Singapore when I asked him to contribute a recipe - jokingly I asked him to come up with one called "Singapore Slurp." He did, and it is a fantastic combination of flavors. While Michael serves the shooters in chilled shot glasses, the oysters are equally as good on the half shell topped with the remaining ingredients - adding a bit more to the experience of "oysterness."
Note: if you can't find quail eggs, crack a hen's egg into a bowl and drizzle 1/2 teaspoon of yolk and white over each oyster.

Half Shell Lori

Michael writes, "I've always enjoyed traveling to the East. In late summer of '99, I headed to Singapore. With a diverse population of people from Singapore, China, and East India, combined with travelers from all over the word, people here eat a wide range of ethnic foods. It was here that I feasted on incredible seafood along the old harbor, as we discussed the role that Singapore will play in the Eastern economy for decades to come."
" My friends from Singapore did not understand why I used cross cultural ingredients in my recipe of a true Singapore oyster dish. But these are some of the pantry flavors from the basic population groups that gave me the idea for this shooter. Beer is mandatory."

Serves 2

- 4   plump, small oysters, freshly shucked
- 1/2   teaspoon light soy sauce
- 1/2   teaspoon sesame habanera oil (or equal parts sesame oil mixed with habanera pepper sauce)
- 4   raw quail eggs
- 4   razor- thin slices jalapeno chili
- Pinch of salt
- Freshly ground black pepper

Place each freshly shucked oyster with its liquor in the bottom of a chilled shot glass. Add drops of soy sauce and the sesame oil. Top with a slice of chili and crack a quail egg over each. Sprinkle with salt and pepper. Let rest for thirty seconds. Enjoy!

"There's nothing in Christianity or Buddhism that quite matches the sympathetic unselfishness of an oyster."
Saki

Shirred Oysters with Saffron
160 Blue, Chicago, IL

Chef Michael Foley of Printer's Row in Chicago contributes this dish from his friend Patrick Robertson of 160 Blue in Chicago. "In the middle of '99 I had occasion to work with two of my chef friends in Osaka, Japan," recalls Michael. "We met some of the most incredible cooks and shared wonderful Japanese foods accompanied by lots of sake at a restaurant called Ichi Dicky . . . where everything we ate quivered. This shirred oyster dish with saffron, from the incredible U.S. Chef Patrick Robinson, brings all of the stories and superb Japanese foods back to mind."

"This dish, with its name "shirred" is based on the method of cooking things 'til they just quiver," Michael continues. "Often this cooking technique refers to eggs, but in this context, it is oysters. You will be amazed at the outcome - not poached, not broiled, not sautéed, but quivering, as only SHIRRING can do. What a cook, Patrick Robertson!"

Preheat oven to 350° F. Heat 2 tablespoon olive oil in a skillet over medium-low heat. Add the leeks; cover and sweat until the leek's aroma develops, about 2 minutes. Add the wine and simmer until mixture is reduced by half. Add 2 cups of the chicken stock; cover and simmer until the leeks are tender, about 7 minutes. Puree the mixture in a blender. Once the leeks are pureed, add the olive oil in a slow, steady stream until the mixture thickens and emulsifies. Season with salt and pepper. Set aside.

For the potato: In a small saucepan, bring the remaining chicken stock to a boil. Place the diced potato in another small saucepan over medium heat; add 1/2 cup chicken broth, stirring well. Gradually add the remaining chicken stock, about 1/2 cup at a time, stirring well after each addition until the liquid is incorporated and the potato is creamy (risotto style). Season with salt and pepper to taste.

For the leek garnish: Bring the 1 cup vegetable oil to 375° F. Fry the julienne leek until it is golden and crisp. Drain on paper towels.

Serves 4

12	small oysters, shucked and drained
3	leeks (white part only) cut into 1-inch dice
1/2	teaspoon saffron threads
1/4	cup dry white wine
4	cups chicken stock
1/2	cup mild flavored olive oil
2	tablespoons lemon juice
	Salt and freshly ground black pepper
1	large russet potato, peeled and cut into 1/4-inch dice

Garnish:

1	leek, cut into 3-inch julienne
1	cup vegetable oil for frying
	Pinch of saffron
	Chervil to garnish

For the oysters: Place the oysters in a lightly oiled casserole dish and cover with about 1/2 cup of the leek sauce. Place in the oven and cook just until firm, about 10 minutes. Distribute the potato into 4 small warm serving bowls, making 5 piles in each bowl. Top each bowl with 3 oysters. Nap with the shirred oyster sauce. Place the crisp leeks in the center of each bowl and garnish with a sprig of chervil.

Whistling Oyster Dip

Named for the famous "Whistling Oyster," of London who, during the 1840s was triumphantly displayed at the Drury Lane Oyster House where he/she was discovered, this tasty dip is delicious on crackers or crostini, or used as a dip for fresh vegetables, including celery, carrots, cauliflower and jicama.

Makes approximately 2 cups

- 12 large oysters, shucked
- 1/2 cup dry white wine
- 1/2 cup cream cheese, softened
- 1-1/2 cups sour cream
- 2 tablespoons finely chopped green onions
- 1 tablespoon chopped fresh thyme
- 1 tablespoon chopped fresh parsley
- 1 tablespoon capers
- Dash of TABASCO® brand Pepper Sauce
- Freshly ground black pepper to taste

Bring the wine to a boil in a saucepan. Reduce to a simmer and drop in the oysters. Cook about 3 minutes, or until the oysters begin to plump. Drain and coarsely chop the oysters.

In a mixing bowl, beat the cream cheese until creamy. Add the sour cream, mixing well. Stir in the green onion, thyme, parsley, and capers mixing well. Gently fold in the oysters. Season to taste with Tabasco and black pepper. Transfer to a serving bowl. Serve at room temperature.

The Whistling Oyster tavern in Quilcene, WA.

Potted Oyster and Shrimp Spread

Potted seafood and meat spreads are a wonderful British Tradition that began as a way to preserve foods. The spreads or "pates" are packed into individual crocks and covered with clarified butter, ready to be spread on bread or crackers. To clarify butter, place unsalted butter in a saucepan over low heat. Let the butter melt, until the white solids drop to the bottom of the pan. Ladle or pour the clear butter off the top into another container. Store at room temperature. Covered in the refrigerator, these will keep up to 4 days.

Place the poached oysters, shrimp and garlic in the bowl of a food processor or blender. Process until mixture forms a smooth paste. Add the softened butter and process until it is incorporated into the mixture. Add the lemon juice and white pepper. Season to taste with salt and Tabasco.

Pack the spread into individual pots and cover with clarified butter. Cover and chill until butter has set. Let warm at room temperature 1/2 hour before serving. Spread on crackers or bread.

Fills four 4-ounce capacity molds or ramekins

- 6 large oysters, shucked and poached (see page 140)
- 6 ounces cooked shrimp meat
- 1 garlic clove, minced
- 6 tablespoons unsalted butter, softened
- 2 tablespoons fresh lemon juice
- 1/2 teaspoon white pepper
  Salt to taste
  Dash of hot red pepper sauce
- 4 ounces (1/2 stick) butter, clarified

Baked Oysters with Beurre Blanc, Spinach and Parsley Gremolata

Anthony's Restaurants, Seattle, WA

Specializing in fresh Northwest seafood and other Northwest specialties, including berries, wines and fresh vegetables, Anthony's Restaurants is a group of fifteen restaurants located in picturesque waterfront locations around the greater Puget Sound region. Each year at their Shilshole Bay restaurant, the restaurant

hosts the annual Oyster Olympics — a fun filled event whose proceeds go to benefit the Puget Sound Alliance — a group dedicated to keeping Puget Sound waters, and shellfish, clean. Both the Beurre Blanc and Gremolata Sauces, as well as the Spinach Saute, can be prepared up to 2 days in advance — so all you have to do the day of serving is shuck the oysters, top them with the sauces, and pop them in the oven to bake.

Serves 4

24 medium oysters in the shell
 1 tomato, finely diced
    Rock salt for lining baking sheet

Spinach Saute:
 1 tablespoon olive oil
 1 tablespoon finely minced shallots
12 ounces spinach leaves, washed
    and dried
1/8 teaspoon salt
    Freshly ground black pepper
    to taste
 1 tablespoon Anisette or Pernod

To make the Spinach Saute: Heat the oil in a skillet over medium heat. Stir in the shallots and cook for 1 minute. Add the spinach, salt, pepper and Anisette. Cook, stirring often, just until leaves are slightly wilted, about 2 minutes. Set aside to cool slightly before using.

The Joy of Oysters

To make the Beurre Blanc: Combine the wine, vinegar, shallots, and pepper in a medium skillet. Bring to a boil and simmer until the liquid has reduced to about 1/2 tablespoon. Stir in the cream and boil until the cream begins to thicken, about 1 minute. Beat in the chilled butter, bit by bit, keeping the sauce just warm enough to absorb the butter. Strain the sauce and keep warm over hot water in a double boiler or in a thermos.

Beurre Blanc Sauce:

- 3 tablespoons dry white wine
- 3 tablespoons white wine vinegar
- 1 tablespoon finely chopped shallots
  Pinch of ground white pepper
- 1 tablespoon heavy cream
- 3/4 cup (1-1/2 sticks) unsalted butter, chilled and cut into 1-inch pieces

To make the Parsley Gremolata: Combine all ingredients in a small mixing bowl. Set aside.

Parsley Gremolata

- 1 cup fresh parsley, finely minced
- 3 garlic cloves, minced
- 2 teaspoons Kosher salt
- 1 teaspoon freshly ground black pepper
- 4 teaspoons lemon zest

Preheat oven to 375° F. Scrub and shuck oysters, reserving their deep cupped shells. Set the deep shells on a baking sheet lined with a bed of rock salt. Line each shell with 1 tablespoon of cooked spinach and set an oyster on each bed of spinach. Top each oyster with 1 teaspoon of diced tomato, 2 teaspoons of Beurre Blanc, and 1/2 teaspoon Gremolata. Bake oysters for 7 to 10 minutes or until oysters are heated through. Serve hot on serving plates lined with rock salt or sea salt.

Recommended wines: Chardonnay, Sauvignon Blanc, Pinot Blanc, Dry Riesling.

Smoked Oysters

Burnished with a smoky sweet glaze, these oysters remain plump and moist after cooking. Part of the secret lies in poaching them before smoking, so the meat plumps and holds its shape. If you don't poach them, the oysters spread out like a pancake on the grill. A seductive brine of real maple syrup and soy sauce is fired with a touch of Tabasco sauce. Plan on marinating the oysters 12 hours to overnight before smoking. To store smoked oysters, cover tightly with plastic wrap or store in zip-lock bags in the refrigerator or freezer. Serve with crackers, or use in recipes calling for smoked oysters.

In a large mixing bowl, whisk together the maple syrup, soy sauce, brown sugar, water and Tabasco® brand hot pepper sauce.

To poach oysters, bring the water and lemon juice to a boil in a large saucepan. Add the oysters and simmer until they plump, about 3 minutes. Using a slotted spoon, transfer the hot oysters to the prepared brine. Partially cover with plastic wrap and chill 12 hours to overnight.

One hour before smoking, remove the oysters from the brine; set on a baking sheet and chill 1 hour. (This creates a firm skin to which the smoke can adhere and seals in the oyster's juice.)

Preheat smoker or barbecue, following directions for temperature, amount of wood chips and time. If using a barbecue, smoke oysters over a very slow fire, occasionally adding dampened hardwood chips or small sticks to produce smoke. Arrange the coals and chips to one side of the barbecue and place the oysters on the opposite side of the grill — not directly over the coals. Cover, leaving small vents for cross ventilation. Cook, about 1 hour, until oysters are a rich, smoky color.

Makes 1 dozen oysters (20 ounces medium oysters)

Brine:
1/4 cup real maple syrup
1/4 cup soy sauce
6 tablespoons brown sugar
2 cups water, room temperature
1/2 teaspoon Tabasco® brand
      hot pepper sauce
3 cups water
1 tablespoon lemon juice

1 dozen medium to large
      oysters, shucked

Baked Oysters with Chanterelle Mushroom Sauce

Friday Harbor House, Friday Harbor, WA

Chefs and partners, Laurie Paul and Tim Barrette, presented this wonderful appetizer at the James Beard House in New York, where they served the oysters on a bed of cedar boughs and fall leaves they had gathered near their home on San Juan Island. In the Pacific Northwest, wild Chanterelle mushrooms appear in late summer and fall. "When they're in season, Chanterelle mushrooms motivate us daily to get out into the woods and forage for them an other fungal gems," says Laurie. "This recipe is a perfect marriage of forest and sea, it's a combination we knew would work even before we tasted it." If you don't have fresh Chanterelles, you can substitute morels, oyster mushrooms, or button mushrooms. The mushroom mixture can be prepared one day in advance and refrigerated until serving time.

Preheat oven to 400° F. Melt butter in a skillet over medium heat. When sizzling, add the shallots and garlic; cook until softened, about 2 minutes. Add the mushrooms and cook until the mushrooms soften and exude their liquid, then begin to reabsorb it. When the mixture turns golden and the liquid is almost evaporated from the pan, add the white wine and cream. Continue to simmer 2 more minutes, or until the mixture thickens slightly, then add the cheese. Simmer until the mixture thickens and will mound on a spoon. Remove from the heat and let cool at room temperature.

Meanwhile, scrub and shuck the oysters, leaving each oyster in its deep, cupped shell. Line a baking pan with rock salt or crinkled aluminum foil, to hold the oysters upright. Arrange oysters on the baking sheet. Spoon a teaspoon or so of the prepared mushroom mixture onto each oyster. Bake for 10 to 12 minutes, until the oysters are heated through and the mushroom mixture is bubbly and golden. Serve warm on plates lined with a bed of rock salt or shredded greens to hold oysters upright.

Recommended wines: Chardonnay, Sauvignon Blanc, Pinot Blanc.

Serves 4 to 6

- 2 tablespoons butter
- 3 large shallots, or one small onion, finely diced
- 2 garlic cloves, minced
- 1 pound Chanterelle mushrooms, cleaned and finely diced
- 3 tablespoons dry white wine
- 1/3 cup whipping cream
- 1/2 cup grated Parmesan cheese
  Sea salt and freshly ground pepper to taste
- 2 dozen small to medium oysters in the shell

Oyster Stuffed Mushroom Caps

Brushed with melted garlic butter and stuffed with freshly shucked oysters, these juicy mushrooms are one of my favorite appetizers. They are quick and easy to prepare, yet mouth-wateringly tasty. These are best served as finger food — popped whole into your mouth; so you can savor all the delicious juices. I usually use either large button mushrooms or darker colored brown button mushrooms. Fresh morels are also very good stuffed with oysters, although you need to bake morels on their sides, as they don't sit upright.
Half Shell Lori

Serves 4

12 extra-small or small oysters, shucked
12 large mushrooms
3 tablespoons butter
1 garlic clove, minced
 Salt and freshly ground black pepper
2 tablespoons finely diced green onions or chives
1/3 cup freshly grated Parmesan cheese

Preheat oven to 350° F. Pull the stems out of the mushroom caps (use stems in another recipe, if desired). Set the caps in a large baking dish. Melt the butter with the minced garlic. With a pastry brush, paint the mushrooms liberally inside and out with the garlic butter. Fill each mushroom cap with an oyster; sprinkle with salt and pepper, diced green onion and Parmesan cheese. Bake the oysters about 15 minutes, until mushrooms are tender and cheese is melted. Let cool slightly before serving.

Recommended wines: Dry Gerwurztraminer, Dry Riesling, Pinot Blanc, Sparkling Wine

Baked Oysters with Toasted Pecan Pesto

The sweet, rich flavor of toasted pecan pesto is delicious with sweet, briny oysters, but you can substitute any of your favorite toasted nuts, such as walnuts, hazelnuts, or almonds.

Serves 4

24 medium oysters in the shell
1/2 cup pecans
2 garlic cloves
3 cups packed fresh basil leaves
3 tablespoons freshly grated Parmesan cheese
1 tablespoon fresh lemon juice
3 tablespoons unsalted butter, softened
2 tablespoons extra-virgin olive oil
 Rock salt to line baking dish

Preheat oven to 325° F. Spread the pecans on a baking sheet and bake until lightly toasted, about 7 minutes. Let cool. Combine the pecans and garlic in the bowl of a food processor, and pulse until pecans are finely chopped. Add the Parmesan cheese and lemon juice, mixing well, then add the butter and olive oil and blend thoroughly.

Increase oven temperature to 400° F. Scrub and shuck the oysters, leaving them in their deep cupped shells. Place the oysters on a baking sheet or individual baking dishes lined with rock salt. Top each oyster with about 1 tablespoon of pesto. Bake until oysters are cooked through and pesto is golden brown, about 10 to 12 minutes.

Recommended wines: Light-bodied Chardonnay, Pinot Gris.

Baked Oysters, Klondike Style

Shaw's Crab House and Blue Crab Lounge, Chicago, IL

Listed by Forbes Magazine as one of the top three oyster bars in the country, Shaw's Crab House is definitely the place to "Royster With the Oyster," during Oyster Hour, held Monday through Friday evenings in the Blue Crab Lounge. Topped with fresh horseradish, bread crumbs and three cheeses, this tasty dish is just one of the oyster specialties of the house.

Preheat oven to 350° F. Rinse the oysters; shuck them, and leave them in the deep shells. Set the oysters on a baking sheet lined with rock salt Sprinkle with paprika and finely grated horseradish. Mix the fresh bread crumbs with the grated Parmesan, Swiss and Edam cheeses and sprinkle over the top of the oysters. Drizzle the oysters with melted butter. Bake 12 to 15 minutes, or until golden brown. Serve on a warm platter lined with rock salt. Garnish with parsley and lemon slices.

Recommended wines: Sauvignon Blanc, Muscadet, Semillon.

Serves 2 to 4

- 1 dozen medium-sized oysters in the shell
  - Paprika
  - Finely grated fresh horseradish
- 1/2 cup bread crumbs
- 1/4 cup Parmesan cheese
- 1/4 cup grated Swiss cheese
- 1/4 cup grated Edam cheese
- 2 tablespoons unsalted butter, melted
  - Parsley sprigs and sliced lemon for garnish

"The Oyster—the mere writing of the word creates sensations of succulence— gastronomic pleasures, nutritive fare, easy digestion, palatable indulgence— then go to sleep in peace."
Lucullus, 1878

Oyster Bill's Baked Stuffed Oysters

Here is Bill's favorite appetizer recipe. Mixed with a flavorful blend of peppers, onions, and herbs, then topped with bacon, these oysters come sizzling-hot out of the oven to be enjoyed with an icy cold beer or glass of crisp white wine.

Serves 4 to 6

24 to 30 medium oysters in the shell
8 strips bacon, cut into 2-inch pieces
1 tablespoon vegetable oil
1 large green pepper, seeded and finely diced
1 large onion, peeled and finely diced
2 cups bread crumbs
2 eggs, lightly beaten
2 tablespoons chopped fresh parsley
Salt and freshly ground black pepper to taste
Paprika to sprinkle on oysters
Rock salt to line baking dish

Preheat oven to 375° F. Heat a skillet over medium-high heat. Add the bacon and cook, stirring often, until it begins to curl, but is not crisp. Remove and drain on paper towels, reserving 1 tablespoon bacon grease. Reduce heat to medium, add the vegetable oil to the bacon grease in the skillet. When oil is hot, add green pepper and onion and cook until softened, about 5 minutes.

Scrub and shuck the oysters, reserving the liquor and the deep cupped shells. Roughly chop the oysters and place them with their liquor in a large mixing bowl. Stir in the bread crumbs, sauteed pepper and onions, eggs, and parsley. Season to taste with salt and pepper.

Place the oyster shells on a baking sheet lined with rock salt. Spoon the oyster mixture into each shell, mounding just above the edges of the shell. Top each oyster with 1 or 2 pieces of bacon and sprinkle with paprika. Bake for 25 to 30 minutes, until the bacon is crisp and sizzling. Serve immediately.

Recommended beverages: Sauvignon Blanc, Pinot Gris, Pinot Blanc, Dry Riesling, Chilled beer.

Oysters Provencal

Shuckers at The Four Seasons Olympic Hotel, Seattle, WA

This simple, but very delicious recipe, hails from Shuckers, one of Seattle's top oyster bars, located in the Four Seasons Olympic Hotel. Use freshly shucked, local oysters, about 2 - 3 inches in length.

Preheat oven to 350° F. In a small bowl, combine the tomato, garlic, herbs, olive oil, salt and pepper. Scrub and shuck the oysters, leaving the meat in deep cupped shells. Line a baking pan with about 1/2-inch rock salt, to hold the oysters upright. Set the shucked oysters in the rock salt. Top each oyster with a teaspoonful of the tomato mixture and sprinkle with cheese. Bake for 7 to 10 minutes, or until bubbling hot. Serve on warm plates lined with rock salt.

Recommended wines: Pinot Gris, Champagne or sparkling wine, Sauvignon (Fume) Blanc.

Serves 4 to 6

1 dozen freshly shucked oysters
   Rock salt for lining baking pan
   and serving plates
1 medium tomato, peeled and
   diced
1 teaspoon minced garlic
1 teaspoon fresh herbs (a mix of
   thyme, basil, parsley or oregano)
2 tablespoons olive oil
1/2 cup grated Asiago or Parmesan
   cheese
   Salt and pepper to taste

"You have never seen the sea, but in an oyster on the shell."
Edmond Rostand

Roasted Oysters with Garlic Parsley Butter

Laced with white wine and cognac, this garlicky parsley sauce is the ultimate on plump, succulent oysters. For a special treat, try this with European Flats or Belons. If you like, serve with good crusty bread to mop up the extra sauces. Plan on refrigerating the Garlic Parsley butter for 2 hours to overnight to marry flavors.

Serves 4 to 6

- 24 small to medium oysters in the shell
- 8 ounces (1 stick) unsalted butter, softened
- 3 garlic cloves, minced
- 1/4 cup minced fresh parsley
- 1 shallot, minced
- 2 teaspoons salt
- 1/2 teaspoon freshly ground black pepper
- 1/4 teaspoon ground nutmeg
- 2 teaspoons Cognac
- 2 teaspoons dry white wine
- Rock salt to line baking dish

Make the Garlic Parsley Butter: In a medium mixing bowl, beat together the butter, garlic, parsley, shallots, salt, pepper, nutmeg, Cognac and wine. Cover and refrigerate at least 2 hours to overnight.

Preheat oven to 400° F. Scrub and shuck the oysters, leaving them in their deep cupped shells. Set the oysters on a baking dish lined with rock salt. Using a stiff knife, fill each oyster with about 1 to 2 teaspoons of the butter mixture. Bake until the oysters are cooked through and butter is sizzling, about 10 to 12 minutes. Serve hot.

Recommended wines: Sauvignon Blanc, Semillon, Champagne or sparkling wine.

Brooklyn Baked Oysters

The Brooklyn Seafood, Steak and Oyster House, Seattle, WA

The circular copper oyster bar in The Brooklyn's main dining room displays a wonderful selection of fresh oysters daily, with an average of ten varieties during oyster season. All oysters are listed on the tasting menu by species, growing method, and tasting notes — always a great learning and tasting experience. Topped

with a creamy mushroom sauce and melted Gruyere cheese, these oysters are one of the Brooklyn's most popular dishes. The chef recommends using either Kumamoto (Crassostrea Sikamea) or small Pacific oysters (Crassostrea Gigas), specifically, Westcott Bay Petites from Friday Harbor, WA, for this recipe. On special occasions, he uses golden, apricot-scented Chanterelle mushrooms, instead of button mushrooms.

Scrub the oysters and shuck them, reserving the liquor. Remove the oysters from their shells, and reserve. Arrange the deep cupped shells in a shallow, ovenproof serving dish lined with 2-inches of rock salt. Place an oyster in each shell.

Clean the button mushrooms by wiping them with damp paper towels; chop them very fine. If using Chanterelles, rinse them briefly under cold water, drain and pat dry. Chop into small pieces.

Melt the butter in a skillet over medium heat. Add the shallots and cook for 1 minute. Stir in the mushrooms and lemon juice and cook for 1 minute more; then add the reserved oyster liquor and black pepper to taste. Stir in the parsley and crème fraîche. Top each oyster with a spoonful of sauce and sprinkle with grated cheese. Place the oysters under a preheated broiler, about 6-inches under the heat source, until the cheese melts and begins to bubble. Serve at once.

Recommended wines: Sauvignon (Fume) Blanc, Chardonnay, Viognier (dry style).

---

*Serves 4 as an appetizer
or 2 as a main dish*

- 16 small oysters in the shell
- 3 cups fresh button or Chanterelle mushrooms
- 2 tablespoons unsalted butter
- 1/2 cup finely chopped shallots
  Juice of 1/2 lemon
- 1 tablespoon finely chopped parsley
- 2 tablespoons crème frâiche or sour cream
- 1/2 cup finely grated Gruyère cheese
  Freshly ground black pepper
  Rock salt for lining baking dish

Hot Oysters with Beurre Blanc, Cucumber and Swiss Chard

Ballymaloe Cookery School, Shanagarry, Ireland

I was very fortunate to study seafood cookery at the Ballymaloe Cookery School in Ireland, under instructor Darina Allen. This was one of my favorite recipes from the class. We used native Irish oysters, but it is delicious with any briny bivalve. To prevent the oysters from sliding around on the plate, Darina served them on a bed of finely shredded Swiss chard or spinach.

Half Shell Lori

Serves 4

Beurre Blanc Sauce
- 3 tablespoons dry white wine
- 3 tablespoons white wine vinegar
- 1 tablespoon finely chopped shallots
- Pinch of ground white pepper
- 1 tablespoon heavy cream
- 3/4 cup (1-1/2 sticks) unsalted butter, chilled and cut into 1-inch pieces

- 1/4 cucumber
- 1/2 cup finely shredded Swiss chard
- 16 medium oysters, rinsed

Make the Beurre Blanc: Combine the wine, vinegar, shallots, and pepper in a medium skillet. Bring to a boil and simmer until the liquid has reduced to about 1/2 tablespoon. Stir in the cream and boil until the cream begins to thicken, about 1 minute. Beat in the chilled butter, bit by bit, keeping the sauce just warm enough to absorb the butter. Strain the sauce and keep warm over hot water in a double boiler or in a thermos.

Peel the cucumber and halve. Use a spoon to scoop out the seeds, then slice the cucumber into fine julienne strips. Combine with the shredded Swiss chard.

Preheat the oven to 400° F. Just before serving, put the oysters on a baking sheet lined with rock salt into the hot oven. Roast until they start to open, about 10 minutes. Remove and discard the top shells. Place a spoonful of the cucumber/chard mixture on each oyster and top with a spoonful of Beurre Blanc. Serve at once.

Recommended wines: Sparkling wine, Chardonnay.

Oysters Rockefeller

Shuckers at The Four Seasons Olympic Hotel, Seattle, WA

Here is Shuker's delicious rendition of the classic Oysters Rockefeller Dish. If you're in the mood for less cooking, simply skip the Hollandaise Sauce. The oysters are great just topped with the sauteed spinach mixture and a dash of Pernod or Anisette.

Heat the oil and butter in a skillet over medium heat. Add the leeks or onions and cook until soft and slightly transparent. Stir in the spinach and cook, stirring often, just until it softens. Stir in cream and simmer until liquid is slightly thickened, about 2 to 3 minutes. Season to taste with salt and white pepper, set aside

Preheat oven to 350° F. Scrub and shuck the oysters, leaving the meat in deep cupped shells. Line a baking pan with about 1/2-inch rock salt, to hold the oysters upright. Set the shucked oysters in the rock salt. Top each oyster with a teaspoon of the spinach mixture. Bake for about 7 to 10 minutes, or until heated through. Top with a teaspoon of Hollandaise. Broil until golden brown and sprinkle with Pernod. Serve on warm plates lined with rock salt.

To make the Hollandaise Sauce: In the top of a double boiler set over hot, but not simmering water, beat the egg yolks with a wire whisk until they begin to thicken and turn pale in color. Slowly add the wine and continue whisking until mixture begins to thicken again. Slowly whisk in the warm melted butter. In order — add lemon juice, Worcestershire sauce, cayenne and salt, continually whisking. Serve at once, or keep sauce warm in a thermos.

---

1 dozen freshly shucked small oysters
2 teaspoons vegetable oil
2 teaspoons butter
2 tablespoons thinly sliced leeks or green onions
1 cup finely shredded or julienned fresh spinach
1/4 cup whipping cream
Salt and white pepper to taste
Hollandaise sauce (recipe follows)
Dash of Pernod or Anisette to top each oyster
Rock salt for lining baking pan and serving dishes.

Hollandaise Sauce

3 egg yolks.
2 tablespoons dry white wine
1 cup (2 cubes) unsalted butter, melted
1-1/2 tablespoons fresh lemon juice
1/4 teaspoon Worcestershire sauce
dash cayenne pepper
1/4 teaspoon salt

Recommended wines: Sauvignon Blanc, Pinot Blanc, Pinot Gris, light-bodied Chardonnay

Poached Oysters with Champagne Cream Sauce

Simple and sophisticated, this is a dish worth having in your files for any occasion. For a special treat, top the oysters with a teaspoonful of your favorite caviar.

Serves 4

24 small to medium oysters in the shell
2 shallots, minced
2 cups whipping cream
1 cup Champagne or sparkling wine
2 tablespoons unsalted butter, chilled
Salt and white pepper to taste
Chopped chives or caviar, optional
Rock salt to line serving dishes

Rinse and shuck the oysters, being careful to reserve their liquor. Place the oysters and their liquor in a sauce pan. Bring to a simmer and cook 2 to 3 minutes, until the oysters plump. Set the deep cupped shells on 4 individual serving dishes lined with rock salt. Remove the oysters from the liquor; place in a warmed bowl and cover to keep warm.

Add the cream, Champagne and minced shallot to the oyster liquor. Bring to a boil over medium-high heat and simmer until the sauce is reduced by one-third, about 10 minutes. Remove sauce from the heat and whisk in the butter. Season with salt and white pepper. Place an oyster in each shell and drizzle liberally with the Champagne sauce. Garnish with chopped chives or caviar.

Recommended wine: Champagne or sparkling wine

Steamed Oysters with Leeks and Saffron Cream Sauce

Use your favorite medium to large-size oysters for this recipe, such as Bluepoints or European Flats. Open any oysters that don't open during steaming with an oyster knife.

In a large saucepan, combine the wine and water. Bring to a boil over high heat. Add the oysters, deep shell down, cover and steam until the oysters start to open, about 10 minutes. As soon as the oysters open, transfer them to a platter, reserving the cooking liquid.

Melt 2 tablespoons of the butter in a saucepan over medium heat. Stir in the leeks and saffron water. Reduce heat to low, cover and cook until leeks are softened, about 8 minutes. Strain the reserved oyster poaching liquid into the leeks. Cook over medium heat until the liquid is reduced to about 1/2 cup. Stir in the heavy cream and simmer until the sauce is thickened, about 3 to 5 minutes. Season with salt and white pepper.

Preheat the broiler. Remove the oysters from their shells, reserving the deep cupped shells. Set the shells on a baking sheet lined with rock salt. Divide the leeks among the oyster shells and set an oyster on top of the leeks in each shell. Whisk the remaining 1 tablespoon of butter and the beaten egg yolks into the cream sauce. Spoon the sauce over the oysters and broil, 4-inches from the heat, just until the sauce is bubbling. Garnish with chopped chives. Serve hot.

Recommended wines: Chardonnay, sparkling wine or Champagne, Pinot Gris.

Serves 4

- 20 medium to large oysters in the shell
- 1 cup dry white wine
- 1/2 cup water
- 3 tablespoons unsalted butter
- 3 leeks, halved and thinly sliced
- 1/2 teaspoon saffron threads soaked in 1 tablespoon boiling water
- 1/2 cup whipping cream
  Salt and ground white pepper to taste
- 2 large egg yolks, lightly beaten
- 1/4 cup finely chopped chives
  Rock salt or crumpled foil to line baking sheet

The Joy of Oysters

Oysters in Sweet Riesling Sauce with Hazelnut-Sage Pesto

I developed this recipe to serve with a dry or semi-dry Riesling wine. Plump, succulent oysters poached in sweet Riesling wine are set on crunchy toast points, topped with a toasty hazelnut-sage pesto, and served in a golden swirl of buttery Riesling sauce. It's an extraordinary combination of flavors and textures. The pesto can be made up to one week in advance and stored in the refrigerator.

Half Shell Lori

Serves 4

12 medium oysters, shucked and drained, reserving juices
3/4 cup semi-sweet or off-dry Riesling wine
3 shallots, minced
2 allspice berries
3 black peppercorns
8 tablespoons (1 stick) unsalted butter, chilled and divided into 8 pieces
12 toast points or baguette rounds
2 tablespoons unsalted butter, melted

Hazelnut Sage Pesto

1/2 cup toasted hazelnuts, finely ground
4 garlic cloves, minced
2 tablespoons rubbed or crumbled dry sage
2 tablespoons extra virgin olive oil
2 tablespoons grated Parmesan cheese

Place the wine, shallots, allspice and peppercorns in a medium saucepan. Bring liquid to a boil, add the oysters and simmer gently for about 2 to 3 minutes, until oysters plump. Remove the oysters with a slotted spoon and set aside. Add the oyster liquor to the wine, bring to a boil and reduce until the liquid is reduced to about 2 tablespoons. Reduce heat to low. Whisk in the butter, one tablespoon at a time (do not let mixture boil), until all butter is incorporated. Strain sauce through a sieve. Keep warm over a double boiler or in a thermos.

Preheat broiler. Brush the toast points or baguette rounds with melted butter and set on a baking sheet. Broil 6-inches from the heat until lightly toasted and golden around the edges. Place an oyster on each toast point. Top each oyster with 1 to 2 teaspoons hazelnut pesto and place under the broiler until oysters are heated through and pesto turns golden brown. Ladle 1/4 cup Riesling sauce onto each plate and top with 2 to 3 oyster toastpoints. Serve at once.

For Pesto: Combine all ingredients thoroughly in a mixing bowl. Covered and stored in the refrigerator, this will keep up to 1 week.

Recommended wine: Dry or Semi-dry Riesling.

Oyster Fritters in Beer Batter

Serve these crispy fritters with wedges of lemon or lime and Jalapeno Tartar Sauce (page 189) or Ginger Sweet & Sour Sauce (page 212). Let the batter sit at room temperature for 1 hour before using to release any air bubbles from the beer. Peanut oil is best for deep frying because it can be heated to higher temperatures without smoking.

Into a mixing bowl, sift together 1/2 cup flour and 1/2 teaspoon salt. Whisk in the melted butter and the beaten egg. Gradually whisk in the beer, mixing just until the batter is fairly smooth. Do not overmix. Let the batter sit at room temperature, covered, for about 1 hour. Just before frying the oysters, beat the egg white until it forms stiff peaks when the beater is lifted out of the bowl. Gently fold the beaten white into the batter, mixing thoroughly.

In a deep-fat fryer or deep skillet, heat 3-inches of peanut oil until it registers 375° F. on a thermometer. Combine the remaining 1/2 cup flour with the salt, pepper and cayenne. Dip the oysters in the flour, shaking off any excess flour, then dip the oysters in the batter. Let the excess batter drain off, then fry the oysters, 5 or 6 at a time, until they are puffed and golden brown, about 3 to 4 minutes. Drain on paper towels and keep warm in a 200° F. oven. Repeat until all the oysters have been fried. Serve hot.

Recommended beverages: Chilled beer, Sauvignon Blanc, Semillon, sparkling wine or Champagne.

Serves 4 to 6

24	medium oysters, shucked drained
1/2	cup all purpose flour
1/2	teaspoon salt
1	tablespoon unsalted butter, melted
1	egg, lightly beaten
1/2	cup dark beer
1	egg white
1/2	cup all purpose flour
1/2	teaspoon salt
1/4	teaspoon freshly ground black pepper
1/4	teaspoon cayenne pepper
	Peanut oil for deep-fat frying
	Lemon or lime wedges

Curry Fried Oysters

*Serve these spicy fried oysters with wedges of fresh lime
and a side dish of your favorite chutney.*

Serves 6 as a appetizer

- 24 medium oysters, shucked and drained
- 1 cup all purpose, unbleached flour
- 1 tablespoon curry powder
- 1/2 teaspoon salt
- 1/4 teaspoon cayenne pepper
  vegetable oil for frying
- 1 tablespoon fresh lime juice
- 1 tablespoon coarsely chopped fresh cilantro leaves
  Chutney

Combine the flour, curry powder, salt and cayenne in a plastic bag. Place several oysters at a time in the bag and shake gently to coat oysters. Set oysters aside and repeat with remaining oysters.

Heat a heavy skillet over medium-high heat. Add enough oil to cover bottom of pan 1/4-inch deep. When oil is sizzling, 350° F., add the oysters in a single layer and cook, turning once, until oysters are golden on both sides, about 2 minutes per side. Using a slotted spoon, transfer oysters to a warm bowl. (If necessary, cook oysters in several batches.) Toss the hot oysters with lime juice and chopped cilantro. Serve warm with lime wedges and chutney.

Recommended beverages: Semillon, Sauvignon Blanc, chilled beer.

Skewered, Grilled and Barbecued Oysters and Accompanying Sauces

Fire up the grill for the ultimate in cooked oysters. For a dramatic presentation, prepare one of our delicious oyster brochette recipes, or simply grill your favorite oysters in the shell and top the plump beauties with a succulent sauce.

Oyster Brochettes
Little Pigs in Blankets
Angels on Horseback
Oyster, Scallop &
*   Mushroom Brochettes*
Beef Tenderloin & Oyster Brochettes
Honey-Mustard Glazed Oyster
*   Brochettes*
Mixed Oyster Grill
Fire-Roasted, Grilled &
*   Barbecued Oysters*
Driftwood Grilled Oysters
South Carolina Oyster Roast
Charcoal Grilled Oysters
Foil Roasted Oysters
Thai Barbecue Oysters
Grilled Oysters with Watercress-
*   Gewürztraminer Sauce*
Cheese & Garlic Butter for
*   Grilled Oysters*
Dorres Foster's Chili-Garlic Dipping
*   Sauce for Grilled Oysters*
Barbecued Oyster Butter
Jalapena Coriander Salsa for
*   Barbecued Oysters*

Oyster Brochettes

*Whether you grill or broil them, Oyster Brochettes always arouse an air of excitement.
There is just something fun about eating food cooked on a stick over a hot fire.
The classic Oyster Brochette recipe is "Angels on Horseback," also known as
"Pigs in a Blanket," in which fresh, plump oysters are wrapped in bacon,
stuck on skewers, and grilled until the bacon is sizzling hot. As you can imagine,
there are endless possibilities. The following are some of our favorites.*

*Note: We recommend poaching oysters before marinating or skewering them.
Light poaching helps the oysters retain their shape during cooking.*

To Poach Oysters: Bring a saucepan filled with 4 cups boiling water seasoned with 1 Tablespoon lemon juice to a boil. Gently drop in the oysters and simmer for about 2 to 3 minutes, or until oysters plump. Remove with a slotted spoon and drain on paper towels.

For these recipes, you can use either bamboo skewers soaked in water, or metal skewers. Grill the oysters over a medium-hot fire, or broil 6-inches from the heat.

Little Pigs in Blankets

This recipe is from Mrs. Rorer's New Cookbook, published in 1902
"This old recipe has been used for a number of years by many American cooks. The oysters are drained and dried and each one wrapped in a very thin slice of bacon, the whole fastened with a small wooden skewer or toothpick. When ready to serve have a large iron baking pan well heated; throw in a few oysters at a time, and as soon as they are browned and the gills curled, take them out, drain in a colander, and continue the frying in the same pan. To eat, pick them up by the skewer with the thumb and finger."

Angels on Horseback

Here is a modern version of this recipe that has remained popular since the nineteenth century. When oysters were not available, cooks substituted scallops, and called them "Archangels on Horseback." In the late James Beard's Seafood Cookbook, he referred to oysters wrapped in bacon as "Devils on Horseback." If you like, serve the cooked oysters on hot buttered toast.

Preheat a grill or broiler. Sprinkle poached oysters with garlic powder and black pepper. Wrap each oyster in a piece of bacon and thread onto a skewer, so that the bacon is secured. Thread 4 oysters onto each skewer. Broil or grill, turning occasionally, until the bacon is crispy. Serve hot.

Serves 6 as an appetizer

- 24 extra small or small oysters, shucked and poached
- 1 teaspoon garlic powder
- 1 teaspoon freshly ground black pepper
- 6 slices bacon, cut in thirds and halved lengthwise
- 6 skewers

Oyster, Scallop and Mushroom Brochettes

Serve these tasty brochettes over rice as an entree, or with tartar sauce and lemon wedges as an appetizer.

Preheat broiler. Dip the oysters and scallops first in the beaten egg, then in the seasoned breadcrumbs, shaking off excess crumbs. Thread alternately on skewers, placing mushrooms at intervals. Set the skewers on a baking sheet and drizzle with melted butter. Broil, turning occasionally, until golden brown, about 5 to 10 minutes.

Serves 4 as an appetizer

- 12 extra small or small oysters, shucked and poached
- 12 medium scallops, rinsed and drained
- 8 small mushrooms, wiped clean
- 2 eggs, beaten
- 2 cups bread crumbs seasoned with 1 teaspoon salt
- 1/2 teaspoon freshly grated pepper
- 1/4 teaspoon cayenne pepper
- 6 tablespoons butter, melted
- 4 skewers

OYSTER RECIPES

Beef Tenderloin and Oyster Brochettes

A twist on the classic Carpetbagger's Steak, which is stuffed with oysters, this combines the best of two worlds — steak and seafood. For a quick, tangy sauce, mix together equal parts of catsup and cream-style horseradish. This is perhaps the only oyster dish where you might serve a red wine, such as a Beaujolais Nouveau or light bodied Pinot Noir.

Serves 4

- 12 extra small or small oysters, shucked and poached
- 12 ounces beef tenderloin, cubed
- Salt and freshly ground black pepper
- 3 tablespoons melted butter
- 1 garlic clove, minced
- 4 skewers

Thread the skewers, alternating with oysters and beef tenderloin. Sprinkle with salt and black pepper. Grill or broil until oysters are just cooked through and beef is lightly browned on the edges.

Melt butter with minced garlic. Place oysters on serving plates and drizzle with melted garlic butter. Serve hot.

The Joy of Oysters

Honey-Mustard Glazed Oyster Brochettes

*Brushed with a thick, honey-mustard glaze and wrapped in smoky bacon,
these savory oyster kebabs are a favorite at the Bay Center Oyster Company
in Bay Center, Washington. Located on picturesque Willapa Bay,
the oyster of choice here, of course, are Willapa Bay oysters.*

Preheat a charcoal or gas grill. Combine the ingredients for the glaze in a saucepan over medium heat. Bring to a boil and simmer about 5 minutes. Remove from the heat and cool slightly. Meanwhile, wrap each oyster in a piece of bacon. Thread oysters and mushrooms alternately on the skewers. Place the skewers on a baking sheet and brush liberally with the glaze. Let the skewers sit 15 minutes, then set them over the hot grill. Cook about 5 minutes, until golden, then turn and brush with glaze. Finish cooking until the oysters are golden brown on all sides. If desired, brush with more glaze before serving.

24 extra-small or small oysters, shucked and poached
12 slices bacon, cut in half
24 medium button mushrooms
4 12-inch skewers

Glaze:
1/3 cup Dijon mustard
1/2 teaspoon dry mustard
3 tablespoons white wine vinegar
3 tablespoons brown sugar
1/3 cup honey
2 teaspoons vegetable oil
2 teaspoons soy sauce

Mixed Oyster Grill

In this recipe, a variation on a recipe developed by Washington's Coast Oyster Company, fresh Pacific oysters are marinated in a red wine mignonette, grilled and served on a bed of grilled vegetables. Served with rice or crusty bread, this makes a great light supper.

Serves 4 as an appetizer

- 24 extra small or small oysters, shucked and poached
- 1 cup dry red wine
- 1/2 cup red wine vinegar
- 3 shallots, minced
- 1-1/2 teaspoons coarsely ground black pepper
- 2 teaspoons fresh lemon juice
- 1 red pepper, seeded and cut into 1/2-inch strips
- 1 green pepper, seeded and cut into 1/2-inch strips
- 1 large zucchini, sliced into 1/2-inch thick pieces
- 12 button mushrooms, halved
- 1/2 cup olive oil
- 2 garlic cloves, minced
- 1 teaspoon salt
- 1/2 teaspoon coarsely ground black pepper

In a shallow, non-reactive bowl, combine the red wine, red wine vinegar, shallots, black pepper and lemon juice. Add the poached oysters and marinate 1/2 hour. In a separate bowl, combine the sliced vegetables with the olive oil, garlic, salt and pepper. Marinate 1/2 hour.

Preheat a charcoal or gas grill. Thread the oysters onto 4 skewers and set aside. Grill the vegetables until tender, turning once, about 10 to 12 minutes. Just before the vegetables are finished cooking, set the oyster skewers over the fire. Grill the oysters until heated through, about 5 minutes, turning occasionally. To serve, place an assortment of grilled vegetables on each serving plate and top with 2 oyster skewers.

Fire-Roasted, Grilled & Barbecued Oysters

Whether you're in South Carolina, roasting oysters over a giant fire on a cast iron slab,
or on the misty Pacific Coast, tossing oysters into a smoky driftwood fire,
oysters cooked over an open fire are incredibly seductive. As the oysters cook,
their sweet, salty juices are reduced to a pure essence of the sea,
while the oyster's earthy, peaty, mushroomy flavors unfold.
Slurped from their smoky shells with a touch of butter or your favorite sauce,
grilled oysters are sure to please nearly everyone — even if they claim they don't like oysters.
There are various methods for roasting, grilling and barbecuing oysters —
each of which has its own merits. We offer instructions for a few different methods,
followed by recipes for sauces specially designed for grilled oysters.
Don't forget the traditional dipping sauce for grilled oysters — melted butter
spiked with hot red pepper sauce. Sauce, Slurp and Enjoy!

Notes:

Before you begin: Scrub oysters shells under cold running water. Keep chilled, covered with a damp towel, until ready to cook.

Always cook oysters deep-shell-down to prevent loss of precious oyster liquor.

Cooked over an open flame, oysters usually open within 10 to 15 minutes. Any that don't open can be pried open easily with an oyster knife. Use the oyster knife to pry off top shells and sever adductor muscles.

Oven mitts or tongs will aide in handling hot oysters.

If the weather is inclement and you're not inclined to cook outdoors, you can roast oysters in a pre-heated 350 F. oven. Place the oysters, deep shell down, in a baking dish lined with rock salt. Bake until they open, about 12 to 15 minutes, or steam them, covered in a steamer basket over simmering water, for about 10 minutes.

Grilled & Roasted Oysters

Driftwood Grilled Oysters

Let a driftwood fire burn down to hot coals. Arrange stones or dampened logs around the fire and rest a metal grill on the stones or logs, over the fire. Place oysters on the grill and let them cook until their shells begin to open, about 12 to 15 minutes. If you like, toss a bit of wet seaweed into the fire to create some extra smoke flavor.

South Carolina Oyster Roast

Place a large cast iron slab on supports, leaving enough space beneath the slab for a giant, roaring fire. Prepare a fire beneath the slab and keep it going two hours or longer. Rinse the oysters well and place them on the iron slab. Soak burlap bags in cold water and cover the oysters with them. Douse the bags with water. Roast, about fifteen minutes, until the oysters start to open.

Charcoal Grilled Oysters

Preheat a charcoal (or gas) grill. When fire has died down to hot coals, place scrubbed oysters, deep shell down, on the hot grill. Roast until oysters begin to open, about 10 to 12 minutes.

Foil Roasted Oysters

Start a camp fire or charcoal grill and let the fire burn down to hot coals. Wrap scrubbed oysters, deep shell down, in aluminum foil (about 4 medium oysters per package), securing the edges well. Place the foil packet on a bed of glowing coals. Roast the oysters about 10 minutes, or until they begin to open. Serve directly from the fire to the table, letting each guest open their own package. To eat, split the foil packet open and remove the oysters' top shells with an oyster knife.

Fried Beach Oysters

British Columbia Food and Wine Writer Gary Faessler

"In late spring my father would occasionally wake me as a boy very early Saturday morning and take me salmon fishing for the weekend. After a long day of fishing we would anchor Dad's twenty-five-foot Lynwood in a small bay off the east coast of Vancouver Island. The water was dead calm in the sheltered bay and at low tide we could easily swim or row our dinghy to the rocky shore to collect beach oysters. One of my most enduring food memories is my dad cooking these large beach oysters for supper. Back on the boat dad shucked the oysters, seasoned them with salt and pepper and dusted them with flour. In a super-heated iron skillet over a small gas cooker he fried them in spitting, bubbling butter, quickly charring the oysters on each side. The scorched butter and oysters tasted wondrously smoky, nutty and sweet and even better with the tang of our only accouterment, ketchup!"

Thai Barbecue Oysters

Flying Fish Restaurant, Seattle, WA

James Beard Award recipient, Chef/Owner Christine Keff, is a master at weaving spicy Asian flavors through a weft of fresh Northwest seafood. Here, hot grilled oysters are topped with a fiery sauce flavored with lime and Thai chilies. Christine shucks the oysters before grilling them, but you can also grill the oysters until they open, about 7 to 10 minutes. Remove the top shells and top them with the sauce. Note: If after 10 minutes, oysters are not opened, use an oyster knife to pry them opened. They will be thoroughly cooked.

Preheat grill. Julienne the daikon and carrot and set aside. In a non-reactive bowl, combine the soy sauce, chilies, fish sauce, lime juice, garlic and Mirin, mixing well.

Place the oysters on a hot grill and cook until the liquor bubbles, but not until the oysters become dry, about 3 to 4 minutes. Pour 2/3 of the sauce over the daikon-carrot mixture, mixing well. Place six oysters each on four plates lined with rock salt. Spoon a teaspoon or so of dressing over each oyster and place a scoop of daikon-carrot salad in the center of each plate. If desired, garnish the edges of the plates with fresh seaweed.

Recommended beverages: Chilled Sake, Sauvignon Blanc, Semillon, Dry Riesling.

Serves 4

- 2 dozen oysters, shucked on the half shell
- 1 large daikon radish
- 1 small carrot, peeled
- 1/2 cup soy sauce
- 5 small Thai chilies, seeded and thinly sliced
- 2 tablespoons Asian fish sauce or oyster sauce
- 2 tablespoons freshly squeezed lime juice
- 1 garlic clove, minced
- 2 tablespoons Mirin (sweet, seasoned rice wine)
  Seaweed for optional garnish

Royster with the Oyster

"Let us royster with the oyster – in the shorter days and moister,
That are brought by brown September, with its roguish final R;
For breakfast or for supper, on the under shell or upper,
Of dishes he's the daisy, and of shell-fish he's the star.

We try him as they fry him, and even as they pie him;
We're partial to him luscious in a roast;
We boil and broil him, we vinegar-and-oil him,
And O he is delicious stewed with toast.

We eat him with tomatoes, and the salad with potatoes,
Nor look him o'er with horror when he follows the coleslaw;
And neither does he fret us if he marches after lettuce,
And abreast of cayenne pepper when his majesty is raw.

So welcome with September to the knife and glowing ember,
Juicy darling of our dainties, dispossessor of the clam!
To the oyster, then a hoister, with him a royal royster,
We shall whoop it through the land of heathen jam."

The Detroit Free Press
October 12, 1889

Grilled Oysters with Watercress-Gewürztraminer Sauce
British Columbia Food and Wine Writer Gary Faessler

Gary recommends using gewürztraminer in this recipe, which he serves as a starter for an elegant dinner party. "Gewürztraminer is one of the most highly perfumed white wines of all and is cultivated in virtually every area of the winemaking world," he explains. "Gewürz means spice, and this variety has a characteristic aroma and flavor of musky roses and sweetness of lychee nuts." He recommends a gewürztraminer from Gray Monk Winery in British Columbia's Okanagan Valley. "It's stylish, delicately spicy, floral fruit taste and character is a great match with this creamy, slightly sweet, peppery watercress sauce and ideal with the smoky flavor the charcoal imparts to the charred oysters. If they are in season, he also suggests using orange, red or yellow Nasturtium flowers for garnish. He says "they are edible as well as a delight to the eye and are from the same family as watercress."

Preheat a grill or barbecue. In a heavy, medium size saucepan bring the 1-1/2 cups wine and shallots to a boil. Reduce to one third. Add the watercress and cream and reduce over medium high heat for about 10 minutes. Remove from the fire and stir in the remaining 2 tablespoons of Gewürztraminer. This intensifies the flavor of the wine in the sauce. Set aside and cover to keep warm.

Brush the oysters with olive oil and season with white pepper. Place on the hot grill until the oyster's sides curl and the oysters are lightly charred, about two minutes on each side.

Spoon the watercress- gewürztraminer cream sauce in the center of six warm plates and arrange three grilled oysters in a star on top of the sauce. Garnish with a nasturtium flower.

Serves six

1-1/2	cups plus 2 tablespoons Gewürztraminer
1	small shallot, minced
2	cups heavy cream
2	bunches watercress, stems removed, chopped very fine
12	plump pacific oysters, shucked and drained
	Olive oil
	White pepper
	Nasturtium flowers for garnish

How to Kill an Oyster

Don't drown him in vinegar
or season him at all,
Don't cover up his shining form
with pepper like a Pall,
But gently lift him from his shell
and firmly hold your breath,
Then with your eager tongue and teeth
just tickle him to death.

Charles Krumling
1910

Cheese & Garlic Butter for Grilled Oysters

Seasoned with fresh parsley and grated Asiago cheese, this flavorful butter melts right into the fresh sea flavor of grilled or roasted oysters.

Cream the butter. Stir in remaining ingredients, blending thoroughly. Brush liberally over hot oysters.

Makes about 1 cup

- 1 cup (2 sticks) unsalted butter, softened
- 2 garlic cloves, minced
- 1/2 teaspoon cracked black pepper
- 1/2 cup freshly grated Asiago or Romano cheese
- 1/4 cup chopped fresh Italian parsley

Dorres Foster's Chili-Garlic Dipping Sauce for Grilled Oysters

My aunt, Dorres Foster, concocted this golden dipping sauce for her husband John Foster's famous grilled oysters — the oysters that initiated me into the club of Elbow Benders when I was just a wee sprite. When Aunt Dorres first cooked this fragrant sauce, she was amazed that it smelled much like oysters. It doesn't taste just like them, but adds a wonderful touch. Look for dried poblano chilies in the international section of your local grocery.

Half Shell Lori

Combine the chicken broth, garlic, turmeric and dried chili in a saucepan. Simmer over medium heat for about 10 minutes. Strain the sauce into a serving dish and cool slightly. Stir in sake just before serving.

Makes about 1-1/4 cups

- 1 cup chicken broth, preferably home made
- 2 garlic cloves, minced
- 1/2 teaspoon ground tumeric
- 1 dried poblano chili, broken into pieces
- 3 tablespoons sake

Barbecued Oyster Butter

Sweet, tangy and garlicky, this is the ultimate on grilled, steamed, or oven-roasted oysters. For quick work, blend the ingredients in a food processor or blender. Covered and refrigerated, this will keep up to 1 week.

Makes about 3/4 cup

1/2 cup unsalted butter, softened
1 garlic clove, minced
2 tablespoons ketchup
2 tablespoons soy sauce
1/2 teaspoon fresh lime juice
1/4 teaspoon freshly ground
   black pepper

Stir the butter with a wire whisk until smooth. Whisk in the garlic, then gradually add the ketchup, soy sauce and lemon juice. Store at room temperature. Brush liberally on hot oysters.

Jalapeno Coriander Salsa for Barbecued Oysters

Spoon this fiery sauce over hot grilled oysters on a chilly fall day and it's sure to warm your bones.

Makes about 2 cups

4 tablespoons butter
2 medium tomatoes, finely
   chopped
1 medium onion, finely diced
2 garlic cloves, minced
1 fresh jalapeno pepper, seeded
   and minced
1/4 cup chopped fresh cilantro
1 tablespoon fresh lime juice
   Few drops TABASCO® brand
   Pepper Sauce
   Salt and freshly ground black
   pepper to taste

Melt the butter in a saucepan over medium heat. Remove from heat, stir in the remaining ingredients. Season to taste with salt and pepper. Spoon hot over oysters right off the grill.

Oyster Stews, Chowders, Bisques & Soups

Piping hot and brimming with plump, succulent oysters, nothing nourishes the soul better than a bowl of steaming oyster stew or chowder. Traditionally eaten on Christmas or New Year's Eve on the Eastern Seaboard, Oyster Stew is elegance in a bowl. We have included a sampling of oyster stew recipes, along with our favorite American and international renditions of oyster chowders, bisques, gumbos and soups. Warm a loaf of crusty bread, pour a glass of beer or wine, dish up your oyster stew and enjoy.

Oyster & Guinness Stew
Louis C. Wachsmuth's Oyster Stew
Puget Sound Oyster Chowder
Oyster Stew - Ye Olde Union Oyster House
Oyster Stew with Brie and Champagne
The Frost Chowder
Curried Oyster and Spinach Stew
Champagne Oyster Stew
Cornet Bay Smoked Oyster Stew
Oyster Creek Inn's Oyster Stew
Cream of Oyster Rockefeller Soup
Toasted Sesame Oyster Soup
Mexican Fish and Oyster Stew
Thai Coconut Soup with Oysters
Pumpkin and Oyster Bisque
Christmas Eve Oyster Bisque
Chanterelle and Oyster Bisque
Creole Oyster Gumbo
*Southern Style Cream of Peanut
        and Oyster Bisque*
Artichoke and Oyster Soup
Oyster, Clam and Shrimp Jambalaya
Cioppino
Oyster, Pepper and Sausage Stew
Duck, Sausage and Oyster Gumbo

Oyster and Guinness Stew

If you enjoy Guinness Stout with oysters, you're bound to savor this creamy stew flavored with Guinness. This recipe is adapted from the Wild Salmon Seafood Market, located at Fishermen's Terminal, in Seattle, WA.

Serves 4

24 small oysters, shucked, reserving liquor
1/2 cup (1 stick) unsalted butter
1 onion, finely diced
2/3 cup dry white wine
1/2 cup all purpose flour
1-1/4 cups fish stock or clam broth
1 cup Guinness Stout
2/3 cup heavy cream
Salt and freshly ground black pepper to taste
Chopped fresh parsley for garnish

Melt half of the butter in a saucepan over medium heat. Add the onion and cook about 5 minutes, or until the onion is softened. Add the wine, bring to a simmer and cook for about 3 minutes. Meanwhile, in a separate saucepan, melt the remaining butter over medium heat. Gradually whisk in the flour and cook for 1 minute. Gradually add the fish stock, stirring constantly, until the mixture is thick and creamy. Stir the stock into the wine and onion mixture. Add the reserved oyster liquor and the Guinness. Bring the mixture to a simmer, then add the cream and oysters. Season to taste with salt and pepper. Cook 2 to 3 minutes, or until oysters plump. Serve in heated soup bowls and garnish with chopped parsley.

Recommended beverage: Guinness Stout.

*The Walrus and the Carpenter, were walking down the Strand,
And all the little Oysters came, and followed hand in hand,*

*"If we but had some Guinness now," they said, "It would be grand!"
The Walrus and the Carpenter, sat down at once to sup,*

*The Oysters, too went smoothly down, and Guinness crowned the cup.
And not a word was spoken more, till all was finished up!*

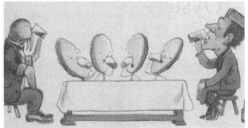

These drawings were used to illustrate the above verse which plays on Lewis Carroll's The Walrus and the Carpenter. From a Guinness advertisement of 1933.

  The Joy of Oysters

The Late Chef Louis C. Wachsmuth's Oyster Stew

Dan & Louis Oyster Bar, Portland, OR

Louis C. Wachsmuth grew up working with his father and brothers on their oyster farm in Oysterville, Washington. His father, Meinert, worked for the Moraghan Oyster Company in California, before moving back to Oysterville in 1881 to set up his own business. Louis learned to shuck oysters at the age of five, developing a lifelong devotion to the succulent bivalves.

In the early 1900s, Louis and his brothers moved to Portland, where Louis worked as a delivery man, cook and oyster shucker, before opening his own seafood store.

During prohibition, in 1919, Louis acquired the food bar from the famous Merchant's Exchange Saloon. He decided that a piping hot oyster stew would be a tasty addition to his tiny menu. Soon the old bar could no longer accommodate the growing number of hungry customers, and

Louis added dining rooms adjacent to the bar. The restaurant is now owned by Louis' Grandson, Doug Wachsmuth, and Great Grandson, Ted Wachsmuth. Great Grandson, M. Keoni Wachsmuth is the chef. At the Oyster Bar, the chef uses "cocktail size" Yaquina Bay oysters, or diced, medium size Pacific Oysters.

Heat the milk and cream in the top of a double boiler until piping hot. Stirring constantly, whisk in 6 tablespoons of butter and the seasoning salt. Add the oysters and simmer the stew for 5 minutes. Stir again and serve in deep pre-warmed bowls. Top each serving with a pat of butter.

Recommended wines: Champagne or sparkling wine, Chardonnay, Sauvignon Blanc, Pinot Gris.

Serves 6

- 1 pint extra small oysters, shucked, reserving liquor
- 8 cups whole milk
- 1 cup whipping cream
- 1 teaspoon Schillings Seasoning Salt
- Salt to taste
- 8 tablespoons (1 stick) butter

Puget Sound Oyster Chowder

Chock full of oysters, bacon, potatoes and other tasty vegetables, this hearty chowder makes a meal served with freshly baked bread and a mug of frosty stout.

Serves 4

24 extra-small or small oysters, shucked, reserving liquor
3 slices bacon, minced
1 tablespoon olive oil
1 onion, diced
1 rib celery, diced
1 large carrot, diced
1/2 red bell pepper, seeded and diced
1/4 cup all purpose flour
1/4 cup dry sherry
1/2 teaspoon dry thyme
2 cups clam juice or chicken stock
2 medium red potatoes, diced
1 cup whipping cream
Salt and freshly ground black pepper to taste
Hot red pepper sauce to taste
Chopped fresh parsley
Lemon wedges

Fry the bacon in a heavy saucepan over medium-high heat for 2 to 3 minutes, or until partially cooked. Add the olive oil, onion, celery, carrot, and red pepper. Reduce the heat to medium. Cook, stirring often, about 10 minutes, or until the vegetables are tender. Add the flour, stirring constantly, until it is thoroughly incorporated. Stir in the sherry, thyme, reserved oyster liquor and clam juice. Add the diced potatoes. Increase the heat and bring the mixture to a boil. Simmer gently until potatoes are tender, about 15 minutes. Add the cream and oysters and cook about 3 minutes, or until oysters are firm and plump. Season the chowder with salt, pepper and hot red pepper sauce. Dish into pre-warmed bowls. Garnish with chopped parsley and lemon wedges.

Recommended beverages: Stout, Sauvignon Blanc.

Oyster Stew

Ye Olde Union Oyster House, Boston, MA

This is the Union Oyster House's recipe for Oyster Stew. Located in Boston, MA, the popular restaurant was established in 1826 and still serves its famous oyster dishes. A century ago in New England a bowl of piping hot oyster stew formed the traditional Christmas Eve supper.

UNION OYSTER HOUSE

Since 1826

America's Oldest Restaurant

Melt the butter in a saucepan over medium heat. Add the oysters and their liquor and cook just until the edges curl, about 5 minutes. Stir in the half and half, and milk. Heat thoroughly until just before the stew reaches the boiling point. Season to taste with pepper, salt. Sprinkle each serving with paprika. If desired, top each serving with a pat of butter. Serve at once with crackers.

Recommended wines: Chardonnay, Pinot Gris.

Serves 4

1 pint freshly shucked oysters (with liquor)
1/4 cup butter
1 cup half and half, scalded
3 cups milk, scalded
  Salt and freshly cracked black pepper
1/2 teaspoon paprika

"He was a bold man that first eat an oyster."

Jonathan Swift
Polite Conversation

Oyster Stew with Brie and Champagne

This is a rich, elegant stew that Oyster Bill serves his guests on special occasions. Pour the remaining Champagne, add a simple salad and some good bread, and you're all set.

Serves 4

8	tablespoons (1-stick) unsalted butter
1/4	cup all purpose flour
4	cups clam juice or chicken stock
2-1/2	cups whipping cream
1/2	teaspoon red pepper flakes
12	ounces Brie cheese, rind removed and cubed
1	cup extra dry or brut Champagne or sparkling wine
20	small oysters, shucked, reserving liquor
1/2	cup finely sliced green onion
	Salt and white pepper to taste

Melt the butter in a large saucepan over medium heat. Gradually whisk in the flour and cook, stirring constantly, for about 3 minutes. Gradually add the clam juice. Bring to a boil, reduce heat and simmer for 10 minutes. Add the cream and red pepper flakes. Simmer 5 minutes. Add the Brie, whisking constantly. When melted, stir in the Champagne, oysters and green onions. Season with salt and white pepper. Turn off the heat, cover and let the stew stand for 10 minutes before serving. Dish into warm soup bowls.

Recommended wines: Champagne or sparkling wine, Chardonnay, Pinot Gris.

The Frost Chowder

Rodney's Oyster House, Toronto, Ontario

When you serve over twenty one-thousand oysters a week, you get to know your guest's desires very well. Here is one of owner Rodney Clark's favorite ways of "appeasing his oyster eaters." The restaurant bottles its own Oyster Stout, "made with the juice of one-thousand oysters" — perhaps the perfect partner for a bowl of steaming oyster chowder.

Melt the butter in a large saucepan over medium heat. Stir in the onions and parsley and cook until the onions are tender, about 5 minutes. Stir in the soy sauce, salt, thyme, bay leaf, and TABASCO® brand Pepper Sauce. Add the oysters and their liquor. Simmer for about 5 minutes, or until the oysters plump and their edges curl. Stir in the milk, cream and wine. Cook until soup is piping hot, but do not let it boil. Remove the chowder from the heat and stir in the grated cheese. Serve in pre-heated bowls as soon as the cheese is melted.

Recommended beverages: Stout, Sauvignon Blanc, Semillon.

Serves 4

- 1 pint (approximately 25 medium) freshly shucked oysters and their liquor
- 2 tablespoons butter
- 1 red onion, diced
- 1/4 cup minced fresh parsley
- 1 tablespoon soy sauce
- 1/2 teaspoon salt
- 1 teaspoon dried thyme
- 1 bay leaf
  Dash of TABASCO® brand Pepper Sauce
- 3 cups whole milk
- 1 cup whipping cream
- 1/2 cup dry white wine
- 2 cups grated cheddar cheese

VILLENEUVE

RODNEY THE OYSTERMAN

Curried Oyster and Spinach Stew
Ray's Boat House, Seattle, WA

Ray's boathouse

For this recipe, Chef Charles Ramseyer prefers extra small Hama Hama oysters from Washington. He serves this hearty stew in large soup plates, with lots of rustic sourdough or Como bread.

Serves 4

26 extra small oysters, shucked, reserving liquor
4 tablespoons butter
4 garlic cloves, minced
1/2 lemon, sliced into 6 paper thin rounds
4 cups whole milk
1/2 cup all purpose flour
1 teaspoon Dijon mustard
1/2 tablespoon chopped fresh basil
2 cups finely chopped spinach leaves
3 green onion tops, finely sliced
1 teaspoon curry powder
Salt and freshly ground black pepper to taste

Melt the butter in a large soup kettle over medium heat. Add the garlic and the oysters with their liquor. Cook, stirring often, until the oysters are plump and their edges curl, about 3 minutes. Remove from the heat. Add the sliced lemon.

In a separate bowl, combine 1 cup of the milk and the 1/2 cup of flour. Whisk until smooth. Whisk in the mustard and set aside. To the oysters, add the basil, spinach, curry, remaining milk, green onion tops, and milk and flour mixture. Season to taste with salt and pepper. Bring the mixture to a simmer over medium heat, and simmer until the stew is piping hot, but not boiling. Serve at once.

Recommended wine: Sauvignon Blanc.

Champagne Oyster Stew
Shaw's Crab House, Chicago, IL

Elegantly seasoned with fresh ginger and Champagne, and luxuriously rich, this is a dish Executive Chef Yves Roubaud saves for special occasions at Shaw's, such as Valentine's Day or Christmas Eve. All you need to complete the meal is a Caesar Salad (see page 269) and more Champagne.

In a saucepan, combine the oysters and their liquor, Champagne, Worcestershire sauce, ginger and celery salt. Bring the mixture to a boil, then reduce the heat and simmer until the oysters are plump and firm, about 2 to 3 minutes. Stir in the cream and heat until the soup is piping hot, but not boiling. Ladle into pre-warmed soup bowls and sprinkle with paprika.

Recommended wine: Champagne or sparkling wine.

Serves 4

- 24 medium oysters, shucked, reserving liquor
- 1-1/3 cups extra dry or brut Champagne or sparkling wine
- 4 teaspoons Worcestershire sauce
- 1 tablespoon grated fresh ginger
- 2 teaspoons celery salt
- 1-1/2 cups whipping cream
- Salt and freshly ground black pepper to taste
- Paprika

Cornet Bay Smoked Oyster Stew

*Thick and smokey, this is perfect for a rainy winter day.
To make your own smoked oysters, see the recipe on page 124 I smoke my own oysters
on my deck overlooking Cornet Bay, on Whidbey Island, WA. It's a peaceful little bay,
where great blue herons and otters come to fish.*

Half Shell Lori

Serves 4

2 slices bacon, diced
1 small onion, finely chopped
   Pinch of saffron threads
1 cup water
4 medium new red potatoes,
   quartered
1 cup fresh or canned corn kernels
1 cup fresh shelled peas or
   petite frozen peas
1 pound smoked oysters
2 cups half and half
   Chopped chives for garnish

Cook the bacon in a saucepan over medium heat until crisp. Drain the bacon on paper towels, reserving the bacon fat. Add the onion to the bacon fat and cook until tender. Meanwhile, soak the saffron threads in 1 cup water. Stir the potatoes into the onions, then stir in the saffron mixture. Simmer the potatoes for approximately 15 minutes, or until they can be pierced with a fork.

Stir in the corn, peas, smoked oysters and half-and-half. Stir in the reserved bacon. Cook the mixture, stirring gently, for about 5 minutes, or until heated through. Ladle into bowls and garnish with chopped chives.

Recommended wines: Sauvignon (Fume) Blanc, Pinot Gris.

Oyster Creek Inn's Oyster Stew

Oyster Creek Inn, Bow, WA

Located on Chuckanut Drive, that winds along the base of Chuckanut Mountain on one side, with a sheer drop-off overlooking the San Juan Islands on the other, the Oyster Creek Inn is a very special place that oyster lovers seek out rain or shine. In the fall, you can watch salmon spawning in the creek below from the restaurant's windows. But forget the scenery — the incredible local oysters, great wines (including Oyster Creek Inn's specially blended wines), and great service are really what people come for.
When we first tasted this creamy stew, we couldn't quite pick out the subtle, but wonderful seasonings, which turned out to be thyme and celery salt. At the restaurant, they accompany this oyster stew with oyster crackers and warm, crusty bread with crocks of herbed garlic butter.

As of presstime in winter of 2000, the Oyster Creek Inn was closed for extensive remodeling.

Chop the oysters into 1/2-inch pieces. Place the oysters with their liquor, and the water in a saucepan and bring to a boil. Reduce heat and simmer about 2 minutes, or until oysters firm and plump. Stir in the milk, whipping cream, celery salt and thyme. Season to taste with salt and white pepper. Heat until soup is very hot, but do not boil. Serve in pre-warmed bowls, topped with a butter pat, and a sprinkle of paprika and parsley.

Recommended beverages: Stout, Oyster Creek Inn White Table Wine, Dry Riesling, Dry Gewurztraminer, Semillon.

Serves 1
(increase portions as necessary)
- 6 small or medium oysters, shucked, reserving liquor
- 3/4 cup water
- 3/4 cup whole milk
- 3/4 cup whipping cream
- 2 shakes TABASCO® brand Pepper Sauce
- 1/2 teaspoon celery salt
- 1/2 teaspoon ground thyme
- Salt and white pepper to taste
- Chilled butter pats
- Paprika
- Minced fresh parsley

Cream of Oyster Rockefeller Soup

*Based on the flavor components of the famous Oysters Rockefeller dish from New Orleans,
this oyster soup is seasoned with fresh spinach and Pernod or Anisette.
Serve with hot, buttered corn bread.*

Serves 6

36 small oysters, shucked, reserving juices
1/2 cup unsalted butter
1 onion, diced
1 garlic clove, minced
2 cups chopped fresh spinach
1/2 cup all purpose flour
4 cups chicken stock, preferably homemade
1 cup whipping cream
1/2 cup chopped green onions
2 tablespoons Pernod or Anisette
Salt and white pepper to taste

Melt the butter in a soup kettle over medium heat. Add the onions and garlic; cook about 5 minutes, until the onions are tender. Add the spinach and cook until wilted, about 3 minutes. Stir in the flour, blending well. Cook, stirring constantly, for several minutes, until the mixture comes to a full simmer. Gradually add the reserved oyster liquor and chicken stock. Bring to a low boil, reduce to a simmer and cook 15 minutes. Add the cream, green onions and oysters. Simmer about 10 minutes, until the soup is heated through and the oysters are firm and plump. Stir in the Pernod and season to taste with salt and white pepper.

Recommended wines: Champagne or sparkling wine, Pinot Gris, Chardonnay.

Toasted Sesame Oyster Soup

Here is a very unusual, yet delicious oyster soup recipe from Japan. The toasted flavor of the sesame seeds highlights the nuttiness of the sweet oysters.

Toast the sesame seeds in a dry skillet over medium heat, stirring constantly until golden brown, about 4 to 5 minutes. Puree the seeds in a blender, together with the reserved oyster liquor and 1 cup of the chicken stock and set aside. Meanwhile, heat the oil in a saucepan over medium heat. When hot, stir in the onions, red pepper, and sliced mushrooms. Cook about 5 minutes, until the vegetables are cooked, but still crisp. Add the sesame liquid and the remaining chicken stock. Season with cayenne, salt and black pepper. Bring the soup to a gently boil. Add the oysters and cook 2 to 3 minutes, or until oysters plump. Serve in warm soup bowls and garnish with chopped chives.

Recommended beverages: Sake, Riesling, Gewurztraminer.

Serves 4

24 small oysters, shucked, reserving liquor
1 cup sesame seeds
2 tablespoons vegetable oil
3 green onions, diced
1/2 red bell pepper, finely sliced
1 cup sliced fresh shiitake or button mushrooms
4 cups chicken stock
1/2 teaspoon cayenne pepper
Salt and freshly ground black pepper to taste
Chopped chives for garnish

The Joy of Oysters   165

Mexican Fish and Oyster Stew

Garnish this spicy stew with slices of fresh avocado, salsa and lime wedges.

Serves 6

- 1 tablespoon olive oil
- 1 onion, diced
- 2 garlic cloves, minced
- 2 14-1/2-ounce cans diced tomatoes in puree
- 2 carrots, finely diced
- 2 celery ribs, finely sliced
- 2 bay leaves
- 7 cups clam juice or fish stock
- 2 potatoes, peeled and diced
- 1 pound red snapper fillets, boned and cut into 1-inch pieces
- 1/2 pound shrimp, peeled and deveined
- 24 extra-small oysters, shucked, reserving liquor
- 2 avocados, peeled and sliced
- Lime wedges
- Salsa

Heat the oil in a sarge saucepan. Add the onion and cook until tender, about 5 minutes. Add the garlic, tomatoes, carrots, celery, bay leaves and clam juice or fish stock. Simmer for 15 minutes. Add the potatoes and cook until tender. Add the fish and simmer for 5 minutes, or just until the fish flakes with a fork. Just before serving, bring the stew to a boil. Add the shrimp and oysters; cook about 3 minutes, until shrimp turns bright pink and oysters plump. Ladle the hot stew into pre-warmed bowls. Top with salsa, sliced avocado and lime wedges.

Recommended beverages: Chilled beer, Sauvignon Blanc, Semillon.

Thai Coconut Soup with Oysters
Flying Fish Restaurant, Bar & Grill, Seattle, WA

Chef Christine Keff frequently visits Thailand, where she gained her inspiration for this creative oyster soup. Her recipe calls for galangal root (also know as Laos), which is a mild-flavored cousin of ginger. Galangal comes fresh, dried and ground, and can be found at Asian markets. If you can't find it, substitute fresh ginger root. Cultivated Shiitake mushrooms have a distinctive, pungent flavor, but the soup is also delicious made with button mushrooms.

Melt the butter in a large kettle over medium heat. Add the shallots, garlic, galangal, and lemon grass. Cover and cook until vegetables are tender, about 5 to 7 minutes. Add the coconut milk, chicken stock, oyster liquor, Mirin, chilies, lime juice, fish sauce, brown sugar, and season to taste with white pepper. Simmer the stock for 1/2 to 1 hour. Stir in the green onions and mushrooms. Adjust seasonings, if necessary. Gently add the oysters and cook 2 to 3 minutes, just until the oysters plump. Ladle into pre-warmed bowls and garnish with sprigs of cilantro.

Recommended wines: Riesling, Gewurztraminer.

Serves 6

- 36 extra small oysters, shucked, reserving liquor
- 2 tablespoons vegetable oil
- 3 shallots, minced
- 2 garlic cloves, minced
- 1-1/2 inch section of fresh galangal or ginger, minced
- 2 blades of lemongrass, finely sliced
- 3 cups unsweetened coconut milk, canned or fresh
- 3 cups low sodium chicken stock or clam juice
  Reserved oyster liquor
- 1/2 cup Mirin (sweet, seasoned rice wine)
- 3 small Thai chilies, thinly sliced with seeds (or 2 teaspoons red pepper flakes)
  Juice of 1/2 lime
- 2 tablespoons Asian fish sauce
- 2 tablespoons brown sugar
  White pepper to taste
- 2 green onions, julienned
- 2 cups sliced Shiitake or button mushrooms
  Cilantro sprigs for garnish

Pumpkin and Oyster Bisque

This is a delicious combination of flavors — perfect for warming your bones on a chilly day.
Oyster Bill and I prepared it one stormy December day after visiting our friends
at Blau Oyster Company in Bow, WA.

Serves 4

- 24 small oysters, shucked, reserving liquor
- 3 tablespoons butter
- 1 large onion, diced
- 1 leek, finely diced
- 1 garlic clove, minced
- 1 16-ounce can pumpkin puree
- 4 cups chicken stock, preferably home made
- 1/2 cup minced fresh parsley
- 1 bay leaf
- 1/4 teaspoon celery salt
- 1/4 teaspoon nutmeg
- 1/4 teaspoon cayenne pepper
- 1 tablespoon fresh lemon juice
- 1-1/2 cups whipping cream
- Salt and white pepper to taste
- Parsley sprigs for garnish

Melt the butter in a large saucepan. Add the onions, leeks and garlic, and cook, about 8 minutes, until softened. Stir in the pumpkin, chicken stock and parsley. Coarsely chop half of the oysters and add to the soup. Puree the mixture in a blender or food processor. Return the bisque to the saucepan. Stir in the bay leaf, celery salt, nutmeg, cayenne, lemon juice and cream. When the bisque is heated through, add the remaining oysters and cook 2 to 3 minutes, until they plump. Season to taste with salt and white pepper. Dish into pre-warmed soup bowls and garnish with a sprig of fresh parsley.

Recommended wines: Riesling, Viognier, Gewurztraminer.

Christmas Eve Oyster Bisque

This is a creamy oyster bisque that's delicately seasoned with shallots and vermouth. I created it for my new neighbor on a blustery Christmas Eve on the Oregon Coast. Victor had never eaten Oyster Bisque before, but he immediately fell in love with this dish.

Half Shell Lori

Serves 4

- 32 small oysters in the shell, shucked, reserving juices
- 2 tablespoons unsalted butter
- 2 shallots, minced
- 1/4 cup dry white vermouth
- 3 tablespoons all purpose flour
- 4 cups half-and-half
- 1/2 teaspoon cayenne pepper
- 1/2 teaspoon white pepper
- Salt to taste
- Hot red pepper sauce

Melt the butter in a saucepan over medium heat. Stir in the shallots; cover and cook until softened, about 5 minutes. Add the vermouth and simmer for 2 minutes. Remove the pan from the heat and whisk in the flour, stirring constantly until it is thoroughly incorporated. Gradually add the reserved oyster liquor, stirring constantly. Return the pan to the burner over medium heat. Whisk in the half-and-half, cayenne pepper, white pepper, and salt to taste. Cook, stirring constantly, until the bisque is slightly thickened. Do not let the mixture boil. Gently add the oysters to the hot bisque and cook 2 to 3 minutes, until oysters plump. Dish into pre-warmed soup bowls and season with a few shakes of hot red pepper sauce.

Recommended wines: Pinot Gris, Chenin Blanc, Pinot Blanc, Melon.

Chanterelle and Oyster Bisque

Golden, apricot-scented Chanterelle mushrooms add a sweet, earthy flavor to this creamy bisque. Serve with hot buttered rolls or crusty sourdough bread.

Serves 4

- 24 small oysters, shucked, reserving liquor
- 1/2 medium onion, finely diced
- 1 pound fresh Chanterelle mushrooms, chopped
- 2 tablespoons fresh chopped basil
- 2 cups chicken stock, preferably homemade
- 2 cups half-and-half
  Salt and freshly ground pepper to taste

Melt the butter in a soup kettle over medium heat. Add the onion and cook until tender, about 5 minutes. Stir in the mushrooms and basil. Cook about 10 minutes, until the mushrooms are tender. Stir in the chicken stock and simmer for several minutes. Remove the bisque from the heat and puree in a blender or food processor. Return the bisque to the saucepan; add the half- and-half and salt and pepper to taste. When the bisque is heated through, add the oysters and poach for about 3 minutes, or until they plump.

Creole Oyster Gumbo

Serve this tasty concoction over steamed rice, with hot bread and plenty of cold beer or wine. Okra are thin, tapered green pods that add flavor and work as a natural thickener. Look for them either fresh, or canned.

Heat the olive oil in a soup kettle over medium heat. When hot, stir in the onion, garlic and red pepper. Cook until the vegetables are tender, about 8 minutes. Stir in the okra, tomatoes, oregano and hot pepper flakes. Add the oyster liquor and clam broth. Bring the mixture to a boil. Reduce heat to a simmer and cook until okra is tender. Stir in the oysters and cook about 2 to 3 minutes, or until oysters plump.

Recommended beverages: Chilled beer, Chardonnay, Pinot Gris.

Serves 4

26 small oysters, shucked, reserving liquor
2 tablespoons olive oil or vegetable oil
1 medium onion, diced
2 garlic cloves, diced
1 red pepper, seeded and diced
1 cup cooked or canned, drained okra
4 ripe tomatoes, diced
1 teaspoon oregano or marjoram
1 teaspoon hot red pepper flakes
Reserved oyster liquor, plus clam broth or chicken stock to equal 4 cups
Salt and freshly ground black pepper to taste

Southern-Style
Cream of Peanut and Oyster Bisque

This delicious soup originated in southern plantation kitchens, where black cooks combined two of their favorite foods — oysters and peanuts. Spiced with cayenne pepper, this reminds me a bit of an Asian peanut sauce — it's definitely a nice twist on oysters. A sprinkle of cilantro and squeeze of fresh lime juice add a bright finish. Corn bread or Savory Cheese Shortbread (page 264) make wonderful accompaniments.

Serves 4

24	small oysters, shucked, reserving liquor
2	tablespoons olive oil
1	onion, finely diced
1	garlic clove, minced
1/2	cup smooth peanut butter
4	cups chicken stock
1/2	cup whipping cream
1/4	teaspoon cayenne pepper
	Salt and freshly ground black pepper to taste
1/4	cup chopped cilantro or parsley fresh lime wedges

Heat the olive oil in a large saucepan over medium heat. Add the onion and cook until tender, about 5 minutes. Add the garlic and the peanut butter, stirring until smooth. Gradually whisk in the chicken stock and reserved oyster liquor. Simmer for about 15 minutes, stirring often. Stir in the cream, cayenne, and salt and pepper to taste. Add the oysters and cook 2 to 3 minutes, or until they plump. Dish into warm soup bowls, sprinkle with chopped cilantro and squeeze a wedge of lime over each portion.

Recommended beverages: Dry Riesling, Gewurztraminer, chilled beer.

Artichoke and Oyster Soup

Acme Oyster House, New Orleans, LA

The Acme Oyster House has been catering to oyster lovers since it first opened in 1910. Now, with three locations, they are happy to please more and more oyster aficionados. This is one of their customer's favorite dishes. The "blond roux" is simply butter and flour cooked together until it binds — a traditional way to thicken sauces. This can be prepared well in advance — up to 2 days. Store, covered, at room temperature.

Heat the olive oil in a large soup kettle over medium heat. When hot, add the onion, celery and garlic. Cook, stirring often, until the vegetables are tender, about 5 to 7 minutes. Add the chopped artichoke hearts and let simmer 2 minutes. Stir in the wine, mixing well. Bring the mixture to a boil, add the cream and oyster juice and simmer rapidly for about 5 minutes. Remove pan from the heat; whisk in the Roux, bit-by-bit, until thoroughly incorporated. Return the soup to the heat and simmer gently, until thickened. Cut the oysters into 1/2-inch pieces and stir gently into the soup. Cook the oysters 2 to 3 minutes, or until firm and plump. Season the soup with thyme, white pepper, Tabasco®, and salt. Serve hot.

Serves 4

- 20 medium oysters, shucked and drained, reserving liquor
- 2 tablespoons olive oil
- 1 onion, diced
- 2 celery ribs, finely diced
- 2 garlic cloves, minced
- 1 14-ounce can artichoke hearts, drained and chopped
- 1/4 cup dry white wine
- Reserved oyster liquor
- 4 cups whipping cream

- Blond Roux (recipe follows)
- 1 teaspoon chopped fresh thyme leaves
- 1 teaspoon white pepper
- Dash of TABASCO® brand Pepper Sauce
- Salt to taste

Melt the butter in a small skillet. Whisk in the flour, just until the flour and butter are combined. Remove from heat and set aside.

Recommended beverages: Chilled beer, Sauvignon Blanc, Semillon.

Blond Roux:

- 1/4 cup unsalted butter
- 1/4 cup all purpose flour

Oyster, Clam and Shrimp Jambalaya

This festive one-dish meal is great for entertaining — all you need to serve with the piping hot stew is crusty bread and a bottle of your favorite wine. Our recipe calls for oysters, clams and shrimp, but you can use any of your favorite shellfish, including crabs and mussels. In New Orleans, where Jambalaya is a classic dish, they hold an annual "blessing of the shrimp fleet," each August. After the archbishop bestows his blessing on the fleet, the village celebrates with steaming pots of Jambalaya cooked over open fires.
Jambalaya is traditionally made with tasso, a highly seasoned Cajun smoked ham.
If you can't locate tasso, use another smoked ham, and add 1/4 teaspoon extra hot red pepper sauce to the dish.

Serves 6

- 2 tablespoons olive oil
- 1/2 cup chopped tasso or other smoked ham
- 1 pound bulk Italian sausage
- 1 onion, diced
- 1 red bell pepper, seeded and diced
- 1 green bell pepper, seeded and diced
- 2 garlic cloves, minced
- 2 bay leaves
- 1/2 teaspoon hot red pepper sauce
- 1-1/2 cups short-grain white rice
- 4 ripe tomatoes, peeled and chopped
- 1/2 cup tomato sauce
- 2 cups seafood stock or chicken stock
- 1/2 teaspoon dried thyme
  Salt and freshly ground black pepper to taste
- 18 fresh Manilla clams in shells, scrubbed
- 18 peeled medium shrimp (about 1/2 pound)
- 18 small oysters, shucked, reserving liquor

In a large saucepan, heat the olive oil over medium heat. When hot, stir in the ham and sausage meat. Cook about 8 minutes, stirring constantly, until sausage is almost cooked through. Stir in the onion, red and green bell pepper, and garlic. Cook until the vegetables are softened, about 5 minutes. Stir in the bay leaves, hot red pepper sauce and rice, mixing well to coat the rice with the mixture. Cook the rice about 5 minutes, stirring constantly, then add the tomatoes, tomato sauce, and gradually whisk in the stock. Season with thyme and salt and pepper to taste. Reduce the heat to low, cover and simmer until the rice is tender, about 30 to 40 minutes. When the rice is done, add the clams, shrimp, and oysters. Cook about 5 to 8 minutes, or until clams open. Serve at once.

Recommended wines: Pinot Gris, Chardonnay, Pinot Noir.

Cioppino

This flavorful fish stew is one of my all time favorites. Serve it with homemade bread, with extra-virgin olive oil for dipping, and a fruity Oregon Pinot Noir.

Saute bacon in a skillet over medium heat until partially cooked. Stir in celery, onions, and carrots. Cook until vegetables are tender. Dissolve saffron in the wine. Stir into the cooked vegetables. Add the garlic, bay leaf, red pepper flakes, cayenne, tomato juice, clam nectar, and diced tomatoes. Heat thoroughly.

To Serve: Place the oysters, fish and shellfish in a heavy-bottomed saucepan. Cover with Cioppino broth. Bring the mixture to a light boil, just until clams and mussels open. Serve immediately.

Recommended wines: Pinot Noir, Chardonnay, Pinot Gris.

Serves 8 - 10

Broth:

- 4 slices bacon, diced
- 1/2 cup diced celery
- 1/2 cup diced onions
- 1/4 cup diced carrots
- 3 strands saffron
- 2 tablespoons dry white wine
- 1 garlic clove, minced
- 1 bay leaf
- 1/2 teaspoon crushed red pepper flakes
- Pinch of cayenne
- 2-1/2 cups tomato juice
- 2-1/2 cups clam nectar
- 42 ounces canned diced tomatoes, with their juice

For Each Serving Allow:

- 6 extra small oysters, shucked
- 2 ounces scallops
- 2 ounces white fish fillet, boned
- 2 prawns, unshelled
- 1/2 Dungeness crab in shell, precooked and cracked
- 5 Manilla clams in shell
- 5 mussels in shell, debearded

Oyster, Pepper and Sausage Stew

*Inspired by a peasant dish from the Emilia-Romagna region of Italy,
this spicy oyster and pepper stew is always a welcome treat.*

Serves 6

- 26 small oysters, shucked and drained
- 1 pound hot Italian sausage links
- 2 pounds green and red peppers
- 2 pounds tomatoes
- 1 teaspoon salt
- 2 tablespoons butter
- 1/4 cup olive oil
- 1 pound small white pearl onions, peeled and thinly sliced
- 1/4 teaspoon freshly ground black pepper

Remove casings from the sausages and break up meat. Heat a skillet over medium high heat and cook thoroughly, stirring often. Remove cooked sausage from skillet, drain and set aside.

Wash and dry peppers. Cut off stems and remove seeds. Slice coarsely. Skin the tomatoes by dipping them briefly in boiling water, peeling, and then cutting in half. Remove water and seeds, then sprinkle the insides lightly with 1/2 teaspoon salt, and place upside down in a colander for 1/2 hour to let excess water drain out. Chop coarsely.

In the same skillet, heat butter and olive oil over medium-high heat. Add the peppers and onions and cook, stirring often, until onions are soft and translucent. Add the tomatoes, cover, reduce the heat, and cook for about 10 more minutes, adding the remaining salt and black pepper. Stir in the cooked sausage and the oysters. Simmer, stirring often, about 5 minutes, until the oysters are plumped. Serve warm with crusty bread.

Recommended wines: Pinot Noir, Chardonnay, Melon.

Duck, Sausage and Oyster Gumbo

Served with a loaf of crusty bread, this makes a wonderful one-dish meal. If you like, you can substitute chicken for the duck. The gumbo won't be quite as rich, but will still be very tasty.

In a heavy skillet, fry the sausage over low heat, turning the slices frequently with a spatula until the sausage is lightly cooked. Increase the heat to moderate and, turning the slices occasionally, continue to fry until the sausage is richly browned. Transfer the sausage to paper towels to drain. There should be about 1/2 cup of fat in the skillet; if not, add vegetable oil to make 1/2 cup.

Pat the pieces of duck completely dry with paper towels and remove any large pieces of fat. Season the birds with 2 teaspoons of the salt and a few cranks of black pepper. Roll the ducks in the flour to coat the pieces on all sides and vigorously shake off the excess flour.

Brown the ducks, five or six pieces at a time, in the hot fat remaining in the skillet. Turn the pieces frequently with tongs and regulate the heat so that they color deeply and evenly without burning. As they brown, transfer the pieces of duck to paper towels to drain.

Warm the roux over low heat in a heavy 12-quart enameled or cast-iron pot. When the roux is smooth and fluid, stir in the onions, scallions and celery. Stirring frequently, cook over moderate heat for about 5 minutes, or until the vegetables are soft. Mix in the green peppers. Then, stirring constantly, pour in the warm water in a slow, thin stream and bring to a boil over high heat.

Serves 8

26 small oysters, shucked and drained
1 pound chorizo, or other hot sausage, skinned and sliced into 1/2-inch thick rounds
Vegetable oil, if needed
2 five pound ducks, rinsed and cut into 8 pieces each
4 teaspoons salt
Freshly ground black pepper to taste
1/2 cup flour
6 tablespoons brown roux (recipe follows)
1 cup finely chopped onions
1/2 cup finely chopped scallions
1 cup finely chopped celery
1 cup finely chopped green peppers
3 quarts warm water
1/2 teaspoon hot red pepper sauce
1-1/2 teaspoons ground cayenne
1/4 cup finely chopped fresh parsley, preferably the flat-leaf Italian variety
File powder (ground sassafras leaves)
6 - 8 cups freshly cooked long-grain white rice

Recipe continued on next page.

Add the sausage, duck, remaining 2 teaspoons of salt, the hot red pepper sauce, and the red pepper. When the mixture returns to a boil, reduce the heat to low and cover the pot partially. Simmer the gumbo for 2 hours. Remove the pot from the heat and, with a large spoon, skim as much fat from the surface as possible. Add the oysters and cook 2 to 3 minutes, or until plump. Stir in the parsley and 2 teaspoons of file powder, and taste for seasoning. The gumbo should be hotly spiced.

Ladle the gumbo into a heated tureen and serve at once, accompanied by the rice in a separate bowl. Traditionally, a cupful of the rice is mounded in a heated soup plate and the gumbo spooned around it.

Roux:
Makes about 11 tablespoons
8 tablespoons unsifted all-purpose flour
8 tablespoons vegetable oil

Combine the flour and oil in a heavy 10-inch skillet and, with a large metal spatula, stir them to a smooth paste. Place the skillet over the lowest possible heat and, stirring constantly, simmer the roux slowly for 30 minutes to an hour.

After 5 minutes or so the mixture will begin to foam and this foaming may continue for as long as 10 minutes. After about half an hour, the roux will begin to darken and have a faintly nutty aroma. Continue to cook slowly, stirring with the spatula, until the roux is a dark rich brown. (During the last 5 minutes or so of cooking, the roux darkens quickly and you may want to lift the pan from the heat periodically to let it cool. Should the roux burn, discard it and make another batch.)

Immediately scrape the contents of the skillet into a small bowl. Let the roux cool to room temperature, then cover with foil or plastic wrap and refrigerate it until ready to use. (It can safely be kept for weeks.)

When it cools the roux will separate and the fat will rise to the surface. Before using the roux, stir it briefly to recombine it. Measure the desired amount into the pan and warm the roux slowly over low heat, stirring constantly. Any liquid that is to be incorporated with the roux must be at least lukewarm or the mixture may separate. If it does, beat it together again with a whisk.

Recommended wines: Pinot Noir, Chardonnay, Pinot Gris.

Oyster Salads, Sandwiches & Luncheon Dishes

One of the most classic oyster sandwiches - the "Oyster Po' Boy" has been a New Orleans favorite for over 200 years, and recipes for oyster loaf (the peacemaker) date back just as far. We have included several classic recipes and many other recipes for delicious oyster sandwiches. Grilled, fried or pickled, oysters also make wonderful toppings for fresh greens, such as Cory Schreiber's tasty Coleslaw with Pan Fried Oysters and Lemon Aioli, and Oyster, Scallop and Shrimp Ceviche.

Coleslaw with Pan Fried Oysters and Lemon Aioli
Oyster-Stuffed Baked Tomato Salad
Oyster, Scallop and Shrimp Ceviche
Warm Oyster and Spinach Salad with Avocado and Ginger Vinaigrette
Cape Cod Pickled Oysters
Jalapeno and Lime Pickled Oysters
Asian Spiced Oysters
Oyster Bill's Oyster Rolls
Oyster Creek Inn Poor Boy
Sourdough Oyster Loaf
Oyster, Bacon and Caramelized Onion Turnovers
Bay Center Oyster, Tomato and Cheese Sandwich

Coleslaw with Pan Fried Oysters and Lemon Aioli

Wildwood Restaurant and Bar, Portland, OR

Chef Cory Schreiber tops a colorful confetti of shredded cabbage, carrots and red onions with crisp fried oysters and a lemony aioli. Make the coleslaw one to three hours in advance to marry flavors. The Lemon Aioli can be prepared up to two days in advance. Cover and refrigerate until ready to use.

To toast fennel seeds: Place them in a small, dry skillet over medium heat. Stir constantly, until lightly browned, about 3 to 4 minutes.

Serves 6
Coleslaw

1 small head cabbage, preferably Savoy cabbage
2 medium carrots, peeled and coarsely grated
1 small red onion, cut in half and thinly sliced lengthwise
1/4 cup chopped fresh Italian parsley leaves
1/4 cup mayonnaise
1/4 cup red wine vinegar
1 tablespoon fennel seed, toasted and chopped
3/4 teaspoon salt
1/2 teaspoon freshly ground black pepper

Remove the tough outer leaves from the cabbage, cut in half, core and thinly slice crosswise. Place cabbage in a large mixing bowl. Stir in carrots, onion and parsley. In a small bowl, whisk together the mayonnaise, vinegar, fennel, salt and pepper. Add to the cabbage mixture and toss. Cover and refrigerate at least one hour before serving.

Lemon Aioli
Makes about 3/4 cup

1/2 cup mayonnaise
1/4 cup fresh lemon juice
1 garlic clove, minced

In a small bowl, whisk together mayonnaise, lemon juice and garlic. Cover and refrigerate until ready to use.

Chef Cory Schreiber

In a mixing bowl, combine the flour, cornmeal, cayenne and salt, mixing well. Toss several oysters at a time in the coating and place on a cooling rack to dry for about 15 minutes. Meanwhile, heat the oil in a heavy 12-inch skillet over medium-high heat. When the temperature reaches 350° F, fry the oysters in small batches, allowing 1 to 2 minutes per side, or until golden. Drain the oysters on paper towels and keep warm in a 200° F. oven. Repeat with remaining oysters.

To assemble salad: Portion coleslaw onto 6 plates. Top the coleslaw with four oysters and drizzle with aioli. Garnish with lemon wedges.

Recommended wines: Semillon, Sauvignon Blanc, Champagne or sparkling wine.

Crispy Fried Oysters

24 medium oysters,
    shucked and drained
1/4 cup all purpose flour
1/4 cup stone ground cornmeal
1/4 teaspoon cayenne pepper
1/4 teaspoon salt
  1 cup canola oil
    Lemon wedges

Oyster Stuffed Baked Tomato Salad

Stuffed with a flavorful blend of oysters, mushrooms and shallots in a rich cream sauce, these oven baked tomatoes make a wonderful first course or side dish.

Serves 8

- 16 small oysters, shucked and drained
- 8 medium ripe tomatoes
- 2 pounds medium button mushrooms
- 6 tablespoons (3/4 stick) butter
- 2 shallots, minced
  Freshly ground black pepper
- 1/4 cup dry white wine
- 2 tablespoons minced fresh parsley
- 1 egg white, lightly beaten
- 1/4 teaspoon ground nutmeg
- 1/2 cup whipping cream
- 1/2 freshly grated Parmesan cheese

Drop the tomatoes into a pot filled with boiling water. Remove after 30 seconds and drop into a bowl of cold water. Once they have cooled enough to handle, peel the tomatoes, core them and hollow out the pulp, leaving a 1 1/2 to 2-inch opening at the top. Salt the tomatoes inside and out, then turn upside down on a plate lined with paper towels. Set aside to drain.

Finely chop the mushrooms. Melt 4 tablespoons of the butter in a skillet over medium heat. Add the mushrooms and simmer, stirring often, until the liquid is evaporated from the mushrooms. Add the shallots and cook, stirring often for 2 minutes. Add the white wine and cook about 2 minutes, until the wine evaporates. Remove from the heat, Stir in the parsley and season with salt and pepper.

Preheat oven to 350° F. Roughly chop the oysters and combine in a mixing bowl with the egg white, nutmeg and cream. Fold in the cooked mushrooms. Fill the tomatoes with the oyster mixture, arrange in a baking dish and sprinkle with Parmesan. Bake 30 minutes, until tomatoes are heated through and tops are golden. Serve warm.

Recommended wine: Champagne or sparkling wine.

Oyster, Scallop and Shrimp Ceviche

In this flavorful Mexican dish, fresh seafood is tossed with tart lime juice, which literally "cooks" the fish. The dish is boldly flavored with fresh garlic, cilantro, and red onions. Serve with your favorite hot salsa on a bed of leafy greens, with fried tortillas or tortilla chips on the side.

In a non-reactive glass or ceramic baking dish or shallow bowl, combine the oysters, scallops, shrimp and lime juice, mixing well. Stir in the garlic, cilantro, onion, salt and jalapena. Cover with plastic wrap and refrigerate 3 hours to overnight. When the dish is ready, the scallops will turn white. Adjust seasonings, if necessary. Line serving plates with leafy greens. Spoon the ceviche over the lettuce and top with a dollop of salsa. Serve with tortilla chips or fried tortillas.

Recommended beverages: Chilled Mexican Beer, Sauvignon Blanc, Semillon.

Serves 8

32	extra small oysters, shucked and drained
1/2	pound sea scallops
32	fresh shrimp, shelled and deveined
1-1/4	cups fresh lime juice
2	garlic cloves, minced
1/4	cup chopped fresh cilantro
1/2	red onion, finely diced
1/2	teaspoon salt
1	fresh jalapena pepper, seeded and finely diced

Warm Oyster and Spinach Salad with Avocado and Ginger Vinaigrette

Serve this warm, main-dish salad for lunch or dinner with plenty of crusty sourdough rolls. The oysters are stuck with a piece of fresh lemon rind before grilling, which adds a touch of unexpected flavor — a trick we learned from the chef at the friendly Longhorn Saloon in the tiny oyster town of Edison, WA.

Serves 4

- 24 small oysters, shucked and drained
- 24 slivers lemon rind, approximately 1/8-inch wide by 1/2-inch long
- Salt and freshly ground black pepper
- 4 slices bacon, diced
- 2 tablespoons vegetable oil
- 4 cups fresh spinach leaves, rinsed and dried
- 2 ripe avocados, peeled, pitted and sliced

Ginger Vinaigrette:

- 1/2 cup extra virgin olive oil
- 3 tablespoons Balsamic vinegar
- 1 garlic clove, minced
- 1 teaspoon coarsely ground Dijon mustard
- 1/2 teaspoon grated fresh ginger root
- 1/4 teaspoon sesame oil
- Salt and freshly ground black pepper to taste

Using a sharp, pointed chopstick or wooden skewer, poke a hole into the rounded end of each oyster, just large enough to insert the sliver of lemon rind, leaving the rind sticking out of the oyster about 1/4-inch. Sprinkle the oysters with salt and pepper and set aside. Fry the diced bacon in a skillet over medium heat. When crisp, drain on paper towels, reserving 2 teaspoons bacon grease. Add the olive oil to the skillet and, when sizzling, fry the oysters, about 2 minutes per side, until golden. Remove from skillet; keep the oysters and bacon warm in a 200° F. oven.

In a small mixing bowl, whisk together all ingredients for the ginger vinaigrette. Just before serving, pour into the skillet and bring to a simmer. Distribute the spinach onto 4 serving plates and drizzle with the hot vinaigrette. Scatter the bacon bits over the spinach and fan the sliced avocado over the top of each salad. Drizzle with more vinaigrette, then top with fried oysters.

Recommended wines: Pinot Gris, Pinot Blanc, Sauvignon Blanc, Champagne or sparkling wine.

Cape Cod Pickled Oysters

Pickling oysters in a seasoned brine is a tradition that goes way back to our European roots. Pickled oysters are delicious by themselves, served on a bed of crisp greens, or mixed with sliced cucumbers for a summer salad. Plan to make this one day in advance so the oysters can marinate overnight. Chilled in the refrigerator, these will keep up to one week. If you prefer, these oysters can be canned. Follow the jar manufacturer's advice for canning oysters.

Drain oysters, reserving liquor. Add enough water to make 1 cup. Pour the liquid into a saucepan and bring to a simmer over medium heat. Add the oysters and cook, about 3 minutes, until they plump. Remove the oysters with a slotted spoon, place in a large non-reactive mixing bowl and set aside. Add the remaining ingredients to the poaching liquid. Bring to a boil, then reduce heat and simmer for 15 minutes. Pour the hot marinade over the oysters. Cover and chill overnight. Serve chilled.

Makes 4 cups

1 quart small or extra small oysters, shucked, reserving liquor water added to liquor to make 1 cup
1 garlic clove, minced
1 tablespoon crushed fennel seed
5 whole cloves
10 whole peppercorns
3 green onions, diced
1/4 cup fresh lemon juice
1 lemon, very thinly sliced (with rind)
1 bay leaf

Jalapeno and Lime Pickled Oysters

From South of the border comes this jalapeno-spiced rendition of plump pickled oysters. Similar to the recipe for ceviche, the oysters are "cooked" in lime juice. Serve chilled with tortilla chips and a tangy margarita or ice cold beer.

Mix all the ingredients together in a non-reactive mixing bowl. Cover and refrigerate 2 hours to overnight. Serve chilled with tortilla chips or fried tortillas.

Serves 4

24 extra small or small oysters, shucked and drained
1 cup fresh lime juice
1 fresh jalapeno pepper, seeded and minced
1 garlic clove, minced
1/2 red onion, finely diced
Salt to taste

Asian Spiced Oysters

Tossed with grated daikon radish in a sauce seasoned with fresh ginger, cilantro, lemon and garlic, these spicy oysters are perfect for a light appetizer served with a glass of chilled sake or white wine, and sesame crackers on the side.

Serves 4

- 24 extra small or small oysters, shucked and drained, reserving liquor
- 1/4 cup rice wine vinegar
- 2 teaspoons soy sauce
- 2 tablespoons minced fresh cilantro
- 2 tablespoons grated fresh ginger root
- 1 garlic clove, minced
- 1/2 teaspoon hot red pepper flakes
- 3/4 cup grated daikon radish
- Lemon wedges

Place the shucked oysters and their liquor in a saucepan over medium heat. Poach gently for 2 to 3 minutes, or until oysters plump. Using a slotted spoon, transfer the oysters to a non-reactive bowl. Discard the liquid. In a separate bowl, mix together the vinegar, soy sauce, cilantro, ginger, garlic and hot pepper flakes. Pour the sauce over the oysters, cover and refrigerate until thoroughly chilled, about 2 hours. To serve: distribute the grated daikon radish among serving dishes. Top with 4 to 6 marinated oysters and a squeeze of fresh lemon. Serve chilled.

Oyster Bill's Oyster Rolls

Growing up on the East Coast, Oyster Bill frequented many little "clam shacks" on the coast, where the specialty was oyster rolls, as well as rolls made with clams, scallops, and lobster. This batter recipe was given to Bill twenty years ago by Ernie Varina of the Mansion Clam House in Westport, Connecticut where, Oyster Bill recalls, you entered the restaurant through the back door, which led into the kitchen. There is something very special about this recipe - it seals in all the oyster's succulent juices, while allowing them to get golden and extra crisp on the outside.

In New England, the rolls - called Frank Rolls, from Frauheufer Baking Company, are baked side-by-side in a large baking sheet. As they bake, the dough rises and the rolls come out of the pan stuck together, so that not every side is browned. This enables the rolls to be grilled on both sides. If you live on the West coast, the closest thing we have are hot dog buns or hoagie rolls. To recreate the effect, you can slice the thin layer of crust off the sides of a hot dog bun.

In a small mixing bowl, whisk together the egg and evaporated milk. Combine the cornmeal and flour in another bowl. Dredge the oysters in the egg mixture, then toss very gently through the flour mixture, coating thoroughly. Gently shake off excess flour. Set oysters on a plate or baking sheet and place in the refrigerator.

Meanwhile, heat 2-inches of oil in a heavy skillet until it reaches 375 º F. When hot, add the oysters and fry about 2 minutes per side, until crisp and golden. Fry in batches if necessary. Drain oysters on paper towels and keep warm in a 200 º F. oven.

To serve: Lightly butter the rolls and grill until golden. Distribute shredded lettuce over the bottom half of the rolls and top with 3 to 4 fried oysters. Spread tartar sauce over the top half of each roll. Serve with extra tartar sauce and lemon wedges.

Recommended beverage: Chilled beer or stout

Serves 6

18-24 small oysters, shucked
and drained
1 egg, beaten
1-1/2 cups evaporated milk
1/2 cup yellow cornmeal
1-1/2 cups all purpose flour
Vegetable oil for frying
6 Frank rolls or hot dog buns,
split
1-1/2 cups shredded lettuce
Tartar Sauce (see page 205 for
recipe)
Lemon wedges

Oyster Creek Inn Poor Boy
Oyster Creek Inn, Bow, WA

This is a favorite of Oyster Creek's guests, who often accompany their Poor Boy with a glass of the house Oyster Creek Inn White Table Wine. The wine is affectionately known as "Domaine Doug," for chef/manager Doug Charles, who oversees the bottling. Each year, Doug's goal is to create the perfect seafood wine — crisp, clean and bright, with no oak. Varietals vary according to vintages, but the end result is always a charmer.
After breading the oysters, the chefs recommend letting them sit 4 to 6 hours. This allows the crumbs to absorb moisture from the oysters so that they brown slowly. If the crumbs are dry, they tend to burn before the oyster is cooked through. If you want a "neon" effect for the Spicy Slaw Dressing, try tossing the mixture with shaved red cabbage several hours in advance. The Oyster Creek Inn closed for extensive remodeling in January of 2000.

For each sandwich:

- 1 6 to 8-inch poor boy or hoagy roll, split
- 5 - 6 small or medium oysters, shucked, drained and breaded
- 2 tablespoons Jalapeno tartar sauce (recipe follows)
- 2 tablespoons Spicy Slaw (recipe follows)
- 1/2 ripe tomato, sliced

To Make Breaded Oysters:

- 1 egg, beaten
- 1 cup evaporated milk
- 1 cup dry bread crumbs mixed with: 1/4 cup flour and 1/2 teaspoon salt
- Vegetable oil for frying

In a mixing bowl, whisk together the beaten egg and evaporated milk. Dip the oysters in the egg mixture, then dredge in the breadcrumb mixture, shaking off extra crumbs. Place the oysters on a baking sheet, cover lightly with plastic wrap and chill for 4 to 6 hours.

To fry oysters: Heat 1/4-inch to 1/2-inch oil in a heavy skillet over medium-high heat. When the temperature reaches 350° F, fry the oysters in small batches, allowing 1 to 2 minutes per side, or until golden. Drain the oysters on paper towels and keep warm in a 200° F. oven. Repeat with remaining oysters.

Combine all ingredients thoroughly in a mixing bowl. Cover and refrigerate up to 1 week.

In a large mixing bowl, combine the mayonnaise, garlic, buttermilk, sugar, vinegar, pepper, milk, and salt to taste. Stir in the cabbage. Cover and chill until ready to use. Store up to 3 days in the refrigerator.

To assemble the Poor Boy:

Butter each side of the roll and grill until lightly browned. Spread tartar sauce on the bottom half of each roll and top with 5 to 6 fried oysters. Spread the top half of the roll with Spicy slaw and top with sliced tomatoes. Serve open-face and let each person assemble their own.

Jalapeno Tartar Sauce:

Makes approximately 1-1/2 cups

- 2 cups mayonnaise
- 1/2 cup dill pickle relish, chopped
- 1 tablespoon capers, chopped
- 1 tablespoon chopped fresh parsley
- 1/2 jalapeno pepper, seeded and finely diced
- 1 garlic clove, minced

Spicy Slaw:

Makes approximately 4 cups

- 2 cups mayonnaise
- 2 garlic cloves, minced
- 1/4 cup buttermilk
- 1 tablespoon sugar
- 3 tablespoons apple cider vinegar
- 2 teaspoons freshly cracked black pepper
- 1 tablespoon milk
  Salt to taste
- 4 cups shredded green or purple cabbage (or a mixture)

Sourdough Oyster Loaf

Steeped in tradition dating back to the 1600s, this great oyster dish has many variations. Legend holds that, in New Orleans, after spending a night away from home, wayward husbands would take an Oyster Loaf home as a peace offering, where it was known as la mediatrice, the mediator. Apparently this tradition was not exclusive in New Orleans. There are stories of this same oyster loaf used by Mrs. James Monroe of Washington, who called it "The Peacemaker." Reputedly, her recipe came from Mrs. George Washington. In San Francisco, the oyster loaf was called "the squarer." Here is our most recent version. What I love about this recipe is its simplicity. A crisp loaf of bread is hollowed out, the breadcrumbs are reserved for coating oysters, then the toasted loaf is filled with fried oysters. Hardly anything tastes better, even if you're just trying to make peace with yourself.

Serves 1

- 8 small or medium oysters, shucked, drained, and dried on paper towels
- 1 4-ounce round loaf sourdough bread
- 2-3 tablespoons butter, melted
- 1 egg, beaten
  Reserved bread crumbs mixed with
- 1/2 teaspoon salt
- 1/4 teaspoon black pepper
- 1/4 teaspoon white pepper
- 1/4 teaspoon garlic powder
  Vegetable oil for frying
  TABASCO® brand Pepper Sauce

Preheat the oven to 350° F. Slice the top off the loaf of bread, about 1/2-inch deep, and reserve. Scoop out the center of the loaf and shred the bread into small pieces into a mixing bowl and season with salt, peppers and garlic powder. Brush the inside of the bread loaf and the underside of the top, liberally with melted butter.

Dip the oysters in the beaten egg, then dredge in the seasoned breadcrumbs. Shake of excess crumbs and set the oysters aside on a plate or baking sheet. Meanwhile, place the buttered loaf of bread in the oven and heat, about 5 to 7 minutes, until the bread is toasty and golden around the edges. Heat the oil in a skillet until it reaches 350° to 375° F. When hot, add the oysters and fry, about 1 to 2 minutes per side, until crisp and golden. Drain on paper towels. Fill the toasted bread case with fried oysters and replace the top. Serve hot. Use a knife and fork to slice the loaf. Season to taste with Tabasco® Sauce.

Recommended wines: Pinot Gris, Champagne or sparkling wine, Chenin Blanc.

Oyster, Bacon and Caramelized Onion Turnovers

*Turnovers are small, individual pastries filled with a sweet or savory filling,
in this case — oysters and caramelized onions. Serve hot as appetizers, or a light lunch
accompanied by a salad or soup. If you can't find extra small oysters,
slice oysters into 1-inch pieces after poaching.*

Preheat oven to 400° F. Place the oysters and their liquor in a saucepan over medium heat. Bring to a boil, reduce heat, and simmer for 2 to 3 minutes, until oysters plump. Drain oysters and set aside. Meanwhile, cook bacon in a skillet over medium heat until crisp. Drain on paper towels, reserving 2 teaspoons bacon grease. Add butter to skillet and return to medium-high heat. When butter is hot, add onion and sugar. Cook, stirring often, until the onion is caramelized, turning a rich golden brown with dark brown edges. Remove from the heat and set aside. Season to taste with salt and pepper.

Roll out the pastry, about 1/8-inch thick on a lightly floured surface. Cut into 2-inch circles. On half of each circle, place 1 oyster (or portion), and 2 teaspoons of caramelized onions. Brush the edges of the pastry with beaten egg, then fold the pastry over. Seal the edges by pressing firmly, then crimp edges with a fork. Place the turnovers on a lightly greased baking sheet and brush lightly with beaten egg to glaze. Bake 10 to 12 minutes, or until pastry is golden brown. Serve hot.

Recommended beverages: Champagne or sparkling wine, Chilled beer, Sauvignon Blanc.

Makes about thirty turnovers

30 extra small oysters, shucked
   and drained, reserving liquor
4 slices bacon, finely diced
2 tablespoons butter
1 onion, cut in half and finely
   sliced into 1/2-rings
1 tablespoon sugar
   Salt and freshly ground
   black pepper
   pastry for 2 crust pie
   (see page 268)
1 egg, beaten

The Joy of Oysters

Bay Center Oyster, Tomato and Cheese Sandwich

This simple, yet very tasty, recipe comes from our friends at Bay Center Oyster Farms in Bay Center, Washington, where they grow some great oysters on Willapa Bay.

Serves 2

12 small or medium oysters, shucked, reserving liquor
Salt and freshly ground black pepper to taste
2 English muffins, split
Butter for spreading
Tartar sauce or mayonnaise
4 slices sharp cheddar cheese
1 tomato, sliced

Place the oysters and their liquor in a saucepan over medium heat. Bring to a boil, reduce heat, and simmer for 2 to 3 minutes, until oysters plump. Drain oysters, sprinkle with salt and pepper and set aside. Meanwhile, butter the English muffins and toast until golden under a broiler. Spread half of each muffin with tartar sauce or mayonnaise. Place 3 oysters on each muffin, top with a tomato slice and then a slice of cheese. Broil until the cheese is melted. Serve hot.

Oyster & Egg Dishes
Oyster Dressings & Stuffings

Which came first, the oyster or the egg? Well, truthfully, oysters begin as microscopic eggs and they have probably been around longer than chickens - oyster's evolutionary longevity dates back 190 million years. Whatever the case, plump little oysters are incredibly delicious tucked or folded into omelets, frittatas and quiches. Enjoy these dishes for breakfast, lunch or a simple dinner. Our favorite oyster dressings and stuffings make wonderful accompaniments for roast turkey or chicken, and are great with salmon, lamb, duck or Cornish game hens.

Shelter Island Oyster Quiche
Hangtown Fry
Chinese Shrimp and Oyster Omelet
Smoked Oyster, Asparagus, and
*   Roasted Red Pepper Frittata*
Eggplant and Oyster Souffle
Half Shell Lori's One-and-a-Half Pound
*   Oyster One Egg Omelet*
Oyster Bill's Hangtown Fry Frittata
Key West Oyster and Eggs Benedict
Dried Cranberry, Hazelnut and
*   Oyster Stuffing*
Corn Bread and Oyster Dressing
Eggplant and Oyster Dressing

Shelter Island Oyster Quiche

*Packed with sautéed vegetables and fresh oysters, this savory oyster quiche
is a favorite of Long Island fishermen. Serve for breakfast, lunch,
or even a light supper, with a fresh green salad.*

Serves 6

- 1 pint extra small oysters, shucked and drained
- 2 tablespoons butter
- 2 green onions, finely chopped
- 2 teaspoons chopped, fresh basil
- 1 tablespoon chopped, fresh parsley
- 1 garlic clove, minced
- 1 cup mushrooms, sliced
- 1/2 red pepper, seeded and sliced
- 1 partially baked 9-inch pie shell (see page 268)
- 6 large eggs, beaten
- 1 cup whipping cream
- 1-1/2 cups grated Swiss Cheese
- 1 teaspoon salt
- 1/2 teaspoon freshly ground black pepper to taste

Preheat oven to 350° F. Melt the butter in a skillet over medium heat. Add the green onions, basil, parsley, garlic, mushrooms and red pepper. Cook, stirring often, until the vegetables are tender, about 10 minutes. Add the oysters and cook until they plump, about 3 minutes. Spoon the mixture into the prepared pie crust, distributing evenly. Whisk together the eggs and whipping cream. Fold in the grated cheese, salt and pepper. Pour the mixture over the oyster and vegetable mixture. Bake for about 50 minutes, or until eggs are set and cheese is lightly browned.

"Oysters are the usual opening to a winter breakfast –
indeed they are almost indispensible."
Almanach des Gourmands

Hangtown Fry

Legend holds that a condemned criminal was faced with his last meal during California's Gold Rush era. With his pockets filled with gold nuggets, he rode into Hangtown (now Placerville, CA), and demanded the finest meal money could buy. In those days, the oysters of choice were probably tiny Olympia oysters, which were shipped by the boat load to California from Washington. It is thought that the eggs used for this dish may have been strong flavored sea bird eggs, which were far cheaper than hen's eggs. If you like, you can cook this in the 49er way, in a cast iron skillet over a camp fire. Serve with a slab of toasted sourdough bread and Stewed Tomatoes on the side.

Dredge the oysters in flour, shaking off any excess. Dip each oyster in the beaten egg and roll it in cracker crumbs. Set aside. Season the eggs with salt and pepper. Melt the butter in a large skillet over medium heat until hot and sizzling. Add the oysters and fry until golden on one side. Turn the oysters over, then pour the beaten eggs over the top. Reduce the heat to low, and cook until the eggs are set. Fold the omelet carefully over into a half circle. Divide into 4 equal portions and top each portion with 2 strips of bacon. Serve with Stewed Tomatoes.

Melt the butter in a skillet over medium heat. Add the tomatoes, basil and garlic. Stew for about 5 minutes. Season with salt, pepper and Tabasco. Serve warm.

Serves 4

16	small oysters, shucked and drained
1/2	cup flour
8	eggs, beaten
3/4	cup fine dry cracker crumbs
1/2	teaspoon salt
1/4	teaspoon freshly ground black pepper
4	tablespoons (1/2 stick) butter
8	strips of bacon, fried crisp

Stewed Tomatoes:

2	tablespoons olive oil
2	large, ripe tomatoes, diced
2	teaspoons minced fresh basil
1	garlic clove, minced
	Salt and freshly ground black pepper to taste
	Dash of hot red pepper sauce

The Joy of Oysters

Chinese Shrimp and Oyster Omelet

Filled with sauteed shrimp, oysters, mushrooms, scallions, and bamboo shoots, this tasty omelet is excellent with steamed Jasmine rice.

Serves 6 to 8

- 16 small oysters, shucked and drained
- 1/2 pound cooked shrimp meat
- 2 tablespoons vegetable oil
- 1/2 cup fresh sliced mushrooms
- 1/4 cup bamboo shoots, sliced
- 2 green onions, minced
- 8 large eggs, beaten with a fork
- 2 tablespoons whipping cream
- 2 teaspoons soy sauce
-    Salt and white pepper to taste
-    Minced fresh chives

Heat the oil in a skillet over medium heat. Stir in the mushrooms, bamboo shoots, and green onions. Cook, stirring often, until vegetables are tender, about 7 minutes. Add the oysters and shrimp. Cook gently for about 3 minutes, until oysters plump. Distribute mixture evenly over the bottom of the skillet. Whisk together the eggs, cream and soy sauce. Season with salt and pepper and pour over the seafood mixture. Cook over low to medium heat, just until the eggs are set. Fold the omelet in half and divide into 4 servings. Sprinkle with minced chives.

Smoked Oyster, Asparagus & Roasted Red Pepper Frittata

Serve with freshly squeezed orange juice and buttered toast for breakfast. To smoke your own oysters, see page 124.

Serves 4

- 1 tablespoon butter
- 1 tablespoon vegetable oil
- 8 eggs
-    Salt and freshly ground black pepper to taste
- 2 green onions, diced
- 1 bunch asparagus, trimmed and steamed until tender
- 1 cup sliced roasted red pepper
- 12 -15 smoked oysters
- 1 cup grated sharp cheddar cheese

Preheat oven to 350° F. Heat the oil in a 12-inch oven-proof skillet over medium heat. Whisk the eggs and pour into the skillet. Reduce heat to low. Arrange the onions, asparagus, roasted red pepper and smoked oysters decoratively over the eggs. Sprinkle with salt and pepper, and top with grated cheddar cheese. Place the skillet in the oven and bake 15 to 20 minutes, or until the eggs are firm. Divide into 4 portions.

Eggplant and Oyster Souffle

Most people who love oysters also like eggplant. The two have a tasty affinity for each other, with their sweet, yet earthy flavors and creamy texture. Here, the eggplant is roasted in the oven until tender and pureed with roasted garlic. Bake this rustic souffle in a large shallow baking dish, allowing it to rise quickly, and evenly.

Preheat the oven to 400° F. Heat the olive oil in a large oven-proof skillet over medium heat. Sprinkle the eggplant pieces with salt and add to the hot oil, mixing well. Transfer the skillet to the oven and roast the eggplant for about 40 minutes, or until tender, stirring occasionally. Meanwhile, wrap the garlic in foil and roast for about 20 minutes, or until softened. Squeeze the garlic from the skins into the bowl of a food processor. Working in batches, if necessary, add the roasted eggplant and puree. Transfer the puree to a large mixing bowl. Season with salt, white pepper, cayenne, and nutmeg. Whisk the egg yolks lightly with a fork or wire whisk, then stir into the eggplant mixture. Stir in 3/4 cup of the grated cheese.

Grease a shallow 9-by-13-inch glass or ceramic baking dish. Beat the egg whites with a pinch of salt until firm peaks form. Fold half of the egg whites into the eggplant mixture, then gently fold in the remaining whites, just until combined. Pour half of the souffle mixture into the baking dish, top with the shucked oysters, then top with the remaining souffle mixture. Sprinkle the reserved Parmesan cheese over the souffle. Bake for about 20 to 25 minutes, or until eggs are puffed and just firm. Serve at once.

Serves 6 as a first course, 4 as a main course
- 24 small oysters, shucked and drained
- 4 tablespoons olive oil
- 1-2 pound eggplant, peeled and diced
- 5 large garlic cloves, unpeeled
- 1/2 teaspoon salt
- 1/2 teaspoon white pepper
- 1/4 teaspoon cayenne pepper
- 1/4 teaspoon ground nutmeg
- 5 large eggs, separated
- 1 cup freshly grated Asiago or Parmesan cheese

Half Shell Lori's
One-and-a-Half Pound Oyster One Egg Omelet

If you've ever wondered what to do with those huge oysters that weigh in over one pound in the shell, try this delicious omelet. This oyster was over 13-inches long and weighed more than my mastiff pup when he was born. The ingredients are very simple, but, often in cooking, the simplest things are the best.

Serves 1

1 tablespoon butter
1 extra large oyster
1 egg
  Salt and freshly ground pepper
  to taste
2 ounces grated sharp cheddar
  cheese
  Hot red pepper sauce
  to taste

Melt the butter over medium heat in a 6-inch non-stick skillet. When sizzling, add the oyster. Cook the oyster about 1-1/2 minutes on each side, until light golden brown. Sprinkle the oyster with salt and pepper. Whisk the egg with a fork and pour over the oyster. Cover, reduce heat to low, and cook about two minutes. Remove cover and sprinkle the egg with salt and pepper. Tip the pan slightly and, using a rubber spatula, lift the cooked egg up slighlty, letting the uncooked egg flow underneath. Replace the cover and cook 1 more minute, or until the egg is nearly set. Remove from the burner and top with grated cheese. Place 6-inches under a hot broiler to melt the cheese. Fold the omelet in half. Season with hot red pepper sauce to taste.

Oysters come in all sizes for those special recipes!

Oyster Bill's Hangtown Fry Frittata

You can always count on Oyster Bill to be creative, especially when it comes to cooking oysters. Here is his twist on the classic Hangtown Fry, made with fresh spinach and mushrooms.

Fry the bacon in an ovenproof skillet over medium heat until almost crisp. Add the oysters, mushrooms, shallots and garlic, and cook for about 4 to 5 minutes, until oysters are plumped and mushrooms are tender. Drain the liquid from the mixture and discard; transfer the oyster-bacon mixture to a bowl and set aside.

Meanwhile, return the skillet to medium heat. Whisk the beaten eggs together with the milk and fold in the shredded spinach. Melt the butter and, when sizzling, add the beaten eggs. When the eggs start to set, top with the oyster-bacon mixture, scattering it evenly over the eggs. Cook over medium heat until eggs are firm on the bottom, then place the frittata under the broiler to finish cooking. Divide into 4 portions and serve hot.

Serves 4

16 extra small oysters, shucked
and drained
 6 strips bacon, chopped
1/2 cup chopped fresh mushrooms
 1 shallot, minced
 1 garlic clove, minced
 1 tablespoon butter
 8 large eggs, beaten
 2 tablespoons milk
1/2 cups shredded fresh spinach

Key West Oyster and Eggs Benedict

Topped with poached eggs and lemony Hollandaise Sauce, this tasty breakfast is a favorite of Key West locals. Serve with sliced tomatoes and steamed asparagus on the side.

Serves 4

- 16 small oyster, shucked
- 2 tablespoons butter
- 1 garlic clove, minced
- 8 slices Canadian bacon
- 4 English muffins, split
- 8 eggs, poached
  Hollandaise Sauce
- 1/4 cup chopped fresh parsley

Melt the butter with the garlic in a skillet over medium heat. Add the oysters and cook until lightly golden on both sides. Set aside and keep warm. Heat the Canadian bacon in a skillet over medium heat. Keep warm. Toast the English muffins and lightly butter. Set two muffin halves on each serving plate. Top with Canadian bacon, and place 2 oysters on top of each muffin. Gently place a poached egg on top of the oysters. Ladle warm Hollandaise Sauce over the top and garnish with chopped parsley.

Hollandaise Sauce:

- 1/4 cup (1/2 stick) unsalted butter
- 1-1/2 tablespoons fresh lemon juice
- 3 egg yolks
- 4 tablespoons boiling water
- 1/4 teaspoon salt
  Pinch of cayenne pepper

Melt the butter in a small saucepan and keep warm. In the top of a double boiler, whisk the egg yolks until they begin to thicken. Place the egg yolks over simmering, but not boiling water, whisking constantly. Whisk in the boiling water, one tablespoon at a time. Whisk in the lemon juice, mixing well. Remove the double boiler from the heat. Whisking constantly with a wire whisk, slowly add the melted butter, until the butter is incorporated and the sauce is creamy and thick. Season with salt and cayenne. Serve at once. Note: If sauce does not bind, whisk in 1 more tablespoon of boiling water.

Dried Cranberry, Hazelnut and Oyster Stuffing

Studded with dried cranberries and toasted hazelnuts, this savory oyster dressing is great with roast chicken or turkey.

Melt the butter in a large skillet over medium heat. When hot, add the onion, celery and garlic. Cook, stirring occasionally, until the vegetables are softened, about 12 minutes. Add the oysters and their liquor and simmer until oysters plump, about 2 to 3 minutes. Remove from the heat.

Toss the bread crumbs, cranberries, hazelnuts, and thyme together in a large mixing bowl. Add the oyster mixture, stirring gently. Season to taste with salt and pepper. Add enough chicken broth to make a moist stuffing that clings together when pressed between your fingers.

Bake in foil for 40 minutes at 350° F. or use to stuff roast chicken or turkey.

Makes 6 cups

- 4 tablespoons (1/2 stick) butter
- 1 onion, chopped
- 3 ribs celery, chopped
- 2 garlic cloves, minced
- 2 dozen small oysters, shucked, reserving liquor
- 5 cups soft bread crumbs
- 2 cups dried cranberries
- 1-1/2 cups chopped, toasted hazelnuts
- 2 tablespoons fresh thyme leaves
  Salt and freshly ground black pepper to taste
  Chicken broth, as needed

Corn Bread and Oyster Dressing

This golden oyster dressing is a holiday staple on Chesapeake Bay, where watermen have been harvesting oysters for over a century. Serve hot with roast turkey or duck.

Preheat oven to 350° F. Melt half of the butter in a skillet over medium heat. When hot, add the onions, celery, sage, and parsley. Cook, stirring occasionally, until the vegetables are soft, about 12 minutes. Set aside. Place the crumbled cornbread in a large mixing bowl. Heat the chicken stock with the remaining 6 tablespoons of butter, until the butter has melted. Pour the hot stock over the cornbread. Stir in the onion mixture, eggs, and cayenne. Season to taste with salt and pepper. Gently fold the oysters into the cornbread mixture. Transfer the dressing to a greased 8 X 8-inch baking dish. Bake for 40 minutes.

Serves 8

- 3 dozen small oysters, shucked and drained
- 12 tablespoons (1-1/2 sticks) butter
- 1 onion, chopped
- 4 ribs celery, chopped
- 2 tablespoons crumbled dried sage
- 1/4 cup chopped fresh parsley
- 6 cups crumbled corn bread
- 1 cup chicken stock
- 2 eggs, lightly beaten
- 1/4 teaspoon cayenne pepper
  Salt and freshly ground black pepper to taste

The Joy of Oysters   201

Eggplant and Oyster Dressing

*This recipe is a favorite of Joe Daniels, who farms oysters on Mats Mats Bay
on Washington State's Olympic Peninsula.*

Makes about 8 cups

2 dozen small oysters, shucked
   and drained
1/4 cup butter or vegetable oil
1 green pepper, seeded and diced
2 onions, chopped
1 medium eggplant, peeled
   and diced
3 ribs celery, chopped
6 cups cubed French bread
6 ounces bulk Italian sausage,
   cooked
1 tablespoon crumbled dried sage
1/2 teaspoon nutmeg
1/2 teaspoon cayenne
1-1/2 teaspoons salt
1/2 teaspoon freshly ground black
   pepper
3 cups chicken stock
   Milk, as needed
   Paprika
1/4 cup chopped fresh parsley

Preheat oven to 350° F. Melt the butter in a large skillet over medium heat. When hot, add the green pepper, onions, eggplant, and celery. Cook, stirring often, until the vegetables are tender, about 15 minutes. Set aside. Place the bread cubes in a large mixing bowl. Stir in the sausage, sage, nutmeg, cayenne, salt and pepper. Add the cooked vegetables and the chicken stock, mixing well. Gently fold in the oysters. If the mixture is dry, add milk to moisten. Transfer to a greased casserole dish. Sprinkle with paprika and chopped parsley. Bake about 35 minutes, or until top is golden brown.

Sauces for Half Shell and Cooked Oysters

For many oyster lovers, a freshly shucked oyster needs no accompaniment other than its own briny nectar. Others prefer a squeeze of fresh lemon or a drop of hot red pepper sauce. (Studies conducted by researchers at Louisiana State University have shown that hot red pepper sauce may counteract harmful bacteria in oysters.) Many Americans were introduced to their first oysters served with ketchup or cocktail sauce, and continue to favor their succulent bivalves topped with a zesty sauce. This comprehensive collection of recipes ranges from classic Mignonette sauces, to a lively Ginger and Pineapple Salsa, a seductive Lemon Butter Sauce, and many more - all wonderful companions to the fresh sea flavor of oysters.

Raspberry Ginger Mignonette Sauce
Long Beach Cranberry Mignonette
Iced Champagne Mignonette
Balsamic Vinegar and Ginger Mignonette
Sparkling Apple Cider Mignonette
Ginger, Lime and Red Chili Mignonette
Elliott's Oyster House Mignonette
Sugaki
Green Chili and Cucumber Sauce
Cucumber, Sour Cream and
*   Horseradish Sauce*
Radish and White Wine Vinaigrette
Ginger and Pineapple Salsa
Buttermilk, Sour Cream and
*   Horseradish Sauce*
Oysters with Lemon and Caviar
Oysters with Smoked Salmon
*   and Lemon*
Oysters with Vodka Cream and Caviar
Oysters on the Half Shell with Guinness

Tarragon Bearnaise Sauce
*   for Fried Oysters*
Spicy Cabbage Sauce
Cocktail Salsa
Ginger Sweet and Sour Sauce
Lemon Butter Sauce
Tartar Sauce with Capers and Orange Zest

Raspberry Ginger Mignonette Sauce

Peter Augusztiny, one of the owners of Westcott Bay Sea Farms, in Friday Harbor, WA, says this recipe from Chef Kathleen Lee-Geist is his all-time favorite sauce for freshly shucked oysters.

Makes about 1-1/4 cups

1-1/2 cups fresh or frozen raspberries
1 cup raspberry vinegar, or white wine vinegar
1 tablespoon freshly grated ginger root
1 large shallot, minced
1 teaspoon brown sugar
Freshly ground black pepper, to taste
Fresh raspberries for optional garnish

Puree the raspberries and press them through a sieve to remove seeds. Combine all the other ingredients in a jar and shake well. (This will keep refrigerated for about 2 weeks.)

To serve: Spoon sauce over oysters and garnish with 1 fresh raspberry per oyster (optional).

Long Beach Cranberry Mignonette

In addition to being famous for briny Willapa Bay oysters, Washington's Long Beach Peninsula is also renowned for its tasty cranberries, which Half Shell Lori used to create this colorful, tart mignonette.

Makes about 1 cup

1/2 cup fresh or previously frozen cranberries, chopped
2 shallots, minced
1/2 cup rice wine vinegar
1/4 cup dry red wine
1/4 cup cranberry juice
1 teaspoon sugar
1/4 teaspoon cracked black pepper
Pinch of salt

Combine all the ingredients in a non-reactive bowl. Served chilled.

Iced Champagne Mignonette

This icy cold mignonette adds sparkle to freshly shucked oysters.
Make it one day ahead, so it has time to freeze overnight.

Combine all the ingredients in a shallow baking dish. Place the dish in the freezer until the mixture becomes slushy, about 1 1/2 to 2 hours. Break up the slush with a fork and place it back in the freezer. Repeat several times, then cover with plastic wrap and freeze overnight. Just before serving, break the ice crystals up with a fork. Spoon 1/2 to 1 teaspoon of the iced mignonette on each freshly shucked oyster.

Makes about 2 cups

- 1/2 cup dry Champagne or sparkling wine
- 1 cup white wine vinegar
- 1/4 cup water
- 2 shallots, minced
- 2 teaspoons finely minced Lemon zest
- 1 teaspoon cracked white pepper

Balsamic Vinegar and Ginger Mignonette

Combine all ingredients in a non-reactive bowl.
Serve chilled.

Makes about 1-1/2 cups

- 3/4 cup Balsamic vinegar
- 3/4 cup soy sauce
- 2 tablespoons grated fresh ginger root
- 2 green onions, thinly sliced

Sparkling Apple Cider Mignonette

Combine all ingredients in a non-reactive bowl.
Serve chilled.

Makes about 1 cup

- 1 cup sparkling apple cider
- 6 tablespoons finely chopped apple, peeled
- 1 teaspoon minced jalapeno pepper
- 1 shallot, minced
- 1 tablespoon chopped fresh parsley
- 1 tablespoon cider vinegar
- 1/2 teaspoon coarsely ground black pepper

Ginger, Lime and Red Chili Mignonette

Makes about 1 cup

1/4 cup sake
Juice of 4 limes
2 tablespoons soy sauce
2 tablespoons grated fresh
ginger root
1 teaspoon hot red chili flakes
1 tablespoon brown sugar

Combine all ingredients in a non-reactive bowl.
Serve chilled.

Elliott's Oyster House Mignonette

Elliott's Oyster House, Seattle, WA

*This simple and very traditional mignonette accompanies oysters on the half shell at
Seattle's popular waterfront restaurant.*

Makes about 1 cup

6 tablespoons red wine vinegar
6 tablespoons rice wine vinegar
2 shallots, minced
2 teaspoons coarsely ground
black pepper

Combine all ingredients in a non-reactive bowl.
Serve chilled.

Sugaki

*This spicy sauce is served with oysters on the half shell at Shiro's,
one of Seattle's most popular sushi restaurants. Daikon is a large, long white radish
that is available in most supermarkets.*

Makes about 1 cup

1/4 cup fresh lemon juice
1/4 cup soy sauce
1/4 cup clam juice
1/2 cup peeled, finely grated
daikon radish
1 teaspoon Asian hot chili-garlic
sauce

Combine all ingredients in a non-reactive bowl.
Serve chilled.

The Joy of Oysters

Green Chili and Cucumber Sauce

Use long, tapered English cucumbers, which have fewer seeds, for this recipe.

Combine all ingredients in a non-reactive bowl.
Serve chilled.

Makes about 1-1/2 cups

1 English cucumber, peeled and grated
1 jalapeno pepper, seeded and minced
3/4 cup rice wine vinegar
3 tablespoons minced fresh cilantro
1/2 teaspoon coarsely ground
black pepper
Pinch of salt

Cucumber, Sour Cream and Horseradish Sauce

Combine all ingredients in a non-reactive bowl.
Serve chilled.

Makes about 1 cup

1 cup finely diced, peeled and seeded
cucumber
1/2 cup sour cream
1/4 cup cider vinegar
1 tablespoon cream style horseradish
1/2 teaspoon freshly ground black
pepper
1 tablespoon minced green onion
Pinch of salt

Radish and White Wine Vinaigrette

Based on a recipe by chef Jean Joho of Everest and Brasserie Jo, in Chicago, this is so simple, yet so good. Use a good quality white wine, such as a Sauvignon Blanc or Chardonnay.

Combine all ingredients in a non-reactive bowl.
Serve chilled.

Makes about 1 cup

3/4 cup finely grated red radish
3/4 cup dry white wine

Ginger and Pineapple Salsa

Flavored with fresh ginger and cilantro, this tropical salsa is a favorite.
Make it several hours in advance so it has time to chill.

Makes about 1 cup

1/4 cup brown sugar
1/4 cup hot water
1/2 cup rice wine vinegar
  2 tablespoons grated fresh
    ginger root
1/4 cup minced fresh cilantro
1/2 teaspoon hot red pepper flakes
1/2 cup finely diced fresh pineapple

Combine the sugar and hot water in a non-reactive bowl. Add all the remaining ingredients, except the pineapple. Cover and chill in the refrigerator. To serve: Place 1 teaspoon of diced pineapple on each oyster. Top with a spoonful of the ginger-vinegar mixture.

Buttermilk, Sour Cream and Horseradish Sauce

For an extra touch, top oysters with a dollop of caviar.
Make the sauce at least 1 hour in advance to marry flavors.

Makes about 1 cup

1/4 cup prepared horseradish
1/2 cup buttermilk
1/2 cup sour cream
  1 green onion, finely sliced
    Caviar, optional

Combine all ingredients in a non-reactive bowl. Serve chilled.

Oysters with Lemon and Caviar

Topped with fresh lemon and a spoonful of caviar,
this Italian oyster dish is fitting for the most elegant occasion.
Serve oysters on a bed of ice decorated with lemon slices and parsley sprigs.

Combine all ingredients in a non-reactive bowl.
Serve chilled, spooned over freshly shucked oysters.

Makes enough to top 2 dozen
freshly shucked oysters

3 tablespoons fine quality caviar
3 tablespoons fresh lemon juice
1/8 teaspoon cayenne pepper

Oysters with Smoked Salmon and Lemon

Topped with a thin slice of nova-style smoked salmon, black pepper, and lemon juice, freshly
shucked oysters are irresistible.

Combine the lemon juice, pepper and parsley in a
non-reactive bowl. Top each oyster with a slice of
smoked salmon, then drizzle with the sauce.

Tops 1 dozen freshly shucked oysters

1/4 cup fresh lemon juice
1/2 teaspoon freshly ground
black pepper
2 tablespoons minced fresh parsley
3 ounces nova-style (or lox)
smoked salmon, cut into
12 pieces

Oysters with Vodka Cream and Caviar

*This was inspired by a menu cooked at the James Beard House, in 1997,
by Chef Alvin Binuya of Ponti Seafood Grill in Seattle, WA. Oysters were just part
of the opening act, accompanied by Nova Smoked Salmon Crostini and
Chili-Garlic Marinated Penn Cove Mussels.*

Tops 2 dozen freshly shucked oysters

1-1/2 cup creme fraiche or sour cream
1/4 cup fine quality vodka
1/2 teaspoon white pepper
2 teaspoons fresh lemon juice
Sevruga caviar as needed

Combine the creme fraiche, vodka, pepper and lemon juice in a non-reactive bowl. Top each oyster with a teaspoon of the sauce and top with a dollop of caviar.

Oysters on the Half Shell with Guinness

*The first time I met "seafood guru" Jon Rowley, of Jon Rowley and Associates in Seattle,
I was interviewing him for Food Arts magazine regarding his highly publicized
"Oyster Wine" competition. Judging took place at Jake's Famous Crawfish ,
in Portland, OR. Following the judging, Jon and I shared a few dozen more oysters,
during which we discovered this wonderful combination.*

Half Shell Lori

For each freshly shucked oyster:

1 to 2 teaspoons chilled Guinness Stout

Top each chilled oyster with Guinness. Lift to your lips and slurp. Drink more Guinness.

Tarragon Bearnaise Sauce for Fried Oysters

This traditional French sauce, flavored with fresh tarragon, is rich and creamy, a beautiful accompaniment for crisp, fried oysters.

In the top bowl of a double boiler, whisk the egg yolks. Gradually add the vinegar, and cream. Season with salt and cayenne. Place the bowl over a pan of simmering water, whisking constantly. When the sauce turns light in color and coats the back of a spoon, stir in the tarragon and garlic. Gradually whisk in the butter, until it is thoroughly incorporated. Serve at once.

Tops 3 dozen fried oysters

- 2 egg yolks
- 1 tablespoon white wine vinegar
- 2 tablespoons cream
- 1/8 teaspoon salt
- 1/8 teaspoon cayenne pepper
- 2 tablespoons chopped fresh tarragon
- 1 garlic clove, minced
- 4 tablespoons unsalted butter, chilled and cut into 1/2-inch pieces

Spicy Cabbage Sauce

This colorful sauce is an East Coast tradition with fried oysters.

Combine ingredients in a non-reactive bowl. Let sit at least 15 minutes before serving to marry flavors.

Makes about 1-1/2 cups

- 2 cup finely shredded purple cabbage
- 1 red pepper, seeded and finely diced
- 1/2 cup mayonnaise
- 1/4 cup whipping cream
- 1/4 cup cider or rice wine vinegar
- 1 teaspoon salt
- 1/2 teaspoon freshly ground black pepper
- 1 teaspoon paprika
- 1 teaspoon celery seed
- 1/2 teaspoon TABASCO® brand hot pepper sauce
- 1 teaspoon fresh lemon juice
- 2 tablespoons brown sugar

The Joy of Oysters   211

Cocktail Salsa

Serve this zesty salsa with fried or half shell oysters

Makes about 1 cup

1/2 cup chili sauce
1/2 cup catsup
1 tablespoon Tabasco sauce
1/4 cup freshly squeezed lime juice
1 tablespoon brown sugar, firmly packed
2 tablespoons prepared horseradish
Salt and freshly ground black pepper to taste

Combine all ingredients in a non-reactive bowl. Serve chilled.

Ginger Sweet and Sour Sauce

Serve this silky, spicy sauce with oyster fritters and fried oysters.

Makes about 1-1/2 cups

1 tablespoon cornstarch
1 teaspoon dry mustard
2 tablespoons cold water
1/4 cup ketchup
1/2 cup brown sugar
1/4 cup cider vinegar
1/4 cup water
3 tablespoons orange marmalade
1 tablespoon grated fresh ginger root
1 tablespoon soy sauce
1 garlic clove, minced
1/2 teaspoon hot red pepper sauce
1 green onion, finely sliced

In a small bowl, whisk together the cornstarch, dry mustard and 2 tablespoons water. Set aside.

Combine the remaining ingredients in a saucepan and bring to a boil over medium-high heat, stirring frequently. Reduce the heat to a simmer. Whisk in the cornstarch mixture, stirring constantly. Simmer until sauce is thickened, about 1 minute. Pour into a serving dish and garnish with green onion. Serve hot.

Lemon Butter Sauce

Elliott's Oyster House, Seattle, WA

At Elliott's the chefs work very quickly, cooking over high heat - and this dish cooks in just 2 to 3 minutes. The secret to this sauce is first pan-frying the oysters in a skillet, then the sauce ingredients are added to the hot drippings left in the skillet. The little bit of flour left in the pan helps bind the sauce. This recipe is designed for home cooks. If you'd like to try the chef's approach, adjust accordingly.

Melt the butter in a skillet over medium heat. Add the garlic and shallots and cook until softened, about 3 minutes. Stir in the wine, stock and lemon juice. Bring to a simmer and cook, stirring often, for 5 or 6 minutes, until reduced by 1/2 volume. Whisk in the chilled butter, piece-by-piece, until the butter is incorporated. Stir in the parsley and season with salt and white pepper. Serve at once or keep warm in a thermos.

Tops two dozen fried oysters

- 1 tablespoon butter
- 1 garlic clove, minced
- 1 shallot, minced
- 1/4 cup dry white wine
- 1/4 cup clam juice or fish stock
- 1/4 cup fresh lemon juice

- 4 tablespoons (1/2 stick) unsalted butter, chilled and cut into 4 pieces
- 2 tablespoons minced fresh parsley
- Salt and white pepper to taste

Tartar Sauce with Capers and Orange Zest

Here is a refreshing twist on a classic oyster sauce.

Combine all the ingredients in a non-reactive bowl. Serve chilled with fried oysters.

Makes about 1 cup

- 1 cup mayonnaise
- 1 teaspoon Dijon mustard
- 1 green onion, minced
- 2 tablespoons chopped, drained capers
- 2 teaspoons fresh orange juice
- 2 teaspoons grated orange zest
- 1/8 teaspoon cayenne pepper
- Salt and white pepper to taste

"A Good Cafe on the Place St. Michel"
from A Moveable Feast, *by Ernest Hemingway*

"I closed up the story in the notebook and put it in my inside pocket and I asked the waiter for a dozen portugaises and a half-carafe of the dry white wine they had there. After writing a story I was always empty and both sad and happy, as though I had made love, and I was sure this was a very good story although I would not know how good until I read it over the next day.

"As I ate the oysters with their strong taste of the sea and their faint metallic taste that the cold white wine washed away, leaving only the sea taste and the succulent texture, and as I drank their cold liquid from each shell and washed it down with the crisp taste of the wine, I lost the empty feeling and began to be happy and make plans."

Oyster Bill samples some fine Chilean oysters at a "A Good Cafe in Puerto Montt, Chile" in December of 1999.

Oyster Entrees

Whether it is something as simple and delicious as an Oyster Pan Roast, or as sophisticated as Oysters Poached in Champagne and Brie Cheese, oysters are the ultimate main dish for breakfast, lunch or dinner. Our collection of oyster entrees offers something for everyone, spanning cultures and cooking styles from oyster sea to shining oyster sea.

Sake Steamed Oysters
Steamed Oysters with Sweet Wine Butter
Wine Steamed Oysters in Curry Sauce
Oysters Poached in Champagne with
*   Cucumbers and Whipped Cream*
Oysters Poached in Champagne and
*   Brie Cheese*
Low Country Oysters with Mushrooms
Xinh's Oyster Saute in Asian Sauce
Oyster Cakes with Caper-Cayenne
*   Mayonnaise*
Oyster Cakes with Remoulade Sauce
Oyster, Bacon and Potato Hash
Oysters Sauteed with Prosciutto
*   and Browned Garlic Butter*
Corn and Oyster Pancakes
Sauteed Oytsters with Green Onion Aioli
Stir-Fried Oysters in Black Bean Sauce
Pan Fried Oysters
Deep South Browned Oysters
Louisiana Pan Fried Oysters with Chili
*   Corn Sauce and Black Bean Salsa*
Seafood Risotto with Pistou
Spicy Cornmeal Fried Oysters with
*   Smoked Chili and Lime Aioli*
Carpetbagger Filet Mignon
Fried Oysters Rector Style with Crab
*   and Lobster*
Creamed Tarragon Oysters in
*   Puff Pastry Shells*
Pan Fried Oysters with Jack Daniel's Sauce
Oyster and Artichoke Casserole
Fried Oysters Served in the Shell with
*   Sauteed Spinach and Chipotle Aioli*

Salad of Field Greens with Crispy Fried
*   Oysters Topped with Aioli and Bacon*
The Davis Family's Scalloped Oysters
Creamy Scalloped Oysters
Olympia Oyster Pepper Pot
Oysters a la Oysterville
Oyster, Goat Cheese and Spinach Gratin
Oysters in Roasted Orange, Melon
*   and Grape Coulis*
Roasted Coho Salmon with Oyster
*   and Bacon Dressing*
Grand Central Oyster Pan Roast
Oyster Rabbit
Oyster Bill's Oysters Au Gratin
*   with Shrimp*
Oysters Baked in Red Peppers
Rodney's Oyster Pie
Smoked Salmon and Oyster Pot Pie
Oyster Pan Roast on Toast
Oysters and Wild Mushrooms Baked
*   in Parchment Paper*
Baked Shellfish in Tomato Garlic Sauce

Sake Steamed Oysters

Oysterville Sea Farms, Oysterville, WA

During the winter months, when low tides tend to occur at night, oysterman Dan Driscoll, from Oysterville Sea Farms on Washington's Long Beach Peninsula, often works his oyster beds in less than desirable weather conditions. He discovered the perfect antidote to biting cold winds and driving rain with his dish of oysters steamed over sake. After steaming the oysters, he pours the hot sake-infused nectar into a mug and drinks it along with the dish.

1-1/2 cups sake
4 dozen small oysters in the shell, scrubbed
1 garlic clove, minced
4 tablespoons (1/2 stick) unsalted butter, melted
Lemon slices

Pour the sake into the bottom of a 2-quart steamer or a large saucepan fitted with a steamer basket. Place the oysters in a layer on the bottom of the steamer, deep cupped shell down.

Cover and bring the sake to a boil, then reduce the heat and simmer for about 10 minutes, or until the oysters begin to open. Dish the oysters into 2 serving bowls and strain the steaming liquid into 2 large mugs.

Combine the minced garlic and melted butter and serve in side dishes for dipping, along with the lemon slices. To open the oysters, insert an oyster knife into the oyster and twist to pry open. Sever the adductor muscle and lift the oyster from the shell.

Recommended beverages: Hot Sake, Chilled Beer or Ale, Sauvignon Blanc.

Steamed Oysters with Sweet Wine Butter
Canlis Restaurant, Seattle, WA

"The sauce that tops these oysters is a variation on the classic buerre blanc," says Executive Chef Greg Atkinson. "This version is delicately sweet thanks to a foundation of late harvest dessert wine, such as Muscat or Riesling." The sauce can be prepared ahead up to 2 hours, to the point where the butter is added. Once the butter is whisked in, serve the sauce at once, or keep warm in a thermos.

C A N L I S
RESTAURANT

To make the sauce: In a saucepan over high heat, bring the wine to a boil and simmer rapidly until it is reduced to 1/4 cup. Stir in the cream. With the mixture simmering gently, whisk in the chilled butter, a few pieces at a time, whisking constantly until all butter is incorporated and the sauce is smooth and creamy. Serve immediately, or keep warm in a thermos.

Scrub the oysters with a stiff brush. Heat the water in a large wok or kettle over high heat. Place the oysters, deep-shell down in the water and steam for about 8 to 10 minutes, or until shells open. Using an oyster knife, remove the tops from the oysters and severe the adductor muscles, leaving the oysters in their deep shells. Arrange the steamed oysters on small plates lined with rock salt. Ladle approximately 1 tablespoon of sauce over each oyster. Serve at once.

Serves 6

36	medium oysters in the shell
1/2 - 1	cup water for steaming
1	cup late harvest Muscat or Riesling wine
2	tablespoons whipping cream
3/4	cup (1-1/2 sticks) unsalted butter, chilled and cut into 1-inch pieces
	Salt and freshly ground black pepper to taste

Wine Steamed Oysters in Curry Sauce

This dish is so simple to prepare, yet extremely elegant and delicious. Serve with crusty bread to mop up extra sauce. Steam the oysters in a German Auslesse or other medium-sweet white wine, such as a Johannisberg Riesling. Make sure the oysters are well scrubbed.

Serves 4

32	extra small or small oysters in the shell
4	tablespoons (1/2 stick) butter
3	shallots, minced
1	cup medium-sweet white wine
1	cup creme fraiche or sour cream
2	teaspoons curry powder
2	teaspoons fresh lemon juice
1/4	cup chopped fresh cilantro

Scrub the oysters thoroughly with a stiff brush under cold, running water. Place the butter in a saucepan large enough to hold the mussels and melt over medium heat. Add the shallots and cook, stirring occasionally, until softened, about 3 minutes. Add the wine and the oysters, deep cupped shell down. Increase the heat to high, cover and cook, shaking the pan occasionally, until the oysters open, about 10 minutes.

Remove the oysters with a slotted spoon and open any that haven't opened with an oyster knife. Shuck the steamed oysters and set aside. Strain the liquid into a bowl, wipe out the pan, then return the liquid to the pan. Bring the liquid to a boil, then whisk in the creme fraiche and curry powder. Reduce the heat to medium-low and add lemon juice. Simmer, stirring often, for about 5 minutes. Taste and adjust the seasonings as necessary. Return the oysters to the pot and stir to reheat. Serve broth and oysters in bowls. Sprinkle with chopped cilantro.

Recommended wines: Chardonnay, Riesling, Gewurztraminer.

Oysters Poached in Champagne
with Cucumbers and Whipped Cream Glaze

Shaffer City Oyster Bar and Grill, New York, NY

Owner A. Jay Shaffer recommends serving these elegant bivalves with a rich premier cru Chablis, preferably one from Fourchaume. For this recipe, he prefers large European Flat oysters.

Preheat oven to 250° F. Scrub the oysters and shuck them, reserving their deep cupped shells. Set the shells on a baking sheet lined with rock salt and place in the oven to warm. Bring the Champagne to a simmer in a saucepan over medium heat. Add the cucumbers and the oysters and poach gently for about 3 minutes, until oysters plump. Drain the oysters and cucumbers. Remove the oyster shells from the oven. Line each oyster shell with julienned cucumber and top with an oyster.

Preheat broiler. Beat the egg yolks in an electric mixer until pale and thick. Whip the cream until soft peaks form. Fold the whipped cream into the egg yolks; season to taste with salt and white pepper. Spoon a tablespoonful of whipped cream sauce over each oyster. Sprinkle with cayenne pepper and place oysters under the broiler, 6-inches from the heat, until golden brown. Serve hot.

Recommended wines: Champagne or sparkling wine, Chardonnay.

Serves 4

- 32 large oysters in the shell
- 2-1/2 cups Champagne or sparkling wine
- 1-1/2 cucumbers, peeled and julienned
- 3 egg yolks
- 2 cups whipping cream
  Salt and white pepper to taste
  Cayenne pepper to sprinkle over oysters
  Rock salt to line baking sheet

The Amorous Oyster
By Gary Faessler

When our briny waters heave and swell with the summer's sun,
The chilly oyster's ivory body becomes amorous and flushed.
Yearning for love and seduction.
With beating heart,
It's delicate black gills flutter
The oyster becomes prey to passion,
Longing to mix with another.

They forget to eat and can't digest
Only hunger to spawn, to woo, to nest
Spatting and spawning, spawning and spattng
The mollusk tired from such fervent loving on seaweed lies
It's frenzied energy spent
Flaccid and sated like all men
Following such pleasure heaven-sent.

Oysters Poached in Champagne and Brie Cheese

Shoalwater Restaurant, Seaview, WA

"This is a rich and beautiful dish," say owners Tony and Ann Kishner. "Even people who aren't great oyster fans love it."

Combine the Champagne, saffron, basil and cayenne in a large saucepan. Bring to a simmer over medium heat. Add the oysters and their liquor. Poach the oysters until the are plump and firm to the touch, about 2 to 3 minutes. Using a slotted spoon, transfer the oysters to 4 warmed serving plates.

Increase heat to high and reduce the poaching liquid by half (to about 1/2 cup). Whisk together the sour cream and whipping cream. Stir into the poaching liquid and heat until mixture begins to simmer. Slice the Brie into 1-inch pieces and add to the simmering sauce. Whisk the sauce until the cheese has melted. Pour over the warm oysters and serve at once.

Recommended wine: Champagne or sparkling wine, Sauvignon Blanc.

Serves 4

- 32 small or medium oysters, shucked, reserving liquor
- 1 cup Champagne or sparkling wine
- 1/2 teaspoon saffron threads
- 1/2 teaspoon dried basil
  Pinch of cayenne pepper (or to taste)
- 1/2 cup sour cream
- 1/2 cup whipping cream
- 4 ounces Brie cheese, trimmed of rind

Low Country Oysters with Mushrooms

This recipe hails from Mrs. Thomas A. Huguenin of Charleston, South Carolina, who first contributed her recipe to "Charleston Receipts," compiled and edited by the Junior League of Charleston, Inc. She serves these creamy oysters from a chafing dish, to spoon over triangles of hot buttered toast. Served with scrambled eggs on the side, this is perfect for a Champagne brunch.

Serves 4

- 32 small or medium oysters, shucked, reserving liquor
- 4 tablespoons butter
- 1/2 pound fresh mushrooms, sliced
- 1/2 cup chopped roasted red pepper or pimento
- 1/4 cup all-purpose flour
- 2 cups whipping cream
- Salt and freshly ground black pepper to taste

Melt the butter in a skillet over medium heat. Add the mushrooms and red peppers and cook, about 10 minutes, until the vegetables have softened. Whisk the flour into the pan, stirring constantly. Gradually add the cream, whisking constantly, until the sauce begins to thicken. Season to taste with salt and pepper. Meanwhile, in a separate pan, simmer the oysters in their own liquor over medium heat, until the oysters begin to plump and edges begin to curl, about 3 minutes. Gently stir the oysters into the mushroom sauce. If desired, transfer to a warmed chafing dish. Serve hot over buttered toast.

Recommended wines: Pinot Gris, Chardonnay, Champagne or sparkling wine.

Xinh's Oyster Saute in Asian Sauce

Xinh's Clam & Oyster House, Shelton, WA

Before opening her own restaurant, Owner and Chef Xinh (pronounced Zin) Dwelley was renowned as the five-time winner of the West Coast Oyster Shucking Championship. A native of Vietnam, Xinh was employed by Taylor Shellfish Farms, the largest shellfish grower/processor in the West, when her culinary talents were first discovered. Cooking on camp stoves, for visiting customers and Taylor employees, Xinh worked her magic, combining fresh shellfish with Asian flavors. This Oyster Saute is one of her specialties.

In a large saucepan, bring 1 quart of salted water to a boil. Add the oysters and simmer gently for 2 to 3 minutes, until oysters plump. Drain oysters and set aside.

Heat the butter in a large skillet over medium heat. Add the garlic, onion, lemon grass, celery and red and green peppers. Cook 2 minutes, stirring often. Add the hoisen sauce, oyster sauce, sherry, lemon juice, sesame oil and soy sauce, mixing well. Gently stir in the oysters, green onion and cilantro. Season with black pepper. Cook, stirring gently until oysters are heated through. Serve warm with steamed rice.

Serves 4

- 32 medium oysters, shucked and drained
- 2 tablespoons butter or vegetable oil
- 3 garlic cloves, minced
- 1/2 onion, chopped
- 1 teaspoon minced fresh lemon grass
- 2 ribs celery, thinly sliced
- 1/2 red bell pepper, seeded and sliced
- 1/2 green bell pepper, seeded and sliced
- 1 tablespoon hoisen sauce
- 1 tablespoon oyster sauce
- 1 tablespoon sherry
  Juice of 1/2 fresh lemon
- 1 tablespoon sesame oil
- 1 tablespoon soy sauce
- 3 tablespoons chopped green onion
- 2 tablespoons chopped fresh cilantro
  Freshly ground black pepper to taste
- 4 cups steamed rice

Oyster Cakes
with Caper-Cayenne Mayonnaise

Packed with sweet oysters, these savory cakes, created by Marie Rizzio of Fraverse City, Michigan, took the grand prize at the 14th annual National Oyster Cook-Off in Leonardtown, Maryland. Marie serves the golden cakes on a bed of shredded lettuce and tops them with Caper-Cayenne Mayonnaise.

Serves 4

- 1 pint medium oysters, shucked and drained
- 1/2 cup bread crumbs, seasoned with
- 1 teaspoon salt and freshly ground black pepper
- 3 green onions, minced
- 1 garlic clove, minced
- 2 tablespoons minced fresh parsley
- 1/4 cup grated Parmesan cheese
- 2 large eggs, lightly beaten
  Vegetable oil for frying

Caper-Cayenne Mayonnaise:

- 3/4 cup mayonnaise
- 1 tablespoon half-and-half
- 2 tablespoons capers, finely chopped
- 1/4 teaspoon cayenne pepper, or to taste

Rinse the oysters and pat them dry on paper towels. Roughly chop the oysters and place in a large mixing bowl. Add the seasoned bread crumbs, green onions, garlic, parsley, Parmesan cheese and eggs. Form the mixture into cakes, about 3-inches across and 1-inch thick. Chill, uncovered, about 30 minutes, or until firm. Meanwhile, prepare the Caper-Cayenne Mayonnaise.

To cook the oyster cakes, heat 1/4-inch of vegetable oil in a heavy skillet over medium-high heat. Add the oyster cakes, being careful not to crowd them. Brown the cakes on both sides, about 3 to 4 minutes per side. Serve cakes on a bed of shredded lettuce with Caper-Cayenne Mayonnaise.

Combine all the ingredients in a small bowl, blending thoroughly. Cover and keep chilled in the refrigerator until serving time.

Recommended beverages: Chilled beer, Sauvignon Blanc, Semillon.

Oyster Cakes with Remoulade Sauce

Shuckers at The Four Seasons Olympic Hotel, Seattle, WA

In this creative recipe, Executive Chef Gavin Stephenson sandwiches plump oysters between layers of scallop-oyster mousse, rolls them in breadcrumbs and fries them until they are crisp and golden. A spicy Remoulade Sauce seasoned with mustard and capers adds the finishing touch.

SHUCKERS

A FINE SEAFOOD TRADITION

Make the mousse: In a food processor or blender, puree the scallops and oysters until smooth. Slowly add the cream. Season with salt and pepper.

Spread out a sheet of waxed paper. Drop a spoonful of mousse mixture onto the waxed paper. Repeat, until you have 12 evenly spaced spoonfuls of mousse (reserving 1/2 of the mixture). Place an oyster on top of each spoonful of mousse. Top each oyster with another spoonful of mousse. Carefully lift up each mousse covered oyster with a spoon and place them in the prepared bread crumbs. Gently cover the oyster cakes with crumbs.

Pat each mousse covered oyster into a round cake and set aside. Heat a large skillet over medium-high heat. Fill 1/8-inch deep with vegetable oil. Fry the cakes until golden brown on both sides, about 2 minutes per side. Serve hot topped with Remoulade Sauce.

To make the Remoulade Sauce: Combine all the ingredients together in a mixing bowl.

Recommended wines: Chardonnay, Pinot Gris, Pinot Blanc, Champagne or sparkling wine.

Serves 2

Scallop Oyster mousse:

- 6 ounces scallops
- 3 ounces oysters, shucked
- 1/4 cup whipping cream
  - Salt and freshly ground pepper to taste
- 12 medium oysters, shucked and drained
- 2 cups bread crumbs
  - Vegetable oil for cooking

Remoulade Sauce:

- 1 cup mayonnaise
- 1 tablespoon whole grain mustard
- 2 teaspoons Dijon mustard
- 1 teaspoon white wine vinegar
- 2 teaspoons capers, chopped
- 2 tablespoons chopped fresh parsley
- 1 tablespoon minced red onion
  - Salt and freshly ground black pepper to taste

The Joy of Oysters

Oyster, Bacon and Potato Hash

Served with scrambled eggs on the side, and plenty of hot, buttered toast, this is a perfect meal for breakfast, lunch or dinner.

Serves 4

24 small or medium oysters, shucked and drained, reserving liquor
8 slices bacon, sliced into 1/2-inch pieces
8 medium new red potatoes, diced, cooked and drained
2 tablespoons vegetable oil
1 onion, diced
2 garlic cloves, minced
2 tablespoons minced fresh parsley
Salt and white pepper to taste
Few drops hot red pepper sauce
Sour cream
Salsa

Place the oysters and their liquor in a saucepan over medium heat. Bring to a simmer and cook until the oysters plump and their edges begin to curl, about 2 to 3 minutes. Drain the oysters and cut them into 1/2-inch pieces. Cook the bacon in a skillet over medium heat. When crisp, drain the bacon on paper towels, reserving 2 teaspoons bacon grease. Return the skillet to the heat, add the vegetable oil and, when hot, add the onions and garlic, cooking them until tender, about 5 minutes. Stir in the cooked potatoes, mixing well. Cook, stirring occasionally, until the potatoes are golden brown on all sides. Stir in parsley and season to taste with salt, pepper and hot red pepper sauce.

Gently fold the oysters and the reserved bacon into the potatoes. Press the mixture down in the pan with a spoon or spatula and cook over medium heat, until the hash is golden brown and lightly crusted on the bottom. Turn the hash, mixing in the browned parts, press down and cook 5 minutes more. Serve hot topped with sour cream and salsa.

Recommended beverages: Bloody Marys, Champagne or sparkling wine.

Oysters Sauteed with Prosciutto and Browned Garlic Butter

Stephanie Inn, Cannon Beach, OR

Located on the rugged Oregon Coast, the Stephanie Inn overlooks one of the world's most dramatic coastlines. Specializing in innovative Northwest fare, Chef John Newman gains inspiration from fresh local seafoods, including his favorite Willapa Bay oysters. Here, they are topped with a golden browned butter sauce and sliced prosciutto.

In a shallow dish, combine flour, cornmeal, salt and pepper. Dredge oysters lightly in the mixture, shaking off excess flour. Heat oil in a skillet over medium-high heat. Gently add the oysters and cook on both sides until golden brown, about 5 minutes per side. Remove the oysters from the oil with a slotted spoon and drain on paper towels. Cover to keep warm.

Discard the cooking oil and wipe the skillet clean with paper towels. Place the skillet over medium-high heat, add the butter and cook until the butter sizzles and turns golden grown. Reduce heat to low, stir in the minced garlic, lemon juice and prosciutto. Place 12 oysters on each warmed serving plate. Drizzle with browned butter, distributing prosciutto evenly over the oysters. Top each oyster with a sprinkling of chopped chives. Serve hot.

Recommended wines: Champagne or sparkling wine, Chardonnay, Pinot Blanc, Pinot Gris.

Serves 2

- 24 small or medium oysters, shucked and drained
- 2 tablespoons all purpose flour
- 2 tablespoons yellow cornmeal
- 1/2 teaspoon salt
- 1/4 teaspoon freshly ground black pepper
- 2 tablespoons vegetable oil for sauteing
- 3 tablespoons unsalted butter
- 1 garlic clove, minced
- 1 tablespoon fresh lemon juice
- 2 ounces prosciutto, sliced into 1/2-inch pieces
- 1 tablespoon finely chopped chives

Corn and Oyster Pancakes

Top these tender buttermilk pancakes, filled with plump oysters, corn and minced red pepper, with sour cream and salsa. For a special treat, skip the salsa and top the sour cream with a teaspoon or so of your favorite caviar. Serve for breakfast or brunch.

Serves 3 - 4

- 12 medium oysters, shucked and drained
- 1/2 cup fresh or frozen corn kernels
- 1/2 cup finely diced red bell pepper
- 1/4 cup finely chopped chives
- Sour cream
- Salsa or caviar
- 1 recipe buttermilk pancake batter

Lightly grease a griddle or large skillet and heat over medium heat. Chop the oysters into 3 to 4 pieces each. Combine the oysters in a mixing bowl with the corn, red peppers and half of the chives. Ladle pancake batter onto the hot griddle to form 4 small pancakes and top each pancake with a portion of the oyster and vegetable mixture. Cook until the edges of the pancakes are dry and bubbles form on top, being careful not to overcook them. Turn the cakes and continue cooking until the bottoms are golden brown and the batter is cooked through. Remove from the skillet and repeat until the batter and oysters are used up.

To serve: Place hot pancakes on each serving dish, overlapping slightly. Top with sour cream, the remaining chives, and salsa or caviar.

Buttermilk Pancake Batter:

Makes 10 - 12 small pancakes
- 1 cup sifted cake flour
- 1 teaspoon sugar
- 3/4 teaspoon baking powder
- 1/2 teaspoon baking soda
- 1/2 teaspoon salt
- 1 cup buttermilk
- 2 tablespoons melted butter

Resift the flour with the sugar, baking powder, baking soda and salt into a mixing bowl. Whisk in the buttermilk and melted butter, just until blended. If necessary, thin with a bit of extra buttermilk.

Recommended wine: Champagne or sparkling wine.

Sauteed Oysters with Green Onion Aioli
Stephanie Inn, Cannon Beach, OR

Seasoned with fresh green onions (scallions), this garlicky aioli adds a fresh bite of heat to sweet, briny oysters. Serve with a crisp green salad and crusty bread. The aioli will keep up to 5 days stored in the refrigerator.

Drain the oysters on paper towels. Sprinkle the oysters with salt and pepper. Heat 2 tablespoons vegetable oil in a skillet over medium-high heat. When the oil is sizzling, quickly place the oysters in the pan, cooking in batches if necessary, so you don't overcrowd the pan. Cook the oysters about 2 to 3 minutes on each side, until golden brown. Keep warm in a 200° F. oven. Serve hot with Green Onion Aioli.

To make the aioli: In the bowl of a food processor, process the egg yolks until pale and thick. Gradually add the lemon juice, then the garlic. Slowly add the olive oil, scraping down sides as necessary. Transfer the mixture to a mixing bowl. Stir in the chopped green onions. Season to taste with salt and white pepper. Cover and store in the refrigerator up to 5 days.

Recommended wines: Sauvignon Blanc, Semillon.

Serves 4

32 medium oysters, shucked and drained
   Salt and freshly ground black pepper
2 tablespoons vegetable oil for cooking

Green Onion Aioli:

Makes about 1 1/2 cups

3 large egg yolks
   juice of 1 lemon
1 cup extra virgin olive oil
3 garlic cloves, minced
1 bunch green onions, finely chopped
   Salt and white pepper to taste

Stir Fried Oysters in Black Bean Sauce

Bathed in luxuriously thick Black Bean Sauce,
freshly shucked oysters take on new dimensions. To complete the meal,
serve steamed Jasmine rice and sauteed long beans. The black bean sauce can be made
up to 5 days in advance and stored in the refrigerator.

Serves 4

32 extra small or small oysters, shucked and drained, reserving liquor

Black Bean Sauce:

1 tablespoon peanut or olive oil
1/2 cup fermented black beans, rinsed and drained
1 garlic clove, minced
1 shallot, minced
1 tablespoon grated fresh ginger
pinch of crushed red peppers
3 dashes hot red pepper sauce
1 ounce sweet sherry
1 cup water or water mixed with oyster liquor
1/8 cup sugar
1/2 cup soy sauce
3 tablespoons cornstarch mixed with 1/2 cup cold water (use as needed)
Sliced green onions and toasted sesame seeds, for garnish

In a saucepan over medium-high heat, saute the black beans, garlic, shallots, ginger, and crushed red pepper in the oil for about 5 minutes, or until the garlic and shallots are tender. Stir in the sherry, scraping down the sides of the pan. Add 1 cup water, sugar and soy sauce. Bring the sauce to a boil and stir in enough of the cornstarch mixture to thicken slightly.

Pour the Black Bean Sauce into a wok or large kettle and bring to a boil over high heat. Gently stir in the oysters, cooking about 5 minutes, or until oysters are plump and heated through. Transfer to a large serving bowl and garnish with diced green onions and toasted sesame seeds.

Recommended beverages: Sake, Riesling, Gewurztraminer, Champagne or sparkling wine.

Pan Fried Oysters
Oysters Out West, Bay City, OR

Located on a pier overlooking Netarts Bay and the oyster beds of Pacific Oyster Company, Oysters Out West is a charming spot to enjoy fresh oysters and other just-caught seafood. The secret to the Chef's crisp fried oysters lies in letting them dry for an hour after breading, to remove extra moisture. Serve the oysters with spicy cocktail sauce, aioli, or Jalapeno Tartar Sauce (page 189).

Combine the cracker meal, salt, pepper and cayenne in a shallow pan. Dip the oysters first in the beaten egg, then dredge in the cracker mixture. Place the oysters on a baking sheet, leaving plenty of space between the oysters. Cover lightly with plastic wrap and refrigerate for at least one hour to dry. Heat 1/8-inch to 1/4-inch vegetable oil in a heavy skillet. When oil is almost smoking, about 375° F., add the oysters and fry on both sides, about 2 to 3 minutes, until golden brown. Drain the oysters on paper towels. Serve hot.

Serves 4

32 medium oysters, shucked and drained
2 eggs, beaten
2 cups cracker meal
1 teaspoon salt
1/2 teaspoon black pepper
1/4 teaspoon cayenne pepper
Vegetable oil for frying

Deep South Browned Oysters

In this old southern recipe, a brown roux is added to cooked oyster juices to make a fantastic, yet simple topping for sauteed oysters. Serve with coleslaw and garlic bread.

Serves 4

32 extra small or small oysters, shucked and drained
4 tablespoons butter
1-1/2 tablespoons all purpose flour
Juice of one lemon
Salt and freshly ground black pepper to taste
1 teaspoon Worcestershire sauce
Dash of hot red pepper sauce, or to taste

Heat 2 tablespoons of the butter in a heavy skillet over medium-high heat. Dredge the oysters in flour, shaking to dislodge extra flour. Brown the oysters in the butter, turning until golden brown on both sides, about 2 to 3 minutes per side. Remove oysters from the pan with a slotted spoon or tongs. Set oysters in a warmed serving dish and cover to keep warm. Strain the frying liquid through a sieve and reserve. Wipe the skillet clean with a paper towel. Melt the remaining butter over medium heat. Add the flour, stirring constantly, until the flour is incorporated and the mixture turns golden brown, about 5 to 8 minutes. Gradually whisk in the oyster-frying liquid and simmer until liquid is incorporated. Remove the sauce from the heat. Add the lemon juice and Worcestershire sauce, then season to taste with salt, pepper and hot pepper sauce. Pour the hot sauce over the cooked oysters. Serve at once.

Recommended wines: Chardonnay, Pinot Gris, Chenin Blanc, Semillon aged Sur Lie.

Louisiana Pan Fried Oysters
with Chili Corn Sauce and Black Bean Salsa
The Brooklyn Seafood, Steak & Oyster House, Seattle, WA

Coated with a blend of spicy seasonings, these crisp fried oysters are served on a bed of Chili Corn Sauce spiked with tequila, and topped with a colorful Black Bean Salsa. Both the Chili Corn Sauce and Black Bean Salsa can be prepared up to 3 days in advance. Reheat the Chili Corn Sauce before serving.

Combine all the ingredients for the Cajun flour in a mixing bowl, blending well. Dredge the oysters in the Cajun Flour, shaking off excess flour. Heat a large skillet over medium high heat. Just before oil starts to smoke, add the oysters. Cook, turning once, until golden brown on both sides, about 2 minutes per side. Drain oysters on paper towels and keep warm in a 200° F. oven.

Place the cooked oysters on a plate lined with hot Chili Corn Sauce and top with Black Bean Salsa.

Serves 4 to 6

30 medium oysters, shucked
and drained

Cajun Flour:

1 tablespoon cayenne pepper
1 tablespoon onion powder
1 tablespoon garlic powder
1 teaspoon ground cumin
1 teaspoon chili powder
1/2 teaspoon dried thyme
1/2 teaspoon dried oregano
1 tablespoon paprika
1 cup masa or fine cornmeal
1 cup all-purpose flour
 Vegetable oil for frying

Heat the oil in a skillet over medium heat. When hot, stir in the peppers, onions, garlic and corn, stirring often until vegetables are tender, about 10 minutes. Increase heat to medium-high; pour in the tequila, bring to a boil and simmer until liquid is reduced to 1/3 cup. Note: If tequila flames, remove from heat and put out flames by covering pan with a lid. Stir in the cream and let the sauce simmer until slightly thickened, about 10 minutes. Serve hot, or cover and store in the refrigerator. Reheat before serving.

Chili Corn Sauce:

2 tablespoons vegetable oil
1/2 red bell pepper, seeded and
 finely diced
1/2 green bell pepper, seeded and
 finely diced
2 green onions, finely diced
1 garlic clove, minced
4 cups corn kernels, fresh or frozen
1 cup tequila
4 cups whipping cream

Black Bean Salsa:

- 3 cups cooked black beans, drained
- 1/2 red onion, finely diced
- 1 bunch fresh cilantro leaves, roughly chopped
- 1 garlic clove, minced
- 2 tablespoons fresh lime juice
- 1/2 cup corn kernels, fresh or frozen
- 2 tablespoons extra virgin olive oil
- Salt and freshly ground black pepper to taste

Combine all ingredients in a mixing bowl. Let sit at least 1/2 hour to marry flavors. Serve chilled or at room temperature.

Recommended beverages: Chilled beer, Sauvignon Blanc, Semillon.

Seafood Risotto with Pistou

I was extremely fortunate to work on a cookbook with Chateau Ste. Michelle Winery's Executive Chef, John Sarich. This recipe didn't make it into our cookbook, but it definitely became a favorite at our table. John prefers Arborio rice for this dish. It's an Italian rice that, when cooked, contributes a wonderful creamy texture to the dish. The cooked rice should be tender, with a slightly firm texture.

Half Shell Lori

Heat a skillet over medium heat. Add the olive oil and, when hot, stir in the fennel, onion, red and yellow peppers, and garlic. Cook, stirring often, until the vegetables are very soft, about 15 minutes. Add 1/2 cup of the chicken stock and the wine. Simmer rapidly until the liquid is reduced by half, about 5 minutes. Stir in the paprika, saffron, lemon zest and rice, stirring until all of the liquid is absorbed. Add another 1/2 cup of stock and stir until the liquid is absorbed again. Repeat, adding broth 1/2 cup at a time, stirring after each addition until liquid is absorbed. When finished, the rice should be cooked al dente — tender but slightly firm.

Add the seafood to the rice mixture. Stir and cover until the clams open, about 5 to 10 minutes. If necessary, add more stock. The rice should be quite moist. Spoon into serving bowls and garnish with Pistou.

Serves 4

- 24 extra small oysters, shucked and drained
- 1/2 pound Manila or steamer clams, scrubbed
- 1 dozen prawns, peeled and deveined
- 2 tablespoons olive oil
- 1 fennel bulb, diced
- 1 medium yellow onion, diced
- 1 red bell pepper, diced
- 1 yellow bell pepper, diced
- 2 garlic cloves, minced
- 2 quarts chicken or fish stock, approximate
- 1/8 cup Pinot Gris, or other dry white wine
- 2-1/2 cups Arborio rice
- 1/8 teaspoon paprika
  Pinch of saffron threads
- 1/8 teaspoon lemon zest
  Salt to taste

Pistou:

Pistou is a pungent garlic and herb sauce that John discovered on his first trip to Provence. In addition to using Pistou as a topping for risotto, he also stirs it into soups and stews, tosses it with pasta and Marinara sauce, and spoons it over fresh sliced tomatoes. Covered tightly, Pistou will keep up to 1 week in the refrigerator.

Makes 3/4 cup

1/2 cup fresh basil leaves
1/2 cup fresh Italian parsley
1/4 cup fresh oregano leaves
3 garlic cloves
3 green onions
1/8 cup extra virgin olive oil
1 teaspoon Balsamic vinegar
Pinch of salt
1/8 cup freshly grated Parmesan cheese

Finely chop the basil, parsley, oregano, garlic and green onions together on a cutting board. Place the herbs in a bowl. Stir in the olive oil, Balsamic vinegar, salt and Parmesan cheese. Let the mixture stand for 15 minutes before using to blend flavors.

Recommended wines: Pinot Gris, Chenin Blanc, Pinot Blanc, Chardonnay.

Spicy Cornmeal Fried Oysters with Smoked Chili and Lime Aioli

Friday Harbor House, Friday Harbor, WA

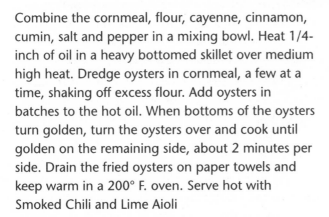

Early each fall, Chefs Laurie Paul and Tim Barrette receive a case of freshly picked chilies from their friends Steve and Linnea Benzel of Nootka Rose Farm on nearby Waldron Island. "We smoke the chilies, combine them with vinegar and other ingredients, and make our yearly supply of hot sauce," say Laurie and Tim. They use the hot sauce to flavor this aioli, which they serve with fried oysters. If you don't have smoked chili hot sauce on hand, you can substitute smoked paprika, or chipotles (which are actually smoked jalapenos). In order to get a really crisp crust on the oysters, Laurie says it is important to bread them just before frying.

Combine the cornmeal, flour, cayenne, cinnamon, cumin, salt and pepper in a mixing bowl. Heat 1/4-inch of oil in a heavy bottomed skillet over medium high heat. Dredge oysters in cornmeal, a few at a time, shaking off excess flour. Add oysters in batches to the hot oil. When bottoms of the oysters turn golden, turn the oysters over and cook until golden on the remaining side, about 2 minutes per side. Drain the fried oysters on paper towels and keep warm in a 200° F. oven. Serve hot with Smoked Chili and Lime Aioli

Combine all ingredients, except the corn oil and cilantro, in the bowl of a food processor. Process for about 30 seconds, to combine all ingredients. With the motor running, gradually add corn oil in a slow, steady stream, until the mixture emulsifies into a medium-thick sauce. Transfer aioli to a serving dish, stir in cilantro. Serve with pan fried oysters.

Recommended beverages: chilled beer, Semillon or Sauvignon Blanc.

Serves 4

- 32 medium oysters, shucked and drained
- 1 cup finely ground cornmeal
- 1/2 cup unbleached all purpose flour
- 1/2 teaspoon cayenne pepper
- 1/2 teaspoon ground cinnamon
- 1/2 teaspoon ground cumin
- 1 teaspoon salt
- 1/4 teaspoon freshly ground black pepper
- Corn oil for frying

Smoked Chile and Lime Aioli

This will keep in the refrigerator up to one week, makes about 3 cups

- 3 large egg yolks
- 1 whole egg
- 1 roasted red pepper, seeded and diced
- Grated zest of 1 lime
- Juice of 3 limes
- 3 garlic cloves, minced
- 1 tablespoon salt, or to taste
- 3 tablespoons salsa
- 2 tablespoons smoked paprika (available in specialty food stores), or 2 tablespoons diced chipotles
- 1 teaspoon white pepper
- 2-1/2 cups corn oil
- 2 tablespoons chopped fresh cilantro

Carpetbagger Filet Mignon

The Brooklyn Seafood, Steak & Oyster House, Seattle, WA

Here is Chef Art Wirz's rendition of a classic oyster dish. At The Brooklyn, the oyster-stuffed filets are topped with a silky, but labor intensive Lemon-Thyme Demi Glace, but at home, you can substitute Lemon Thyme Butter (recipe follows). Serve with rice or potatoes and a green salad or steamed vegetables.

Serves 6

6   8-ounce filet mignon steaks
12 small oysters, shucked and drained
6   strips bacon
    Salt and freshly ground black pepper
12 6-inch bamboo skewers
4   ounces vegetable oil

Lemon Thyme Butter

4   ounces (1/2 stick) unsalted butter, softened
1   tablespoon fresh thyme leaves, chopped
2   teaspoons fresh lemon juice

Cut a pocket into each filet by inserting a sharp paring knife into one side of the filet and slicing horizontally, cutting just far enough to insert two small oysters. Place a medium skillet over high heat. Add 2 tablespoons oil. When the oil is hot, carefully add the oysters, shake the pan constantly to keep the oysters from sticking. Cook about 30 seconds, or just until the oysters begin to plump. Remove from the heat and cool slightly. Stuff each filet with 2 oysters, then wrap each filet with a strip of bacon. Use bamboo skewers to hold the bacon in place. Season steaks with salt and pepper.

Place the filets under a pre-heated broiler, 6-inches from the heat. Cook to desired doneness. Meanwhile, cream the butter with the thyme and lemon juice. Top each filet with 1 tablespoon of Lemon Thyme butter. Serve hot.

Recommended wines: Pinot Noir, Chardonnay, Champagne or sparkling wine

Fried Oysters Rector Style with Crab and Lobster

Shaw's Crab House, Chicago, IL

Located in the heart of downtown Chicago, Shaw's ambience is reminiscent of days-gone-by, when over-sized martinis were the drink of choice, and rousing conversation was considered entertainment. Rolled in a savory mixture of fresh crab, lobster and bread crumbs, these crisp, fried oysters are sure to spark conversation around your table. If you like, use just crab or lobster meat instead of a combination. The oysters can be prepared up to 2 hours in advance, and kept chilled, covered, in the refrigerator.

Season the oysters with salt and pepper and roll in the cracker crumbs. In a mixing bowl, whisk together the eggs, mustard, Worcestershire sauce and 2 tablespoons oyster liquor. In a separate bowl, mix together the crab, lobster and bread crumbs.

Heat a skillet over medium-high heat. Add the oil and butter. Dip the oysters one-at-a-time in the egg batter, then roll them in the crab mixture to coat. With your fingers, pack the crab mixture onto each oyster. When the oil is sizzling, add the oysters, working in batches if necessary, and fry on both sides until golden brown, about 2 minutes per side. Serve on warm plates garnished with parsley and lemon slices.

Recommended wines: Chardonnay, Champagne or sparkling wine, Pinot Gris.

Serves 2

- 16 medium oysters, shucked and drained, reserving liquor
- 30 Saltine crackers, finely crushed
- 2 eggs, beaten
- 1 teaspoon Dijon mustard
- 1 teaspoon Worcestershire Sauce
- 1 cup crab meat, shredded
- 1 cup lobster meat, shredded
- 3/4 cup breadcrumbs
- 2 tablespoons vegetable oil, such as Saffola
- 1 tablespoon butter
- 1/4 up chopped fresh parsley lemon slices

Creamed Tarragon Oysters in Puff Pastry Shells

This ethereal concoction is something I used to serve to special guests when I worked as a chef. It's delicious served with steamed asparagus and a glass or two of Champagne.

Half Shell Lori

Serves 6

24 extra small oysters, shucked, reserving liquor
2 sheets (8 1/2 X 13-inches) puff pastry, chilled
1 egg, beaten
2 tablespoons butter
2 garlic cloves, minced
1/2 cup finely chopped leeks
2 cups sliced mushrooms
1/2 cup diced red pepper
2 tablespoons chopped fresh tarragon
1/2 cup Champagne
1 cup whipping cream
8 tablespoons (1 stick) unsalted butter, chilled and cut into 1-inch pieces
Salt and freshly ground black pepper to taste
Few drops hot red pepper sauce

Preheat oven to 400° F. Place the two sheets of puff pastry one atop the other, and cut into 3-inch squares. Place the squares on a baking sheet, leaving space between them. Brush the top of the pastry lightly with beaten egg. Bake the pastry until it is golden brown, about 12 to 15 minutes. Keep warm, or re-heat before serving.

Melt the butter in a heavy saucepan over medium-high heat. Add the garlic, leeks and mushrooms, red pepper, and tarragon. Cook, about 10 minutes, or until vegetables are softened. Stir in the Champagne. Add the cream, bring to a rapid simmer and cook, until the liquid is reduced to 1/2 volume, about 12 minutes. Add the oysters and the oyster liquor, mixing well. Cook, about 2 to 3 minutes, or until the oysters plump. Gently swirl in the chilled butter, 1 to 2 tablespoons at a time, constantly swirling the pan until all the butter is incorporated. Remove sauce from the heat; season to taste with salt, pepper and Tabasco. Place a pastry square in the center of each serving plate, remove the top half of the pastry and fill with oysters and cream sauce. Top with the remaining pastry and serve hot.

Recommended wines: Champagne or sparkling wine, Chardonnay.

Pan Fried Oysters with Jack Daniel's Sauce
Elliott's Oyster House, Seattle, WA

Located on Pier 56 along Seattle's bustling waterfront, Elliott's Oyster House is one of Seattle's top seafood restaurants. A twenty-one foot oyster bar features up to forty varieties of oysters at a time. Whether they are fried, baked, or served on the half shell, Elliott's customers definitely love oysters. One elbow bender consumed 262 oysters at one sitting — setting a record for Elliott's.

Mix flour, salt and pepper together. Heat cooking oil until very hot in a flat sauté pan. Dredge the oysters in seasoned flour, shaking off any excess and place in the hot oil. Cook oysters until edges start to curl. Flip the oysters over and continue to cook until crispy and golden brown. Remove from heat and drain. Serve immediately with warm Jack Daniel's Sauce.

Serves 4

- 36 extra small oysters, shucked and drained
- 3/4 cup cooking oil (such as peanut or Canola oil)
- 1 cup flour
- 2 teaspoons kosher or good quality sea salt
- 1/2 teaspoon freshly cracked black pepper
- 3/4 cup Jack Daniel's Sauce (recipe follows)

Blend together all ingredients in a sauce pan and heat until sugar has melted. Serve warm.

Jack Daniel's Sauce:

- 1/4 cup Dijon mustard
- 1-1/2 tablespoons soy sauce
- 1/4 cup Jack Daniel's Bourbon
- 2 teaspoons Worcestershire sauce
- 1/3 cup brown sugar

Oyster and Artichoke Casserole

There is something magical about the combination of artichokes and oysters. The sweet, nutty flavor of each ingredient seems to highlight the other. This is a great dish to make ahead and bake just before serving. The artichokes need to cook about 1 1/2 hours, so plan ahead. They can be cooked up to 2 days in advance.

Serves 6

36 small or medium oysters, shucked, reserving liquor
6 whole fresh artichokes
8 tablespoons (1 stick) butter
3 tablespoons all purpose flour
1 onion, diced
2 garlic cloves, minced
Reserved oyster liquor
Dry white wine, as needed
1/2 cup finely chopped parsley
1 teaspoon ground thyme
1/2 teaspoon ground nutmeg
1 teaspoon paprika
Juice of 1/2 lemon
Salt and white pepper to taste

2 cups bread crumbs seasoned with
1 teaspoon salt
1/2 teaspoon freshly ground black pepper
1/2 teaspoon garlic powder
1/4 cup freshly grated Asiago or Parmesan cheese

Place the artichokes in a large saucepan. Cover with salted water, bring to a boil and cook until tender, about 1 1/2 hours. Drain the artichokes and let them cool until they can be handled. Scrape the tender pulp from the artichoke leaves into a mixing bowl. Trim the heart and slice it into 1/2-inch pieces; add to the mixing bowl. Melt the butter in a skillet over medium heat. Whisk in the flour and cook, stirring constantly, until the mixture is smooth and well blended. Add the onion and garlic and cook until soft, about 4 minutes.

Preheat oven to 400° F. Pour the reserved oyster liquor into a measuring cup; add white wine, as necessary to make 2 cups. Gradually whisk the liquids into the onion mixture, stirring constantly. Stir in the parsley, thyme, nutmeg, paprika, lemon juice, salt and pepper to taste. Simmer gently for 15 minutes, stirring occasionally. Add the oysters and simmer, about 2 to 3 minutes, or until the oysters plump. Add the artichokes, mixing well. Spoon the mixture into 6 individual greased casserole dishes. Combine the bread crumbs with the seasonings and the grated cheese, and sprinkle over each casserole. Bake about 20 minutes, or until casseroles are bubbling and the crumb topping is golden brown. Serve hot.

Recommended wines: Sauvignon Blanc, Semillon.

Fried Oysters Served in the Shell with Sauteed Spinach and Chipotle Aioli

Shaffer City Oyster Bar and Grill, New York, NY

A. Jay Shaffer, owner of Shaffer City Oyster Bar and Grill, recently began harvesting his own "Shaffer Cove," oysters, which he fondly refers to as "our own little gems." Here is one of Jay's favorite recipes for " these briny little creations." Chipotle chilies are smoked jalapeno chiles, which come in a variety of different styles, including dried, canned and canned in sauce. For this recipe, look for canned Chipotles in sauce. To accompany this dish, Jay recommends a crisp Pinot Blanc or Sauvignon Blanc from New Zealand.

A. Jay Shaffer of Shaffer City

Scrub and shuck the oysters, reserving deep cupped shells. Drain the oysters on paper towels. Combine the semolina, flour, chili powder, cumin, cayenne and salt in a shallow pan. Dredge the oysters in the flour mixture, shaking off excess. Set on a cooking rack to dry slightly.

Mix the chipotles with the mayonnaise and garlic. Cover and refrigerate until ready to use.

Meanwhile, heat water in a skillet over medium high heat. When water is boiling, stir in spinach, shallots and garlic. Cover and steam about 3 minutes, or until spinach is tender. Drain; season with salt and pepper, and cover to keep warm.

To finish: Preheat oven to 200° F. Line serving plates with rock salt and place 8 oyster shells on each plate. Heat the shells in the oven. Meanwhile, heat the vegetable oil in a large skillet over medium-high heat. When sizzling, add the oysters (working in batches if necessary). Cook about 3 minutes on each side, until oysters are golden brown. Drain on paper towels and keep warm in the oven.

To serve: Fill each warm oyster shell with 1 to 2 tablespoons cooked spinach. Top with a hot fried oyster and a dollop of Chipotle Aioli.

Recommended wines: Pinot Blanc, Sauvignon Blanc.

Serves 4

- 32 medium to large oysters in the shell
  Rock salt to line serving plates
- 1/2 cup semolina flour
- 1 cup all purpose flour
- 2 tablespoons chili powder
- 2 teaspoons cumin
- 1/2 teaspoon cayenne pepper
- 1/2 teaspoon salt

Chipotle Aioli:

- 1/2 cup (8 ounces) canned chipotle chilies in sauce, rinsed and finely diced
- 1-1/2 cups homemade or prepared mayonnaise
- 1 garlic clove, minced

Spinach Saute:

- 1/4 cup water
- 1 cup finely chopped spinach
- 1 shallot, minced
- 1 garlic clove, minced
  Salt and freshly ground black pepper to taste

Salad of Field Greens with Crispy Fried Oysters Topped with Aioli and Bacon

Wildwood Restaurant & Bar, Portland, OR

Chef/ owner, Cory Schreiber, a James Beard Award recipient, comes from a long line of oyster growers and restaurateurs. His family has been involved in the Pacific Northwest oyster business since the mid 1800s with their Oregon Oyster Company. When Cory was born, his family had already ventured into the restaurant business, with what has since become a Northwest institution, Portland's Dan & Louis Oyster Bar. By age eleven, Cory had begun his restaurant career at the Oyster Bar. He opened his own restaurant, Wildwood, in 1994, after working with well known chefs across the country. With an emphasis on dishes that celebrate the freshness and flavor of regional Northwest foods, Wildwood has become nationally acclaimed as one of the country's top restaurants.

Note: At Wildwood, Cory serves this salad on a crepe seasoned with fresh herbs. To make herbed crepes, follow your favorite recipe for crepes, folding 1/4 cup finely chopped fresh tarragon, chives and Italian parsley into the batter. Both the Red Wine Vinaigrette and Aioli can be prepared up to five days in advance.

Serves 6

10 cups baby salad greens, washed and dried
12 slices bacon, cooked until crisp and drained on paper towels

Red Wine Vinaigrette:

1/3 cup extra virgin olive oil
3 tablespoons red wine vinegar
1 teaspoon Dijon mustard
1/2 teaspoon salt
1/2 teaspoon freshly ground black pepper

In a medium, non-reactive bowl, combine the Vinaigrette ingredients, mixing well. Cover and refrigerate up to five days. Shake or mix well before using.

In a small bowl, whisk together mayonnaise, milk, lemon juice and garlic. Cover and refrigerate until ready to use.

Aioli:

1/4 cup mayonnaise
2 tablespoons milk
1 tablespoon fresh lemon juice
1 garlic clove, minced

In a mixing bowl, combine the flour, cornmeal, cayenne and salt, mixing well. Toss several oysters at a time in the coating and place on a cooling rack to dry for about 15 minutes. Meanwhile, heat the oil in a heavy 12-inch skillet over medium-high heat. When the temperature reaches 350° F, fry the oysters in small batches, allowing 1 to 2 minutes per side, or until golden. Drain the oysters on paper towels and keep warm in a 200° F. oven along with the bacon. Repeat with remaining oysters.

Crispy Fried Oysters:

24 medium oysters, shucked and drained
1/4 cup all purpose flour
1/4 cup stone ground cornmeal
1/4 teaspoon cayenne pepper
1/4 teaspoon salt
1 cup canola oil

To assemble the salad: Toss the greens with the Red Wine Vinaigrette in a large salad bowl. (If using crepes, place one crepe on each of 6 plates.) Portion the greens onto each plate and top with three hot oysters. Place two strips of bacon over each serving and drizzle the oysters with aioli. Serve at once.

Recommended wines: Pinot Gris, Pinot Blanc, Chardonnay.

The Davis Family's Scalloped Oysters

*No one in Lori's extended family — the Davis family of Montana — can quite remember
if it was their Dad (Loren) or Mom (Florence) who cooked this creamy oyster dish
more often. What they do recall is that it was always one of their favorites.
It was their cousin, Dolores Halsted, who finally printed the recipe out
some years ago to include in the community's recipe booklet.*

Serves 4

1-1/2 cups crushed Saltine crackers
2 pints small oysters in their liquor
4 tablespoons (1/2 stick) unsalted butter
1 cup half-and-half
1/4 cup dry sherry

Preheat oven to 350° F. Lightly grease a 2-quart casserole dish. Sprinkle 1/2 cup of cracker crumbs over the bottom of the dish and top with half of the oysters and their liquor. Dot the oysters with one-third of the butter and pour 1/2 cup of the half-and-half over them.

Add another layer of cracker crumbs, oysters, butter, and half-and-half. Sprinkle with sherry, and top with the remaining cracker crumbs and butter. Bake for about 30 minutes, or until golden.

Recommended wines: Chenin Blanc, Pinot Blanc, Chardonnay.

Creamy Scalloped Oysters
Union Oyster House, Boston, MA

The oldest restaurant in Boston, and the oldest restaurant in continuous service in the United States, since its doors first opened in 1826, the historic Union Oyster House is currently owned by the Milano family. It was at Union Bay's famous oyster bar that Daniel Webster, a loyal customer and oyster lover, consumed his daily quota of three or more dozen oysters downed with tumblers of brandy and water. Served in their shells and topped with a cream sauce seasoned with white wine and Dijon mustard, this is Union's wonderful rendition of a classic dish — Scalloped Oysters.

Since   1826

America's Oldest Restaurant

To make the Cream Sauce: Melt the butter in a medium saucepan. Add the garlic and cook until softened, about 3 minutes. Stir in the white wine, mixing well. Add the cream, salt and pepper, Dijon mustard and thyme. Simmer rapidly until sauce is reduced by 1/2 volume and is thickened.

Meanwhile, place the oyster shells on a baking pan lined with rock salt. Line the bottom of each shell with a pinch of bread crumbs. Top the breadcrumbs with 1 to 2 teaspoons of cream sauce. Set an oyster in each shell and top the oysters with more sauce. Place the oysters under a broiler, 6-inches from the heat. Broil for 3 to 5 minutes, or until oysters become lightly browned and bubbly. Serve hot.

Recommended wines: Champagne or Sparkling wine, Chardonnay.

Serves 2

Cream Sauce:

1 tablespoon butter, melted
1 garlic clove, minced
2 tablespoons dry white wine
1 cup whipping cream
  Salt and pepper to taste
1 teaspoon Dijon mustard
  Pinch of dried thyme

24 small or medium oysters, scrubbed and shucked, reserving deep cupped shells
1/2 cup breadcrumbs
1/2 teaspoon salt
1/4 teaspoon freshly ground black pepper
  Rock salt to line baking dish

Olympia Oyster Pepper Pot

Olympia Oysters (Ostrea lurida) are the only oyster native to the Pacific Northwest. Averaging about the size of a quarter, the little oysters are loved by many for their ambrosial, metallic sea flavor. During the 1800s, these oysters were shipped by the tons to San Francisco (sometimes used as ballast on ships) and nearly depleted. Thanks to heroic efforts on the part of Northwest oystermen, Oly's are once again available. Shucked Olympia Oysters are available mail-order from Taylor Shellfish (see growers directory, page 310).

Serves 4

1 pint shucked Olympia oysters
   in their liquor
4 tablespoons (1/2 stick)
   unsalted butter
2 green onions, minced
1/2 cup finely chopped green
   pepper
2 tablespoons fresh lemon juice
2 tablespoons catsup
1 teaspoon Worcestershire sauce
   Salt and freshly ground black
   pepper to taste
4 slices lightly buttered
   pumpernickel or sourdough
   toast

Melt the butter in a large skillet over medium heat. Stir in the onions and green pepper, cover and cook until tender, about 5 minutes. Add the lemon juice, catsup, Worcestershire sauce, salt and pepper. Gently stir in the oysters and their liquor and simmer just until oysters are firm and plump, about 2 to 3 minutes. Remove oysters from the heat and ladle them and their sauce over hot toast.

Recommended wines: Pinot Blanc, Chenin Blanc, Dry Riesling.

Oysters a la Oysterville
Oysterville Sea Farms, Oysterville, WA

"When in Honolulu buy pineapples. When in Oysterville buy oysters," says the handpainted sign outside Oysterville Sea Farms, the last operating oyster farm in historic Oysterville. Located in the original cannery, built in 1939 on the shores of Willapa Bay, the hands-on business is run by Dan Driscoll and his wife Katherine, who live right next door. As you can imagine, the Driscolls eat lots of oysters. Here is one of their favorite recipes.

Preheat oven to 350° F. In a shallow bowl, combine the bread crumbs, Italian seasoning and Parmesan cheese. Place the spinach in a saucepan with 1/4 cup water. Bring water to a boil, reduce heat to a simmer, cover and steam until spinach is just cooked, about 2 to 3 minutes. Gently squeeze the spinach to remove excess moisture. Grease a shallow, oven proof casserole. Distribute the spinach over the bottom of the pan. Coat the oysters with the bread crumb mixture and arrange the oysters over the spinach.

Melt the butter in a saucepan over medium heat. Add the green onions and cook until tender, about 3 minutes. Whisk in the flour, stirring constantly, and gradually whisk in the hot milk. Cook, stirring constantly until sauce is thickened. Stir in the ham and season with salt and pepper. Spoon the sauce over the oysters and top with any remaining bread crumbs. Bake, uncovered, for about 40 minutes, or until breadcrumbs are golden and sauce is bubbling.

Recommended beverages: Chardonnay, Sauvignon Blanc, Pinot Gris, Pinot Blanc.

Serves 4

- 32 extra small or small oysters, shucked and drained
- 1 cup bread crumbs
- 1 tablespoon Italian Seasoning, or mixed oregano, thyme and basil
- 1/4 cup freshly grated Parmesan cheese
- 2 bunches fresh spinach leaves, rinsed and chopped
- 2 tablespoons butter
- 1/2 cup sliced green onions
- 2 tablespoons all purpose flour
- 1 cup milk, scalded
- 1 cup diced ham
- Salt and freshly ground black pepper to taste

Oyster, Goat Cheese and Spinach Gratin

If you prefer, this gratin mixture can be divided among individual ramekins before baking.
Serve with plenty of crusty bread and a crisp green salad.

Serves 4

32 small or medium oysters, shucked, reserving liquor
2 cups fresh spinach leaves, washed and dried
1/4 cup water
6 tablespoons (3/4 stick) unsalted butter, softened
1 onion, diced
1/3 cup all purpose flour
reserved oyster liquor
1/2 cup dry white wine
1 cup whipping cream
2 large egg yolks, beaten
Salt and white pepper to taste
4 to 5 ounces soft goat cheese (chevre)
1/4 cup chopped fresh parsley

Place the spinach in a large saucepan. Add water, cover and steam over medium heat until spinach is wilted, stirring often, about 4 minutes. Drain well and set aside.

Return saucepan to the burner and melt 3 tablespoons butter over medium heat. Add the onion and cook until tender, about 5 minutes. Whisk in the flour and cook about 2 minutes, whisking constantly, until flour is incorporated and butter is thickened. Remove the saucepan from the heat. Gradually whisk in the reserved oyster liquor and wine. Whisk in the whipping cream. Return the saucepan to medium heat and simmer until the sauce thickens, stirring often, about 5 minutes. Remove the saucepan from the heat. Whisk in the remaining butter and egg yolks. Season the sauce to taste with salt and white pepper. Stir in the cooked spinach.

Preheat oven to 375° F. Lightly grease a 2-quart capacity gratin dish or baking dish. Arrange the oysters over the bottom of the dish, then spoon the spinach and cream mixture over the oysters. Sprinkle with chopped parsley and dot with chunks of goat cheese. Bake about 30 minutes, or until the gratin is hot and bubbly around the edges. Serve hot.

Oysters in Roasted Orange, Melon and Grape Coulis
Moby Dick Hotel and Restaurant, Nahcotta, WA

Chef Rocio Ariste, a native of Santiago, Chile, arrived on Washington's Long Beach Peninsula, home to the region's famed Willapa Bay oysters, after cooking stints in London and Washington D.C. She has a wonderful knack for combining local foods with delicious and unusual flavors from her eclectic culinary background. In this delightful recipe, she roasts oranges, then purees them with melon and red grapes to make a complex flavored, beautifully colored sauce for the hotel's house-raised oysters.

In a large saucepan, bring 1 quart salted water to a boil. Add the oysters, deep cupped shell down, and the rosemary and steam until the oysters open, about 10 minutes. Open any oysters that don't open with an oyster knife. Shuck all oysters and set aside.

Meanwhile, preheat oven to 400° F. Place the oranges on a baking sheet and roast until they are brown, even a little charred, about 20 minutes. Let the oranges cool slightly, then squeeze the juice and scoop the pulp into a saucepan. Bring the juice to a boil and simmer for 2 minutes. Add the honey, melon, grapes, shallots and brown sugar. Bring mixture to a boil, then reduce heat and simmer for 10 minutes. Puree the fruit mixture in a blender or food processor, then pass through a sieve back into the saucepan. Let the sauce cook another 1 minutes, stirring constantly, until slightly thickened; eason with salt and pepper. Serve warm. (Sauce may be prepared ahead up to 2 days in advance and re-heated.)

Melt 2 tablespoons butter in a skillet over medium heat. Add the steamed oysters and cook for 3 to 5 minutes, until oysters are golden brown and heated through. Ladle 1/4 cup of sauce onto each serving plate; top with 6 oysters and sprinkle with chopped chives. Serve at once.

Recommended wines: Dry Riesling, Dry Gewurztraminer, Chardonnay.

Serves 6

- 36 medium oysters in the shell
- 1 bunch fresh rosemary
- 2 oranges, whole
- 1 tablespoon honey
- 1/2 ripe cantaloupe or honeydew melon, peeled, seeded and cubed
- 1 bunch red seedless grapes, halved
- 1 shallot, minced
- 1 cup brown sugar
- Salt and freshly ground black pepper to taste
- 2 tablespoons butter
- 1/4 cup finely chopped fresh chives

Roasted Coho Salmon
with Oyster & Bacon Dressing

Stuffed with a smokey Oyster & Bacon Dressing, this spectacular Roasted Coho Salmon makes a dramatic and delicious entree for any special occasion. I like to accompany the salmon with steamed Brussel sprouts, and cranberries cooked in port with orange rind and fresh pears. Coho, a dense, flavorful salmon, is my favorite, but you can use any variety of fresh salmon.

Half Shell Lori

Serves 4 to 6

4 to 5 pound salmon, skin on — head off, rinsed

Oyster Bacon Dressing:

- 6 slices bacon, diced
- 1 onion, diced
- 1 cup chopped fresh spinach
- 1 teaspoon lemon zest
- 2 teaspoons lemon juice
- 4 tablespoons butter, melted
- 3 cups cubed sourdough bread
- 15 extra small or small oysters, shucked and drained
- 2 eggs, beaten
  Salt and freshly ground black pepper to taste

Fry the bacon until crisp in a large skillet over medium heat. Drain on paper towels, reserving bacon grease. Return skillet to the heat, stir in onion and cook about 5 minutes, until tender. Stir in spinach, lemon zest, and lemon juice and cook until spinach is tender, about 2 minutes. Remove from the heat. Stir in cubed bread, oysters, and beaten eggs. Season with salt and pepper.

Preheat oven to 325° F. Oil a piece of foil large enough to hold the salmon and set the foil on a large baking sheet. Place the salmon on the foil. Stuff the salmon as full as possible with the Oyster Dressing, wrapping the foil around the salmon to hold in the dressing, but not covering the top of the salmon. Wrap any remaining dressing in foil and bake along side the salmon.

Bake the salmon for about 1 1/2 to 2 hours, or until the salmon is cooked through. To test for doneness: Lift the salmon open with a fork and break off a piece of meat near the center of the fish. The meat should flake easily but should still be very moist. To serve, divide the stuffed salmon into 2 1/2-inch slices. Serve with extra dressing on the side.

Recommended wines: Pinot noir, Chardonnay, Pinot Gris, Champagne or sparkling wine.

Grand Central Oyster Pan Roast

Grand Central Oyster Bar, New York, NY

Next to Oyster Stew, this is the Grand Central Oyster Bar's most celebrated dish, which patrons have been clamoring for since the restaurant first opened in 1913 . If you've been lucky enough to sit counterside at the Oyster Bar, you've watched the chefs prepare this creamy concoction in the restaurant's steam-jacketed bowls. At home, a double boiler works great.

Place the oysters and their liquor, 1 tablespoon butter, chili sauce, Worcestershire sauce and celery salt in the top of a double boiler over boiling water. Don't let the top of the boiler touch the water below. Whisk mixture briskly and constantly for about 1 1/2 minutes, until the edges of the oysters begin to curl. Add the cream and continue stirring briskly until mixture is hot and small bubbles form along the rim of the pan. Do not boil. Place the toast in a soup plate and pour the hot oyster and cream mixture over the toast. Top with the remaining 1 tablespoon of butter and sprinkle with paprika.

Recommended beverages: Champagne or sparkling wine, Pinot Gris, Sauvignon Blanc, Pinot Blanc, Viognier, Dry Riesling.

Ingredients per serving:

- 8 medium oysters, scrubbed and shucked, reserving liquor
- 2 tablespoons (1/4 stick) unsalted butter
- 1 tablespoon chili sauce
- 1 tablespoon Worcestershire sauce Dash of celery salt
- 1/2 cup cream
- 1 slice dry sourdough or pumpernickel toast
- 1/2 teaspoon paprika

Oyster Rabbit

Our Grandma Armstrong loved to make Rarebits or "Rabbits," as she called them, seasoned with lots of cheese and local beer. As kids, we weren't used to the taste of beer, so this wasn't our favorite dish, but it certainly is welcome on our tables now.

Half Shell Lori

Serves 4

32 extra small or small oysters, shucked and drained
2 tablespoons butter
3 cups grated sharp cheddar cheese
1 teaspoon salt
1 teaspoon paprika
2 teaspoons dry mustard
1 cup beer, room temperature
4 to 6 pieces lightly buttered toast
1/4 cup finely chopped green onion

Melt the butter in the top of a double boiler over simmering water. Stir in the grated cheese, salt, paprika, and mustard. Cook, stirring constantly, until the cheese begins to melt. Stir in the warm beer, stirring constantly. Before the mixture becomes smooth, add the oysters and cook for about 2 to 3 minutes, or until the oysters plump and the cheese is smooth. Serve over hot toast and sprinkle with chopped green onion.

Recommended beverages: Chilled beer, Viognier, Chenin Blanc, Pinot Gris.

"A lusty bit of nourishment."
M. F. K. Fisher
Consider the Oyster

The Joy of Oysters

Oyster Bill's Oysters Au Gratin with Shrimp

In addition to his many talents, including preparing mouthwatering oyster dishes, Co-author, Oyster Bill, is a very talented musician, who often plays with the local symphony orchestra. This is a dish he prepared for couples who bid on his fund-raising dinner to benefit the orchestra.

Preheat oven to 425° F. Scrub the oysters well and shuck them, reserving their liquor and deep cupped shells. Set aside. Shell and de-vein the shrimp, rinse under cold water and pat dry with paper towels. Coarsely chop the shrimp. Melt 2 tablespoons of the butter in a skillet over medium heat. Add the shrimp and cook 2 to 3 minutes, or until they turn bright pink. Remove from the heat and set aside.

Pour the oyster liquor into a measuring cup and add enough milk to make 1 3/4-cup. Heat the remaining butter in a heavy skillet over medium heat. Whisk in the flour, mixing thoroughly. Gradually stir in the milk, oyster liquor, and wine. Cook, stirring constantly, until the sauce boils and starts to thicken. Reduce heat to low and simmer for about 3 minutes. Whisk about 1/4 cup of the hot sauce into the beaten egg yolk, then whisk the yolk mixture back into the sauce. Season with pepper and salt to taste. Stir in the chopped, cooked shrimp and the bacon; remove sauce from the heat.

Cover the bottom of a shallow baking pan with 1/2-inch of rock salt. Set the oyster shells on the rock salt. Spoon about 1 tablespoon of the shrimp sauce into the bottom of each shell; top with an oyster, then cover the oyster with another spoonful of sauce.

Bake for about 10 minutes, or until sauce starts to bubble. Remove the oysters from the oven and top them with the breadcrumbs and grated cheese. Bake another 4 to 5 minutes, until the crumbs turn golden brown. Sprinkle the oysters with chopped parsley. Serve hot.

Recommended wines: Sauvignon Blanc, Pinot Blanc, Chenin Blanc, Chardonnay.

Serves 4

- 24 medium oysters in the shell
- 1/2 pound medium-sized raw shrimp
- 6 tablespoons (3/4-stick) butter
- 1/2 -1 cup whole milk
- 1/4 cup dry white wine
- 3 tablespoons all-purpose flour
- 1 large egg yolk, beaten
- 1/4 teaspoon freshly ground black pepper
  Salt to taste
- 3 slices cooked bacon, drained and finely chopped
- 1/2 cup fresh bread crumbs
- 3/4 cup freshly grated Gruyere cheese
- 1/4 cup chopped fresh parsley
  Rock salt to line baking pan

Oysters Baked in Red Peppers

This easy to make dish is bursting with flavor. Serve for lunch or dinner with a crisp green salad and a side of scalloped potatoes.

Serves 2

24 extra small oysters, shucked
and drained, reserving liquor
 2 large red or green bell peppers
1/2 cup crushed saltine crackers
 4 tablespoons (1/2 stick)
butter, melted
Salt and freshly ground black
pepper
 2 tablespoons minced fresh
parsley

Preheat oven to 375° F. Half the peppers lengthwise and scoop out seeds. Place peppers, hollow side up, in a greased baking dish. In a mixing bowl, combine the cracker crumbs and the melted butter. Place a thick layer of crumbs in the bottom of each pepper. Fill each pepper with 3 oysters. Season the oysters with salt and pepper and drizzle with reserved oyster liquor. Top oysters with another layer of crumbs, then repeat with more oysters and another layer of crumbs. Moisten with a little more of the oyster liquor and sprinkle with minced parsley. Bake about 20 minutes, or until peppers are tender and crumbs are golden brown. Serve hot.

Recommended wines: Sauvignon Blanc, Chardonnay, Pinot Gris.

The Joy of Oysters

Rodney's Oyster Pie
Rodney's Oyster House, Toronto, Ontario

According to Owner Rodney Clark, the culinary focus of his famed Oyster House is "shellfish, both mollusks and crustaceans — from your ankles to your neck." His creamy oyster pie is brimming with plump oysters, bacon, mushrooms, corn and red peppers, and topped with a flaky golden crust. All you need is a simple salad or slaw and a glass of your favorite beer or wine to round out the meal.

Preheat oven to 400° F. Grease a 1-quart capacity (1.2-liter) baking dish or souffle dish. Place the oysters and their liquor in a saucepan and bring to a simmer over medium heat. Cook until the oysters begin to plump, about 3 to 5 minutes. Set oysters and liquor aside. Meanwhile, saute the bacon in a large skillet. When crisp, remove from the heat and drain on paper towels, reserving the bacon grease. Add the vegetable oil to the bacon grease and heat over medium heat. When oil is hot, stir in onion, mushrooms, red pepper and corn. Cook, stirring often, for 2 to 3 minutes, or until vegetables are slightly tender. Stir in the flour and cook, stirring constantly for about 3 minutes. Strain the oyster liquor gradually into the vegetable mixture, stirring constantly. Season with salt, pepper and cayenne. Simmer for about 5 minutes, or until mixture is thickened. Gently stir in the bacon and oysters. Pour the mixture into the greased baking dish.

Roll out the pastry crust, cutting several vents to allow steam to escape. Lay the pastry gently over the filling; trim edges so that pastry extends 1/2-inch over edges of baking dish. Crimp edges to seal. Bake for 25 to 30 minutes, or until pastry is golden brown.

Dish into warm bowls.

Recommended beverages: Stout, Chardonnay, Pinot Blanc, Pinot Gris.

Serves 4 to 6 (Fills one 1-quart capacity baking dish.)

- 36 medium oysters, shucked, reserving liquor
- 8 slices bacon, sliced into 1-inch pieces
- 1-2 tablespoons vegetable oil, as needed
- 1 large onion, diced
- 6 ounces button mushrooms, sliced
- 1 red pepper, seeded and diced
- 1 cup corn kernels (fresh or frozen)
- 2 ounces all purpose flour
- 4 tablespoons chopped parsley
- Salt and freshly ground pepper to taste
- Pinch of Cayenne pepper
- Pastry for single crust pie (see page 268)

Smoked Salmon & Oyster Pot Pie

*When I worked as a chef, I used to make this same Smoked Salmon and Oyster filling to serve in pre-baked individual patty shells made with puff pastry.
Either way, it's a delicious meal for lunch or dinner.*

Half Shell Lori

Serves 4

- 20 extra small or small oysters, shucked and drained
- 6 ounces hot-smoked salmon, divided into bite-size pieces
- 3 tablespoons butter
- 3 tablespoons flour
- 3/4 cup chicken broth, preferably homemade
- 3/4 cup half & half
- 1/2 teaspoon chopped fresh thyme
- 1/4 teaspoon white pepper
  Salt to taste
- 1 cup cooked peas
- 1 cup chopped cooked carrot
- 4 medium new potatoes, diced and cooked until tender
- 1 sheet prepared puff pastry (available in the frozen food section)

Preheat the oven to 400° F. Melt the butter in a saucepan over medium heat, blend in the flour and then gradually stir in the chicken broth and cream. Bring the mixture to a boil, stirring constantly. Season with thyme, white pepper and salt. Simmer for five minutes.

Gently stir in the oysters, smoked salmon, peas, carrots and potatoes. Turn the mixture into a one-and-one-half quart deep baking dish, or 4 individual deep ramekins. Cut the puff pastry to fit the top of the casserole, allowing an extra 1/2 inch to drape over the edges of the casserole dish. With a sharp knife, cut a 1/2-inch round steam hole in the center of the pastry. Then, without slicing clear through the pastry, make decorative spirals running from the center hole out to the edge of the pastry.

Brush the rim of the casserole with cream and set the pastry over the filling, pressing slightly along the rim to secure the pastry. Brush the pastry lightly with cream. Place in the preheated oven and bake approximately twenty minutes, or until the pastry is golden brown.

Recommended wines: Champagne or sparkling wine, Chardonnay.

Oyster Pan Roast on Toast

Shaw's Crab House and Blue Crab Lounge, Chicago, IL

When it comes to cooking, simplicity is often the best thing. While it's one of the simplest recipes for an Oyster Pan Roast that we've come across, Shaw's is also one of our favorites.

Place the oysters and their liquor in a skillet over medium heat. Top with butter and season with salt and pepper. Bring the mixture to a simmer and cook until oysters are plump and firm to the touch, about 3 minutes. Place 2 pieces of toast on each serving plate. Distribute the warm oysters over the toast and pour the butter sauce over the oysters. Sprinkle with chopped parsley. Serve at once.

Recommended wines: Champagne or sparkling wine, Pinot Gris, Pinot Blanc.

Serves 2

24 small or medium oysters, shucked, reserving liquor
2 tablespoons butter
Salt and freshly ground black pepper to taste
1/4 cup chopped fresh parsley
4 slices buttered toast

"An oyster, that marvel of delicacy, that concentration of sapid excellence, that mouthful before all other mouthfuls, who first had faith to believe it, and courage to execute? The exterior is not persuasive."
Henry Ward Beecher

Farewell to Innocence
By Andrew Wiegardt

Oh, the Oyster. Oh, the shimmering beauty of this briny bivalve. And oh, the life affirming sensation of its heavenly kiss.

To this initiate, such is required that one muster one's inner courage, and quell for a moment the imaginations shuddering at the half naked sight. Then, with raised elbow and heroic resolution, to plunge ahead, no looking back. Thereby granting oneself the experience of titillating delight found only upon prying apart and diving between its two firmly secretive shells.

Having once indulged the palate's senses, and succumbed to the naturally luscious potation of this seemingly innocent creature, one most commonly finds all former apathy turns into a natural craving. And so, such valiant boldness as is required when venturing into the unknown domain of this enchantingly mysterious mollusk, is forever rewarded by the delightful discovery of its subtle, yet seductively potent, succulence.

This new-found ecstasy could easily be passed off to momentary fantasy, but for the next rapturous encounter being only a raised shell and a slurp away. Thus, in innocence started, a new-found passionate desire necessitates the frequent partaking of the ever inviting, oyster on the half shell.

Oysters and Wild Mushrooms Baked in Parchment Paper

Baking oysters in parchment paper seals in the oyster's sweet briny juices, which mingle with the earthy flavor of wild mushrooms. Our favorite wild mushrooms for this dish are chanterelles, porcini, or morels. You can also substitute cultivated mushrooms, such as portabellas, or common button mushrooms. Parchment paper is great for baking because it doesn't react with acidic foods, such as lemon. Look for parchment paper at your local kitchen shop or grocer. If you can't find it, substitute well greased aluminum foil (don't use waxed paper; the wax will melt in the oven). Serve with steamed rice.

Preheat oven to 400° F. Heat olive oil in a heavy skillet over medium heat. Add the leeks and mushrooms and cook, stirring often, until they begin to soften, about 5 minutes. Remove from the heat, stir in the lemon juice, thyme and wine. Season to taste with salt and pepper.

Fold each piece of parchment paper in half and trim into an oval. Divide 1/2 of the mushroom mixture evenly between the 4 pieces of parchment. Top each packet with 8 oysters, then top the oysters with the chopped bacon and the remaining mushroom mixture. To seal the packets: Brush the edges with beaten egg white and press to seal edges together. Roll the edges over on themselves, in toward the center of the packets, to create a 1/2-inch border. Place the packets on a baking sheet and bake for 15 to 20 minutes, or until they are hot and golden. To serve, place a hot packet on each serving plate. Open the packets with a sharp knife and empty the contents onto the plate, discarding the parchment. Serve with steamed rice.

Recommended wines: Champagne or sparkling wine, Chardonnay, Pinot Gris, Viognier.

Serves 4

- 32 small oysters, shucked and drained
- 4 slices bacon, drained and chopped
- 3 tablespoons olive oil
- 1 leek, thinly sliced
- 3/4 pound mushrooms, cleaned and sliced
- 3 tablespoons fresh lemon juice
- 1 teaspoon minced fresh thyme
- 1/4 cup dry white wine
  Salt and freshly ground black pepper
- 4 tablespoons (1/2 stick) unsalted butter
- 4 pieces parchment paper or foil, 12 x 14-inches
- 1 egg white, beaten

The Joy of Oysters

Baked Shellfish in Tomato Garlic Sauce

In Madrid, fishermen make this dish with their catch of the day, which usually includes clams, mussels, and oysters. If you have large shellfish, you may wish to remove the top shell from each mollusk before covering them with sauce. Serve with crusty garlic bread, pitchers of your favorite beer or wine, and plenty of napkins.

Serves 6

2 dozen extra small oysters, scrubbed clean

2 dozen manilla clams, cleaned

2 dozen mussels, debearded and cleaned

1 cup dry white wine or water

4 tablespoons olive oil

1 large onion, diced

2 tomatoes, seeded and diced

2 garlic cloves, minced

1 tablespoon all purpose flour

2 tablespoons chopped fresh parsley

Salt and freshly ground black pepper to taste

Preheat oven to 400° F. Place the cleaned shellfish in a large saucepan, pour in the wine, cover and cook over medium-high heat, for about 8 to 10 minutes. As soon as shellfish open, remove them, using tongs or a slotted spoon, and place in a large oven proof baking dish. Continue cooking the shellfish in the pot until they open. When the mussels and clams are all open, pry open any remaining oysters with an oyster knife. Reserve cooking liquid.

Heat a skillet over medium heat. Add the olive oil and, when hot, add the onion and cook until it is tender, about 4 minutes. Stir in the tomatoes and cook until most of the liquid has evaporated, about 3 minutes. Add the garlic and parsley, mixing well. Whisk in the flour and cook, stirring constantly, for 1 minute. Strain the shellfish cooking liquid through a sieve into the tomato sauce, mixing well. Season with salt and pepper. Pour the sauce over the shellfish and bake for 10 to 15 minutes, or until shellfish is heated through and the sauce is bubbling.

Recommended beverages: Chilled beer, Sauvignon Blanc, Pinto Blanc, Semillon.

262   *The Joy of Oysters*

Oyster Accompaniments

Like the Walrus and the Carpenter, oyster lovers rarely need much more than a crusty loaf of bread a glass of wine or beer to enjoy a meal of Blue Points, Samish Bay Pacifics or tasty Kumamotos. Often, regional specialties dictate side dishes, so we have limited our offerings to a few tasty breads and a classic Caesar salad. When in Boston, add some baked beans, then some Indian pudding for dessert. If you're in New Orleans, indulge in an oyster Po' Boy and a glass of frosty beer. In South Carolina, help yourself to cornbread and banana pudding. In the Pacific Northwest, a crisp Northwest Sauvignon Blanc or Pinot Blanc will match just fine with oysters and a crusty loaf of bread, until the fresh blackberry cobbler arrives to finish the meal.

Savory Cheese Shortbread
Dijon Spice Bread
Ballymaloe Brown Soda Bread
Sourdough Pumpernickel Bread
Focaccia
Rich Pastry Dough
Classic Caesar Salad

Savory Cheese Shortbread

Serve these buttery shortbread crackers with oysters on the half shell and Champagne. Stored in an airtight container, these will keep up to 3 days.

Makes about 12 dozen

2-1/4 cups all-purpose flour

1/4 teaspoon cayenne pepper

1 cup (2 sticks) butter, chilled and cut into small pieces

2 cups grated sharp cheddar cheese

1/2 cup milk

1 tablespoon Worcestershire sauce

Place the flour and cayenne in the bowl of a food processor; pulse to combine. Add the butter and pulse until the mixture is reduced to a coarse meal, about 8 to 10 seconds. Transfer the mixture to a large mixing bowl. Stir in the grated cheese, mixing well. Using a fork, stir in the milk and Worcestershire sauce until well combined. Roll the mixture into two 1-inch-diameter logs, wrap in plastic wrap or waxed paper and chill until very firm, at least 1 hour.

Preheat oven to 350° F. Lightly grease 2 baking sheets, or line with parchment paper. Remove the logs from the refrigerator, and slice each one into 1/4-inch thick rounds. Place the rounds on the baking sheets, leaving 1-inch between them. Bake the shortbread about 12 minutes, or until they are golden brown. Cool on wire racks.

Dijon Spice Bread

This dense, spicy bread, from the Dijon region of France, is especially delicious served with hot Italian sausage and freshly shucked oysters (see page 116). For the best results, let the batter age for 3 to 8 days at room temperature after mixing.

Combine the honey, sugar, and baking soda in water that is hot but not boiling. Blend well. Stir in the anise seeds, orange rind and salt, sift in flour gradually, beating well between additions. To be at its best, batter should age from 3-8 days. (You may eliminate this step, but it does greatly improve the flavor.)

Preheat oven to 350° F. Turn the batter into 2 well oiled 7-inch loaf pans. Bake for about 1 hour, or until a toothpick inserted in the center comes out clean. Brush the loaves with hot milk as soon as they are pulled from the oven. Cool on racks.

Makes 2 -7-inch loaf cakes

- 1 cup dark honey
- 1 cup sugar
- 1 tablespoon baking soda
- 1 cup hot water
- 1 tablespoon crushed anise seeds
- Grated rind of 1 orange
- Pinch of salt
- 1 cup rye flour
- 3 cups unbleached flour
- 1/4 cup hot milk

OYSTER RECIPES

Ballymaloe Brown Soda Bread

This dense, nutty soda bread, found on nearly every Irish table, is excellent with seafood, especially freshly shucked oysters. It's a recipe I learned from Darina Allen at her wonderful Ballymaloe Cookery School in Ireland. Slice it very thin and spread it lightly with butter.

Half Shell Lori

Makes 1 large or two small loaves

4-1/2 cups stone-ground whole wheat flour
3-1/4 cups unbleached white flour
1/4 cup oat bran or oatmeal
1 egg, beaten
2 tablespoons butter, softened
2 rounded teaspoons salt
2 rounded teaspoons baking soda
3 cups buttermilk, approximate

Preheat the oven to 400° F. Mix the dry ingredients together in a large mixing bowl. Cut in the butter. Make a well in the center and add the beaten egg, then immediately add most of the buttermilk, mixing well. The dough should be soft but not sticky. Add more buttermilk if necessary. Turn out onto a floured surface and knead lightly, just enough to shape into a round loaf (or loaves). Flatten slightly, to about 2 1/2-inches. Place the bread on a lightly greased baking sheet. Using a knife, slash a deep cross in the top of the bread. Bake at 400° F for 15 minutes, then reduce the heat to 350° F. Continue baking (about 20 minutes for small loaves, longer for large loaf) or until the bread is golden on top and sounds hollow when tapped. Cook on racks.

Sourdough Pumpernickel Bread

This is a very dense loaf flavored with caraway seeds and coffee. The recipe was given to me by a Czechoslovakian couple who owned a small bakery on the Oregon Coast where I worked as the baker. Sliced thin and spread with butter, it is a delicious accompaniment for oysters on the half shell. Plan to start the dough at least 8 hours in advance.

Half Shell Lori

Place the caraway seeds in a large mixing bowl. Pour the hot coffee over the seeds and let the mixture cool to room temperature. Stir in the sourdough starter and rye flour, mixing well. Cover with plastic wrap and let sit in a warm place for at least 8 hours, to overnight.

Stir in the molasses, oil, salt, dissolved yeast, and milk. Gradually add flour, until a soft dough is formed. Turn onto a floured surface and knead, adding flour as necessary, for about 10 minutes, until the dough forms a firm ball. Turn into an oiled bowl; cover with plastic and let rise in a warm place until doubled in bulk, about 1-1/2 to 2 hours. Punch the dough down; cover and let rise again until doubled.

Turn the dough out onto a floured surface. Divide in two. Shape each portion into a firm round loaf, by tucking the dough in on itself toward the center until it becomes firm. Turn the loaf over, placing the seam on the bottom. Using the inner edges of your upward-turned hands, shape the dough into a round by firmly pushing in toward the center around the bottom of the loaf. Brush the tops lightly with flour. With a very sharp knife or razor blade, cut horizontal slits 1/4-inch apart across the top of each loaf. Let the bread rise until doubled, about 30 minutes. Meanwhile, preheat oven to 350° F. Bake about 30 to 40 minutes, or until the tops are golden brown and the loaves sound hollow when tapped with a finger. Let cool on racks before slicing.

Makes 2 large or 4 small round loaves

1-1/2	cups sourdough starter
1	tablespoon caraway seeds
1-1/4	cups strong, hot coffee
2-1/4	cups rye flour
1/2	cup molasses
1/2	cup vegetable oil or melted butter
1-1/2	tablespoons salt
1	package dry yeast dissolved in
1/4	cup warm water
1-1/2	cups whole milk, room temperature
8-1/2	cups (approximate) unbleached all-purpose flour

Focaccia

Studded with garlic and fresh rosemary, this fragrant loaf is drenched in thick green olive oil and sprinkled with kosher salt. Serve it hot out of the oven with freshly shucked oysters.

Makes 1 round loaf

- 2 teaspoons dry yeast
- 2 teaspoons sugar
- 1 cup warm water
- 1/2 teaspoon salt
- 2-1/2 cups (approximate) unbleached all-purpose flour
- 3 tablespoons fresh rosemary needles
- 4 garlic cloves, peeled and thinly sliced lengthwise
- 3 tablespoons extra virgin olive oil Kosher salt

Place the yeast and sugar in a large mixing bowl. Pour the warm water over the yeast and let sit, about 5 minutes, until yeast is dissolved. Stir to mix. Add the salt and enough flour to form a soft dough. Turn onto a floured surface and knead, adding flour as necessary, for about 10 minutes, until the dough forms a firm ball. Turn into an oiled bowl; cover with plastic and let rise in a warm place until doubled in bulk, about 1-1/2 to 2 hours.

Preheat oven to 350° F. Turn the dough out onto a floured surface. Shape into a circle and, using a rolling pin, roll out to 1/2-inch thickness. Transfer to an oiled baking sheet. Let the dough rise, about 20 minutes, or until doubled in bulk. With your fingers, poke indentations over the bread, about every inch. Insert a sliver of garlic and several rosemary needles into each indentation. Drizzle the olive oil over the bread and sprinkle with Kosher salt. Bake for 15 to 20 minutes, or until golden brown. Serve warm with extra olive oil for dipping.

Rich Pastry Dough

Makes one 9 or 10 inch single crust

- 1-1/2 cups unbleached flour
- 1/2 teaspoon salt
- 1/2 cup unsalted butter, chilled and divided into 1/2-inch pieces
- 1/2 teaspoon salt
- 1 egg yolk
- 1-2 tablespoons cold water, as needed

Place the flour, salt, and butter in a food processor. Pulse until butter is reduced to pea-size bits. With processor running, add egg yolk, then add cold water, 1 tablespoon at a time, until mixture comes together to form a stiff dough. Turn out onto a floured surface, knead lightly and form into a pancake, about 1/2-inch thick. Let rest 10 minutes, then roll out as needed.

Classic Caesar Salad

Every time I eat oysters, I find myself craving Caesar Salad. I learned to make this from a delightful chef in Cozumel, Mexico. The chef's name was Lennin, and he studied cooking in Mexico City. He prepared the whole salad, even the croutons at table-side. To this day, it is the best Caesar Salad I have ever eaten. Traditionally, the salad is made with whole leaves of romaine from the center of the lettuce. The salad is eaten with the fingers, by wrapping a crouton in each lettuce leaf.

In a large salad bowl, combine the anchovies with one crouton. Using a wooden spoon, break the anchovies up into small bits and crush the crouton, forming a sort of paste. Add the lime juice, olive oil, and garlic, mixing well. Gently fold in the lettuce leaves. To coddle the egg: Set the egg in a saucepan and cover with warm water. Bring the water to a boil over medium high heat. Remove the egg from the heat 30 seconds after the water reaches a boil. Rinse under cold water. Crack the egg over the salad, using a spoon to remove it from the shell. Sprinkle the cheese over the salad and toss gently. Dish the salad out onto large plates. Top with croutons and sprinkle with black pepper.

Serves 2

Homemade croutons (recipe follows)
4 to 8 anchovy fillets
   Juice of 1 lime
  3 tablespoons extra virgin olive oil
  2 garlic cloves, minced
 20 small whole romaine leaves (4 -5 inches in length)
  1 egg, coddled
  4 tablespoons freshly grated Parmesan cheese
   Freshly ground black pepper

For croutons: Preheat oven to 325° F. Toss all the ingredients together in a mixing bowl. Transfer to a baking sheet and bake, stirring often, for about 15 minutes, or until golden brown. Serve warm.

Croutons:

  2 cups French bread, cut into 1/2-inch cubes
1/4 cup extra virgin olive oil
  1 garlic clove, minced
  1 teaspoon dried thyme
   Salt and freshly ground black pepper to taste

Acme Oyster House

724 Iberville St., New Orleans, LA 70130
(504) 522-5973 • www.acmeoyster.com
In the heart of the French Quarter, ACME has been a destination for oyster lovers, fine diners and revelers since 1910. The historic building where the Acme Oyster House serves its famous Po-Boys, Poopas and oysters on the half shell was constructed as an elegant townhouse in 1814. Open daily for lunch and dinner. Check out their website for logo apparel, menus and fun information.

Anthony's Restaurants

Multiple locations in the Puget Sound region of Washington State: downtown Seattle waterfront, Shilshole Bay, Kirkland, Edmonds, Everett, Des Moines, Tacoma, Olympia & Chinook's at Salmon Bay. www.anthonys.com
Anthony's HomePorts and their other fine restaurants all feature water-side dining and the freshest Northwest seafood. Their own whole-sale seafood company buys direct from fisher-men and growers to supply each location with the freshest fish and shellfish daily. Leading the fight for water quality in the Puget Sound, Anthony's annual Oyster Olympics is a benefit for the Puget Soundkeeper Alliance.

Ballymaloe Cookery School

Shanagarry, Midleton, County Cork, Ireland
353 (0) 214646785
Famed for sharing the secrets of Irish cookery with professional chefs and ambitious home cooks in classes and special programs held throughout the year. Visit the school on the web at: www.ballymaloe-cookery-school.com

The Brooklyn Seafood, Steak & Oyster House

1201 3rd Ave., Seattle, WA 98101
(206) 224-7000
In the heart of downtown Seattle, The Brooklyn serves delicious fresh seafood, great steaks and the city's widest selection of half shell oysters at their popular oyster bar. Cozy surroundings and a fine assortment of local beers and ales (each paired with an oyster selection) make this a great destination for lunch or dinner. Their annual Oyster Appreciation Day in May is a tradition of Northwest oyster revelry.

Canlis

2576 Aurora Ave. N., Seattle, WA 98109
(206) 283-3313 • www.canlis.com
Perched on a high bluff overlooking Lake Union and Seattle's skyline, Canlis is renowned as Seattle's most exclusive restaurant. Featuring exemplary "contemporary Northwest cuisine," from Executive Chef Greg Atkinson, who has a special affinity for oysters, the restaurant draws diners from around the world, as well as dedi-cated locals. Sommelier Rob Bigelow presides over the restaurant's Wine Spectator award-winning list of over 1,100 wines.

Dan & Louis Oyster Bar

208 SW Ankeny St., Portland OR 97204
(503) 227-5906
Louis C. Wachsmuth founded his namesake
oyster bar and restaurant in downtown Portland
in 1907 expanding into the current location in
1919, by taking over the Merchant's Exchange
Saloon at the advent of prohibition. Thanks to
his family's ongoing dedication, his delicious
oyster stews, fresh seafood and inimitable
nautical decor are still favorites with locals and
visitors alike to this day. Lunch and dinner daily.

Elliott's Oyster House

1203 Alaskan Way, Pier 56, Seattle, WA 98101
(206) 623-4340 • www.elliottsoysterhouse.com
A favorite with Northwest oyster lovers, Elliott's
serves a wide selection of half shell oysters along
with signature Dungeness crab and salmon
dishes. Northwest wines and ales are offered as
the perfect accompaniment to fresh fish and
shellfish. Elliott's Oyster New Year takes place in
October. Open daily for lunch and dinner.

Flying Fish

2234 1st Ave., Seattle, WA 98121
(206) 728-8595 • www.flyingfishseattle.com
Chef Christine Keff traveled the world learning
the secrets of fine seafood cookery before
opening Flying Fish in Seattle's Belltown neighborhood. Her delectable preparations often lean
toward to her Asian cooking background. Superb
oyster dishes and a delectable selection of wine
and beers. Lunch and dinner served daily.

Friday Harbor House

130 West St., Box 1385,
Friday Harbor, WA 98250
(360) 378-8455
www.fridayharborhouse.com
Chefs Laurie Paul and Tim Barrette
are partners in the kitchen and
partners in life. They also
marry fine Northwest ingredients
with skill and creativity for the patrons of this
upscale inn and restaurant on Puget Sound's San
Juan Island.

Grand Central Oyster Bar

Lower Level, Grand Central Station
New York, NY 10017 • (212) 490-6650
The oldest oyster bar in New York City and a
mecca for oyster lovers from around the world,
this subterranean seafood palace has been
serving the finest fruits of the sea to a sellout
crowd since it opened in 1913. Since then,
every president of the United States has dined
here and celebrities, from Diamond Jim Brady
and Lillian Russell to Lauren Bacall and Jaason
Robards have feasted on oysters and other
seafood specialties. Elbow up to the oyster bar
and take your pick from dozens of oysters from
around the world. They all lie heaped on beds
of ice, just waiting for the thrust of the shucker's
knives.

"If it isn't fresh, it isn't Legal!"

Legal Sea Foods

33 Everett St., Allston, MA 02134
(800) 343-5804 • www.lsf.com
Restaurant locations in Massachusetts, Rhode Island, New York, Maryland, Virginia, Washington, D.c., and Florida.
George Berkowitz opened his seafood market in Cambridge, MA in 1950 promising his customers the finest fresh seafood for their home preparation. Soon, the family expanded the shop with a few picnic tables so they could serve cooked seafood specialties and the rest is history. Legal Sea Foods has become the flag bearer for quality, freshness and safety in American seafood. More locations open each year.

Moby Dick Hotel and Oyster Farm

P.O. Box 82, 25814 Sandridge Rd.
Nahcotta, WA 98637 • (360) 665-4543
www.nwplace.com/mobydick.html
A small hotel and restaurant (and oyster farm) on the shores of Washington's Willapa Bay. Gourmet cuisine is served at this outpost of fine dining on Willapa Bay.

Oysters Out West

5150 Oyster Drive, P.O. Box 3030,
Bay City, OR 97107 • (503) 377-2323
This company store and restaurant, located above the oyster beds at Pacific Oyster Co. on Oregon's Tillamook Bay, serves fresh oysters prepared the way Northwest oyster lovers like 'em. Other specialties include clam chowder, cioppino and a smoked seafood sampler.

Oysterville Sea Farms

P.O. Box 6, Oysterville, WA 98641
(360) 665-6585
(800) CRANBERRY
Operating from the historic oyster capitol of Willapa Bay, Oysterville Sea Farms offers fresh Pacific oysters, smoked oysters, cooking spices, baking mixes, condiments and other culinary favorites.

Printer's Row Restaurant

550 South Dearborn St.
Chicago, IL
(312) 461-0780
Located in Chicago's historic
Printer's Row district, Printer's
Row restaurant, under the direction of award-
winning Chef/Owner Michael Foley, has long
been renowned as one of our country's top
dining establishments. His creative menu
features the highest quality, seasonal ingredients
available, paired with a great selection of wines
from around the world. A dedicated oyster lover,
Michael searches out the best oysters wherever
he travels, from America's eastern and western
shores, to France, Asia and in-between.

Ray's Boathouse

6049 Seaview Ave. NW, Seattle, WA 98107
(206) 789-3770 • www.rays.com
One of Seattle's finest seafood houses and a
monument to NW seafood. Chef Charles
Ramseyer creates fine seafood cuisine featuring
oysters, salmon, crab and other specialties. Ray's
also offers their guests a superb selection of
Northwest wines.

Rodney's Oyster Bar

209 Adelaide St. E., Toronto, ONT
(416) 363-8105
1228 Hamilton St., Vancouver, BC
(604) 609-0080
Rodney Clark is a master of the oyster and other
seafood, too. He operates his Toronto and
Vancouver, B.C. Oyster Bars serving up to 15
different types of oysters each day. His own
oyster beds are located off Prince Edward Island.

Shaffer City

5 West 21st St., New York, NY 10010
(212) 255-9827• www.shaffercity.com
Chef/owner Jay Shaffer has claimed a top spot in
New York for fresh seafood, and specifically fresh
oysters. The finest shellfish, great service and live
jazz Wednesday through Saturday keeps 'em
coming back to Shaffer City.

Shaw's Crab House

21 E. Hubbard St., Chicago, IL 60611
(312) 527-2722 • www.shaws.com
Shaw's Crab House was instrumental in elevating
the quality and service of seafood in the Mid-
west. Serving the finest fresh oysters, succulent
crab and perfect finfish is a passion at Shaw's.
Their annual Royster with the Oyster festival is
classic, week-long oystermania at its finest.

The Shoalwater Restaurant

P.O. Box A, Seaview, WA 98644
(360) 642-4142 • www.shoalwater.com
Located in the historic Shelburne Inn, The
Shoalwater restaurant celebrates the bounty of
the Pacific Northwest. Serving oysters from the
namesake Shoalwater (Willapa) Bay nearby,
owners Tony and Anne Kischner please guests
with creative preparations, the finest service and
elegant surroundings.

Shuckers – Four Seasons Olympic Hotel

411 University St., Seattle, WA 98101
(206) 621-1984
A quintessential Northwest oyster bar located just off the lobby of Seattle's grande dame hotel. This cozy, intimate restaurant features fresh NW seafood, local oysters, regional microbrews and fine wines. Open daily for lunch and dinner (no lunch service on Sunday).

Stephanie Inn

2740 S. Pacific, P.O. Box 219
Cannon Beach, OR 97110 • (503) 436-2221
The Stephanie Inn offers Oregon Coast visitors the elegance and charm of fine country inns in Europe and New England. Superb service and attention to detail, combined with exemplary regional cuisine make this a popular destination for locals and visitors from around the globe.

America's Oldest Restaurant

Ye Olde Union Oyster House

41 Union St., Boston, MA 02108
(617) 227-2750 • www.unionoysterhouse.com
How would you like to slurp your oysters at the same bar that served Daniel Webster (and dozens of other personalities)? Americas oldest restaurant offers lots of personality, great New England charm and delicious seafood. The building dates back before the Revolutionary War and it still rings with echoes from the voices of early American heroes.

Wildwood Restaurant & Bar

1221 NW 21st Ave., Portland, OR 97209
(503) 248-9663
Executive Chef and Operating Partner Cory Schreiber is the creative force behind Wildwood Restaurant. A James Beard Award recipient for "Best Chef of the Northwest" in 1998, Schreiber is passionate about fresh, regional foods, especially oysters. His family has been involved in the Pacific Northwest oyster business since the mid-1800s as owner of the Oregon Oyster Company and Dan & Louis Oyster Bar, a Portland institution. Schreiber's innovative menu is a showcase for the best of the Pacific Northwest.

Xinh's Clam & Oyster House

221 Railroad Ave., Suite D, Shleton, WA 98584
(360) 427-8709 • www.taylorshellfish.com
Xinh Dwelley worked as a teenager in an American Army kitchen in her native Vietnam. In the Pacific Northwest, she is a legendary oyster shucker (five-time West Coast champion) and has gained a wide reputation for her culinary creations utilizing NW shellfish and finfish.

The Joy of Oysters

Other Notable Oyster Bars and Restaurants

Aquagrill
210 Spring St., New York, NY, (212) 274-0505

Awful Arthur's Oyster Bar
Mile Post 6 on The Beach Road
Kill Devil Hills, NC • (252) 441-5955

A. W. Shucks Seafood Restaurant
State Street in the Market
Charleston, SC • (843) 723-1151

Aw Shucks Oyster Bar
3601 Greenville Ave., Dallas, TX
(214) 821-9449

Big Daddy's Crab Shack & Oyster Bar
339 Elgin St. & 780 Baseline, Ottawa, Canada
(613) 569-5200, (613) 228-7011

Bluepoint Oyster Bar
741 W. Randolph, Chicago, IL (312) 207-1222

Casamento's
4330 Magazine St., New Orleans, LA
(504) 895-9761

Drago's Seafood Restaurant
3232 N Arnoult Rd., Metairie, LA
(504) 888-9254

East Coast Grill
1271 Cambridge St., Cambridge, MA
(617) 491-6568

Elm Street Oyster House
11 West Elm St., Greenwich, CT
(203) 629-5795

Emmett Watson's Oyster Bar
1916 Pike Place, Seattle, WA (206) 448-7721

Felix's Restaurant & Oyster Bar
739 Iberville, New Orleans, LA (504) 522-4440

Hyde St. Seafood House & Raw Bar
1509 Hyde St., San Francisco, CA
(415) 928-9148

Maestro S. V. P.
3615 St. Laurent, Montreal, Quebec
(514) 842-6447

McCormick & Kuleto's Restaurant
Beach St., Ghirardelli Square, San Francisco, CA
(415) 929-1730

Nick's Cove
Marshall, CA
(415) 663-1033

Old Ebbitt Grill
675 15th St. NW, Washington, D.C.
(202) 347-4800

Oscar's Old Florida Grill
Intracoastal Waterway
Villano Beach, FL • (904) 829-3794

P.J.'s Oyster Bed
737 Irving St., San Francisco, CA (415) 566-7775

Salty's on Alki
1936 Harbor Ave. SW, West Seattle, WA
(206) 937-1600

Sansom Street Oyster House
1516 Sansom St., Philadelphia, PA
(215) 567-7683

72 Market Street Oyster Bar & Grill
72 Market St., Venice, CA (310) 392-8720

Slider's Oyster Bar
218 1st St., Neptune Beach, FL (904) 246-0881

Sooke Harbor House
1528 Whiffen Spit Road, RR 4, Sooke, BC
(250) 642-3421

Spoto's Oyster Bar
125 Datura St.
West Palm Beach, FL • (561) 835-1828

Swan Oyster Depot
1517 Polk St., San Francisco, CA
(415) 673-1101

Uglesich's Restaurant & Bar
1238 Baronne St., New Orleans, LA
(504) 523-8571

Water Grill
544 South Grand Ave., Los Angeles, CA
(213) 891-0090

The Whistling Oyster
807 S. Broadway, Baltimore, MD
(410) 342-7282

Whistling Oyster Tavern
Quilcene, WA 98376, (360) 765-9508

Oyster Festivals and Events

Throughout oyster growing regions of every corner of the world, festivals and events are held to celebrate the oyster, its life, and the history involved with oystering. From Galway, Ireland to South Bend, Washington, these local activities are as unique as the places in which they are held, with the exception of the common thread that weaves through them all – OYSTERS! There are oyster shucking, slurping, and eating contests, street dances, classic car and motorcycle shows, cook-offs, wine tastings, oyster identification competitions, harbor cruises, art exhibits, displays of traditional oystering tools and related memorabilia, and tours of both older restored, as well as today's working oyster boats. Kayak races, children's live "touch tanks," carnival rides, sales of cookbooks, oyster fashion shows, musical entertainment, and environmental exhibits promoting clean water are all part of these events.

Probably the most enjoyable element of these gatherings is the food! Oysters prepared in every way imaginable are consumed by festival goers. Raw oysters, grilled oysters, baked oysters, barbecued oysters, oyster shooters, steamed oysters, skewered oysters, stir-fried oysters, pan-fried oysters, deep-fried oysters, oyster stews, oyster chowders, oyster bisques, oyster fritters, stuffed oysters, oyster cocktails, oyster salads, oyster rolls, oyster po'boys and oyster poopahs are just a sampling of what can be had at an oyster festival. Throw in a beer tent, an area for dancing, and a good live band, and you have yourself a party!

Most oyster events are sponsored by local community or historical organizations that recognize the importance oystering has played in the economic growth of the area. Seafood restaurants and oyster bars are also instrumental in promoting oysters, oyster wines and accompaniments through special dinner presentations and featured oyster selections from around the world. Anthony's Restaurants, a group of waterfront eateries in the Puget Sound area of Washington State, even holds an "Oyster Olympics." This event marks the finale of their annual month-long Oyster Festival, which not only promotes locally-grown oysters, but also raises funds for the Puget Soundkeeper Alliance, an organization devoted to the protection of the Puget Sound ecosystem.

Other groups that promote oyster events range from non-profit groups to music promoters who feel that eating oysters evokes a special feeling that goes well with certain styles of music. While the majority of these festivities take place along coastal waters, an event in Clinton, Montana (nearly 500 miles from a salt water estuary) offers an unusual twist by celebrating an entirely different type of oyster.

So let's pack up the kids, grandma, and Uncle Louie (he LOVES oysters), and visit some of these Oyster Festivals and events, enjoying some great fun and delicious food along the way.

Anglesey Oyster & Shellfish Fayre - Anglesey, Wales

Follow the oyster trail through North Wales on the first weekend of October. Events at this spirited local festival include an oyster cooking competition, waiters race and Family Open Golf Tournament. Local hotels and J.W. Lees pubs feature local oysters and Guinness throughout oyster week, as well as local musicians and other entertainment.

Amite Oyster Festival - Amite, LA

For more information on the Amite Oyster Festival contact:
Amite Oyster Festival
P.O. Box 1064
Amite, LA 70422
(504) 748-5537

North of New Orleans is the Pearl of Tangipahoa Parish, the town of Amite City, Louisiana (pronounced ay-meat). For twenty-five years the town has been celebrating their status as "the oyster shucking capitol of the world" by celebrating the Amite Oyster Festival in March. Several events take place during the month offering everyone a chance to participate in his or her specialty.

Beauty contests for six different age categories are judged and celebrated early in the month. The southern tradition of featuring local beauties is an important part of the festivities. Miss Amite Oyster Queen is crowned at the pageant on Saturday night.

Other activities commence later in the month with a weekend of music, carnival rides, a chili cook-off, oyster eating contest, firemen's competitive games and pig roast, horseshoe throwing contest, and lots of oysters and boiled crawfish for the hungry attendees. Arts and crafts booths and live entertainment welcome everyone to the Tangipahoa Parish Fairgrounds after the parade through town at 10 AM.

Anthony's Oyster Olympics

*Anthony's Oyster Olympics
Seattle, WA
Annual event held in March
Contact: (425) 455-0732
Web: www.anthonys.com
Team competitions in oyster
identification, oyster wine
identification and oyster
shucking for speed and
quality.*

Imagine a yearly oyster occurrence held at one of the most popular seafood restaurants in Seattle, Washington, with an unsurpassed view of Puget Sound, its islands, and the majestic snow covered Olympic Mountains rising above the horizon. An event that brings out both serious competitiveness and crazy antics of the participants, and brings to one place the growers of the finest oysters in North America, the makers of wines that have established the Pacific Northwest as a leader in wine production, and the chefs and food service managers who love seafood and have taken its preparation to heights never before imagined. It doesn't get any better than this.

This particular oyster happening is "Anthony's Oyster Olympics," a fun filled, one day festivity that began in 1990 as the finale to the annual Oyster Festival, which takes place at the many Anthony's-owned seafood restaurants in the Puget Sound

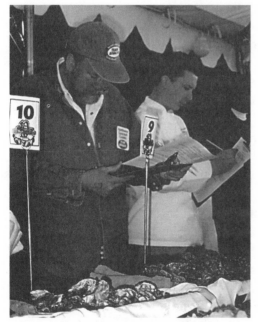

*Oyster Bill of Team Bivalve identifying
oysters as part of the Oyster Olympics.*

region. The Oyster Olympics not only features oysters, seafood and beverages, but is also a fund raiser for the Puget Soundkeeper Alliance, an organization whose members serve as stewards for the protection and enhancement of Puget Sound through public education, close monitoring of the sound and its hundreds of miles of shoreline, and celebration of the health and diversity of the Puget Sound ecosystem. For a single fixed-price admission, those attending the Olympics have the opportunity to watch local Seattle personalities compete during the "Celebrity Oyster Slurp Competition," see wine and shellfish enthusiasts tasting and scrutinizing their way through both the "Oyster Wine Identification," and "Oyster Identification" contests, judge the outrageous attire of the "Oyster Fashion Show," and experience the speed and finesse demonstrated by professional shellfish handlers at the shucking competition.

The Anthony's location that hosts the Oyster Olympics is their HomePort restaurant on the waterfront at Shilshole Bay in Seattle. Throughout the multi-leveled building, buffet tables containing hot and cold seafood appetizers, cheeses and fresh fruits are provided for those in attendance. A barbecue area outside prepares oysters and salmon, and shellfish growers from the United States and Canada let you sample and compare many of the

Ode to the Noble Oyster

By Chris Carlson & Duffy Bishop - 1993
Performed at Anthony's Oyster Olympics

Ode to the Noble Oyster - The liver of the sea
How wonderfully snug in your beds you filter fishies' pee
And when you get all fat and plump, a lighter shade of shale
A gal like me will suck you up and wash you down with ale

Oyster, oyster - You look just like a loogie
Oyster, oyster - You make me want to boogie
Oyster, oyster - Creamy like a loogie
Oyster, oyster - You make me want to boogie.

Just who was this person that first partook your flesh
What had they been drinkin - with what were they possessed
Perhaps they saw a seagull drop you with a splat!
Sez them, "Oh my, that does look good, I'll have some of that!"

Oyster, oyster - You look just like a loogie
Oyster, oyster - You make me want to boogie
Oyster, oyster - Creamy like a loogie
Oyster, oyster - You make me want to boogie.

You're eaten many ways, Oyster - why there's even oyster pie
And thanks to modern science we can eat you in July
Now it's time to end this song and bring you to my table
Hope I don't get a rotten one that tastes just like a stable

Oyster, oyster - You look just like a loogie
Oyster, oyster - You make me want to boogie
Oyster, oyster - Creamy like a loogie
Oyster, oyster - You make me want to boogie.
(repeat)

varieties and species of fresh oysters that are available. Numerous local wineries and microbreweries are also represented, allowing you to taste beers and wines as you amble through the event. A strolling magician performs special oyster magic and sleight of hand tricks while you sip and nibble, and later in the afternoon, a live band performs for your dancing pleasure.

The Oyster Olympics is a very special occasion, and benefits an equally special association, the Puget

Grilled oysters are served up by the hundreds on Anthony's outside deck.

Soundkeeper Alliance. "We're excited to be hosting the Oyster Olympics for the tenth year in a row," said Budd Gould, owner of Anthony's Restaurants, at the 1999 Olympics. "We fully support the Puget Soundkeeper Alliance's efforts to maintain clean water in Puget Sound. Clean water is essential to all of us who love this area, but especially to us at Anthony's - a waterfront seafood restaurant company specializing in Northwest seafood."

Anthony's Oyster Olympics is held during the latter part of March at Anthony's HomePort restaurant on Shilshole Bay in Seattle. Visit Anthony's website to find out more about the Oyster Olympics: www.anthonysrestaurants.com.

Oo-Aah Oysters
By Susan Paynter, Seattle P-I, 1994

Cheers to the oyster!
Is anything moister
than those silken pleasures
which lie in their beds?

If given the choicester
of something to hoister
would you really pick up
McNuggets instead?

Not yet deemed illegal in the land of the eagle,
the oyster can boisterously still be fed
to one's mouth by another, who isn't your mother
of what else so juicy can that still be said?

Acknowledged bi-valvuals, from non-Limbaugh gene pools,
they spread to the right and far left if unquelled.
So shuck 'em! Ursurp 'em! It's high time to slurp 'em.
Gratify oral pleasures which beckon, half-shelled.

Oyster Parade
By Kathy Casey & Ann Manly, 1994
(to the tune of Easter Parade - by Irving Berlin, 1931

In your Oyster bonnet,
With all the shells upon it,
You'll be the grandest mollusk
In the shellfish parade.

I'll be all in seaweed,
When the Oysters filter food,
I'll be the proudest bivalve,
In the Oyster Parade.

On the waterfront, Quilcene waterfront,
The shuckers will snap you
Jon Rowley will map you
In the list of nomenclature

In June the Oysters swoon,
They'll be out of season soon,
You'll be sitting lonely
While the Oysters honeymoon!

The Joy of Oysters

The Brooklyn Seafood, Steak & Oyster House
Oyster Appreciation Day, Oyster & Microbrew Festival

The Brooklyn Seafood,
Steak and Oyster House
1212 Second Ave.
Seattle, WA 98101
(206) 224-7000

In Seattle, Washington, both local residents and visitors from out of town who appreciate fine microbrews served with the freshest oysters obtainable, head to The Brooklyn Seafood, Steak & Oyster House. Located in a historic building adjacent to the new Seattle Symphony's Benaroya Hall and the Seattle Art Museum, The Brooklyn features contemporary Northwest cuisine combining a classic French foundation with Pacific Rim and local influences. The atmosphere and decor evoke the congenial ambiance of the grand old restaurants that were popular during the 1920s through 1940s. The circular oyster bar in the main dining room frequently displays the largest selection of fresh oysters in Seattle. As many as fifteen different oysters may be available each day.

The Brooklyn offers a menu of oyster and beverage pairings developed to assist patrons in obtaining the total dining experience by comparative tasting. These pairings are served on platters containing four of the day's fresh oysters on the half shell, each accompanied by a sample of either an award-winning oyster wine or microbrew. Also available is an oyster with caviar and vodka sampler. The servers at The Brooklyn know their oysters and will help in your selection if you are intimidated by the extensive variety. Other menu items include duck, dry-aged steaks, lamb, fish and vegetarian dishes.

Three yearly happenings at The Brooklyn attract large crowds of enthusiastic seafood lovers. Oyster Appreciation Day is held each May, with a decree from the State of Washington honoring the local oyster industry and lots of activities for attendees. An oyster-slurping contest is followed by live entertainment and lots of oyster eating. Roughly 6,000 oysters are consumed with the proceeds benefitting the Pacific Coast Shellfish Growers Association.

The annual Northwest Oyster and Microbrewery Festival takes place throughout the month of November. In recent years, as many as 40 varieties of oysters and Northwest microbrews have been served. The festival celebrates the return of the Pacific oyster to its prime, and salutes the hand-crafted craft beers of the Pacific Northwest.

In August, The Brooklyn hosts its annual Wild Salmon Festival. At this time, special lunch and dinner entrees are prepared featuring several species of wild salmon, including red king, silver, white king and sockeye. Salmon appetizers, soups, sandwiches and salads complete the menu. A wild salmon sampler is also available, offering a smaller portion of each of the wild species. Visit The Brooklyn Seafood, Steak & Oyster House in Seattle during these three festive occasions, or enjoy a wonderful dining and beverage experience any time of the year.

Chincoteague Oyster Festival - Chincoteague Island, VA

Held each year in October at the Maddox Family Campground on Chincoteague Island. Call or write for more information:
Chincoteague Chamber of Commerce
P.O. Box 258
Chincoteague, VA 23336
(757) 336-6161

A tradition at the Maddox Family Campground since 1972, the Chincoteague Oyster Festival is an all-you-can-eat celebration of oysters and other shellfish from the waters surrounding this famous barrier island. Families come from miles around bringing their folding chairs, coolers with favorite beverages and a hearty appetite for Chincoteague oysters prepared in just about every way imaginable, steamed crabs, clam fritters, hush puppies, potato salad and cole slaw. Proceeds from the $30 per person admission benefit the island's chamber of commerce. A dessert booth is presented by the Chincoteague Oyster and Maritime Museum as a benefit fundraiser for the museum.

Clarenbridge Oyster Festival - Clarenbridge, Ireland

For information on both Ireland oyster festivals, contact the Irish Tourist Board in New York City at (212) 418-0800.

The calmer cousin of the Galway Festival, this feast takes place in the lovely bay-side village of Clarenbridge in early September. If you want to avoid the raucous revelry of the larger event, but still enjoy these wonderful oysters, this festival is a good bet. Festivities include a ladies international oyster shucking competition.

Elliott's Oyster Celebration

For information on events at Elliott's Oyster House, please call 206-623-4340 or 206-224-7157

Elliott's Oyster House
Pier 56
Seattle, WA 98101

This event was formerly known as Elliott's Oyster New Year, where hundreds of oyster lovers gathered on Seattle's Pier 56 for a night of beer, bivalves and revelry. Due to a number of concerns relating to space availability, safety and costs, the event has been re-invented to accommodate a smaller group inside the restaurant. Beer, wine and up to 20 varieties of Northwest oysters are offered for true shellfish aficionados to consume. We commend Elliott's for their consistent leadership in providing the Seattle waterfront's largest variety of half shell oysters at their newly-remodelled oyster bar. Call the restaurant for information on their annual oyster extravaganza.

Florida Seafood Festival - Apalachicola, FL

Held each year the first weekend in November at Battery Park in Apalachicola. For more information call or write:
Florida Seafood Festival
P.O. Box 758
Apalachicola, FL 32320
(888) 653-8011
floridaseafoodfestival.com

Nearly 90% of all commercially harvested oysters in Florida come from the waters around Apalachicola and the surrounding barrier islands. Oysters are such a large part of the area's history and economy that even the local radio station's call letters are "WOYS" - Oyster Radio! The Florida Seafood Festival in Apalachicola began in 1963, and is one of the oldest seafood festivals in the south. Over 20,000 attendees are on hand to enjoy local Apalachicola Bay oysters and a variety of festivities. A local personality heads the celebration as King Retsyo (oyster spelled backwards) and leads the festival through three days of good eatin', fun and games and civic events. The festival begins on Friday with the blessing of the fleet, as local clergymen, King Retsyo and Miss Florida Seafood bless the parade of fishing, oystering, shrimping and recreational vessels as they pass by in the marina.

On Saturday, the activities heat up beginning with the annual Redfish Run, a 5K race through the streets of historic Apalachicola. At the park, live entertainment goes all day as background for lots of eating at the food booths, browsing the arts and crafts booths, and getting ready to cheer competitors in the oyster shucking contest and oyster eating contest. The winner of the shucking contest goes on to compete at St. Mary's County for the national title. The oyster eating competitors just try to keep the dozens (or hundreds) of oysters down to win the title. As the sun sets, revelers head over to the Armory for the annual King Retsyo Ball.

Sunday is a more relaxed day with local bands backing up the eating and browsing activities until the 4 PM closing.

Galway International Oyster Festival & Oyster Opening Contest - Galway, Ireland

The Galway International Oyster Festival takes place each year on the last weekend of September. Visit their web page at: www.galwayoysterfest.com

For *serious* oyster festival goers, the International Oyster Festival in Galway, Ireland is the ultimate, since it is the grand patriarch of them all. The International Festival has been celebrated by residents of Galway and their multinational guests since 1954. This four-day affair of gluttonous feasting is a seafood free-for-all, so be prepared to eat whatever comes up from King Neptune's watery realm. The bays and estuaries surrounding Galway are known for their oysters and scallops, and if you still haven't developed a taste for these treats of the deep, try washing them down with a pint of Guinness or a "Black Velvet" (Guinness and Champagne).

Sweden's Per Olafsson, 2000 shucking champion.

The mayor of Galway begins the festivities by shucking the first oyster of the season, then gulps it down with experienced vigor. Champion oyster shuckers from around the world compete for the World Championship to see who can shuck 30 oysters in the least amount of time . . . but you don't have to be a professional to enjoy the oysters! Oyster season in Ireland is September through December, and at the time of the festival, the last weekend in September, the oysters are just waking up in time for dinner!

Jazz bands and street entertainers join in the celebration while patrons follow music and song along the Guinness "pub trail." Each year a young lady is chosen as the "Oyster Pearl" who presides over ceremonies and events. An added venue for the year 2000 is the New Millennium Marquee, where the Mardi Gras party was held. Ladies, dress in your finest for the international judging of the "Elegant Lady" competition. The black tie ball follows the announcement of the

Olivia Lynch, 2000 Guinness "Oyster Pearl."

Guinness World Oyster Opening Champion, and then the party *really* gets underway. Gourmet experiences, fine wines and liqueurs, golf, sailing and yacht racing, and more Guinness with oysters complete the weekend. This is truly a world class event that sets the standard for all other oyster festivals.

The Joy of Oysters

Annual Milford Oyster Festival

Activities located at various places in Milford, CT. Call for information at (203) 878-5363.

Approximately four nautical miles northeast of the mouth of the Housatonic River on the Connecticut side of Long Island Sound, lies the entrance to Milford harbor. A short distance upriver and you're in the city of Milford, home of the Annual Milford Oyster Festival. Like so many other towns along this area of coastal Connecticut, oystering played an important role in Milford's history. The Milford Oyster Festival was organized in 1974 to promote community pride and civic awareness among Milford's residents, business owners, non-profit organizations, and community leaders. The festival accomplishes this by providing an opportunity for these non-profit groups to raise money, as well as making the public aware of their services and charitable causes.

The one-day event is held on the third Saturday in August, and has several festival locations throughout the town. The day begins with a canoe and kayak race at the Milford boat ramp, and continues with a classic car and motorcycle show at Harbor Landing. The non-profit area is located on the Milford Green, with the lower green featuring exhibits by local businesses, service organizations, environmental and health groups. Along "Main Street USA" attendees have the opportunity to meet

The Annual Milford Oyster Festival.

and speak with business owners one-on-one. The upper green is the site of Connecticut's largest one-day arts and crafts show, with over 200 vendors from the entire eastern seaboard. Separate stages provide a variety of entertainment for all ages, and include '50s and '60s contests, demonstrations, music and dancing at the Swinging Soiree. The main stage features performances by nationally-known musical groups. Children's entertainment runs continuously throughout the day at several locations, with amusement rides, ponies, clowns, and games found at The Fowler Pavilion.

An oyster festival wouldn't be complete without FOOD! Of course there are oysters to eat, along with clams, lobster rolls, sausage and pepper grinders, Italian ices, burgers, pita pockets, soft drinks, desserts, and beer and wine. The Food Court is on Fowler Field adjacent to the pavilion. Festival souvenir booths offer tee shirts, hats and mugs for sale, along with the Milford Bank sponsored "Oysters and Other Shellfish" cookbook.

Staffed entirely by volunteers, the Annual Milford Oyster Festival has become a traditional summer classic, and for over twenty-five years has allowed families and individuals to enjoy a wide variety of activities, food and entertainment.

North Carolina Oyster Festival - Shallotte, NC

Takes place on the third weekend in October at South Brunswick Islands (West Brunswick High School) off Highway 17. For more information, contact:
NC Oyster Festival
P.O. Box 1185
Shallotte, NC 28459
(800) 426-6644

What began as a small oyster roast almost 20 years ago has grown into a popular family event for residents and vacationers of the South Brunswick Islands. Taking place Saturday and Sunday at West Brunswick High School, the festival features over 100 arts and crafts booths, live entertainment and an abundance of delicious seafood. The prescribed method of oyster consumption at this festival is "steamed by the bucket." Hungry oyster lovers take their bucket of steamed bivalves to a stand-up table where they shuck and consume the lightly cooked delicacies by the dozen.

Oyster lovers shucking their buckets of oysters.

An important part of the event is the North Carolina Oyster Shucking Championship which takes place on Saturday right after the amateur shucking contest. The winner of the Championship goes on to St. Mary's County, Maryland to compete for the right to represent the U.S. at the International Oyster Opening Contest in Galway, Ireland.

The North Carolina Oyster Festival also offers 5K and 10K races at Ocean Isle Beach on Saturday morning, and a one mile fun run for the less competitive.

This festival is a great opportunity to participate in a traditional Carolina Oyster Roast, but on a slightly larger scale than Uncle Louie might have known!

Norwalk Seaport Association Oyster Festival - Norwalk, CT

Held each September on the weekend after labor Day at Veterans Memorial Park, in East Norwalk. For Oyster Festival information, write:
The Norwalk Seaport Association
132 Water St.
South Norwalk, CT 06854
(203) 838-9444
Visit the Seaport Association's web page at www.seaport.org

In September 1978, the Norwalk Seaport Association inaugurated its Oyster Festival in Norwalk, Connecticut. That initial event drew approximately 60,000 people from around the Northeast. In the ensuing years, the festival has grown to become the largest festival in the State of Connecticut and the 46th largest in the United States, with well over 100,000 in attendance in recent years. The Norwalk Seaport Association and its Oyster Festival grew out a group of concerned citizens who wanted to revitalize the city's

  The Joy of Oysters

decaying urban waterfront and recapture some of South Norwalk's past glory as a thriving seaport. At one time steamboats carried freight and passengers from Norwalk to New York City, only 40 miles (64 km) away, and prior to steam, large schooners sailed from Norwalk wharves to ports around the world.

Harbor tours are offered to see the historic Sheffield Lighthouse.

During the 19th century Norwalk enjoyed a reputation as a shipbuilding center and boasted a large oystering industry. During the first half of the 20th century, Norwalk's waterfront and maritime industries slowly declined. The rebirth of South Norwalk as a maritime center began in the 1970s with the Association being formed in 1978. The Oyster Festival highlights the revitalized historic district featuring Victorian-era buildings housing numerous shops, restaurants and entertainment centers.

The Oyster Festival begins on Friday evening with the annual Children's Parade taking place on Saturday. The weekend is a continuous stream of events, eating, exhibits, education and entertainment for young and old. Visitors can learn about Norwalk's oyster industry, learn to shuck oysters and cheer their favorite celebrity at the Oyster Slurp-Off. Walking along the bank of the Norwalk River at Veterans Park, you can look across the water to the beautiful building that is home to the largest and most up-to-date oyster company in the world. Tallmadge Brothers, Inc. is a leader in oyster cultivation and harvesting. Tied up next to their facility are several of Tallmadge's twenty-plus wooden oyster boats, all working vessels beautifully maintained to yacht-like condition. The same building also houses the Norwalk Seaport Association.

Recent festivals have included nationally-recognized music performers such as Little Richard, Maynard Ferguson, The Four Tops and Latin percussionist Tito Puente and his Jazz All-Stars. Sea chanteys, ballads, traditional dance tunes and other songs of the sea are performed by Mystic Seaport Museum musicians. Other activities include a Big Boy Toy Show and a juried arts and crafts show highlighting over 225 booths featuring works from artists from around the country.

Local civic organizations prepare tasty eats at booths set up around the festival site. Choose from oysters, clams, Greek sandwiches and pastries, barbecued pork, clam chowder, New England lobster, mussels, burgers, Philly Cheese Steaks – "Uncle Louie! Don't eat so much. Save room for dessert!" Enjoy a cold beer or a glass of wine, dance to a great rhythm & blues band, or just kick back and watch the sun set over the Norwalk waterfront while taking a harbor cruise.

The Norwalk Oyster Festival is certainly an event not to be missed. During this extremely busy weekend, no parking is available at the site, but free shuttle buses transport visitors to the festival from nearby parking lots.

The Walrus and the Carpenter

By Lewis Carroll

(from Through the Looking-Glass and What Alice Found There, 1872)

The sun was shining on the sea,
Shining with all his might:
He did his very best to make
The billows smooth and bright—
And this was odd, because it was
The middle of the night.

The moon was shining sulkily,
Because she thought the sun
Had got no business to be there
After the day was done--
"It's very rude of him," she said,
"To come and spoil the fun!"

The sea was wet as wet could be,
The sands were dry as dry.
You could not see a cloud, because
No cloud was in the sky:
No birds were flying overhead--
There were no birds to fly.

The Walrus and the Carpenter
Were walking close at hand;
They wept like anything to see
Such quantities of sand:
"If this were only cleared away,"
They said, "it would be grand!"

"If seven maids with seven mops
Swept it for half a year.
Do you suppose," the Walrus said,
"That they could get it clear?"
"I doubt it," said the Carpenter,
And shed a bitter tear.

"O Oysters, come and walk with us!"
The Walrus did beseech.
"A pleasant walk, a pleasant talk,
Along the briny beach:
We cannot do with more than four,
To give a hand to each."

  The Joy of Oysters

Four other Oysters followed them,
And yet another four;
And thick and fast they came at last,
And more, and more, and more--
All hopping through the frothy waves,
And scrambling to the shore.

The Walrus and the Carpenter
Walked on a mile or so,
And then they rested on a rock
Conveniently low:
And all the little Oysters stood
And waited in a row.

"The time has come," the Walrus said,
"To talk of many things:
Of shoes–and ships--and sealing-wax–
Of cabbages–and kings--
And why the sea is boiling hot–
And whether pigs have wings."

"But wait a bit," the Oysters cried,
"Before we have our chat;
For some of us are out of breath,
And all of us are fat!"
"No hurry!" said the Carpenter.
They thanked him much for that.

"A loaf of bread," the Walrus said,
"Is what we chiefly need:
Pepper and vinegar besides
Are very good indeed--
Now if you're ready, Oysters dear,
We can begin to feed."

"But not on us!" the Oysters cried,
Turning a little blue.
"After such kindness, that would be
A dismal thing to do!"
"The night is fine," the Walrus said.
"Do you admire the view?"

"It was so kind of you to come!
And you are very nice!"
The Carpenter said nothing but
"Cut us another slice:
I wish you were not quite so deaf--
I've had to ask you twice!"

"It seems a shame," the Walrus said,
"To play them such a trick,
After we've brought them out so far,
And made them trot so quick!"
The Carpenter said nothing but
"The butter's spread too thick!"

"I weep for you," the Walrus said:
"I deeply sympathize."
With sobs and tears he sorted out
Those of the largest size,
Holding his pocket-handkerchief
Before his streaming eyes.

"O Oysters," said the Carpenter,
"You've had a pleasant run!
Shall we be trotting home again?"
But answer came there none--
And this was scarcely odd, because
They'd eaten every one.

Annual Oyster Festival - Oyster Bay, Long Island, NY

Held each year on the third weekend in October. For more information on the Oyster Festival at Oyster Bay, visit their website at www.oysterbay.com or write:

Oyster Bay Chamber of Commerce
P.O. Box 21
Oyster Bay, NY 11771
(516) 624-8082

The town of Oyster Bay, located on Long Island's north shore, is just 30 miles (48 km) from midtown Manhattan, so it's no surprise that its Annual Oyster Festival attracts nearly 300,000 visitors during the Saturday and Sunday celebration. Held during the third weekend of October, this oyster festival dates back to 1984, and presents itself as an old-fashioned street fair throughout the downtown area. Oysters are unique to the community of Oyster Bay, where they have been harvested commercially for over 200 years. The founding sponsor of the festival, Oyster Bay's Frank M. Flower & Son, provides oysters for the event. Oyster growers since 1887, Flower Oyster is the only surviving oyster harvesting company in New York State.

The Oyster Bay Chamber of Commerce, organizer of the festival, is pleased to be able to share this particular bounty of the sea with thousands of people who attend. This Annual Grandaddy of Long Island Festivals is a joint effort linking business, government, and the non-profit sectors of the community.

This "OYSTERific Event" serves oysters in every imaginable form – fried, in chowders and stews, and over 50,000 are eaten on the half shell. Along with the oysters, local fraternal and civic organizations prepare a tempting array of specialty food items. Sweet potato pie,

funnel cakes, bratwurst, fried clams, calamari, shrimp cocktails, littleneck clams, steamed clams, calzones, and apple pie are available to satisfy the hunger pangs that develop as soon as visitors enter the Food Pavilion. For the most part, food at the Oyster Festival is prepared in local kitchens by the volunteers who run the booths. This gives every festival guest the experience of eating food made from the freshest possible ingredients and according to regional recipes.

Restored oystering sloop Christeen.

Among the highlights of the Oyster Festival are the oyster eating and oyster shucking contests, which always draw large crowds of spectators who marvel at the feats being accomplished on stage. The Festival's oyster eating record was set in 1998 by David Leonard of Central Islip, Long Island with 480 oysters eaten in two minutes, five seconds! The Festival shucking record was established in 1985 when Rodney Dow and Andy Schuller tied with each man shucking 57 oysters in the allotted time of four minutes, forty seconds. In order to break the tie, a shuck-off was held, and in the additional two minutes, Dow won with an additional 22 oysters shucked.

The Joy of Oysters

Oyster eating contest at Oyster Bay Festival.

Music, music, music . . . on four performance stages, is heard all weekend with styles including jazz, blues, funk and classic rock. A family-oriented children's entertainment area offers interactive arts and crafts, rides, magicians, contests and web site demonstrations. A large arts and crafts exhibit can be found in two locations of downtown Oyster Bay featuring painting, glass, photography, woodworking, jewelry and many seasonal and general crafts. On the waterfront, a historic boat exhibit features free tours of classic vessels on display at the marina. An arctic exploration ship, a Grand Banks fishing schooner, and the oyster sloop Christeen – newly restored to her original 1883 design – are among the boats that can be seen in the picturesque harbor. With a backdrop of beautiful fall foliage, the views of these lovely boats will delight visiting photographers and artists. Harbor cruises are also available aboard a historic paddle boat.

Oysterfest - Chesapeake Bay Maritime Museum, St. Michael's, MD

Osyterfest takes place the first Saturday in November, 10 AM to 4 PM. For more information call:

Chesapeake Bay Maritime Museum
(410) 745-2916

Located on Maryland's Eastern Shore, St. Michael's is a historic town that is woven together with the lives of the watermen of the Chesapeake. The Chesapeake Bay Maritime Museum is a remarkable complex of nine waterfront buildings that illustrate this lifestyle of hard work on the Bay.

Monthly classes and programs are held to educate and entertain, all of which center around boating, local history or enjoying the bounty of the Bay. Oysterfest is among the latter, offering oysters on the half shell, steamed or fried along with instruction in shucking, tonging and nippering. Museum admission gains you access to the event, additional charges apply for food, beverages and boat rides.

Don't miss the Museum Store to stock up on quality gifts and artwork centered around the Chesapeake Bay theme.

The Oyster Run – NW Washington State
Leather, Lace, Chrome ... and Oysters!

For information on the Oyster Run, call (425) 259-2661, or just show up in North Everett, Washington on the last Sunday of September between 6:00 and 10:00 AM. See you there!

What began 20 years ago as a local motorcycle club's ride through the beautiful crisp fall countryside – sampling oysters and beer along the way – has turned into the largest annual motorcycle run in the State of Washington and the Pacific Northwest. The "Oyster Run" is held on the last Sunday of September and has attracted more riders and spectators each year since it began in 1982. The 1999 event attracted in excess of 20,000 motorcycles, a lineup of almost 50 miles if ridden single file with one bike-length spacing out the riders. With an average of almost two riders per bike, plus hundreds of non-riding adults and children who attend just to experience the sight (and sound) of these beautiful iron stallions, we're talking a lot of people!

First, an explanation for those gentle readers not familiar with a motorcycle "run." A run is a ride taken by a group of motorcyclists that usually has a purpose or a theme attached to it. The run normally follows a pre-determined route along various scenic highways and back roads. A route sheet with directions is distributed to the riders prior to

Bikes line up outside the Conway Pub.

departure. One of the oldest types of run is a "poker run," in which a playing card is given to each rider at designated points along the way. At the end of the run, the cards are turned in and the riders with the best poker hand are winners. There are many types of runs including toy runs to collect toys for needy children during the Christmas season, fun runs, love runs, benefit runs, lobster runs in Maine, and the Northwest's own Oyster Run. The end of a run usually brings the riders to some type of gathering or party (usually with copious amounts of food), and the Oyster Run is no exception.

The Oyster Run is a well-organized event that begins with a pancake breakfast in Everett, Washington, approximately 30 miles (48 km) north of Seattle. The run has no definite route so groups of riders begin at

Oysters are grilled for hundreds of hungry riders.

other locations such as Granite Falls and Stanwood. The run follows a loose course through the picturesque Skagit Valley and the towns of Conway, Clearlake, Edison, Sedro Woolley,

Oyster Shooters are brought out by the dozen at each stop of the Oyster Run.

Bow and on into the beautiful seaport town of Anacortes. Along the way, many participating watering holes serve oysters prepared in various ways. Most are consumed as "shooters," a raw oyster in a shot glass, downed with a beer chaser, but many of the pubs offer them grilled, steamed, or fried.

On this run you can ride at your own pace, there's no time schedule and no required route, but you'd better be in Anacortes for the afternoon events. The entire downtown area is reserved for cycles only, and starting around 1:00 PM thousands of pedestrians line the streets to gawk at the beauty and number of bikes. If the sun shines, leather jackets and chaps are stripped away, revealing many tattooed limbs, torsos, and other parts of the human body in a colorful display of ink and flesh. Live bands perform from stages assembled in the streets, motorcycle drill teams demonstrate their riding skills and intricate maneuvers, vendors hawk cycle-related wear, bikers for Jesus preach the word and even more oysters are devoured at beer gardens, food booths and concession stands. Ribs, burgers, corn on the cob, curly fries, and ice cream can also be found, but the oyster is the champ at this run.

Sponsors for the Oyster Run include Western Washington Harley-Davidson dealers, along with participating bike accessory shops, local restaurants, cafes, markets and, of course, Blau Oyster Company of nearby Samish Island. The run is organized and promoted by "Limp Lee" and other members of the Oyster Run Committee, and is held every year – rain or shine.

The Oyster Stampede

The Oyster Stampede South Bend, Washington Presented annually on the Memorial Day Weekend by the South Bend Chamber of Commerce.
For more information, call: 360-875-5874.

The arrival of Memorial Day weekend marks the unofficial start of the summer season to many people. Communities all across America honor their servicemen and women with parades down Main Street, barbecues in the back yard, and family picnics and camping trips during the long weekend. To the historic community of South Bend, Washington however, Memorial Day weekend means one thing, and only one thing, the Annual "Oyster Stampede," a four day festival celebrating the stampeding oysters of Willapa Bay.

Continued on next page.

The Joy of Oysters 295

Legend has it that during the late spring, just before they begin to spawn, the oysters in the bay get very restless. So restless, in fact, that they have been known to spring from their beds and "stampede" to every corner of Willapa Bay in search of a mate! The lives of the oystermen are at risk during this time, since they may easily be trampled by the mating masses of mollusks as they stampede throughout the bay. To offer the oystermen an escape route, tall poles have been placed in high stampede areas so the men can quickly climb out of harm's way, avoiding serious injury. During this period of total chaos in the water, you will see oystermen perched atop these poles shouting this warning to others as the oysters stampede by: "Here they come again!"

Local favorite Brady's Oyster Company serves up a variety of oysters and oyster dishes.

The Oyster Stampede was established in 1985 to observe this very dangerous time of year for local oystermen, and to recognize the important role that oystering has played in the history of South Bend. The town of South Bend is nestled along a gentle curve of the Willapa River on its south shore. Large signs on either end of town proclaim South Bend "The Oyster Capital of the World." Just a short distance downstream to the west, the river widens and empties into Willapa Bay, where highly productive oyster beds are found in shallow protected estuaries of the bay. Coast Oyster Company operates out of South Bend, and its plant is open to the public for tours during the Stampede. The seafood pavilion directly across the street from the oyster company offers a culinary sampling of oysters and other seafood dishes at a variety of concession stands and food booths. South Bend is the Pacific County seat, and the beautiful courthouse overlooking the river offers guided tours during the festival. Other events during the Oyster Stampede include a Sunday morning pancake breakfast, Native American pow-wow, a teen dance, arts and craft displays, softball tournament, story telling, oyster eating and shucking contests, a carnival, and entertainment for the entire family. On Friday evening the festival begins with a multi-course gourmet dinner accompanied by Washington State wines. While attending the Oyster Stampede, visit the Pacific County Museum, which houses many exhibits relating to the local history and development of the county, including an extensive display on oystering in Willapa Bay.

If you happen to be venturing through southwest Washington in late May, stop by the Annual Oyster Stampede for a great family weekend. Just be sure to watch out for those oysters— they'll run right over you! "Look! Uncle Louie!—Here they come again!"

The Joy of Oysters

Shaw's Crab House "Royster with the Oyster" Festival - Chicago, IL

"Royster with the Oyster" is held each October. For more information contact:
Shaw's Crab House
21 East Hubbard
Chicago, IL 60611
(312) 527-2722
www.shaws.com

An oyster festival in Chicago? Get outta town! Your heard right, and it all happens at Shaw's Crab House, a Chicago dining institution which has hosted their "Royster with the Oyster" festival since 1989. Each October, oyster lovers rejoice as Shaw's presents a week-long festival filled with fresh oysters and oyster specials daily, live bands, and special events nightly. The festival highlight is Friday night's big "Royster with the Oyster" celebration in the giant tent outside the restaurant.

"Royster with the Oyster" is now a Chicago tradition, featuring daily events and promotions in Shaw's Blue Crab Lounge. Special prices on half shell oysters and live "Oyster Blues" nightly keep regulars coming in, while daily oyster slurping contests culminate in the championship competition on Friday night. The head chefs at Shaw's serve up oyster specialties all during the week including fried oysters, hangtown fry, oyster stew, oyster bisque, barbecued oysters and oyster biscuits. Recent "Royster" nights have included multi-course dinners with elaborate food and wine pairings, microbrew tastings, and the recent "Taste of Tabasco" night.

Oyster lovers enjoy their favorite food and drink at Shaw's Royster with the Oyster!

The excitement of the Friday night "Royster with the Oyster" Hubbard Street Tent Party is overwhelming with live Chicago blues, tons of freshly shucked oysters, jambalaya, catfish sandwiches, beer, wine AND the final heat of the Championship Slurp-Off. There is no cover charge for the event in the tent! Chicago and "Royster with the Oyster" . . . sounds like my kind of town!

Oyster eating in Chicago, a long and colorful tradition, has been revived to new heights at Shaw's Crab House featuring the freshest oysters procured from both coasts daily.

Shelton Oysterfest
West Coast Oyster Shucking Championship and
Washington State Seafood Festival

In 1982, the Skookum Rotary Club of Shelton, Washington and the Pacific Coast Oyster Growers Association co-sponsored a weekend festival that surpassed the expectations of all who organized the event that first year. Within hours after the gates opened on that first Saturday morning, the fairgrounds where the festival took place were taken over by eager patrons sampling the food, enjoying the entertainment and exhibits, and anxiously awaiting an opportunity to see professional oyster shuckers competing for the honor of West Coast Oyster Shucking Champion. On the Sunday of that inaugural festival, the very popular United States Senator Henry "Scoop" Jackson was on hand for an appearance. That first year they ran out of tickets, food, ice, and parking spaces, and the organizers were overwhelmed by the tremendous public response shown at the initial Oysterfest. The event has grown in both number of exhibitors and public attendance since 1982, making the Oysterfest in Shelton one of the most popular annual celebrations in the state. It is held on the first weekend of October at the Mason County Fairgrounds.

Information about Oysterfest can be found on its web page, www.oysterfest.org, or through the Shelton/Mason County Chamber of Commerce at: 360-426-2021,
or write:
OYSTERFEST
P.O. Box 849
Shelton, WA 98584

Getting the crowd warmed up for the oyster shucking competition.

The highlight of the weekend is the oyster shucking competition, which consists of two categories: speed shucking, and half shell presentation. Speed shucking is based on time only, while half shell presentation, although a timed event, takes into account the quality of the shucked oyster, and its final appearance for eating on the half shell. It's the half shell competition that determines the West Coast Champion. Preliminary heats of these events take place throughout the two-day festival, with the finals being held on Sunday afternoon. Spectators are encouraged to cheer and root for their favorite shucker, and the shells begin to fly at the sound of the starting gun. The winner of the West Coast shucking competition shows off his or her skills several weeks later at the National Oyster Shucking Championship in Leonardtown, Maryland, and the winner of that event flies to Galway, Ireland to compete for the title of International Oyster Shucking Champion. This is serious business, folks.

While the main outdoor stage alternates between the shucking competition and the great variety of family entertainment, elsewhere at the fairgrounds people line up at the many food stands to purchase oysters, oysters, and more oysters! Shooters, fritters, spicy grilled oysters, cajun oyster sandwiches, Oysters Rockefeller, and bacon wrapped oysters are just a few of the tempting preparations available. Since this is a seafood festival as well, try the shrimp tempura, linguine with clam sauce, lobster, shrimp gumbo, chowders, shrimp puffs and steamed mussels. "Hey Uncle Louie, they've got Geoduck Burgers over here!" "What is a geoduck?", you ask! Pronounced gooey-duck, it is a large... no, a VERY large clam found along coastal areas of the Pacific Northwest. When properly prepared, they make for excellent eating. Other goodies include BBQ beef sandwiches, scones & jam,

caramel apples, pies, burgers, rootbeer floats, and baked potatoes. Beer and wine is available and the entertainment stage nearby offers the grown ups a place to listen and dance to live blues, rock, and country bands.

Each exhibit hall at the fairgrounds has displays ranging from art and photography galleries to environmental demonstrations. Since water quality is so important to the success of aquaculture and marine life, many exhibits offer information and literature on how the public can contribute to

Lots of oysters are served up to hungry festival-goers.

the cause of clean water. Boating organizations offer classes on boating safety, while sport fishermen share their secrets to successful casting. Both amateurs and professionals compete on the Oysterfest Cook-off stage, as the audience sips wine and beer provided by the many fine wineries and microbreweries in the area. For salty dogs and landlubbers alike, the Oysterfest has something for everyone. The vendors and exhibitors at Oysterfest are non-profit organizations, and their commitment to the community of Shelton and the state of Washington is evident by the wonderful enthusiasm shown during the weekend.

The Mason County Fairgrounds, on Washington's scenic Olympic Peninsula, is located on Highway 101 about 20 miles (32 km) north of Olympia, adjacent to the Shelton airport (Sanderson Field). Parking is free, RV space is available, and shuttle transportation to Oysterfest is provided from locations in downtown Shelton, a few miles away.

When the first Oysterfest opened it's gates on that brisk Saturday in October, 1982, our own author, Oyster Bill, was there- oyster knife in hand, ready to compete against (unknown to him at that time) PROFESSIONAL shuckers. Thinking that he was pretty good at removing oysters from their shells without doing too much damage, he proceeded to come in dead last in the first preliminary heat, eliminating him from any further competition. Head judge John Blau told him at the time, "Your oysters looked real good, you just need to do it a little faster." Not being one to take defeat lying down, Oyster Bill returned the following year, but instead of entering the shucking competition, he participated in the cook-off, taking home a prize ribbon for his creamed oyster and spinach bisque.

St. Mary's County Oyster Festival – Leonardtown, MD

Held each year on the third weekend in October at the county fairgrounds. Write or call for more information:
The Oyster Festival Office
P.O. Box 766
California, MD 20619
(301) 863-5015

To receive a copy of the 1999 Oyster Cook-Off Cookbook, send $4.00 to:
Oyster Cook-Off Cookbook
P.O. Box 653
Attn: EDC
Leonardtown, MD 20650

Just a short drive southeast of the nation's capitol, lies a small rural peninsula known as St. Mary's County, Maryland. Bordered by the Potomac and Patuxent Rivers and Chesapeake Bay, this beautiful area surrounded by over 400 miles (640 km) of shoreline and acres of unspoiled park land offers the perfect getaway destination for a weekend of family fun. During the third weekend of October, the county fairgrounds near Leonardtown is the site of a two-

day jubilee that has grown to become one of the leading folk festivals on the Eastern Seaboard – the annual St. Mary's County Oyster Festival. Presented by the Rotary Club of St. Mary's County, Lexington Park, the festival celebrates the opening of the oyster season on Chesapeake Bay, and provides a means for local charities and community non-profit organizations to raise money. Held since 1967, the Oyster Festival has come to mean great food, fantastic entertainment, and family fun. More than 20,000 visitors attend the event each year.

The Joy of Oysters

Country and western, barbershop, swing, classical, square dancing, and bluegrass are all part of the musical entertainment that performs continuously during the two days of the festival. Children enjoy clowns, pony rides, carnival games and a Chesapeake Bay balladeer. Oyster shucking lessons are given daily, arts and crafts vendors provide items for curious shoppers, and who knows what you'll find at "King Oyster's Treasure Chest," a yard sale of immense proportion.

The real reason for all of the excitement centers around King Oyster! While strolling the fairgrounds, you can sample fried oysters, oyster stew, half shell oysters, oyster shooters, and scalded oysters. Soft shell crab (an item that is unfamiliar to many West Coasters), catfish sandwiches, seafood chowder and delightful homemade desserts are all available to tempt every palate. Be sure to try a stuffed ham sandwich, a local St. Mary's specialty not to be missed!

In 1980, a new feature was added to the festival. The National Oyster Cook-Off recipe competition attracts cooks from across the country, and features twelve finalists whose recipes are chosen from more than 200 entries. Categories of the competition include oyster main dishes, oyster hors d'oeuvres, oyster soups & stews and outdoor oyster cookery. The best overall recipe is selected from the top winner in each category with the champion taking home the $1,000 grand prize. Visitors can sample the contestants dishes and can purchase a cookbook celebrating 20 years of oyster recipes.

The St. Mary's Oyster Festival also determines the winner of the National Oyster Shucking Contest. On both Saturday and Sunday, competitors for this contest are eliminated by several shucking heats until two finalists (one male, one female) remain. To finish the event, the champion woman shucker competes against the men's champ for the Grand Prize – cash and all-expense paid trip to Galway, Ireland, where he or she will represent the United States in the International Oyster Shucking Championship.

The St. Mary's Oyster Festival is a wonderful way to spend a fall weekend with friends and family. Exhibits sponsored by the county, private community organizations and the local U.S. Naval Air Station are both entertaining and educational, and guarantee an increased appreciation for the star of this festival, King Oyster. Located 55 miles (88 km) south of Washington, D.C. and 75 miles (120 km) southeast of Baltimore.

Testicle Festival - Rocky Mountain Oyster Feed

Held the third weekend in September each year at Rock Creek Lodge P.O. Box 835 Clinton, MT 59825 (406) 825-4868 www.testyfesty.com

"Have a ball at the Testicle Festival!" proclaims the poster for this once-a-year gathering in Clinton, Montana - 22 miles east of Missoula. At Rod Lincoln's Rock Creek Lodge the name of the main course is Rocky Mountain Oysters — Montana Tendergroin — also known as bull's testicles, specially prepared for the thousands of party goers that arrive during the third weekend in September. Lincoln shares much of the preparation technique as follows: "The meat arrives frozen. First, I skin the membrane off, slice the meat and soak it in brine for 48 hours. I take them out of the brine and them marinate them in beer for 24 hours. The meat is dehydrated in a cooler, then battered and quick frozen. The batter includes the secret combination of herbs and spices added for flavoring." As the orders are prepared, cooks at the Rock Creek Lodge deep fry the delicacies at 300° F. and serve it with a special dipping sauce.

Rod Lincoln

The annual party features events like a hairy chest contest, wet t-shirt contest and various games of skill involving pitching bull dung. A sponsor of the event is Rainier Beer, giving some idea that a little attitude adjustment is necessary for tipping testicles.

If you just have a desire for the memorabilia, you can order hats, shirts, key chains, posters and dozens of other logo items from Rod Lincoln's website at www.testyfesty.com. Note that the website features photos of exposed men and women enjoying various events.

J. Millard Tawes Oyster & Bull Roast, Crisfield, MD

At the Somers Cove Marina, third Saturday in October, 1 to 5 PM. Call for more information:
Crisfield Heritage Foundation
(410) 968-2501

Named for former Maryland Governor J. M. Tawes, a resident of Crisfield, this all-you-can-eat, waterside event offers oysters and pit-roasted beef to hungry Crisfielders and visitors alike. Founded in 1662, Crisfield is on Maryland's Eastern Shore and has strong ties with the crabbing and oystering industries.

Urbanna Oyster Festival – Urbanna, VA

The festival takes place the first weekend in November on Friday and Saturday. For more information call or write:
Urbanna Oyster Festival Foundation
P.O. Drawer C
Urbanna, VA 23175
(804) 758-0368
www.urbanna.com

The community of Urbanna, Virginia was founded in 1680 with the name honoring England's Queen Anne. Located on Urbanna Creek and the Rappahannock River, the town is just a few miles from Chesapeake Bay and the bounty of seafood that has made the area famous for over three centuries.

Taking place in one of America's oldest settlements, it is appropriate that the Urbanna Oyster Festival is among America's oldest Oyster Festivals as well. The festival began in 1958 and is now the official Oyster Festival of the Common-wealth of Virginia. The two-day event draws over 75,000 people from near and far who arrive by both land and sea. Oysters are served raw, roasted, steamed, stewed, fried and frittered. Crab cakes, ham biscuits, and other treats for young and old are available. Many venues throughout the picturesque community offer entertainment, arts and crafts, children's entertainment, ship tours and other waterfront activities.

The Friday night Fireman's Parade draws fire and rescue units from around Virginia and thousands line the streets of town for the extravaganze of flashing lights and sirens. The Oyster Festival Parade takes place on Saturday afternoon presenting the Oyster Festival Queen and Little Miss Spat chosen for citizenship, personality and academics by interviews throughout the summer.

Serious oyster lovers never miss the official Virginia Oyster Shucking Contest which takes place on the Firehouse Stage on Saturday morning. The winner of this contest partici-pates in the St. Mary's County, Maryland championship leading to the international contest in Galway, Ireland.

Water Music Festival, Oysters & Jazz - Long Beach, WA

For information on the Water Music Festival, contact the Long Beach Peninsula Visitor's Bureau at (800) 451-2542. Tickets may be obtained by writing:
Water Music Festival
P.O. Box 524
Seaview, WA 98644-0524

Visit the Water Music Festival web page at: www.watermusicfestival .com or the Visitor's Bureau web page at: www.funbeach.com

As the busy months of summer wane toward a more relaxed time of year, the beautiful Long Beach Peninsula in southwest Washington State plays home to one of the most unique music festivals in the United States. An annual event since 1985, the Water Music Festival celebrates chamber music with a series of diverse concerts in venues that allow the audience to participate with the musicians in their virtuosity and creativity. This offers listeners the chance to hear beautiful music performed in towns along the lower Columbia River as well as on the peninsula, and in locations that are enhanced by the natural beauty of the area. Several of the concerts are offered free of charge so that everyone has access to the music.

Although the chamber music concerts take place in October, the kick-off to the festival is the "Jazz and Oysters" concert held on a Sunday afternoon in August on the sprawling lawn of the historic one-room Oysterville Schoolhouse. Food available at the concert includes oysters on the half shell, grilled oysters, cheeses, pates and breads, desserts created by the peninsula's finest chefs, plus wines, beers and soft drinks. The music, performed by various groups of instrumentalists and vocalists, ranges from hot jazz to cool blues to foot-stompin' soul. This is a very popular concert, so plan to arrive early.

The Jazz and Oysters concert is always on the the Sunday afternoon preceding the week-long Washington State International Kite Festival, which is held on the peninsula during the third full week of August. The chamber music concert series takes place during the fourth weekend in October.

The Joy of Oysters

Support Your Local Oyster Feed

As your travels take you along back roads of the more rural oyster growing areas of North America, you will discover hidden treasures of local gastronomy. There are hundreds of establishments that you won't find listed in any restaurant guides or tour books. These places include beach side shacks, social clubs, grange halls, pubs and taverns, and elbow to elbow standing-room-only seafood bars. Many of these joints have special days throughout the year honoring the oyster.

The advertising for these shindigs usually consists of leaflets hung on windows and bulletin boards around town. Sometimes it's just "word of mouth" that passes the information along. Searching for these eating frenzies can be an adventure in itself. Ask around while visiting local waterfronts, and keep an eye out for posted flyers, which will usually contain phrases such as "All-You-Can-Eat!," or Oyster Feed!" These down home get togethers are out there, and they're wonderful. You just have to find them!

Astoria, Oregon is home to one of these many oyster indulgences. Jeffers Gardens Inn, located on Old Highway 101 out by the airport, has one or two oyster feeds a year. There's no particular weekend, just whenever they want to have one. Might be November, might be February. You need to call them ahead to find out when the next one will be.

This local gathering place has been around for years, and its business card reads: "Jeffers Gardens Inn, Restaurant and 18 Hole Mini Golf Course-Children Welcome." On Oyster Feed night, owners Mark Chilson and his mother Betty grill oysters out back, and when they're done, deliver them on a

Mark and Betty of Jeffers Gardens Inn

large tray to the pool table, which is transformed to a buffet table for the evening. Accompanied by coleslaw and garlic bread, the oysters disappear as fast as they're brought out, with a fresh supply arriving in short order.

The beer is cold, and the oysters are hot, and both Betty and Mark will make even first time visitors feel like old friends within no time at all. The scenic beauty of the area, with the mouth of the Columbia River just minutes away, make Jeffers Gardens Inn worth visiting, especially during one of their all-you-can-eat Oyster Feeds. Call Mark at 503-325-4352 for more information. Jeffers Gardens, 34635 Highway 105, Astoria, OR 97103.

Love on the Half Shell
Eat Oysters, Love Longer

In the James Bond movie "You Only Live Twice," a sultry femme fatale offers Agent 007 some oysters. "Well, I don't need these!" he says resolutely. Agent 007 obviously realized that oysters are an aphrodisiac, but, rather than let anyone think he needed help in the sexual arena, he passed on the tasty morsels.

Let us consider Casanova, who regularly downed at least fifty oysters in the nude before playing oyster "games of the tongue" in the bathtub with his two special ladies, Armelline and Emilie. Casanova, who referred to oysters as "a spur to the spirit and to love," described his oyster antics in writing: "We amused ourselves in eating oysters after the voluptuous fashion of lovers. We then sucked the oysters in, one by one, after placing the oyster on the other's lips. Voluptuous readers, try it and tell me whether it is not the nectar of the gods!" For the record, this was one of the least sexy games he played with oysters. We leave the rest to imagination.

From both a medical and psychological standpoint, no food has been held in greater regard as an aphrodisiac throughout history than oysters. Our term aphrodisiac (which means stimulating or intensifying sexual desire) is derived from ancient Greek *aphrodisiados* (of sexual love). Aphrodite, who sprang forth from the sea on the half shell, received her name from this term for love, combining the Greek terms *aphros*, meaning "of the foam," and *aphrite* (a pearly calcite).

Casanova is just one example of how slurping can enhance our sexual prowess. As early as 5 B.C., gluttonous Romans, who prized oysters as delights of lust and pleasure, always included great quantities of oysters in their elaborate feasts. Intoxicated by oysters and wine, the promiscuous Romans often ended their feasts with sexual orgies. Diamond Jim Brady, known for his womanizing, demanded at least five-dozen oysters before dinner and any post-dining "exercise." Oysters were lustful Louis XIV's favorite food; he never slurped less than 100 at a time. Oysters were also a favorite of Queen Elizabeth. We can only imagine how they affected her. "Lett me not fayle of oysters," wrote her friend, Sir Francis Walsingham, who took oysters to her every time he visited. We could continue, but surely you get the idea: Oysters turn people on.

Galen, a noted Greek physician (130 - 200 A.D.) often prescribed oysters to men and women who needed a boost with their sex lives. And modern day Dr. David Reuben, author of *Everything You Always Wanted to Know About Sex*, recommends oysters as a sexual stimulant. What is it about oysters that gives them their sexual reputation? Quite a few things contribute to an oyster's powers as a love potion.

To start, there is the mystique about the oyster's own sexual life. Their reproductive capacity is extremely robust: During spawning season, a healthy female emits roughly 100 million unfertilized eggs in just one season. Topping that, males release over one billion sperm. Furthermore, oysters can live up to forty years and they remain as prolific in old age as they are in youth. Also, there is the oyster's intriguing capability of changing sexes. Most of them change sex once or more during their lifetime.

Mystique aside, few foods are better balanced nutritionally than oysters. They are one of the richest sources of vitamins and minerals and, as we know, when we feel healthy and active, our sex lives are usually much improved. Containing just 75 calories per dozen, oysters contain beneficial Omega 3 fatty acids, which lower bad cholesterol. They are also packed with vitamins and minerals — containing Vitamins A, B1, B2, C and D, and minerals: including calcium, iodine, magnesium, iron potassium, copper, sodium, phosphorous, manganese, sulphur and zinc.

Zinc, which is considered essential for the metabolism of testosterone, is found in great quantities in oysters. They absorb high concentrations of zinc from seawater and store it in their mantle and gills. Zinc is vital for the functioning of the male prostate gland, which is essential for sex. In fact, the prostrate gland requires more zinc than any other organ in the body. Many claim that oysters are nature's Viagra.

Lovemaking is also enhanced by an oyster's dopamine content. Like the beneficial chemical endorphin, which our bodies release during exercise, dopamine is a neurotransmitter that enhances our intensity of sensation by heightening brain activity and increasing sexual desire. Many people are also aroused by looking at freshly shucked oysters due to their physical resemblance to human genitalia. Some are reminded of male apparatus, while most compare oysters on the half shell to a female's private parts.

As you see, there are many great reasons for eating oysters. If you are still not convinced, we hope you will follow the sound advice from a doctor to his 98-year-old patient. His recommendation "For long life and a happy heart, eat oysters."

In celebration of love on the half shell, we leave you with a bawdy poem by 16th century French humorist and satirist, Francois Rabelais:

"Drink! I know I shall be wed.
How my wife will love her bed!
The pot snaps shut, the stout eel wriggles,
Lord, What a juicy framblefriggles!
Marriage? Marriage is my oyster!
Harder, deeper, lower, moister.
Toss them down and drain them dry.
Hail the hymeneal urge
Of the perfect groom, Panurge!
Hail to marital relations!
Hail to joyous copulation!"

North American Oyster Growers

The following list of growers includes those that replied to our questionnaires or were recommended by industry associates.

Alabama

Bay Harvest Oysters
15055 Zirlott Road
Coden, AL 36523-0342
334-873-4347

Blackies Oysters
14085 Shell Belt Road
Bayou La Batre, AL 36509-0236
334-824-7705

Seaman Oysters
Highway 188
Coden, AL 36523
334-824-3100

Alaska

Aquabionics, Inc.
Jack M. Van Hyning
P.O. Box 80165
Fairbanks, AK 99708
907-479-2476
E-Mail: jvanhnring@compuserve.com

Elfin Cove Oysters
Elfin Cove, AK 99825
907-239-2224

Oyster Cove Sea Farms
Homer, AK 99603
907-235-8032

Pristine Products
P.O. Box 1272
Seward, AK 99664
907-255-2340

Qutekcak Shellfish Hatchery
P.O Box 369
Seward, AK 99664
907-224-5181

Sitka Sea Farm
Madelon Mottet, Ph.D.
704 Sawmill Creek Blvd.
Sitka, AK 99835
907-747-3862
E-Mail: madelon@ptialaska.net

Tatitlek Mariculture
P.O. Box 171
Tatitlek, AK 99677
907-325-2311

Tenass Pass Shellfish Co.
Rodger Painter
P.O. Box 20704
Juneau, AK 99802
907-463-3600
E-Mail: seacultu@eagle.ptialaska.net

California

Hog Island Oyster Co.
John Finger, Michael Watchorn, Terry Sawyer
P.O. Box 829, 20215 State Route No 1
Marshall, CA 94940
415-663-9218
E-Mail: hogislnd@svn.net

Tomales Bay Oyster Co.
15479 Highway 1
Marshall, CA 94940
415-663-1242

Johnson Oyster Co.
17171 Sir Francis Drake Bl
Inverness, CA 94937-0972
415-669-1149
Web: seadriftrealty.com/oysters.htm

Point Reyes Oyster Co.
11101 Highway 1
Point Reyes Station , CA 94956
415-663-8373

Connecticut

Tallmadge Brothers, Inc.
132 Water Street
South Norwalk, CT 06854
Port Norris, NJ

Norm Bloom and Company
7 Edgewater Place
East Norwalk, CT
203-866-7546

Florida

Buddy Ward & Sons
Walter Ward
Post Office Box 697
Apalachicola, FL 32329
850-653-8932
Fax 850-653-2184

David's Seafood
David Sasnett
472 C Highway 98
Eastpoint, FL 32328
850-670-4530
Fax 850-670-4814

Joe Taranto & Son Seafood
Anthony Taranto
Post Office Box 387
Apalachicola, FL 32329
850-653-9328

Lynn's Quality Oysters
Lynn Martina
Post Office Box 247
Eastpoint, FL 32328
850-670-8796
Fax 850-670-8548
E-Mail: lynnmartina@digitalexp.com

Milas Inc.
Anthony Koromilas
3640 Alan Drive
Titusville, FL 32789
407-269-1931
E-Mail: akoromilas@aol.com

R.M. Seafood, Inc.
Rocky Moore
Post Office Box 580
Eastpoint, FL 32328
850-670-8679
Fax 850-670-4363

Webbs Seafood, Inc.
Robert Webb
12603 Hwy. 231
Youngstown, FL 32466
850-722-9598
Fax 850-722-1010

Cooke's Oysters
Mr. & Mrs. Richard Cooke
Post Office Box 21
Cedar Key, FL 32625
352-543-5948

Oyster Co-op, Inc.
Danny Juskowski
4609 Westconnett Boulevard
Jacksonville, FL 32210
904-779-6999
Fax 904-908-9992

Louisiana

Ameripure Oyster Companies
P.O. Box 308
Kenner, LA 70063
800-EAT M RAW (328-6729)
Fax 504-467-0450
Web: ameripure.com

M. J. Bilich Oyster Co.
2331 N. Rampart St.
New Orleans, LA 70117
504-949-5544

Oyster Farms, Inc.
5917 Hopedale Hwy.
Yscloskey, LA 70003
504-676-3309

P & J Oysters
1039 Toulouse St.
New Orleans, LA 70112
504-523-2651

Maine

Glidden Point
Barb Scully
707 River Road
Edgecomb, ME 04556
207-633-3599
E-Mail: barb@oysterfarm.com

Spinney Creek Shellfish
Lori and Thomas L. Howell
P.O. Box 310, 2 Howell Lane
Eliot, ME 03903
207-439-2719
Fax 207-439-7643
E-Mail:
LAHowell.Spinneycreek@RSCS.net

Massachusetts

Aquaculture Research Corp.
Richard Kraus
P.O. Box 2028
Dennis, MA 02638
508-385-3933
Fax 508-385-3935
E-Mail: arc@capecod.net

Barnstable SeaFarms
Les Hemmila
P.O. Box 321
Cummaquid, MA 02637
508-362-2137
E-Mail: bsfarms@capecod.net

Billingsgate Shellfish Co.
Bob Wallace
P.O. Box 454
South Wellfleet, MA 02663
508-349-7556
E-Mail: rwallace@C4.net

Cuttyhunk Shellfish Farms, Inc
Seth Garfield
P.O. Box 51
Cuttyhunk, MA 02713
508-990-1317

Valli Enterprises
Brent Valli
255 Cahoon Hollow Road
Wellfleet, MA 02667
508-237-0737
Fax 508-349-3143

Waquoit Shellfish Corp.
Denise Kelley
P.O. Box 413
East Falmouth, MA 02536
508-548-2683

Wellfleet Oyster & Clam
Irving Puffer
P.O. Box 1439
Wellfleet, MA 02667
800-72-9227
Fax 508-349-2717

Woodbury's Inc.
Patrick and Barbara Woodbury
P.O. Box 828
Wellfleet, MA 02667
508-349-9852
E-Mail: pbsnwood@capecod.net

Maryland

Bivalve Oyster Packing Co.
Princess Anne, MD 21853
410-651-2383

Maryland Crab & Oyster
2460 Bennett Point Road
Queenstown, MD 21658
410-827-5400

McNasby's Oyster Company
723 2nd Street
Annapolis, MD 21403-0332
410-280-2722

Metompkin Bay Oyster Co.
Dock Street
Crisfield, MD 21817
410-968-0662

Mississippi

J & R Oysters
Sones Chapel Road
Picayune, MS 39466
601-798-3907

New York

Frank M. Flower & Son
Oyster Bay, NY
Bayville, NY

Oregon

Bay Ocean Oyster
603 Garibaldi Avenue
Garibaldi, OR 97118
503-322-0040

Clausen Oysters
811 N Bay Drive, Bldg. A
North Bend, OR 97459-0957
541-756-3600

Coos Bay Oyster Co.
5055 Boat Basin Drive
Coos Bay, OR 97420
541-888-5525

The Last Place On Earth LLC.
PO Box 1477
Newport, OR 97365
503-931-3601
Fax 541-265-3966
E-Mail: mikemarshall@whoever.com

Newport Pacific Oyster Growers
6224 S Bay Road
Toledo, OR 97391-0975
541-867-4414

Oregon Oyster Farms, Inc.
Liv Xin, John Becker, Tom Ragghianti
6878 Yaquina Bay Road
Newport, OR 97365
541-265-5078
Fax 541-265-2401
E-Mail: oregonoyster@actionnet.net

Oysters Out West
Pacific Oyster Co.
Cindy Gardner
P.O. Box 3030, 5150 Oyster Dr.
Bay City, OR 97107
503 -377-2323
Fax 503-377-4237

Pearl Point Oyster Co.
Mark and Melody Wittwer
9810 Whiskey Creek Road
Tillamook, OR 97141
503-842-6371
Fax 502-842-1764
E-Mail: pearlpoint@wbrgalaxy.com

Qualman Oyster Farms
4898 Crown Pt. Rd.
Coos Bay, OR 97420
541-888-3145

Umpqua Aquaculture
P.O. Box 1287
Winchester Bay, OR 97467
541-271-5684

Winchester Bay Oysters Ltd.
75318 US Highway 101
Reedsport, OR 97467-0973
541-271-5224

Texas

Hillman Oyster Co.
Rt. 3 Box 409
Dickinson, TX 77539
281-339-1506
Fax 281-339-1509
800-582-4416
Web: www.iqfoysters.com

Washington - Hood Canal

Coast Seafoods
14711 NE 29th Place
Bellevue, WA 98007
425-702-8800
Fax 425-702-0400
Hatchery at Quilcene, WA

K & P Oyster Co.
Kenneth & Patricia Gaul
246 Robinson Road
Brinnon, WA 98320
360-796-4962
E-Mail: sunnybeach@worldfront.com

Kelly Oyster Co.
James E. Kelly
P.O. Box B, 305504 Hwy 101
Brinnon, WA 98320
888-437-3062
Fax 360-796-3062
Web: www.kellyoyster.com

Rock Point Oyster Co.
R. N. (Dick) Steele
1611 Dabob P.O. Road
Quilcene, WA 98376
360-765-4664
Fax 360-765-3676
E-Mail: rpoco@olypen.com

Washington - North Puget Sound

Baywater, Inc.
Joth and Karen Davis
15425 Smoland Lane
Bainbridge Island, WA 98110
206-842-0894
E-Mail: Jdavis@wolfenet.com

Blau Oyster Company
E.E. Blau and Sons
11321 Blue Heron Road
Bow, WA 98232
360-766-6171
Fax 360-766-6115

Buck Bay Shellfish Farm
Jay and Janet Booth
119 E. J. Young Road
Olga, WA 98279
360-376-2091

Jamestown Seafood
3820 W Sequim Bay Road
Sequim, WA 98382
360-683-2025
Web: www.shellfishnw.com

Neptune Sea Farm, Inc.
Erin and Walter Ruthenstiener
P.O. Box 781
Freeland, WA 98249
360-331-7783
E-Mail: erinwalt@whidbey.com

Scow Bay Oysters and Clams
Bernie Mueller/Ralph Rush
5073 Flagler Road
Nordland, WA 98358

Wescott Bay Sea Farms
4071 Westcott Drive
Friday Harbor, WA 98250
360-378-2489
Fax 360-378-6388
Web: www.westcottbay.com

Western Oyster Co.
Jerry Yamashita
902 E. Allison St.
Seattle, WA 98102
206-325-1659
Fax 206-325-6654

Washington - South Puget Sound

J.J. Brenner Oyster Co.
Bruce Brenner
1601 Cooper Point Rd. #112
Olympia, WA 98502
360-866-7761
Fax 360-866-4613
Web: www.jjbrenner.com

Chelsea Farms
Linda & John Lentz
6438 Young Road NW
Olympia, WA
360-866-8059
Fax 360-866-4003

Little Skookum Shellfish Growers
P.O. Box 1157
Shelton, WA 98584
360-426-9759
Fax 360-426-5272
Web: www.skookumshellfish.com

Olympia Clams, Inc.
Vince Perelli-Minetti
4820 Sunset Dr. NW
Olympia, WA 98502
360-866-7582
E-Mail: vincenzopm@earthlink.net

Olympia Oyster Co,
Tim McMillin
1042 SE Bloomfield Road
Shelton, WA 98584
360-426-3354
Fax 360-427-0122

Taylor Shellfish
Bill and Paul Taylor, Jeff Pearson
SE 130 Lynch Road
Shelton, WA 98584
360-426-6178
Fax 360-427-0327
Web: www.taylorshellfish.com

Schreiber Shellfish
Glenn Schreiber
350 SE Mell Road
Shelton, WA 98584
360-426-7942
Fax 360-432-9906
E-Mail: shellstock@aol.com

Washington - Willapa Bay

Bay Center Farms
Dick and Jan Wilson
P.O. Box 356, 306 Dike Rd.
Bay Center, WA 98527
360-875-5519
360-875-5937
E-Mail: bcfarms@willapabay.org

Brady's Oysters
3714 Oyster Place E.
Aberdeen, WA 98520
1-800-572-3252
E-Mail: bradys@techline.com

Kemmer Oyster Co.
Robert Kemmer
31006 SR 103, P.O.Box 33
Ocean Park, WA 98640
360-665-4128

Nahcotta Oyster Farm
Larry Warnberg
27002 Sandridge Road
P.O. Box 43
Nahcotta, WA 98637
360-665-2926

Nisbet Oyster Co.
David and Maureen Nisbet
P.O. Box 338
Bay Center, WA 98527
360-875-6629
E-Mail: dnisbet@willapabay.org

Northern Oyster Co.
Richard and Ruth Sheldon
P.O. Box 365
Ocean Park, WA 98640
360-665-4886

Oysterville Sea Farms
Dan and Katherine Driscoll
P.O. Box 6
Oysterville, WA 98641
360-665-6585
Fax 360-665-3425

Pristine Bay Oysters
Bruce Urquhart
2776 Hollywood
Tokeland, WA 98590
E-Mail: urquhart@techline.com

Wiegardt Brothers, Inc.
Ken Wiegardt
P.O. Box 309
Ocean Park, WA 98640
(360) 665-4111
Fax (360) 665-4950

British Columbia - Canada

Baynes Sound Oyster Co.
5848 Island Hwy
Union Bay, BC V0R3B0
250-335-2111

Coopers Cove Oyster Farm
6377 Belvista Pl
Sooke, BC V0S1N0
250-642-3153, 250-642-4553

Fanny Bay Oysters, Ltd.
P.O. Box 209
Union Bay, BC V0R3B0
250-335-0125, Fax 250-335-1211
www.fannybayoysters.com

Great Little Oyster Company
Eric Boucher
3470 Tweedsmuir Ave.
Powell River, BC V8A 1C3

Island Scallops Ltd. Hatchery
5552 West Island Highway,
Qualicum Beach, B.C. V9K 2C8
250-757-9811, Fax 250-757-8370
E-Mail: islandscallops@bcsupernet.com

Macs Oysters, Ltd.
7162 Island Hwy
Fanny Bay, BC V0R1W0
250-335-2233

Madrona Shellfish Ltd.
Dave Mitchell
Box 329
Errington, BC V0R 1V0

The Oyster Man
Brent Petkau
Box 235
Whaletown, Cortes Island, BC
V0P 1Z0
250-354-4576, Cell 250-287-0363
Email: bpetkau@netidea.com

Pearl Seaproducts
Sam Bowman, Drew Standfield
Box 1792, 5878 Marine Way
Sechelt, BC V0N 3A0
604-740-0465, Fax 604-740-0467
Email: pearl@pearlsea.com

Timothy Oyster Co.
5035 Paton Rd
Ladysmith, BC V9G1M6
250 245 3213

Village Bay Mariculture Ltd.
Roberta Stevenson
Box 32
Heriot Bay, BC V0P 1H0

Brent Petkau harvesting oysters on Cortes Island, B.C.

Prince Edward Island - Canada

Burleigh Brothers Seafood
224 Burleigh Road
Ellerslie, Prince Edward Island
902-831-2349
Web: www.burleigh.pe.ca

Prince Edward Island Oyster Co.
Raspberry Point Oysters
Charlottetown, Prince Edward Island
800-565-2697
Web: www.raspberrypoint.com

Nova Scotia - Canada

Bay Enterprises
Charles Purdy
RR#1, 2642 Malagash Road
Malagas, NS B0K 1E0
902-257-2690

Dunphy's Oysters
Alex Dunphy
RR#2, Shore Road
Dingwall, NS B0C 1G0
902-383-2701

Fish Haven
Bill McDonald
RR#2
Baddeck, NS B0E 1B0
902-295-1781

Har-Wen Farms Limited
John/Krista Harding
P.O. Box 127
Port Medway
Queen's Co. NS B0J 2T0
902-677-2758
Fax 902-677-2052

Highhead Shellfish Growers, Ltd.
Shawn d'Entremont
P.O. Box 190 West Pubnico, Yarmouth
County, Nova Scotia, Canada
B0W 3S0
902-762-3301
Fax 902-762-2484
E-Mail: tipaul@klis.com

SFT Venture
Frank de Waard
RR#1 Hubbards
Blandford, NS B0J 1T0
902-228-2579
Fax 902-228-2297

North American Oyster Grower, Shellfish and Aquaculture Associations

Shellfish Institute of North America

c/o National Fisheries Institute , 1901 North Ft. Myer Drive Ste 700 , Arlington VA 22209
(703)524-8880   Fax (703)524-4619
This group began as the Oyster Growers and Dealers Association of North America in 1908, but now works with the aquaculture industry and environmental agencies to unite growers and dealers, educate consumers and provide spokesmen for the industry on issues of water quality and pollution control.

Pacific Coast Shellfish Growers Association

120 State Ave. NE PMB #142, Olympia, WA 98501 USA
(360) 754-2744   Fax (360) 754-2743, E-Mail pcsga@olywa.net, www.pcsga.org
Robin Downey, Executive Director , Connie Smith, Programs Coordinator
The Pacific Coast Shellfish Growers Association is the largest shellfish association in North America. They represent the local, state and federal interests of oyster, clam, mussel, scallop and geoduck growers from Alaska, British Columbia, Washington, Oregon, California, Mexico and Hawaii. Involvement includes: environmental protection, shellfish safety and health issues and technological advances, and international marketing and research.
The PCSGA touts the clean waters of Pacific Coast and the wide variety of quality shellfish produced by the members for international distribution.

British Columbia Shellfish Growers Association

321 St. Julian Street, Duncan, BC V9L 3S5 Canada
250-748-9688, Fax: 250-748-1707
E-mail: bcsga@island.net, www.island.net/~bcsga/
Shellfish farming has primarily been a small scale activity in British Columbia, but this is changing due to technological improvements, expanded markets and general awareness of shellfish farming as a business opportunity. The BCSGA is helping to organize a rapidly growing industry that has great economic potential.

World Aquaculture Society

143 J. M. Parker Coliseum, Louisiana State University, Baton Rouge, LA 70803 (USA)
225-388-3137, Fax 225-388-3493
The World Aquaculture Society (WAS) is an international non-profit society with over 4,000 members in 94 countries. Founded in 1970, the primary focus of WAS is to improve communication and information exchange within the diverse global aquaculture community. The World Aquaculture Society, through its commitment to excellence in science, technology, education, and information exchange, offers as a goal to contribute to the progressive and sustainable development of aquaculture throughout the world.

Other Aquaculture Associations:

Florida Bureau of Seafood and Aquaculture Marketing
2051 East Dirac Drive, Tallahassee, FL 32310, 850-488-0163
www.fl-seafood.com

Maine Aquaculture Association
Joseph B. McGonigle, 141 North Main Street, Suite 203, Brewer, Maine 04412
207-989-5310, Fax 207-989-5795, meaqua@aol.com

Maryland Aquaculture Association
Richard Pelz, President, 42366 Manor Drive, Mechanicsville, MD 20659
301-373-8662

Maryland Sea Grant College
Merrill Leffler, 0112 Skinner Building, College Park, MD 20742
301-405-6376
Email: leffler@mdsg.umd.edu   (Maryland Aquafarmer Newsletter)

Massachusetts Aquaculture Association
Richard Nelson, P.O. Box 209, Barnstable, MA 02630
508-362-2511

New York State Aquaculture Association
Norman Soule, P.O.Box 29, Cold Spring Harbor, NY 11724
516-692-6768, nsoule_cshfha@juno.com

South Carolina Aquaculture Association
Betsy Sheehan, P.O. Box 11280, Columbia, SC 29211
803 734-2210, Fax 803-734-2192, betsy@scda.state.sc.us

Nova Scotia Aquaculture Association
PO Box 802 Suite M, 1657 Barrington St., Suite 310,
Halifax, Nova Scotia, Canada B3J 2V2, 902-422-6234, 902-422-6248
aquans@fox.nstn.ca

Newfoundland Aquaculture Industry Association
PO Box 23176, 176 Nagles Hill, St. John's, Newfoundland, Canada A1B 4J9
709-754-2854, Fax 709-754-2981

Healthy Oysters from Healthy Waters

North, south, east and west, water quality in salt water bays and estuaries is a problem throughout North America. Large population centers dumping sewage into waterways, industrial discharge and pollution from recreational sources are three major problems that the oyster industry must contend with. Federal and local governments have attacked the problem in two ways. First, water quality monitoring by a variety of agencies is helping to restrict pollution and clean up the rivers and bays. Second, monitoring of commercial seafood and related processing companies is revealing problem areas and suggesting solutions from several angles.

Oyster lovers interested in preserving the quality of the shellfish they enjoy can volunteer for one of the following organizations and can urge their local seafood purveyor to observe ISSC and HACCP guidelines for processing shellfish.

Long Island Soundkeeper

www.soundkeeper.org • Soundkeeper, 7 Edgewater Place, PO Box 4058, Norwalk, CT 06855 203-854-5330, Fax: 203-866-1318, Toll Free: 1-800-933-SOUND

The motto of this group is "To protect and preserve Long Island Sound." Working with volunteers and local funding, the Soundkeeper is leading the way to maintain water quality in Long Island Sound. Lending support to the Yankee Oyster Project (developing hatchery programs for oysters along L.I. Sound), working to provide sewage pumpout services for recreational boaters, and taking on New York City and the huge amount of sewage issued from the metropolis.

Chesapeake Bay Foundation

www.cbf.org • 162 Prince George Street, Annapolis, MD 21401 410-268-8816, 410-269-0481 (from Baltimore), 30-261-2350 (from D.C. metro)

Bringing back Chesapeake Bay to conditions that support marine life and local wildlife is the challenge facing this organization. In the middle of a very fast-growing population area with encroachment along many shorelines, Chesapeake Bay is just holding its own against further degradation of water quality. Volunteers are very important to this organization's achievements.

Puget Soundkeeper Alliance

www.Pugetsoundkeeper.org • 1415 W. Dravus, Seattle, WA 98119, 206-286-1309, Fax: 206-286-1082

The Puget Soundkeeper Alliance brings together concerned citizens, businesses and government agencies to solve marine environmental issues in a responsible and balanced manner. Recently splitting responsibility for patrolling the waterways of three major Puget Sound cities – Tacoma, Seattle and Bellingham – the group continues to evolve as the protector of water quality in the area.

American Oceans Campaign

www.americanoceans.org, 600 Pennsylvania Ave SE, Suite 210, Washington DC 20003
(202)544-3526 - FAX (202)544-5625 -

The mission of American Oceans Campaign is to safeguard the vitality of the oceans and our coastal waters. AOC is committed to scientific information in advocating for sound public policy. We are equally committed to developing partnerships with all entities interested in protecting the environment. AOC seeks to ensure healthy sources of food and coastal recreation as well as protect the ocean's grandeur for future generations.

Interstate Shellfish Sanitation Conference

www.issc.org
115 Atrium Way, Suite 117, Columbia, SC 29223-6382
803-788-7559, Fax 803-788-7576, E-Mail: info@issc.org,

The National Shellfish Sanitation Program (NSSP) was developed in 1925 when the U. S. Public Health Service responded to a request for assistance from local and state public health officials in controlling disease associated with the consumption of raw shellfish (oysters, clams, and mussels).

The public health control procedures established by the Public Health Service were dependent on the cooperative and voluntary efforts of State regulatory agencies. These efforts were augmented by the assistance and advice of the Public Health Service (now the Food and Drug Administration) and the voluntary participation of the shellfish industry. These three parties combined to form a tripartite cooperative program. The guidelines of the program have evolved into the NSSP Handbook which is managed and updated by the Interstate Shellfish Sanitation Conference (ISSC).

The Interstate Shellfish Sanitation Conference (ISSC) was formed in 1982 to foster and promote shellfish sanitation through the cooperation of state and federal control agencies, the shellfish industry, and the academic community. To achieve this purpose the ISSC:

Adopts uniform procedures, incorporated into an Interstate Shellfish Sanitation Program, and implemented by all shellfish control agencies;

Gives state shellfish programs current and comprehensive sanitation guidelines to regulate the harvesting, processing, and shipping of shellfish;

Provides a forum for shellfish control agencies, the shellfish industry, and academic community to resolve major issues concerning shellfish sanitation;

Informs all interested parties of recent developments in shellfish sanitation and other major issues of concern through the use of news media, publications, regional and national meetings, internet, and by working closely with academic institutions and trade associations.

The ISSC promotes cooperation and trust among shellfish control agencies, the shellfish industry, and consumers of shellfish; and insures the safety of shellfish products consumed in the United States.

U.S. F.D.A. - Center for Food Safety and Applied Nutrition
http://vm.cfsan.fda.gov/~lrd/haccp.html

Hazard Analysis and Critical Control Point (HACCP)

The goal of this arm of the FDA, created in 1997, is to achieve a "science-based level of safety assurance" by working with the seafood industry. This program requires seafood processors, repackers and warehouses—both domestic and foreign exporters to this country—to follow a modern food safety system known as Hazard Analysis and Critical Control Point, or HACCP (pronounced hassip). This system focuses on identifying and preventing hazards that could cause food-borne illnesses rather than relying on spot-checks of manufacturing processes and random sampling of finished seafood products to ensure safety.

This is the first time that the HACCP system is being required for the processing and storage of a U.S. food commodity on an industry-wide basis.

Seafood safety could be further ensured if seafood retailers integrate HACCP in their operations. Although seafood retailers are exempt from the HACCP regulations, FDA, through its 1997 edition of the Food Code, encourages retailers to apply HACCP-based food safety principles, along with other recommended practices. The Food Code serves as model legislation for state and territorial agencies that license and inspect food service establishments, food vending operations, and food stores.

These efforts will be accompanied by seafood safety programs already in place, such as ongoing research by FDA's seafood safety experts and others, and the National Oceanic and Atmospheric Administration's voluntary fee-for-service inspection program.

A shellfish certification tag for oysters grown by Spinney Creek Shellfish in Newcastle, Maine. Every oyster shipment in the United States must carry such a tag and each handler of the product must adhere to the rules for tracking the shellfish.

Online Oyster Resources

Given the rapid growth of computer-assisted living these days, we thought our readers would find some internet resources about oysters to be a useful addition to The Joy of Oysters. We have tried to divide these links up into sections so each person can find what they are looking for with the greatest speed. Buying Oysters offers websites from oyster growers and some seafood retailers who will ship live oysters in the shell and shucked oysters in the jar via air freight to your doorstep. Other Oyster Sites lists a variety of academic, historical, technical and culinary sites that should serve as a springboard for the web surfer to spend many happy hours researching oysterdom. As most internet users anticipate, some of these sites may be "down" or otherwise unavailable at the time you try to log on, but we have tested all links as of press time for The Joy of Oysters.

Buying Oysters

Bay Center Farms, WA - www.willapabay.org/~bcfarms/Seasonalsf.html
Oysters and clams from Willapa Bay can be ordered through this site.
E-Mail or phone 888-905-9079.

Brady's Oysters, WA - www.techline.com/~broyster/
Online ordering for shucked oysters, smoked oysters or smoked salmon. 800-572-3252

J. J. Brenner Oyster Company, WA - www.jjbrenner.com
Order oysters in the shell or Manila clams online.

Burleigh Brothers Seafood - www.burleigh.pe.ca/
This seafood firm on Prince Edward Island has a long history and sells Malpeque oysters, clams, Arctic char, trout and smelt. 902-831-2349

Fanny Bay Oysters, BC - www.fannybayoysters.com
Find out about Fanny Bay oysters, then E-Mail your order or call 250-335-0125

Glidden Point Oyster Company, ME - www.oysterfarm.com
Online ordering of Glidden Point oysters (and accessories) from the Damariscotta River in the great state of Maine.

Hog Island Oyster Company, CA - www.saturdaymarket.com/intertidal.htm
Information provided on products. E-Mail or call the phone numbers to order.

Jamestown Seafood, WA - www.shellfishnw.com
This company is based at Dungeness on the Strait of Juan de Fuca. Check the site then call for information on ordering. 360-683-2025

Little Skookum Shellfish Growers, WA - www.skookumshellfish.com
Several species of oysters as well as clams and mussels are available seasonally from this southern Puget Sound grower. E-Mail or call for ordering. 360-426-9759

 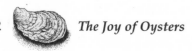

Louisiana Oysters - crawfish.cc/oysters.htm
Louisiana Oysters from Black Bayou are available online at this site. 504-712-0190

Oregon Oyster Farms, OR - www.oregonoyster.com/
You can E-Mail or call in an order for Yaquina Bay oysters -shucked, in-shell, oyster cocktails - or steamer clams. 541-265-5078

The Last Place on Earth, OR - www.tlpoe.com/
Contact owner Mike Marshall by E-Mail for information on where to find his Yaquina Bay single cultured oysters. 503-931-3601

Oysterville Sea Farms, WA - www.oysterville.net/   Order smoked oysters and other specialty food products. 360-665-6585

Pearl SeaProducts, BC - www.pearlsea.com/
Detailed descriptions of the operation and products available from this British Columbia grower. Products are mostly sold wholesale, call for more information. 604-740-0465

Prince Edward Island Oyster Co., Raspberry Point Oysters, www.raspberrypoint.com/
Raspberry Point PEI oysters by phone (800-565-2697) or online

Sitka Sea Farm, AK - www.ptialaska.net/~madelon/sitka.htm
Information provided about product. E-Mail or call to order. 907-747-3862

Taylor Shellfish, WA - www.taylorshellfish.com
Order many species of oysters shucked or in-shell, smoked oysters and smoked salmon, crabs, clams and mussels through this large Puget Sound grower. 360-426-6178

Westcott Bay Sea Farms, WA - www.westcottbay.com
Place orders online for Petite or No. 1 Pacific Oysters or Westcott Bay "Belons" (European Flats) 360-378-2489

Yaquina Bay Oysters - www.lighthousedeli.com/oysters.html
This seafood deli on the Oregon coast will ship you shellfish from their area. 541-867-6800

Other Oyster Company Sites

Goose Point Oyster Company, WA - www.sbpac.com/goosept1.html
No ordering, but some information about Goose Point Oysters.

Johnson Oyster Co., CA - www.seadriftrealty.com/oysters.htm
A web page about this long-time grower in California's Point Reyes area.

Other Oyster Sites

Below are a few links to some government or industry sponsored sites that are dedicated to improving oysters and other shellfish in the U.S. There are lots of other sites (many links from the ones mentioned below) for you to follow your own particular interests in oysters and shellfish. Sites are sorted by most general to most specific.

Oysters - Maryland Sea Grant's site about oysters in general and their restoration to Chesapeake Bay and other coastal waters in particular. Partly designed as a site for teachers to show biology students something about shellfish.
www.mdsg.umd.edu/oysters/

Oysterstew - Washington State Oysters - Washington Sea Grant created this site to tell everything about oysters in Washington State. Describes oyster biology, history of Washington oystering, recipes, much more.
www.wsg.washington.edu/oysterstew/OysterStew_intro.html

Oysters, Oysters, Oysters - A fun set of pages from Global Gourmet that describe the preparation and serving of oysters. Recipes, storage, other information.
www.globalgourmet.com/food/egg/egg0298/oysters.html

Washington State Shellfish Gathering - Booklet on public shellfish gathering sites in Puget Sound can be downloaded as .pdf files at this location.
http://www.doh.wa.gov/ehp/sf/sf10maps.htm

Pacific Coast Shellfish Growers Association - Information about oyster growing on the Pacific Coast with links, recent news, historic photos, etc.
www.pcsga.org

British Columbia Shellfish Growers Association - Lots of information on the fast-growing B.C. oyster growing business. www.island.net/~bcsga/

Aquaculture Network Information Center - Site for finding papers and other academic sources for aquaculture including oysters.
http://aquanic.org/

Oyster Disease Research - Details about the research being undertaken as part of the University of Maryland's Sea Grant program.
www.mdsg.umd.edu:80/NSGO/research/oysterdisease/index.html

Oregon State University Molluscan Broodstock Program - Lots of information about how hatcheries spawn oysters. www.hmsc.orst.edu/Projects/mbp/index.html

Seafood Network Information Center - Clearinghouse for links to seafood information. Includes research, commercial, educational and other sites.
http://www.seafood.ucdavis.edu/home.htm

Haskin Shellfish Research Laboratory, Bivalve NJ, Cape Shore NJ - This facility was begun at Rutgers University in 1888 and has been continuously providing information and assistance to oyster growers on Delaware Bay and other areas of New Jersey. Growth in the 1950s included research and development programs to address MSX disease in local oyster populations.
www.hsrl.rutgers.edu/

Japan's Pearl Industry - a one-page site about pearl growing in Japan.
http://jin.jcic.or.jp/atlas/nature/nat27.html

Washington Biotoxin Beach Closures - A list of beach closures due to biotoxins in Washington State. Following is the URL for a similar site for British Columbia, Canada.
www.doh.wa.gov/ehp/sf/biotoxin.htm
For B. C. - www.pac.dfo-mpo.gc.ca/ops/fm/shellfish/Biotoxins/biotoxins.htm

OysterWorld.cc Andrew Wiegardt and friends are launching this ambitious website that features the world's best oysters, lessons on handling and preparation, impressive oyster trivia, helpful trip planning to visit an oyster farm or festival, oyster-related restaurant, wine and beer reviews, and invaluable insights into oysters and your love life. Scheduled to be up and running by spring of 2001.

Oyster Knives:
Carvel Hall Cutlery Company., MD - www.crisfield.com/carvelhall/oysterkn.htm
Oyster knives in many styles are available from this venerable firm.

Williams Sonoma, CA- www.williamssonoma.com
Half Shell Lori swears by the French oyster knives she gets from Williams Sonoma.

Oyster Museums

The Maritime Aquarium at Norwalk,

10 N. Water Street, Norwalk, CT 06854   (203) 852-0700 www.maritimeaquarium.org/

The Maritime Aquarium at Norwalk is one of the few in the country solely devoted to one body of water: in this case, Long Island Sound. The Aquarium features more than 1,000 marine animals native to the Sound and its watershed. Tanks portray successive levels of life in the Sound, from shallow tidal areas filled with oysters, sea horses, lobsters and small fish to the 110,000-gallon Open Ocean tank with 9-foot sharks, bluefish, striped bass, rays and other creatures found in the Sound and the ocean beyond. A large exhibit on oystering features some photos by Oyster Bill.

Suffolk Marine Museum

PO Box 184, West Sayville, NY 11796 (516) 567 1733

Explore turn-of-the-century maritime activities on the shores of the Great South Bay. Overlooking the Fire Island Lighthouse and Captree Bridge, this museum features seamans' crafts, shipwreck artifacts, life saving equipment, ship models, and Long Island shellfish. The Oyster House demonstrates how oysters were processed. This was West Sayville's main industry until the hurricane of 1938 wiped out the oysters. At the docks, visitors can view the schooner, Priscilla; the sloop, Modesty, and tugboat, Charlotte and Alice V. And the authentic West Sayville Dutch Cottage illustrates the bayman's family life in the 1890s. Open Wednesday thru Saturday, 10 am - 3 pm, Sunday 12:00 - 4:00. Closed Monday and Tuesday.

Directions: I-495 East to exit 57 South. Memorial Hwy. to Lakeland Ave. south (just before McArthur Airport). Lakeland Ave. to Rt. 27A (Montauk Hwy.). West on 27A to entrance for Suffolk County Park/Suffolk Marine Museum.

The Chesapeake Bay Maritime Museum

Mill Street, P.O. Box 636, St. Michaels, MD 21663
(410) 745-2916 Fax: (410) 745-6088 Web: www.cbmm.org/

The Chesapeake Bay Maritime Museum occupies nine exhibit buildings on 18 water-front acres in scenic St. Michaels, Maryland. You step back in time as you enter the fully restored 1879 Hooper Strait lighthouse and feel what it must have been like to be on station at this beacon, guiding ships to safety. You may choose to climb aboard the skipjack Rosie Parks and experience the daily drudgery of sailing a large wooden boat while hauling up heavy oysters in freezing temperatures and high winds. With a working boatyard, an impressive collection of decoys and a new interactive waterman's shanty, there's something of interest for everyone. The museum offers fun-filled festivals, engaging special exhibitions, hands-on boatbuilding classes, and outdoor summer concerts.

The Waterman's Museum

20880 Rock Hall Ave., Rock Hall, MD 21661 (410) -778-6697

The concept for the Waterman's Museum began in 1990, when a committee of representatives from the Rock Hall community and Haven Harbour Marina decided that the watermen needed their own unique center of recorded history. Today the museum includes exhibits on oystering, crabbing, and fishing. A reproduction of a shanty house is on display, along with historical photographs, local carvings, and, of course, boats.

There is no charge to visit the museum, though donations are accepted. All donations benefit the Maryland Waterman's Association. Open seven days a week.

Barnegat Bay Decoy & Baymen's Museum

Tip Seaman Park on US 9 (From exit 58 on the Garden State Parkway, follow county road 539 southeast to Tuckerton.) Phone (609) 296-8868

At the entrance porch to the museum is a replica hunting shanty with a lifelike display of "master" carver, Harry V. Shourds, a world class decoy carver and one of Tuckerton's famous baymen. Museum exhibits illustrate the life of a Barnegat Bay bayman—hunting, fishing, clamming, oystering, boat building, decoy carving, charter fishing—and the history of the U.S. Life Saving Service along the Jersey shore. The museum is open Wednesday through Sunday from 10:00am to 4:30pm.

Oyster and Maritime Museum

7125 Maddox Blvd. , P.O.Box 352 , Chincoteague, VA 23336
(757)336-6117, www.chincoteaguechamber.com / oyster / omm.html

One of the most fascinating activities on Chincoteague Island is a visit to the Oyster and Maritime Museum located at the side of the road just before the bridge to Assateague. Here you'll find a truly unique collection of rare and unusual shells, fossils, and artifacts from Virginia's barrier islands and from around the world. At the museum, you'll find not only examples of the traditional tools used in the oyster industry, but also a wealth of information on the gathering and processing of oysters. A good place to start is the sight and sound diorama that explains oystering - from breeding and growing to harvesting, packing, and shipping. You'll see models of oyster boats and an oyster dock and hear an excellent narration. Open daily 10am-5pm, Memorial Day-Labor Day. Open Saturday 10am-5pm, Sunday noon-4pm, March 1 through the day before Memorial Day and the day after Labor Day through November 30.

Pacific County Historical Society & Museum
1008 W Robert Bush Drive (Highway 101) , South Bend, Washington
Phone: (360) 875-5224

The museum features displays on Pacific County communities, cultural life, ethnic groups, indigenous peoples and trade, and economic activities. Located on Willapa Bay, one of the last unpolluted estuaries in the continental United States, the museum interprets noteworthy local industries such as oyster farming, tree farming, and cranberry growing. Significant collections include the largest photographic collection in the area, comprising over 10,000 images, and an important collection of charts and maps. The Indian basket collection includes representative examples from local craftspersons. Open 11 AM to 4 PM, seven days. Closed Christmas and Thanksgiving.

The Willapa Bay Interpretive Center
Nahcotta, WA

The town of Nahcotta, located on the shores of Willapa Bay, got the rail teminus its northern neighbor Oysterville coveted. The narrow-gauge lines enabled Nahcotta (named after Chinook Indian Chief Nahcati) to become the Long Beach Peninsula's northern hub for pedestrian transportation, logging, fishing, and oyster shipping. Today, the oyster industry here is a shell of its former self, but a replica of an oyster station house successfully transports visitors back to the boom times. The Willapa Bay Interpretive Center offers walls covered with quotes, notes and anecdotes, along with a film about the oyster industry and Willapa Bay ecology. The Center is open Fridays through Sundays, beginning in May. Center visitors enjoy access to the rocky shores of Willapa Bay. It's one of just two publicly-owned spots (Leadbetter Point is the other) with access to the bay.

The Prince Edward Island Shellfish Museum
Bideford Road, Prince Edward Island, Canada Route 166, Just off of Route 2 (Lady Slipper Drive) Ellerslie http://westcountry.peicaps.org/museum.htm

The Prince Edward Island Shellfish Museum portrays the fascinating story of the shellfish industry on PEI. The historical importance of the shellfish to the Island economy reaches back to the mid 1800s when the Malpeque Oyster won their fame at the world's fair in Paris! The Prince Edward Island Shellfish Museum boasts a new story line, interpretive displays, and modern exhibits. Visitors delight in viewing the aquariums that house many varieties of shellfish such as oysters, quahogs, scallops, and everyone's favorite - lobster! With the touch tank, children can experience the feel of the spiny starfish or the hard shell of a quahog. Open Monday to Saturday, 9AM to 5PM; Sunday, 1AM to 5PM; June 30 to September 1.

Other Oyster References and Recommended Reading on Oysters

The Rise and Decline of the Olympia Oyster, by E.N. Steele Copyright 1957, by the Olympia Oyster Growers Association

The Immigrant Oyster, by E.N. Steele Copyright 1964, by E.N. Steele (out of print, but may be downloaded as a .pdf file from Washington Sea Grant's Oysterstew website)

Oysterville, by Willard R. Espy Copyright 1977, by Willard R. Espy

Oystering from New York to Boston, by John M. Kochiss Copyright 1974 by Mystic Seaport, Inc.

The Eastern Oyster Crassostrea virginica, by Victor S. Kennedy, Roger I.E. Newell, and Alfred F. Eble, editors Copyright 1996, by Maryland Sea Grant College

The Celebrated Oysterhouse Cookbook, by Frederick J. Parks Copyright 1985, by Frederick J. Parks

O is for Oysters, by Sydney Stevens Copyright 1998, by Sydney Stevens

NOAA Technical Report NMFS 127, Volume 1, Atlantic and Gulf Coasts September 1997 (not copyrighted)

NOAA Technical Report NMFS 128, Volume 2, Pacific Coast and Supplimental Topics December 1997 (not copyrighted)

The Oysters of Locmariaquer, Copyright 1959, by Eleanor Clark

Consider the Oyster, by M.F.K. Fisher, Copyright 1941, Duell, Sloan & Pearce

WoodenBoat Magazine, Number 151 Copyright 1999 by WoodenBoat Publications

Index

(Recipe Index Begins on Page 333)

The Joy of Oysters

Recipe Index

(General Index Begins on Page 330)

The Joy of Oysters

The Joy of Oysters

The Joy of Oysters   335

RECIPE INDEX